Peter F. Drucker

# Management

an abridged and revised version of
**Management: Tasks, Responsibilities, Practices**

## BUTTERWORTH HEINEMANN

Oxford    Auckland    Boston    Johannesburg    Melbourne    New Delhi

Butterworth-Heinemann
Linacre House, Jordan Hill, Oxford OX2 8DP
225 Wildwood Avenue, Woburn MA 01801-2041
A division of Reed Educational and Professional Publishing Ltd

A member of the Reed Elsevier plc group

First published 1974
Reprinted 1974 (twice), 1982
Paperback edition 1988
Reprinted 1994, 1995, 1997
Reissued with new cover 1999
Transferred to digital printing 2001

**British Library Cataloguing in Publication Data**
Drucker, Peter F. (Peter Ferdinand), *1909–*
    Management: tasks, responsibilities, practices
    1. Management – techniques    I. Title
    **658**

ISBN 0 7506 4389 7

For information on all Butterworth-Heinemann publications
visit our website at www.bh.com

Printed in Great Britain by Antony Rowe Ltd, Eastbourne

# Contents

31966

# Preface: Management as Profession and Commitment

As a subject management is multidimensional. It is first a discipline in its own right. It is a young discipline; modern organisations are barely a century old, and management arose with them. But while there is still a great deal we do not know, we know that management is not just common sense. It is not just codified experience. It is, at least potentially, an organized body of knowledge. This book tries to present what we know so far. But it also tries to present the much larger body of our "organized ignorance"—that is, the areas in which we know that we need new knowledge in which we can define what we need, but in which we do not as yet possess the knowledge. Yet practicing managers cannot wait. They have to manage as the problems and needs arise. This book therefore attempts to develop approaches to the areas of our ignorance; to think through policies, principles and practices; to accomplish the managerial tasks. This book tries to equip the manager with the understanding, the thinking, the knowledge, and the skills for today's and also tomorrow's job.

Management is tasks. Management is a discipline. But management is also people. Every achievement of management is the achievement of a manager. Every failure is the failure of a manager. People manage, rather than "forces" or "facts." The vision, dedication, and integrity of managers determines whether there is management or mismanagement.

This book therefore focuses on the manager as a person. It focuses on what people do and what people achieve. Yet it always tries to integrate people and tasks. For the tasks are objective and impersonal. It is "managers" who perform. But it is "management" that determines what is needed and what has to be achieved.

Management is work. Indeed it is the specific work of a modern society, the work that distinguishes our society from all earlier ones. For management is the work that is specific to modern organization and makes modern organization perform. As work, management has its own skills, its own tools, its own techniques. Many of these are discussed in this book—a few in some detail.

But management is also different work from any other. Unlike the work of the physician, the stonemason or the lawyer, management must always be done in an organization—that is, within a web of human relations. The manager, therefore is always an example. What he does is important. But equally important is who he is—far more important than it is with respect to the physician, stonemason or even lawyer. Only the teacher has the same twofold dimension, the dimension of skill and performance, and the dimension of personality, example and integrity. In this book, therefore, there is equal stress on the manager's tasks and on his character.

This book and its approach have been developed and tested in more than thirty years of teaching management to many different kinds of students in colleges, universities, and executive programmes and seminars. But the subject matter of the book itself has largely been developed out of nearly forty years of working closely with managers on all levels as a consultant, with managers in large and small businesses, and with managers in government agencies, in hospitals and in schools. Most of this experience has been in America, and with American businesses and public service institutions—although I have worked also with managements of businesses and nonbusinesses alike outside the United States, especially in Great Britain, Western Europe, Japan, and Latin America. The book therefore tries to include what every manager needs to know—but in a form in which it is also accessible to people who themselves have not yet worked as managers or even as employees in managed institutions. The user of this book can therefore be sure of two things: everything in the book has been developed in management practice and found both effective in it and central to it; and everything has been tested by students of management and found to be meaningful to them, as well as easily accessible.

*Peter F. Drucker*

*Claremont, California*
*New Year's Day, 1987*

# 1 Introduction: Management and Managers Defined

Management may be the most important innovation of this century – and the one most directly affecting the young educated people in colleges and universities who will be tomorrow's 'knowledge workers' in managed institutions, and their managers the day after tomorrow. But what is management? Why management? How do you define 'managers?' What are their tasks, their responsibilities? And how has the study and discipline of management developed to its present state?

When the first business schools in the US opened around the turn of this century, they did not offer a single course in management. About that same time the word 'management' was first popularized by Frederick W. Taylor, to describe what he had formerly (and more accurately) called 'work study' or 'task study'; we call it 'Industrial Engineering' today. But when Taylor meant to talk about what we now call 'management' and 'managers' he said 'the owners and their representatives'.

The roots of the disciplines of management go back 150 years (see the note on the Roots and History of Management at end of this chapter). But management as a function, management as a distinct work, management as a discipline and area of study – these are all products of this century. And most people only became aware of management after World War II.

Within the life span of today's old-timers, our society has become a 'society of organizations'. In this century, the major social tasks have come to be performed in and through an organized institution – business enterprises, large and small; school systems; colleges and universities; hospitals; research laboratories; governments and government agencies of all kinds and sizes; and many others. And each of them in turn is entrusted to 'managers' who practice 'management'.

## What is management?

Management and managers are the specific need of all institutions, from the smallest to the largest. They are the specific organ of every institution. They are what holds it together and makes it work. None of our institutions could function without managers. And managers do their own job – they do not do it by delegation from the 'owner'. The need for management does not arise just because the job has become too big for any one person to do alone. Managing the business enterprise or a public service institution is inherently different from managing one's own property or from running a practice of medicine or a solo law practice.

Of course many a large and complex business enterprise started from a one-man shop. But beyond the first steps growth soon entails more than a change in size. At some point (and long before the business becomes even 'fair-sized') quantity turns into quality. At this point 'owners' no longer run 'their own' business even if they are the sole proprietors. They are then in charge of a *business enterprise* – and if they do not rapidly become *managers* they will soon cease to be 'owners' and be replaced, or the business will go under and disappear. For at this point the business turns into an organization and requires for its survival different structure, different principles, different behaviour, and different work. It requires managers and management.

Legally management in the business enterprise is seen still as a delegation of ownership, even in the Soviet system; under Soviet Law the State controls because it is the 'owner' and has replaced private stockholders. But the doctrine that already determines practice, even though it is still only evolving in law, is that management precedes and even outranks ownership. The owner has to subordinate himself to the enterprise's need for management and managers. There are, of course, many owners who successfully combine both roles, that of owner-investor and that of top management. But if the enterprise does not have the management it needs, ownership itself is worthless. And in enterprises that are so big or play such a crucial role as to make their survival and performance matters of national concern, public pressure or governmental action will take control away from an owner who stands in the way of management. Thus the late Howard Hughes was forced by the US government in the 1950s to give up control of his wholly-owned Hughes Aircraft Company, which produces electronics crucial to US defence. Managers were brought in because he insisted on running the company as 'owner'. Similarly the German government in the 1960s put the faltering Krupp Company under autonomous management even though the Krupp family owned 100 per cent of the stock.

The change from a business which the owner-entrepreneur can run with 'helpers' to a business that requires management is a sweeping change. It can be made only if basic concepts, basic principles, and individual vision are changed radically.

One can compare the two kinds of business to two different kinds of organisms: the insect, which is held together by a tough, hard skin; and the vertebrate animal, which has a skeleton. Land animals that are supported by a hard skin cannot grow beyond a few inches in size. To be larger, animals must have a skeleton. Yet the skeleton has not evolved out of the hard skin of the insect; for it is a different organ with different antecedents. Similarly, management becomes necessary when a business reaches a certain size and complexity. But management, while it replaces the 'hard-skin' structure of the owner-entrepreneur, is not its successor. It is, rather, its replacement.

When does a business reach the stage at which it has to shift from 'hard skin' to 'skeleton'? The line lies somewhere between 300 and 1,000 employees in size. More important, perhaps, is the increase in complexity. When a variety of tasks have all to be performed in cooperation, synchronization, and communication, an organization needs managers and management. One example would be a small research lab in which 20 to 25 scientists from a number of disciplines work together. Without management, things go out of control. Plans fail to turn into action. Or worse, different parts of the plans get going at different speeds, different times, and with different objectives and goals. The favour of the 'boss' becomes more important than performance. At this point the product may be excellent, the people able and dedicated. The boss may be – and often is – a person of great ability and personal power. But the enterprise will begin to flounder, stagnate, and soon go downhill unless it shifts to the 'skeleton' of managers and management structure.

The word 'management' is centuries old. But to apply it to the governing organ of an institution and particularly to a business enterprise is specifically American – and the American meaning of 'management' has no counterpart in any other language. (The English usually speak of 'the Board' or 'the executive', when Americans speak of 'management'). Management denotes both a function and the people who discharge it. It denotes a social position and authority, but also a discipline and field of study.

Even in American usage, 'management' is not an easy term, for institutions other than business do not speak of management or managers, as a rule. Universities or government agencies have administrators, as have hospitals. Armed services have commanders. Other institutions speak of executives, and so on.

Yet all these institutions have in common the management function, the management task, and the management work. All of them require management. And in all of them, management is the effective, the active organ.

Without the institution there would be no management. But without management there would be only a mob rather than an institution. The institution is itself an organ of society and exists only to contribute a needed result to society, the economy, and the individual. Organs, however, are never defined by what they do, let alone by how they do it. They are defined by their contribution. And it is management that enables the institution to contribute.

Management is tasks. Management is a discipline. But management is also people. Every achievement of management is the achievement of a manager. Every failure is a failure of a manager. *People* manage rather than 'forces' or 'facts'. The vision, dedication, and integrity of managers determine whether there is management or mismanagement.

# Who are the managers?

Most people, when asked what they mean by 'manager', will reply 'a boss'. But when the sign over the shoeshine stand in an airport reads 'John Smith, Manager', everybody (at least in America) knows that this means that Mr Smith is not the boss, but a hired hand with a minimum of authority and a salary just above that of the workers who shine the shoes.

Early in the history of management a manager was defined as someone who is 'responsible for the work of other people'. This definition distinguished the manager's function from that of the owner. It made clear that managing was a specific kind of work which could be analysed, studied and improved systematically. The definition focused on the essentially new, large, and permanent organization emerging to perform the economic tasks of society.

Yet, the definition is not at all satisfactory. In fact, it never was. From the beginning, there were people in the enterprise, often in responsible positions, who were clearly management and yet did not 'manage', that is, were not responsible for the work of other people. The treasurer of a company, the person responsible for the supply and use of money in the business, may have subordinates and in that sense be a manager in terms of the traditional definition. But clearly, the treasurer alone does most of the treasurer's job – working with the company's underwriters, with the financial community, and so on. The treasurer is an 'individual contributor' rather than a manager. But treasurers are members of top management. Also, the definition focuses on the tools for a task rather than on the task itself. The person in charge of market research in a company may have a large number of subordinates and is thus a manager in the traditional sense. But it really makes no difference to his or her function and contribution whether there is a large staff, a small staff, or no staff at all. The same contribution in terms of market research and market analysis can well be made by a person to whom no one reports. In fact, the market researcher may even make a greater contribution when not forced to spend a great deal of time with subordinates and on their work. He or she thus may make market research more effective in the business, better understood by management associates, and more firmly built into the company's basic business decisions.

The most rapidly growing group in today's businesss enterprise is composed of people who are management in the sense of being responsible for contribution to and results of the enterprise but who are not responsible for the work of other people. They are individual professional contributors of all kinds who work by themselves (perhaps with an assistant and a secretary) and yet have impact on the company's wealth-producing capacity, the direction of its business, and its performance.

Such people are not to be found only in technical research work, though it was here that they first emerged as a distinct group. The senior chemist in the laboratory has major responsibility and makes major decisions, many of them irreversible in their impact. But so also does the person who works out and thinks through the company's organizational structure and designs managerial jobs. Here also belongs the senior cost accountant who determines the definition and allocation of costs. By defining the measurements for management, he, in effect, largely decides whether a certain product will be kept or will be abandoned. Other people in the same category are the men charged with the development and maintenance of quality standards for a company's products, the woman working on the distributive system through which the company's products are being brought to the market, and the advertising director, who may be responsible for the basic promotion policy of a company, its advertising message, the media it uses, and the measurements of advertising effectiveness.

The traditional definition of management is responsible for the fact that the individual professional contributor presents a problem within the structure and a problem to himself. His or her title, pay, function, and career opportunities are confused, ambiguous, and a cause of dissatisfaction and friction. Yet the number of these career professionals is increasing fast.

## The new definition of a manager

What really defines a manager ? Who should be considered management ? The first attempt at answering these questions, made in the early 1950s, merely supplemented the old definition of the manager by recognizing the 'individual professional contributor' and calling for 'parallel paths of opportunity' for both. This made it possible to pay properly for advanced 'professional' work rather than make higher pay dependent upon promotion into a position of responsibility for the work of others.

Yet this formula has not fully solved the problem. The companies that have adopted it report that individual professional contributors are only slightly less dissatisfied than they were before. They remain convinced that true opportunities for advancement still exist primarily within the administrative structure, and that one has to become a 'boss' to 'get ahead'. Above all, the separation of the managerial world into two groups serves to emphasize the inferiority of those who do their own work as compared with those responsible for the work of others. The emphasis is still on power and authority rather than on responsibility and contribution.

Any analysis which does not start out from the traditional definition but looks at the work itself will come to the conclusion that the traditional definition of a manager as one responsible for the work of others emphasizes a secondary, rather than a primary, characteristic.

As we will see a little later, one can divide the work of a manager into planning, organizing, integrating, measuring, and developing people. Career professionals – for example, a market researcher who works alone, or a senior cost accountant – also have to plan, to organize and to measure results against objectives and expectations. What they do and how they do it has considerable impact on how people develop, especially if they also act as teachers to others in the organization. Career professionals also have to integrate their work with the work of other people in the organization. Above all, if they are to have results, they have to integrate 'sideways', that is, with people in other areas and functions who have to put their work to use.

The traditional definition of the manager focuses on 'integrating downwards' that is on integrating the work of subordinates. But even for managers who have subordinates, 'sideways' relationships with people over whom they have no supervisory authority are usually at least as important in the work, and usually more important in terms of decision and information. The district sales manager has to work closely with production scheduler, sales analyst, and cost accountant – and they in turn have to work closely with the district sales manager. Most of the day-to-day decisions these people have to make are decisions that affect their 'peers' rather than their subordinates. Integrating, in other words, is important because people work in organizations and with other people rather than because they have subordinates.

The essence of the job of the first-line supervisor in plant or office – the foreman on the assembly line or the forelady of the key-punch room in the insurance company – is indeed the management of people. But then the first-line supervisor is only marginally a 'manager' – which is the reason why first-line supervision presents so many 'problems'. First-line supervisors, whether in the factory or in the office, are not commonly expected to plan and to organize, or to take much responsibility for their contribution and results. They are expected to deliver according to objectives set for them by others. In the typical mass-production plant this is all the supervisor possibly can or should do.

It would, therefore, seem appropriate to stress that the first criterion in identifying those people within an organization who have management responsibility is not command over people. *It is responsibility for contribution. Function rather than power has to be the distinctive criterion and the organizing principle.*

But what should these people be called? Many organizations have experimented with new definitions or have tried to give old terms a new meaning. Perhaps the best thing is not to coin a new term but to follow popular usage that speaks of the 'management group.' Within the management group there will be people whose function includes the traditional managerial function, responsibility for the work of others. There will be others who do not carry this responsibility within their specific assignment. And there will be a third group, somewhat ambiguous and in between: people whose job is that of a team leader or task force captain, or people who combine the function of advisor to top management with supervisory and administrative responsibility over a staff in a given area. Managers will move into situations where they are not superiors, and career professionals will sometimes serve as task force leaders.

This is not a neat, let alone a perfect, solution. In every organization there are people who are true specialists and who, while anything but rank-and-file workers, do not see themselves as part of management either. Their allegiance is to their technical or professional skill, rather than to their organization. The psychologist within a personnel department would prefer to be thought of as a professional – that is, a member of the world of a particular academic specialty – rather than as an executive of this or that company (or even as a faculty member of this or that university). And so does the computer specialist.

Nevertheless, this definition enables us to call 'manager' all the people who perform management tasks, whether or not they have power over others.

## What do managers do?

Most managers spend most of their time on things that are not 'managing'. A sales manager makes a statistical analysis or handles an important customer. A foreman repairs a tool or fills out a production report. A manufacturing manager designs a new plant layout or tests new materials. A company president works through the details of a bank loan or negotiates a big contract – or spends hours presiding at a dinner in honour of long-service employees. All these pertain to a particular function. All are necessary and have to be done well.

But they are apart from the work which is common to all *managers*, whatever their function or activity, rank or position. We can apply to the job of manager the systematic analysis of 'Scientific Management'. We can isolate that which a person does because he or she is a manager. We can divide the work into its constituent operations. And everybody can improve his or her performance as a manager by improving performance of these activities.

There are five basic operations in the work of the manager. Together they result in the integration of resources into a viable growing organism.

A manager, in the first place, sets objectives. He or she determines what the objectives should be. He determines what the goals in each area of objective should be. He decides what has to be done to reach these objectives. He makes the objectives effective by communicating them to the people whose performance is needed to attain them.

Second, a manager organizes. He or she analyses the activities, decisions, and relations needed. He classifies the work. He divides it into manageable activities and further divides the activities into manageable jobs. He groups these units and jobs into an organization structure. He or she selects people for the management of these units and for the jobs to be done.

Next, a manager motivates and communicates. He or she makes a team out of the people that are responsible for various jobs. He does that in his own relations to the people with whom he works. He does it through his 'people decisions' on pay, placement, and promotion. And he does it through constant communication, to and from his subordinates, and to and from his superior, and to and from his colleagues. This is the manager's integrating function.

The fourth basic element in the work of the manager is measurement. The manager establishes targets and yardsticks – and few factors are as important to the performance of the organization and of every person in it. He or she sees to it that each person has measurements available which are focused on the performance of the whole organization and which, at the same time, focus on the work of the individual. The manager analyses appraises, and interprets performance. As in all other areas of this work, he or she communicates the meaning of the measurements and their findings to subordinates, superiors, and colleagues.

Finally, a manager develops people, including himself or herself.

Every one of these categories can be divided further into subcategories, and each of the subcategories could be discussed in a book of its own. Moreover, every category requires different qualities and qualifications.

Setting objectives, for instance, is a problem of balances: a balance between business results and the realization of the principles one believes in; a balance between the immediate needs of the business and those of the future; a balance between desirable ends and available means. Setting objectives clearly requires analytical and synthesizing ability.

Organizing, too, requires analytical ability. For it demands the most economical use of scarce resources. But it deals with human beings, and therefore stands under the principle of justice and requires integrity. Both analytical ability and integrity are similarly required for the development of people, but there is a need also for human perception and insight.

The skill needed for motivation and communication is primarily social. Instead of analysis, integration and synthesis are needed. Justice dominates as the principle, economy is secondary. And integrity is of much greater importance than analytical ability.

Measuring requires, first and foremost, analytical ability. But it also demands that measurement be used to make self-control possible rather than abused to control people from the outside and above – that is, to dominate them. It is the common violation of this principle that largely explains why measurement is the weakest area in the work of the manager today. For example, measurements are sometimes used as a weapon of an internal secret police that supplies audits and critical appraisals of a manager's performance to the boss without even sending a carbon copy to the appraised manager. As long as measurements are abused as a tool of control, measuring will remain the weakest area in the manager's performance.

Setting objectives, organizing, motivating and communicating, measuring, and developing people are formal, classifying categories. Only a manager's experience can bring them to life, and make them concrete and meaningful. But because they are formal, they apply to every manager and to everything he or she does as a manager. They can therefore be used by all managers to appraise their own skill and performance and to work systematically on improving themselves and their performance.

Being able to set objectives does not make a manager, any more than the ability to tie a small knot in a confined space makes a surgeon. But without the ability to set objectives a person cannot be an adequate manager, just as no one can do good surgery without tying small knots. And as a surgeon becomes a better surgeon by improving the knot-tying skill, so a manager becomes a better manager by improving skill and performance in all categories of the work.

## The manager's resource: people

The manager works with a specific resource: people. And the human being is a unique resource requiring peculiar qualities in whoever attempts to work with it.

'Working' with the human being always means developing him or her. The direction which this development takes decides whether the human being – both as a person and as a resource – will become more productive or cease, ultimately, to be productive at all. This applies, as cannot be emphasized too strongly, not alone to the person who is being managed but also to the manager. Whether he or she develops subordinates in the right direction, helps them to grow and become bigger and richer persons, will directly determine whether he or she will develop, will grow or wither, become richer or become impoverished, improve or deteriorate.

One can learn certain skills in managing people – for instance, the skill to lead a conference or to conduct an interview. One can set down practices that aid development – in the structure of the relationship between manager and subordinate, in a promotion system, in the rewards and incentives of an organization. But when all is said and done, developing people still requires a basic quality in the manager which cannot be created by supplying skills or by emphasizing the importance of the task. It requires integrity of character.

There is tremendous stress these days on liking people, helping people, getting along with people, as qualifications for a manager. These alone are never enough. In every successful organization there are bosses who do not like people, who do not help them, and who do not get along with them. Cold, unpleasant, demanding, they often teach and develop more people than anyone else. They command more respect than the most likable person ever could. They demand exacting workmanship of themselves and other people. They set high standards and expect that they will be lived up to. They consider only what is right and never who is right. And though often themselves persons of brilliance, they never rate intellectual brilliance above integrity in others. The manager who lacks these qualities of character – no matter how likable, helpful, or amiable, no matter even how competent or brilliant – is a menace who is unfit to be a manager.

What a manager does can be analysed systematically. What a manager has to be able to do can be learned. But one qualification the manager cannot acquire but must bring to the task. It is not genius: it is character.

## Management: a practice, not a science

During the last fifty years, every developed country has become a society of institutions. Every major social task, whether economic performance or health care, education or the protection of the environment, the pursuit of new knowledge or defence, is today being entrusted to organizations, designed for long life and managed by their own managements. On the performance of these institutions, the performance of modern society – if not the very survival of its members – increasingly depends. The performance and the survival of the institution depend on the performance of management.

The individual has a direct stake in the performance of managers and management. Nine out of every ten of the people who go to college beyond high school go to work as employees in organizations. Their effectiveness and performance, their satisfaction, their achievement, and their growth as human beings largely depend on the performance of management in the employing institution. And a good many of these 'knowledge workers' will themselves become managers so that their own capacity to perform and to achieve will depend on their knowledge of management and on their skill as practitioners of management.

In view of this it would be comforting to be able to speak of management as a 'science'. But in fact we can only do harm by believing that management can ever fully be a 'science'.

To be sure, the work of the manager can be systematically analysed and classified. There are, in other words, distinct professional features and a scientific aspect to management. Management is not just a matter of experience, hunch or native ability. Its elements and requirements can be analysed, organized systematically, and learned by anyone with normal intelligence. Altogether this entire book is based on the proposition that the days of the 'intuitive' manager are numbered. This book assumes that managers can improve their performance in all areas of management, and on all levels of management – from the trainee position to the level of the chief executive officer of the giant multinational corporation – through the systematic study of principles, the acquisition of organized knowledge, and the continuing analysis of performance in all areas of work. Nothing can contribute so much to skill, to effectiveness, and to performance as a manager. And underlying this theme is the conviction that the impact of the manager on modern society and its citizens is so great as to require of the manager the self-discipline and the high service standards of the true professional.

And yet the ultimate test of management is performance. Achievement rather than knowledge remains, of necessity, both aim and proof. Management is a practice rather than a science or a profession, though containing elements of both. Only damage to society and economy could result from the attempt to 'professionalize' management by limiting access to management to people with a special academic degree. The end would be the replacement of managers by bureaucrats and the stifling of innovation, entrepreneurship, and creativity.

Anyhow we still know far too little to put management into the straitjacket of a 'science' or to make the practice of management into a licensed professional monopoly. For the study of management is no older than management itself – and that means that it has barely begun.

But we do know a good deal – though as this book will make clear, the areas of ignorance and searching exceed the areas in which we have truly firm, truly tested knowledge, and the 'right answer'.

We know, first, a good many things which, however plausible they may seem, do *not* work in the practice of management. We further know that management is not confined to one country or to one culture. Indeed, a century ago when the first managed institutions arose – the transcontinental railroad in America, for instance – management as a practice and management as a discipline were tackled by people of many nationalities. In the years following World War II it sometimes seemed to many observers that management was an American invention. This was a mistake – and shortly proven to be such by the rapid recovery of Western Europe and Japan. The management function, the work of management, its tasks and its dimensions are universal and do not vary from country to country. But the way the work is done is strongly influenced by national traits, national traditions, national history – and sometimes determined by them, as in such important areas as the relationship between government and business management, the do's and dont's in managing people, or the structure of top management.

Management is a social function, embedded in a tradition of values, customs, and beliefs, and in governmental and political systems. Management is – and should be – culture-conditioned; in turn, management and managers shape culture and society. Thus, although management is an organized body of knowledge and as such applicable everywhere, it is also 'culture'. It is not 'value-free' science.

Above all we know that managers practise management. They do not practise economics. They do not practise quantification. They do not practise behavioural science. These are tools for managers. But they no more practise economics than a physician practises blood testing. They no more practise behavioural sciences than a biologist practises the microscope. They no more practise quantification than a lawyer practises precedents. Managers practise management.

Thus there are specific managerial skills which pertain to management, rather than to any other discipline. One of these is communication within organizations. Another is the making of decisions under conditions of uncertainty. And there is also a specific entrepreneurial skill: strategic planning.

As a specific discipline, management has its own basic problems, its own specific approaches, its own distinct concerns. A manager who understands the discipline of management will still be an effective – and may even be a first-rate – manager with no more than minimum competence in managerial skills and tools. A person who knows only the skills and techniques, without understanding the fundamentals of management, is not a manager but merely a technician.

Management is a practice rather than a science. In this, it is comparable to medicine, law, and engineering. It is not knowledge but performance. Furthermore, it is not the application of common sense, or leadership, let alone financial manipulation. Its practice is based both on knowledge and on responsibility.

## Note: the roots and history of management

Some recent writings on management give the impression that their authors consider management to be an invention of the last thirty years since World War II, and an American invention at that. True, before World War II interest in, and study of, management was confined to small groups – the popular interest in management as a discipline and a field of study – what is sometimes called the 'management boom' – is fairly recent. But management, both as a practice and as a field of study has a respectable history, in many different countries, going back almost two centuries.

When the early economists – from Adam Smith (1723–1790) to Karl Marx (1818–1883) did their work, management did not exist. To them, the economy was impersonal and governed by objective economic forces. As a modern spokesman for the classical tradition, the Anglo-American Kenneth Boulding (b. 1910) phrases it: 'Economics deals with the behaviour of commodities, rather than with the behaviour of men.' Or, as with Marx, impersonal laws of history were seen to dominate. Humanity can only adapt. It can, at best, optimize what the economy makes possible; at worst, it impedes the forces of the economy and wastes resources. The last of the great English classical economists, Alfred Marshall (1842–1924), did indeed add management to the factors of production, land, labour, and capital. But this was a half-hearted concession. Management was still not a central factor.

From the beginning there was however, a different approach which put the manager into the centre of the economy and which stressed the managerial task of making resources productive. J. B. Say (1767–1832), the brilliant French economist, was an early follower of Adam Smith. But in his own works the pivot is not the factors of production. It is the entrepreneur – a word Say coined – who directs resources from less productive into more productive investments and who thereby creates wealth. Say was followed by the 'utopian socialists' of the French tradition, especially Francois Fourier (1772–1837) and that eccentric genius, the Comte de Saint-Simon (1760–1825). At that time there were no large organizations and no managers, but both Fourier and Saint-Simon anticipated developments and 'discovered' management before it actually came into being. Saint-Simon in particular saw the emergence of organization. And he saw the task of making resources productive and of building social structures. He saw managerial tasks.

It is for their stress on management as a separate and distinct force, and one which can act independently of the factors of production as well as the laws of history, that Marx vehemently denounced the French. But it is the French – and above all Saint-Simon – who, in effect, laid down the basic approaches and the basic concepts on which every socialist economy has actually been designed. No matter how much the Russians today invoke the name of Marx, their spiritual ancestor is Saint-Simon.

In America too management was early seen as central. Alexander Hamilton's (1757–1804) famous 'Report on Manufactures' starts out with Adam Smith, but then Hamilton gave emphasis to the constructive, purposeful, and systematic role of management. He saw in management, rather than in economic forces, the engine of economic and social development; and in organization, the carrier of economic advance. Following him, Henry Clay (1777–1852) with his famous 'American system' produced what might be called the first blueprint for systematic economic development.

A little later, an industrialist in Scotland, Robert Owen (1771–1858), actually became the first manager. In his textile mill, Owen, in the 1820s, first tackled the problems of productivity and motivation, or the relationship of worker to work, or worker to enterprise, and of worker to management – to this day key questions in management. With Owen, the manager emerges as a real person. But it was a long time before Owen had successors.

## The emergence of large-scale organization

What had to happen first was the rise of large-scale organization. This occurred simultaneously – around 1870 – in two places. In North America the transcontinental railroad emerged as a managerial problem. On the continent of Europe, the 'universal bank' – entrepreneurial in aim, national in scope, and with multiple headquarters – made obsolescent traditional structures and concepts and required management.

One response was given by Henry Towne (1844–1924) in the United States, especially in his paper *The Engineer as Economist*. Towne outlined what might be called the first programme for management. He raised basic questions: effectiveness as against efficiency; organization of the work as against the organization of workers; value set in the marketplace and by the customer as against technical accomplishment. With Towne begins the systematic concern with the relationship between the tasks of management and the work of management.

At roughly the same time, in Germany, Georg Siemens (1839–1901), in building the Deutsche Bank into the leading financial institution of continental Europe, first designed an effective top management, first thought through the top-management tasks, and first tackled the basic problems of communications and information in the large organization.

In Japan, Eiichi Shibusawa (1840–1931), a statesman turned business leader, in the 1870s and 1880s first raised fundamental questions regarding the relationship between business enterprise and national purpose, and between business needs and individual ethics. He tackled management education systematically. Shibusawa first envisioned the *professional* manager. Japan's rise to economic leadership in this century is largely founded on Shibusawa's thought and work.

A few decades later, in the years before and after the turn of the century, all the major approaches to modern management were fashioned. Again the developments occurred independently in many countries.

In the 1880s Frederick W. Taylor (1856–1915), the self-taught American engineer, began the study of work. It is fashionable today to look down on Taylor for his outdated psychology, but Taylor was the first man in history who did not take work for granted, but looked at it and studied it. His approach to work is still the basic foundation. And, although Taylor in his approach to the worker was clearly a man of the nineteenth century, he started out with social rather than engineering or profit objectives. What led Taylor to his work and provided his motivation throughout was first the desire to free the worker from the burden of heavy toil, destructive of body and soul. And then it was the hope to make it possible to give the labourer a decent livelihood through increasing the productivity of work.

Around the same time in France, Henri Fayol (1841–1925), head of a coal mine which for its time was a very large company, first thought through organization structure and developed the first rational approach to the organization of enterprise: the functional principle. In Germany, Walter Rathenau (1867–1922), whose early training had been in a large company, asked: 'What is the place of the large enterprise in a modern society and in a modern nation? What impact does it have on both? And what are its fundamental contributions and its fundamental responsibilities?' Most present questions of the social responsibilities of business were first raised and thought through by Rathenau in the years before World War I. Also in Germany, at the same time, the new discipline of *Betriebswissenschaft* (literally, the science of enterprise), was developed by such men as Eugen Schmalenbach (1873–1955). The management sciences developed since – managerial accounting, operations research, decision theory, and so on – are largely extentions, though in the main, unconscious ones, of the *Betriebswissenschaft* of those years before World War I. And in America, German-born Hugo Muensterberg (1863–1916) first tried to apply the social and behavioural sciences, and especially psychology, to modern organization and management.

## The first management boom

After World War I there came what might be called the first management boom. It was sparked primarily by two of the most highly respected statesmen of the period, the American Herbert Hoover (1874–1964) and the Czech Thomas J. Masaryk (1850–1937). Hoover, the Quaker engineer, had vaulted to worldwide prominence by applying principles of management to the first massive foreign-aid operation in history. He planned the feeding of hundreds of thousands of starving people: first, before America's entry into World War I in his Belgian Relief Operation, and then after the end of World War I in the relief operations in Central and Eastern Europe. But it was Masaryk, the historian, who had become the first president of the new Czech Republic, who

conceived the idea that management would be able to restore the
economies of Europe after their destruction by war – an idea that
then found its realization twenty-five years later in the Marshall
Plan after World War II. These two men founded the international management movement and tried to mobilize management as a major social force.

But the period between the two World Wars was not congenial
to such an idea. It was a period of stagnation, a period in which
the highest goal which any national government or any economy
– except the United States – could conceive was a return to what
had been. It rapidly became a world in which mounting political,
social, and economic tensions paralysed will as well as vision.

## The work of the twenties and thirties

The first management boom fizzled out. Its high hopes were replaced by frustration. Yet behind the apparent stagnation, work
went on. It was in those years that the foundations for the sweeping management boom of the post-World War II period were
put in place.

In the early twenties, Pierre S. du Pont (1870–1954) at the Du
Pont Company, followed by Alfred P. Sloan, Jr (1875–1966) at
General Motors, first developed the organization principle for
the new 'big business', the principle of decentralization. Du Pont
and, even more, Sloan also first developed systematic approaches
to business objectives, to business strategy, and to strategic planning. Also, in the United States, Sears, Roebuck – led first by
Julius Rosenwald (1862–1932) and then by Robert E. Wood
(1879–1969) – built the first business to be based on the marketing approach. In Europe shortly thereafter, the architects of the
Dutch-English merger that resulted in the Unilever Companies
designed what to this day may well be the most advanced structure for the multinational corporation and came to grips also with
the problem of multinational business planning and multinational marketing.

The discipline of management was also further developed. In
the United States there were the successors to Taylor, the hus-

band and wife team of Frank and Lillian Gilbreth (1868–1924, 1878–1972), and Henry Gantt (1861–1919). In Great Britain Ian Hamilton (1853–1947), reflecting on his experiences as a military leader during World War I, realized the need to balance formal structure with policies that give 'soul' to an organization. Two Americans, Mary Parker Follett (1868–1933) and Chester Barnard (1886–1961), first studied the process of decision-making in organizations, the relationships between formal and informal organizations, and the role and function of the executive. Cyril Burt (1883–1972) in England and the Australian Elton Mayo (1880–1949), working at Harvard, developed, respectively, industrial psychology and human relations and applied each to enterprise and management.

Management as a discipline also began to be taught in the interwar years. The Harvard Business School first began in the thirties to teach courses in management – though still mainly in production management. And the Massachusetts Institute of Technology started, at the same time, advanced management work with young executives in mid-career.

The American James McKinsey (1889–1937) and the Englishman Lyndall F. Urwick (b. 1891) started management consulting, that is, consulting no longer confined to technical problems, but dealing with fundamental management concerns such as business policy and management organization. Urwick also classified and codified the work on the structure of management and on the function of the executive that had been done until that time.

## Summary

Our society has in this century become a society of organizations. Organizations depend on managers, are built by managers, directed and held together by managers, and made to perform by managers. Once an organization grows beyond a very small size, it needs managers who practice professional management. This means management grounded in a discipline and informed by the objective needs of the organization and of its people, rather than management based on ownership or on political appointment. Every organization needs people – managers – who do the specific work of management: planning, organizing, integrating, measuring, and developing people. It needs managers who take responsibility for contribution. Responsibility for contribution, rather than rank or title, or command over people, defines the manager. And integrity rather than genius is the basic requirement.

# Part One
# Business Performance

W do not yet have a genuine theory of business and no integrated discipline of business management. But we know what a business is and what its key functions are. We understand the functions of profit and the requirements of productivity. Any business needs to think through the question: What is our business and what should it be ? From the definition of its mission and purpose, a business must derive objectives in a number of key areas, and it must balance these objectives against each other and against the competing demands of today and tomorrow. A business needs to convert objectives into concrete strategies and to concentrate resources on them. Finally, it needs to think through its strategic planning, the decisions of today that will make the business of tomorrow.

# 2 The Dimensions of Management

Business enterprises – and public-service institutions as well – are organs of society. They do not exist for their own sake, but to fulfil a specific social purpose and to satisfy a specific need of society, community, or individual. They are not ends in themselves, but means. The right question to ask in respect to them is not: What are they? but: What are they supposed to be doing and what are their tasks?

Management, in turn, is the organ of the institution. It has no function in itself, indeed, no existence in itself. Management divorced from the institution it serves is not management.

There are three tasks – equally important but essentially different – that face the management of every institution:

—to think through and define the specific purpose and mission of the institution, whether business enterprise, hospital, or university

—to make work productive and the worker achieving

—to manage social impacts and social responsibilities

These might be called the dimensions of management.

## Purpose and mission

An institution exists for a specific purpose and mission, a specific social function. In the business enterprise this means economic performance.

With respect to this first task, the task of specific performance, business and nonbusiness institutions differ. In respect to every other task, they are similar. But only business has economic performance as its specific mission. It is the definition of a business that it exists for the sake of economic performance. In all other institutions – hospital, church, university, or armed services – economics is a restraint. In those institutions the budget sets limits to what the institution and the manager can do. In business enterprise, economic performance is the rationale and purpose.

Business, while by no means the only task to be discharged in society, is a priority task, because all other social tasks – education, health care, defence, and the advancement of knowledge – depend on the surplus of economic resources. Only successful economic performance can produce these profits and other savings. The more of these other satisfactions we want, and the more highly we value them, the more we depend on economic performance of business enterprise.

Business management must always, in every decision and action, put economic performance first. It can justify its existence and its authority only by the economic results it produces. A business management has failed if it fails to produce economic results. It has failed if it does not supply goods and services desired by the consumer at a price the consumer is willing to pay. It has failed if it does not improve, or at least maintain, the wealth-producing capacity of the economic resources entrusted to it. And this, whatever the economic or political structure or ideology of a society, means responsibility for profitability.

The first definition of business management is that it is an economic organ, the specifically economic organ of an industrial society. Every act, every decision, every deliberation of management, has economic performance as its first dimension.

But business management is no different from the management of other institutions in one crucial respect: it has to *manage*. And managing is not just passive, adaptive behaviour; it means taking action to make the desired results come to pass.

The early economist conceived of the businessman's behaviour as purely passive; success in business meant rapid and intelligent adaption to events occurring outside, in an economy shaped by impersonal, objective forces that were neither controlled by the businessman nor influenced by his reaction to them. We may call this the concept of the 'trader'. Even if he was not considered a parasite, his contributions were seen as purely mechanical: the shifting of resources to more productive use. Today's economist sees the businessman is choosing rationally between alternatives of action. This is no longer a mechanistic concept; obviously the choice has a real impact on the economy. But still, the economist's 'businessman' – the picture that underlies the prevailing economic 'theory of the firm' and the theorem of the 'maximization of profits' – *reacts* to economic developments. The businessperson is still passive, still adaptive – though with a choice between various ways to adapt. Basically, this is a concept of the 'investor' or the 'financier' rather than of the manager.

Of course, it is always important to adapt to economic changes rapidly, intelligently, and rationally. But managing implies responsibility for attempting to shape the economic environment; for planning, initiating, and carrying through changes in that economic environment; for constantly pushing back the limitations of economic circumstances on the enterprise's ability to contribute. What is possible – the economist's 'economic conditions' – is therefore only one pole in managing a business. What is desirable in the interest of economy and enterprise is the other. And while humanity can never really 'master' the environment, while we are always held within a tight vise of possibilities, it is management's specific job to make what is desirable first possible and then actual. Management is not just a creature of the economy; it is a creator as well. And only to the extent to which it masters the economic circumstances, and alters them by consciously directed action, does it really manage. To manage a business means, therefore, to *manage by objectives*.

## Productive work and Worker achievement

The second task of management is to make work productive and the worker achieving. Business enterprise (or any other institution) has only one true resource: people. It performs by making human resources productive. It accomplishes its performance through work. To make work productive is, therefore, an essential function. But at the same time, these institutions in today's society are increasingly the means through which individual human beings find their livelihood, find their access to social status, to community, and to individual achievement and satisfaction. To make the worker achieving is, therefore, more and more important and is a measure of the performance of an institution. It is increasingly a task of management.

Organizing work according to its own logic is only the first step. The second and far more difficult one is making work suitable for human beings – and their logic is radically different from the logic of work. Making the worker achieving implies consideration of the human being as an organism having peculiar physiological and psychological properties, abilities, and limitations. It implies consideration of the human resource – as persons and not as things, and as having – unlike any other resource – personality, citizenship, control over whether they work, how much and how well, and thus requiring responsibility, motivation, participation, satisfaction, incentives and rewards, leadership, status, and function.

Management, and management alone, can satisfy these requirements. For workers, whether machine tenders or executive vice-presidents, must be satisfied through their achievement in work and job – that is, within the enterprise; and management is the activating organ of the enterprise.

The enterprise, by definition, must be capable of producing more or better than all the resources that comprise it. It must be a genuine whole: greater than – or at least different from – the sum of its parts, with its output larger than the sum of all inputs.

The enterprise cannot therefore be a mechanical assemblage of resources. To make an enterprise out of resources it is not enough to put them together in logical order and then to throw the switch of capital, as the nineteenth-century economists firmly believed (and as many of their successors among academic economists still believe). What is needed is a change of the resources into a more productive form. This requires management.

But it is also clear that the 'resources' capable of enlargement can only be human resources. All other resources stand under the laws of mechanics. They can be better utilized or worse utilized, but they can never have an output greater than the sum of the inputs. People, alone of all resources, can grow and develop. Only the directed, focused, united effort of free human beings can produce a real whole.

When we speak of growth and development we imply that the

human being himself determines what he contributes. Yet, we habitually define rank-and-file workers – as distinguished from managers – as people who do as they are directed, without responsibility or share in the decisions concerning their own work. This indicates that we consider workers in the same light as other material resources and, as far as their contribution to the enterprise is concerned, as standing under the laws of mechanics. This is a serious misunderstanding. The misunderstanding, however, is not in the definition of rank-and-file *work*, but rather in the failure to see that rank-and-file *jobs* are potentially managerial, or would be more productive if made so.

Human resources acquire the capacity to grow, to develop, to contribute through management. We speak of 'organization' – the formal structure of the enterprise. But what we mean is the organization of managers and of the functions they manage; neither brick and mortar nor rank-and-file workers are the stuff of organization structure. We speak of 'leadership' and of the 'spirit' of a company. But leadership is given by managers and effective primarily within management; and the spirit is made by the spirit within the management group. We talk of 'objectives' for the company, and of its performance. But the objectives are goals for management people; the performance is management performance. And if an enterprise fails to perform, we rightly hire not different workers but a new president.

## Social impacts and social responsibilities

The third task of management is managing the social impacts and the social responsibilities of the enterprise. None of our institutions exists by itself and as an end in itself. Every one is an organ of society and exists for the sake of society. Business is no exception. 'Free enterprise' cannot be justified as being good for business. It can be justified only as being good for society.

Every one of our institutions today exists to contribute outside of itself, to supply and satisfy nonmembers. Business exists to supply goods and services to customers and economic surplus to society, rather than to supply jobs to workers and managers, or even dividends to shareholders. Jobs and dividends are necessary means but not ends. The hospital does not exist for the sake of doctors and nurses, but for the sake of the patients whose one and only desire is to leave the hospital cured and never come back. The school does not exist for the sake of teachers, but for the students. For a management to forget this is mismanagement.

To discharge its job, to produce economic goods and services, the business enterprise has to have impacts on people, on communities, and on society. It has to have power and authority over people, for example, employees, whose own ends and purposes are not defined by and within the enterprise. It has to have impact on the community as a neighbour, as the source of jobs and tax revenue but also of waste products and pollutants. And, in increasingly, in our pluralist society of organizations, it has to add to its fundamental concern for the quantities of life (economic goods and services) a concern for the quality of life, for the physical, human, and social environment of modern man and modern community.

This dimension of management is inherent in the work of managers of *all* institutions. University, hospital, and government agency equally have impacts, equally have responsibilities – and by and large have been far less aware of them, far less concerned with their human, social, and community responsibilities than business has. Yet, more and more, we look to business management for leadership with regard to the quality of life. Managing social impacts is, therefore, becoming a third major task and a third major dimension of management.

## Which task is most important?

Managing these three tasks always has to be done at the same time and within the same managerial action. It cannot even be said that one of the three tasks predominates or requires greater skill or competence. True, economic performance comes first – it is the aim of the enterprise and the reason for its existence. But if work and worker are grossly mismanaged there will be no economic performance, no matter how good the chief executive may be in managing the business. Economic performance achieved by mismanaging work and workers is illusory and actually destructive of capital, even in the fairly short run. Such performance will raise costs to the point where the enterprise ceases to be competitive. It will, by creating class hatred and class warfare, make it impossible in the end for the enterprise to operate at all. And mismanaging social impacts eventually will destroy society's support for the enterprise – and with it the enterprise as well.

Each of these three dimensions has a primacy of its own. Managing a business has primacy because the enterprise is an economic institution; but making work productive and workers achieving has importance precisely because society is not an economic institution and looks to management for the realization of basic beliefs and values. Managing the enterprise's social impacts has importance because no organ can survive the body which it serves; and the enterprise is an organ of society and community.

## The time dimension

One complexity is ever-present in every management problem, every decision, every action – not, properly speaking, a fourth task of management, and yet an additional dimension: time.

Management always has to consider both the present and the future; both the short run and the long run. A management problem is not solved if immediate profits are purchased by endangering the long-range health, perhaps even the survival, of the company. A management decision is irresponsible if it risks disaster this year for the sake of a grandiose future. The all too common case of the great man in management who produces startling economic results as long as he runs the company but leaves behind nothing but a sinking hulk is an example of irresponsible managerial action and of failure to balance present and future. The immediate economic results are actually fictitious and are achieved by destroying capital. In every case where present and future are not both satisfied, where their requirements are not harmonized, or at least balanced, capital – that is, wealth-producing resource – is endangered, damaged, or destroyed.

There are two reasons why the time dimension is of particular importance in management's job, and of particular difficulty. In the first place, through economic and technological progress, the time span for the fruition and proving out of a decision is steadily lengthening. Edison, in the 1880s, needed two years or so between the start of laboratory work on an idea and the start of pilot-plant operations. Today it may well take Edison's successors fifteen years. A half century ago, a new plant was expected to pay for itself in two or three years; today, with capital investment per worker twenty times that of 1900, the payoff period often runs to ten or twelve years. A human organization, such as a sales force or a management group, may take even longer to build and to pay for itself.

The second peculiar characteristic of the time dimension is that management has to live always in both present and future. It must keep the enterprise performing in the present – or else there will be no enterprise capable of performing in the future. And it has to make the enterprise capable of performance, growth, and change in the future. Otherwise it has destroyed capital – that is, the capacity of resources to produce wealth tomorrow.

For the manager the future is discontinuity. And yet the future, however different, can be reached only from the present. The greater the leap into the unknown, the stronger the foundation for the takeoff has to be. The time dimension gives the managerial decision its special characteristics.

## Administration and entrepreneurship

Managers always have to administer, to manage and improve what already exists and is already known. But there is another dimension to managerial performance. Managers also have to be entrepreneurs. They have to redirect resources from areas of low or diminishing results to areas of high or increasing results. They have to slough off yesterday and to make obsolete what already exists and is already known. They have to create tomorrow.

In the ongoing business markets, technologies, products, and services exist. Facilities and equipment are in place. Capital has been invested and has to be serviced. People are employed and are in specific jobs, and so on. The administrative job of the manager is to optimize the yield from these resources.

This, we are usually told, (especially by economists) means efficiency, that is, doing better what is already being done. It means focus on costs. But the optimizing approach should focus on effectiveness. If focuses on opportunities to produce revenue, to create markets, and to change the economic characteristics of existing products and markets. It asks not, How do we do this or that better? It asks, Which of the products really produce extraordinary economic results or are capable of producing them? Which of the markets and/or end uses are capable of producing extraordinary results? It then asks, To what results should, therefore, the resources and efforts of the business be allocated so as to produce extraordinary results rather than the 'ordinary' ones which is all efficiency can possibly produce?

Of course efficiency is important. Even the healthiest business, the business with the greatest effectiveness, can die of poor efficiency. But even the most efficient business cannot survive, let alone succeed, if it is efficient in doing the wrong things, that is, if it lacks effectiveness. No amount of efficiency would have enabled the manufacturer of buggy whips to survive.

Effectiveness is the foundation of success – efficiency is a minimum condition for survival after success has been achieved. Efficiency is concerned with doing things right. Effectiveness is doing the right things.

Efficiency concerns itself with the input of effort into all areas of activity. Effectiveness, however, starts out with the realization that in business, as in any other social organism, 10 or 15 per cent of the phenomena – such as products, orders, customers, markets, or people – produce 80 to 90 per cent of the results. The other 85 to 90 per cent of the phenomena, no matter how efficiently taken care of, produce nothing but costs (which are always proportionate to transactions, that is, to busy-ness).

The first administrative job of the manager is, therefore, to make effective the very small core of worthwhile activities which is capable of being effective. At the same time, he or she neutralizes (or abandons) the very large number of ordinary transactions – products or staff activities, research work or sales efforts – which, no matter how well done, will not yield extraordinarily high results.

The second administrative task is to bring the business all the time a little closer to the full realization of its potential. Even the most successful business works at a low coefficient of performance as measured against its potential – the economic results that could be obtained were efforts and resources marshalled to produce the maximum yield they are inherently capable of.

This task is not innovation; it actually takes the business as it is today and asks, What is its theoretical optimum? What prevents us from attaining it? Where (in other words) are the limiting and restraining factors that hold back the business and deprive it of the full return on its resources and efforts?

At the same time, inherent in the managerial task is entrepreneurship: making the business of tomorrow. Inherent in the task is innovation.

Making the business of tomorrow starts out with the conviction that the business of tomorrow will be and must be different. But it also starts out – of necessity – with the business of today. Making the business of tomorrow cannot be a flash of genius. It requires systematic analysis and hard, rigorous work today – and that means by people in today's business and operating within it.

Success cannot, one might say, be continued forever. Businesses are, after all, human creations which have no true permanence. Even the oldest businesses are creations of recent centuries. But a business enterprise must continue beyond the lifetime of the individual or of the generation to be capable of producing its contributions to economy and to society. The perpetuation of a business is a central entrepreneurial task – and ability to do so may well be the most definitive test of a management.

## Summary

There are three basic tasks – they might be called dimensions – in management. There is the first task of thinking through and de-

fining the specific purpose and mission of the organization –
whether business enterprise, hospital, school, or government
agency. There is the second task of making work productive and
the worker achieving. There is finally the task of managing social
impacts and social responsibilities. In respect to the second and
third task, all institutions are alike. It is the first task that distinguishes the business from the hospital, school, or government
agency. And the specific purpose and mission of business enterprise is economic performance. To discharge it, managers always
have to balance the present against an uncertain and risky future,
have to perform for the short run and make their business capable
of performance over the long run. Managers always have to be
stewards of what already exists; they have to be administrators.
They also have to create what is to be; they have to be entrepreneurs, risk-takers, and innovators. For a modern business can
only produce results, both for society and for its own people, if it
can survive beyond the life span of a person and perform in a new
and different future.

# 3 Managing a Business: The Sears Story

There are hundreds, if not thousands, of books on the management of the various functions of a business – production, marketing, finance, engineering, purchasing, personnel, public relations, and so forth. But what it is to manage a business, what
management is supposed to do and how it should be doing it,
are subjects which are rarely discussed.

This oversight is no accident. It reflects the absence of both a
useful theory of business enterprise and an adequate discipline of
management. Therefore, rather than theorizing, we shall first

look at the conduct and behaviour of an actual business enterprise. There is no better illustration of what a business is and what managing it means than one of America's most successful enterprises: Sears, Roebuck and Company.

With sales in excess of $15 billion, Sears is the largest retailer in the world. It is by far the most profitable retail business anywhere and altogether one of the most profitable companies in the American economy, by any yardstick. Only Marks & Spencer in Great Britain can compare with Sears in terms of success (see Chapter 6). But Marks & Spencer is not only much smaller – barely one-tenth of Sears; it also admittedly owes much of its success, especially in its earlier years, to imitating Sears.

Sears, Roebuck has always been a major growth company, even though its industry, the retail business, is old and well established, and totally lacking in the glamour of high technology or scientific innovation. No other business in America, not even General Motors, has shown such a consistent and sustained growth pattern.

Sears became a business around the turn of the century, with the realization that the American farmer represented a separate and distinct market. Separate because of his isolation, which made existing channels of distribution virtually inaccessible to him; distinct because of his specific needs, which were different from those of the city consumer. Although farmers' purchasing power was individually low in total it represented a tremendous, and almost untapped, buying potential.

To reach the farmer, a new distribution channel had to be created. Merchandise had to be produced to answer his needs and wants. It had to be brought to him at a low price, and with a guarantee of regular supply. He had to be given a warranty of reliability and honesty on the part of the supplier, since his physical isolation made it impossible for him to inspect merchandise before delivery or to obtain a refund if cheated.

To create Sears, Roebuck as a business required analysis of customer and market, and especially of what the farmer considered 'value'. Furthermore, it required major innovation in a number of distinct areas.

First, it demanded systematic 'merchandising', that is, the finding and developing of sources of supply for the particular goods the farmer needed, in the quality and quantity he needed, and at a price he could pay. Second, it required a mail-order catalogue capable of serving as adequate substitute for the shopping trips to the big city the farmer could not make. For this reason, the catalogue had to become a regular publication, rather than an announcement of spectacular bargains at irregular intervals. It had to break with the entire tradition of selling by mail and learn not to high-pressure the farmer into buying by exaggerated claims, but to give him a factual description of the goods offered. The aim had to be to create a permanent customer by convincing him of the reliability of the catalogue and of the company behind it. The catalogue thus became the 'wish book' for the farmer.

Third, the age-old concept of 'let the buyer beware' had to be changed to 'let the *seller* beware' – the meaning of the famous Sears policy of 'your money back and no questions asked'. Fourth, a way had to be found to fill large quantities of customer orders cheaply and quickly. Without the mail-order plant, conduct of the business would have been physically impossible.

Finally, a human organization had to be built – and when Sears, Roebuck started to become a business, most of the necessary human skills were not available. There were, for instance, no buyers for this kind of operation, no accountants versed in the new requirements of inventory control, no artists to illustrate the catalogues, no clerks experienced in the handling of a huge volume of customer orders.

Richard Sears (1863–1914) gave the company his name. He understood the needs of the customer, and he brilliantly improvised to satisfy these needs. But it was not he who made Sears, Roebuck into a business enterprise. In fact, Richard Sears' own operations could hardly be called a business. He was a shrewd speculator, buying up distress-merchandise and offering it, one batch at a time, through mail advertising. Every one of his deals was a complete transaction in itself. When finished, it liquidated itself and the business with it. Sears might have made a lot of money for himself, but his way of operating could never have founded a business, let alone perpetuate it. Indeed his success almost bankrupted him, as it pushed his company far beyond the limit of his managerial capacity. His company was about to go under when he sold it to a total outsider, the Chicago clothing merchant Julius Rosenwald (1862–1932).

Between 1895, when he took control, and 1905, when the Chicago mail-order plant was opened, Rosenwald made a business enterprise out of Sears. He analysed the market, began the systematic development of merchandise sources, and invented the regular, factual mail-order catalogue and the policy of 'satisfaction guaranteed or your money back'. He built the productive human organization, and gave management people a maximum of authority and full responsibility for results. Later he gave every employee an ownership stake in the company, bought out of profits. Rosenwald is the father not only of Sears, Roebuck but of the distribution revolution which has changed the world economy in the twentieth century and which is so vital a factor in economic growth.

Only one basic contribution to the early history of Sears was not made by Rosenwald. The Chicago mail-order plant was designed by Otto Doering in 1903. Five years before Henry Ford's, it was the first modern mass-production plant, complete with the breakdown of all work into simple repetitive operations, with an assembly line, conveyor belt, standardized interchangeable parts – and, above all, with planned plant-wide scheduling.

The next phase of the Sears story began in the mid-twenties. The first chapter was dominated by Julius Rosenwald; the second chapter was dominated by General Robert E. Wood (1879–1969). When Wood joined Sears, the original Sears market was changing rapidly. The farmer was no longer isolated; the automobile had enabled him to go to town and to shop there. He no longer formed a distinct market but was, largely thanks to Sears, rapidly modifying his way of life and his standard of living to conform to those of the urban middle class.

Wood had made this analysis even before he joined Sears. Out of it came the decision to switch Sears' emphasis to retail stores – equipped to serve both the motorized farmer and the city population.

A whole series of innovations had to be undertaken to make this decision work. Merchandising had to add two new major functions: the design of products, and the development of manufacturers capable of producing them in large quantity. Products originally designed for the high-income consumer – for instance, refrigerators in the 1920s – had to be redesigned for a mass market with limited purchasing power. Suppliers had to be created – often with Sears money and Sears-trained management – to produce these goods. This required another important innovation: a basic policy for the relations between Sears and its suppliers, especially those who depended on the company's purchases for the bulk of their business. Merchandise planning and research had to be invented; hundreds of small suppliers capable of producing for a mass market had to be built up. These factors are as basic to mass distribution in Sears' second phase as mail order and catalogues were in its first, and they were as distinct a contribution to the American economy.

Retail selling also meant getting store managers. Mail-order selling did not prepare a person for the management of a retail store. The greatest bottleneck for the first ten or fifteen years of Sears's retail operation – almost until World War II – was the shortage of store managers. The most systematic innovation had to be in the field of manager development; and the Sears policies of the thirties became the starting point for all the work in manager development now going on.

Expansion into retail selling also meant radical innovations in organization structure. Mail-order selling is highly centralized; but retail stores cannot be run from headquarters two thousand miles away. They must be managed locally. Only a few mail-order plants were needed to supply the country; Sears today has over a thousand stores, each with its own market in its own locality. Methods of structuring and managing a decentralized company, measuring the performance of store managers, and maintaining both corporate unity and local autonomy – all had to be devised to make retail selling possible. And new compensation policies had to be found to reward store managers for performance.

Finally, Sears had to innovate in store location, architecture, and physical arrangement. The traditional retail store was unsuited for the Sears market. It was not just a matter of putting the Sears store on the outskirts of the city and of providing it with an adequate parking lot. The whole concept of the retail store had to be changed. In fact, few people even at Sears realize how far this innovation has gone and how deeply it has influenced the shopping habits of the American people, as well as the physical appearance of our towns. The suburban shopping centre which appeared in the fifties as a radical innovation in retail selling is just a logical extension of the concepts and methods developed by Sears during the thirties.

In 1954 General Wood retired, though he retained influence in the company for another ten years. No other long-term dominant chief executive has emerged to replace him. Since Wood's retirement, Sears has been run by a small team of men – a chairman, a president and an executive vice-president. Without exception, these members of the top team retire after five to seven years in office.

The changes brought about by these successive managements have redefined Sears' business. Under General Wood, Sears was moving from being a seller to being a buyer. Under his successors, Sears has redefined itself as a maker for the American family. Increasingly the emphasis is on Sears as the informed, responsible producer who designs the things the American family needs and wants. Today Sears's largest capital investment is in the manufacturing plants it owns or controls – even though retail-store expansion has been pursued vigorously.

Sears again and again changed the definition of its market in line with the shifting patterns of the American population. Rosenwald made available mass goods to a new, emerging mass market. Wood made available to this mass market what earlier had been class-market goods, for example, kitchen appliances. Sears now operates on the assumption that the American middle class is, in its economic behaviour, actually an upper class. Sears has thus greatly widened its product scope. Of course, Sears still carries appliances in its stores – and they probably are still the largest-selling product category. But Sears has also become the world's biggest diamond merchant, one of the country's biggest booksellers, and a large buyer and seller of original art objects, such as drawings, prints, and paintings.

Julius Rosenwald and General Wood had moved into controlling key manufacturers as the only way to make sure of the quality Sears needed, of the quantities its tremendous distribution system required, and of the lowest possible price for the customers. This is still the rationale given at Sears for ownership or control of manufacturing sources. But it would probably be more correct to describe the present relationship between Sears and its suppliers as procurement rather than buying. The emphasis has steadily shifted towards a long-range strategy that anticipates what tomorrow's American family will be and what it will require, and then designs and develops the appropriate products or services. Sears today may be the first truly marketing-focused manufacturing business in the US. It practises the total marketing approach which most manufacturing businesses so far only preach. To this marketing strategy, focused on creating the sources of supply rather than on selling products to the public, Sears owes both its tremendous growth in sales and its profitability.

Yet Sears today faces new challenges which will require innovation and strategic thinking fully as much as the developments of the past.

From the beginning Sears has been keenly aware of basic population trends in the United States. Wood's favourite management tool was a 'little black book' full of population statistics and projections. Julius Rosenwald, too, had built his business on population analysis and population trends. The Sears policy, all along, has been to find the majority market and to convert it into a true mass market.

There is a market shift ahead in America, and Sears may not be strategically positioned for it. Young educated families, whose breadwinners make their living as knowledge workers have now come to dominate the American market. Even if Sears can transfer to them the special relationship it has had with their parents (the blue-collar workers of the big industrial cities) Sears does not make, buy, or sell in the areas in which their needs may be greatest and their spending likely to go up the fastest. Sears is still primarily thing-focused, primarily a maker, buyer, and seller of manufactured goods. The young educated families have a healthy appetite for goods; but the major growth areas in their budgets may be information and education, health care, travel and leisure, reliable financial advice and services, and guidance on job and career choices. By and large, these are not areas in which Sears has established itself as the responsible maker and buyer.

If Sears wants to maintain its leadership position and its capacity to grow, it faces major new challenges and may have to redefine what its business is, where its markets are, and where innovations are needed.

The right answers are always obvious in retrospect. The basic lesson of the Sears story is that the right answers are likely to be anything but obvious *before* they have proven themselves. 'Everybody knew' around 1900 that to promise 'satisfaction guaranteed or your money back' could bring only financial disaster to a retailer. 'Everybody knew' around 1925 that the American market was sharply segmented into distinct income groups, each buying different things in different places. 'Everybody knew' – as late as 1950 – that the American consumer wanted to shop downtown, and so on.

Even more important as a lesson from the Sears story is the knowledge that the right answers are not the result of brilliance or of 'intuition'. Richard Sears had both – and almost failed. The right answers are the result of asking the right questions. And this in turn requires hard, systematic work to understand what a business is and what 'our' business is.

## Summary

Sears, Roebuck has been more successful and has been successful longer than any other major American business. Yet when Julius Rosenwald, a Chicago clothing merchant without mail-order experience, bought out Richard Sears in 1895, the company was

on the brink of bankruptcy. Rosenwald thought through what
Sears' business was by asking: who are the customers? what do
they need? what is value for them? where and how do they buy?
And within a decade, Sears, Roebuck had become the leader and
a household word. Rosenwald's successor, General Robert E.
Wood, then asked the same questions again in the mid-1920s.
He redefined Sears and made it into a very different business.
Since Wood's retirement in 1954, a succession of Sears' top managements has again re-defined Sears' business by asking the
same questions. Every time these questions were asked, they
yielded different answers. Every time, the answers flew in the face
of what 'everyone knew' at the time. And every time, the right
answers were reached by hard systematic work rather than by
'intuition'.

# 4 What is a Business?

The Sears story shows that a business enterprise is created and
managed by people and not by forces. Economic forces set limits
to what management can do. They create opportunities for management's action. But they do not by themselves determine what
a business is or what it does. Nothing could be sillier than the oft-
repeated assertion that 'management only adapts the business to
the forces of the market'. Management not only has to find these
forces, it has to create them. It took a Julius Rosenwald to make
Sears into a business enterprise eighty years ago and a General
Wood thirty years later to change its basic nature and thus ensure
its growth and success. Now another management generation
will have to make new decisions that will determine whether
Sears is going to continue to prosper or going to decline, to sur-

vive, or eventually to perish. And that is true of every business.

Another conclusion is that a business cannot be defined or explained in terms of profit. Asked what a business is, the typical businessman is likely to answer, 'An organization to make a profit'. The typical economist is likely to give the same answer. This answer is not only false, it is irrelevant.

The prevailing economic theory of business enterprise and behaviour is the maximization of profit – which is simply a complicated way of phrasing the old saw of buying cheap and selling dear. It may adequately explain how Richard Sears operated. But it cannot explain how Sears, Roebuck or any other business enterprise operates, nor how it should operate. The concept of profit maximization is, in fact, meaningless.

Profit and profitability are indeed crucial – for society even more than for the individual business. Yet profitability is not the purpose of, but a limiting factor on, business enterprise. Profit is not the explanation, cause, or rationale of business decisions, but the test of their validity. If archangels instead of business people sat in directors' chairs, they would still have to be concerned with profitability, despite their total lack of personal interest in making profits.

The first test of any business is not the maximization of profit but the achievement of sufficient profit to cover the risks of economic activity and thus to avoid loss.

The root of the confusion is the mistaken belief that the motive of an individual – the so-called profit motive of the businessman – is an explanation of his behaviour or his guide to right action. Whether there is such a thing as profit motive at all is highly doubtful. It was invented by the classical economists to explain an economic reality which their hypothesis of static equilibrium could not explain. There has never been any evidence for the existence of the profit motive. We have long since found the true explanation of the phenomena of economic change and growth which the profit motive was first put forth to explain.

It is irrelevant for an understanding of business behaviour, profit, and profitability whether there is a profit motive or not. That Jim Smith is in business to make a profit concerns only him and the Recording Angel. It does not tell us what Jim Smith does and how he performs. We do not learn anything about the work of a prospector hunting for uranium in the Nevada desert by being told that he is trying to make his fortune. We do not learn anything about the work of a heart specialist by being told that she is trying to make a livelihood, or even that she is trying to benefit humanity. The profit motive and its offspring, maximization of profits, are just as irrelevant to the function of a business, the purpose of a business, and the job of managing a business.

In fact, the concept is worse than irrelevant: it does harm. It is a major cause for the misunderstanding of the nature of profit in our society and for the deep-seated hostility to profit which are among the most dangerous diseases of an industrial society. It is largely responsible for the worst mistakes of public policy, which are squarely based on the failure to understand the nature, function, and purpose of business enterprise. And it is in large part responsible for the prevailing belief that there is an inherent contradiction between profit and a company's ability to make a social contribution. Actually, a company can make a social contribution only if it is highly profitable. A bankrupt company is not likely to be a good company to work for, nor likely to be a good neighbour and a desirable member of the community.

## The purpose of a business

To know what a business is we have to start with its *purpose*. Its purpose must lie outside of the business itself. In fact, it must lie in society, since business enterprise is an organ of society. There is only one valid definition of business purpose: *to create a customer*.

It is the customer who determines what a business is. It is the customer alone whose willingness to pay for a good or for a service converts economic resources into wealth, things into goods. What the business thinks it produces is not of first importance – especially not to the future of the business and to its success. The typical engineering definition of quality is something that is hard to do, is complicated, and costs a lot of money! But that isn't quality; it's incompetence. What the customer thinks he or she is buying, what he or she considers value, is decisive – it determines what a business is, what it produces, and whether it will prosper. And what the customer buys and considers value is never a product. It is always utility – that is, what a product or service does for him or her. And what is value for the customer is, as we shall see in the next chapter, anything but obvious.

Customers are the foundation of a business and keep it in existence. They alone give employment. To supply the wants and needs of a customer, society entrusts wealth-producing resources to the business enterprise.

## The two entrepreneurial functions

Because its purpose is to create a customer, the business enterprise has two – and only these two – basic functions: marketing and innovation. Marketing and innovation produce results; all the rest are 'costs'.

Marketing is the distinguishing, unique function of the business. A business is set apart from all other human organizations by the fact that it *markets* a product or a service. Neither church, nor army, nor school, nor state does that. Any organization that fulfils itself through marketing a product or a service is a business. Any organization in which marketing is either absent or incidental is not a business and should never be managed as if it were one.

The first person in the West to see marketing clearly as the unique and central function of the business enterprise, and the creation of a customer as the specific job of management, was Cyrus H. McCormick (1809–1884), the founder of the International Harvester Company. The history books mention only that he invented the first effective mechanical harvester. But he also invented the basic tools of modern marketing: market research and market analysis, the concept of market standing, pricing policies, the service salesman, parts and service supply to the customer, and instalment credit. He had done all this by 1850, but not till fifty years later was he widely imitated.

The economic revolution of the American economy since 1900 has in large part been a marketing revolution. Creative, aggressive, pioneering marketing is still far too rare in American business. Few businesses are even abreast of the Sears of 1925, let alone of the Sears of 1970. Yet fifty years ago the typical attitude of the American businessman towards marketing was 'the sales department will sell whatever the plant produces'. Today it is increasingly, 'It is our job to produce what the market needs'. However deficient in execution, the attitude has by itself changed our economy as much as any technical innovation.

Marketing is so basic that it cannot be considered a separate skill or work within the business. Marketing requires separate work, and a distinct group of activities. But it is a central dimension of the entire business. It is the whole business seen from the point of view of its final result, that is, from the customer's point of view. Concern and responsibility for marketing must permeate all areas of the enterprise.

Among American manufacturing companies the outstanding practitioner of the marketing approach may well be IBM; and IBM is also the best example of the power of marketing. IBM does not owe its meteoric rise to technological innovation or product leadership. It was a Johnny-come-lately when it entered the computer field, without technological expertise or scientific knowledge. But while the technological leaders in the early computer days (Univac, GE, and RCA) were product-focused and technology-focused, the punch-card salesmen who ran IBM asked: 'Who is the customer? What is value for him? How does he buy? And, what does he need?' As a result, IBM took over the market.

## From selling to marketing

Despite the emphasis on marketing and the marketing approach, marketing is still talk rather than reality in far too many businesses. 'Consumerism' proves this. For what consumerism demands of business is that it actually market. It demands that business define its goal as the satisfaction of customer needs. That consumerism could become a powerful popular movement proves that not much marketing has been practiced. Consumerism is the 'shame of marketing'.

But consumerism is also the opportunity of marketing. It may force businesses to become market-focused in their actions as well as in their words.

Above all, consumerism should dispel the confusion which largely explains why there has been so little real marketing. When managers speak of marketing, they usually mean the organized performance of all selling functions. This is still selling. It still starts out with 'our products'. It still looks for 'our market'. *True* marketing starts out the way Sears starts out – with the customers, their demographics, realities, needs, and values. It does not ask, 'What do we want to sell?' It asks, 'What does the customer want to buy?' It does not say, 'This is what our product or service does'. It says, 'These are the satisfactions the customer looks for'.

Ideally, marketing should result in a customer who is ready to buy. All that should be needed then is to make the product or service available. We may be a long way from this ideal. But consumerism is a clear indication that the right motto for business management should increasingly be, 'from selling to marketing'.

## The enterprise as the organ of economic growth and development

A business enterprise can exist only in an economy which considers change both natural and acceptable. And business is the specific organ of growth, expansion, and change.

The second function of a business is, therefore, *innovation* – the provision of different economic satisfactions. It is not enough for the business to provide just any economic goods and services; it must provide better and more economic ones. It is not necessary for a business to grow bigger; but it is necessary that it constantly grow better.

Innovation may result in a lower price – the factor with which the economist has been most concerned, for the simple reason that it is the only one that can be handled by quantitative tools. But the result may also be a new and better product, a new convenience, or the definition of a new want.

The most productive innovation is a *different* product or service that creates a new potential of satisfaction. Typically this new and different product costs more – yet its overall effect is to make the economy more productive.

The antibiotic drug costs far more than the cold compress which is all yesterday's physician had to fight pneumonia. The computer costs far more than an adding machine or a punch-card sorter, the typewriter far more than a quill pen, the Xerox duplicator far more than a copy press or even a mimeograph copier. And if and when we get a cancer cure, it will cost more than even a first-class funeral.

The price of the product is thus only one measurement of the value of an innovation, or of economic value altogether. We may relate price to unit output, compare the price of a drug to the saving it produces in days of hospital stay and in added years of working life. But even that is hardly adequate. We really need a value measurement. What economic value does innovation give the customer? The customer is the only judge; he or she alone knows the economic reality.

Innovation may be finding new uses for old products. A salesman who succeeds in selling refrigerators to Eskimos to prevent food from freezing would be as much of an innovator as if he had developed brand-new processes or invented a new product. To sell Eskimos a refrigerator to keep food cold is finding a new market; to sell a refrigerator to keep food from getting too cold is actually creating a new product. Technologically this is, of course, only the same old product; but economically there is innovation.

Above all, innovation is not *invention*. It is a term of economics rather than of technology. Nontechnological innovations – social or economic innovations – are at least as important as technological ones. (On this see Chapter 37 'The Innovative Organization'.)

In the organization of the business enterprise, innovation can no more be considered a separate function than marketing. It is not confined to engineering or research but extends across all parts of the business, all functions, all activities. It cannot be confined to manufacturing business. Innovation in distribution and service have been as important as innovation in manufacturing.

The leadership in innovation with respect to product and service has traditionally been focused in one functional activity that is responsible for nothing else. This has been particularly true for businesses with heavy engineering or chemical technology. In an insurance company, too, a special department charged with leadership responsibility for the development of new kinds of coverage may be in order; and there might well be other such departments charged with innovation in the organization of sales, the administration of policies, the settling of claims, and the investment of company funds. All these are the insurance company's business.

But the best way to organize for systematic, purposeful innovation is as a business activity rather than as functional work. At the same time, every managerial unit of business should have responsibility for innovation and definite innovation goals. It should be responsible for contributing to innovation in the company's product or service. In addition, it should strive consciously to advance the art in the particular area in which it is engaged: selling or accounting, quality control or personnel management.

Innovation can be defined as the task of giving human and material resources new and greater wealth-producing capacity. Innovation is particularly important for developing countries. These countries have the resources. They are poor because they lack the capacity to make these resources wealth-producing. They can import technology, but they have to produce their own social innovations to make imported technology work.

Managers must convert society's needs into opportunities for profitable business. That, too, is a definition of innovation. It needs to be stressed today, when we are so conscious of the needs of society, schools, health-care systems, cities, and environment. These needs are not too different in kind from those which the nineteenth-century entrepreneur converted into growth industries – the urban newspaper and the streetcar; the steel-frame skyscraper and the school textbook; the telephone and pharmaceuticals. Our new needs similarly demand the innovating business.

## The productive utilization of wealth-producing resources

The enterprise must utilize wealth-producing resources to discharge its purpose of creating a customer. It is, therefore, charged with productive utilization of these resources. This is the administrative function of business. In its economic aspect, it is called productivity.

Productivity means the balance between *all* factors of production that will give the greatest output for the smallest effort. This is quite different from productivity per worker or per hour of work. Such traditional standards only vaguely reflect true productivity. They are still based on the eighteenth-century belief that manual labour is the only productive resource. The standards still express the mistaken idea that all human achievement could eventually be measured in units of muscle effort. Increased productivity in a modern economy is never achieved by muscle effort. It is always the result of doing away with muscle effort, of substituting something else for the labourer. One of these substitutes is, of course, capital equipment, that is, mechanical energy.

At least as important, though unnoticed until very recently, is the increase in productivity achieved by replacing manual labour, whether skilled or unskilled, by knowledge work. This results in a shift from labourers to managers, technicians, and professionals.

A little reflection will show that the rate of capital formation, to which economists give so much attention, is a secondary factor. Someone must plan and design the equipment – a conceptual, theoretical, and analytical task – before it can be installed and used. The basic factor in an economy's development must be the rate of 'brain formation' – the rate at which a country produces people with imagination and vision, education, and theoretical and analytical skills.

However, the planning, design, and installation of capital equipment is only a part of the increase in productivity through the substitution of brain for brawn. At least as important is the contribution made through the direct change of the character of work. The old way requires the manual labour, skilled and unskilled, of many people; the new way requires theoretical analysis and conceptual planning, without investment in capital equipment.

The greatest opportunities for increasing productivity are surely to be found in knowledge work itself, and especially in management. The vocabulary of business – especially of accounting – in talking about productivity has become so obsolete as to be misleading. What accountants call productive labour is manual workers tending machines; this is actually the least productive labour. What they call nonproductive labour – all the people who contribute to production without tending a machine – is a hodgepodge. It includes pre-industrial, low-productivity brawn labour like sweepers; some traditional high-skill, high-productivity labour like toolmakers; new industrial high-skill labour like maintenance electricians; and industrial high-knowledge personnel like foremen, industrial engineers, and quality control experts. Finally, what the accountants lump together as overhead contains what should be the most productive resource, the managers, researchers, planners, designers, innovators. But it may also contain purely parasitical, if not destructive, elements in the form of high-priced personnel needed only because of poor organization, poor spirit, or confused objectives, that is, because of mismanagement.

We need a concept of productivity that considers together all the efforts that go into output and expresses them in relation to their result, rather than one that assumes that labour is the only productive effort. But even such a concept – though a big step forward – would still be inadequate if its definition of effort were confined to the activities measurable by accountants as visible and direct costs. There are factors of substantial if not decisive impact on productivity that never become visible cost figures.

First there is knowledge – the most productive resource if properly applied, but also the most expensive one, and totally unproductive, if misapplied. The knowledge worker is, of necessity, a high-cost worker. Having spent many years in school, he or she also represents a very high social investment.

Then there is time – business's most perishable resource. Whether people and machines are utilized all or only part of the time will make a difference in their productivity. There is nothing less productive than idle time of expensive capital equipment or wasted time of highly paid and able people. Equally unproductive may be cramming more productive effort into a time period than it will comfortably hold – for instance, the attempt to run three shifts in a congested plant or on old or delicate equipment.

The most productive – or least productive – time is that of the manager. Yet it is usually the least known, least analysed, least managed of all factors of productivity.

Productivity is also a function of the product mix, the balance between various kinds of output from the same resources. As every manager should know, differences in the market values of various product mixes are rarely proportional to the efforts that go into making up the combinations. A company turning out a constant volume of goods with unchanging use of materials and skills and a constant amount of direct and indirect labour may reap fortunes or go bankrupt, depending on the product mix. Obviously this represents a considerable difference in the productivity of the same resources – but not one that shows in costs or can be detected by cost analysis.

There is also an important factor which I would call 'process mix'. Is it more productive for a company to buy a part or to make it, to assemble its product or to contract out the assembly process, to market under its own brand name or to sell to independent wholesalers using their own brands ? What is the company good at ? What is the most productive utilization of its specific knowledge, ability, experience, reputation ?

Finally, productivity is vitally affected by organization structure and by the balance among the various activities within the business. If a lack of clear organization causes managers to waste their time trying to find out what they are supposed to do rather than doing it, the company's scarcest resource is being wasted. If top management is interested only in engineering (perhaps because that's where all the top people came from) while the company needs major attention to marketing, it lacks productivity. The resulting damage will be greater than could be caused by a drop in output per worker-hour.

We therefore not only need to define productivity so as to embrace all these factors affecting it, but also need to set objectives that take all these factors into account. We must develop yardsticks to measure the impact on productivity of the substitution of capital for labour, and of knowledge for both. We need the means to distinguish between creative and parasitical overhead, and to assess the impact on productivity of time utilization, product mix, process mix, organization structure, and the balance of activities.

Not only does individual management need adequate concepts and measurements for productivity, the economy needs them. Their lack is the biggest gap in our economic statistics and seriously weakens all economic policy. It frustrates out attempts to fight depression and inflation alike.

## The functions of profit

Profit is not a cause but a result – the result of the performance of the business in marketing, innovation, productivity. It is a needed result, serving essential economic functions. Profit is, first, the test of performance – the only effective test, as the communists in Russia soon found out when they tried to abolish it in the early 1920s. Indeed, profit is a beautiful example of what engineers mean when they talk of feedback, or the self-regulation of a process by its own results.

Profit has a second function which is equally important. It is the premium for the risk of uncertainty. Economic activity, because it is activity, focuses on the future; and the one thing that is certain about the future is its uncertainty, its risks. The word 'risk' itself is said to mean 'earning one's daily bread' in the original Arabic. It is through risk-taking that any business earns its daily bread. Because business activity is economic it always attempts to bring about change. It always saws off the limb on which it sits; it makes existing risks riskier or creates new ones.

As the Sears story showed, the future of economic activity is a long one; it took fifteen or twenty years for basic Sears decisions to become fully effective, and for major investments to pay off. 'Lengthening the economic detour' has been known for a hundred years to be a prerequisite to economic advance. Yet while we know nothing about the future, we know that its risks increase in geometric progression the farther ahead we commit ourselves to it.

Profit and profit alone can supply the capital for tomorrow's jobs, both for *more* jobs and for *better* jobs.

And finally profit pays for the economic satisfactions and services of a society, from health care to defence, and from education to the opera. They all have to be paid for out of the surplus of economic production, that is, out of the difference between the value produced by economic activity and its cost.

Businesspeople these days tend to be apologetic about profit. This is a measure of the dismal job they have done explaining profit – above all to themselves. For there *is* no justification and no rationale for profit as long as one talks the nonsense of profit motive and profit maximization.

No apology is needed for profit as a necessity of economy and society. On the contrary, what a businessman should feel guilty about, what he should feel the need to apologize for, is failure to produce a profit appropriate to the economic and social functions which profit, and only profit, can develop.

What, then, is managing a business ? It follows from the analysis of business activity as the creation of a customer through marketing and innovation that managing a business must always be entrepreneurial in character. There is need for administrative performance. But it follows the entrepreneurial objectives. Structure follows strategy.

It also follows that managing a business must be a creative rather than an adaptive task. The more a management creates economic conditions or changes them rather than passively adapts to them, the more it manages the business.

But an analysis of the nature of a business also shows that management, while ultimately tested by performance alone, is a rational activity. Concretely this means that a business must set objectives that express what is desirable of attainment rather than aim at accommodation to the possible (as the maximization-of-profit theorem implies). Once objectives have been set by fixing one's sights on the desirable, the question can be raised as to what concessions to the possible have to be made. This requires management to decide what business the enterprise is engaged in, and what business it should be engaged in.

## Summary

The purpose of a business is not to make a profit. Profit is a necessity and a social responsibility. A business, regardless of the economic or legal arrangements of society, must produce enough profit to cover the risks of committing today's economic resources to the uncertainties of the future; to produce the capital for the jobs of tomorrow; and to pay for all the noneconomic needs and satisfactions of society from defence and the administration of justice to the schools and hospitals, and from the museums to the boy scouts. But profit is not the purpose of business. Rather a business exists and gets paid for its economic contribution. Its purpose is to create a customer. A business therefore has two, and only two, basic functions: marketing and innovation. To discharge these functions, the enterprise must make productive the wealth-producing resources of people, capital, natural resources (including time), and management.

# 5 Business Purpose
# and Business Mission

All the great business builders we know of – from the Medici of
Renaissance Florence and the founders of the Bank of England
in the late seventeenth century down to IBM's Thomas Watson
in our day – had a clear theory of the business which informed all
their actions and decisions. Not intuition, but a clear, simple and
penetrating theory of the business characterizes the truly successful entrepreneur, the person who not just amasses a large
fortune but builds an organization that can endure and grow.

The individual entrepreneur does not need to analyse concepts
and explain a theory of the business to others, let alone spell out
the details. He or she is in one person thinker, analyst, and executor. Business enterprise, however, requires that the theory of the
business be thought through and spelled out. It demands a clear
definition of business purpose and business mission. It demands
asking, 'What is our business and what should it be ?'

Today's theory of the business always becomes obsolete – and
usually pretty fast. Unless the basic concepts on which a business
has been built are visible, clearly understood, and explicitly expressed, the business enterprise is at the mercy of events. Not
understanding what it is, what it represents, and what its basic
concepts, values, policies, and beliefs are, it cannot rationally
change itself. The history of Henry Ford and the early Ford
Motor Company shows how rapidly even the most brilliant entrepreneurial idea can become outdated – only fifteen years
elapsed between the origin of an entrepreneurial idea in 1907
that literally transformed economy and society and its obsolescence in the early 1920s, when General Motors, with a new
and different business theory, took over as the market leader
and almost drove Ford out of the market.

Only a clear definition of the mission and purpose of the business makes possible clear and realistic business objectives. It is
the foundation for priorities, strategies, plans, and work assign-

ments. It is the starting point for the design of managerial jobs, and above all, for the design of managerial structures. Structure follows strategy. Strategy determines what the key activities are in a given business. And strategy requires knowing 'what our business is and what it should be'.

## Decisions are made at all levels of management

In sharp contrast to the organizations of the past, today's organization brings together many people of knowledge and skill, at practically every level. But knowledge and skill also mean decision-impact on how the work is to be done and on what work is actually being tackled. Managers make, by necessity, risk-taking decisions. And the computer does not alter this fact. In fact, it makes the decisions of top management even more dependent on the decision input from lower levels – which is what then becomes the data of the computer.

When the computer first arrived in the early 1950s, we heard a good deal about the coming disappearance of the middle manager. Instead, the next two decades brought a tremendous growth of middle management in all developed countries. And, unlike traditional middle managers, the new middle people are largely decision-makers rather than executors of decisions made on high.

As a result, decisions affecting the entire business and its capacity to perform are made at all levels of the organization, even fairly low ones. Risk-taking decisions – what to do and what not to do; what to continue to work on and what to abandon; what products, markets or technologies to pursue with energy and what markets, products, and technologies to ignore – are in the reality of today's business enterprise (especially the large one) made every day by a host of people of subordinate rank, very often by people without traditional managerial title or position. Research scientists, design engineers, product planners, and tax accountants: all these people base their decisions on some theory of the business, however vague.

Common vision, common understanding, and unity of direction and effort of the entire organization require definition of 'what our business is and what it should be'.

## 'What is our business' - never obvious

Nothing may seem simpler or more obvious than to know what a company's business is. A steel mill makes steel, a railroad runs trains to carry freight and passengers, an insurance company underwrites fire risks, a bank lends money. Actually, 'What is our business' is almost always a difficult question and the right answer is usually anything but obvious.

One of the earliest and most successful answers was worked out seventy years ago by Theodore N. Vail (1845–1920) for the American Telephone and Telegraph Company (also known as the Bell System): 'Our business is service.' This sounds obvious once it has been said. But first there had to be the realization that a telephone system, being a natural monopoly, was in danger of nationalization; a privately owned telephone service in a developed and industrialized country was exceptional and needed community support for its survival. Second, there had to be the realization that community support could not be obtained by propaganda campaigns or by attacking critics as 'un-American' or 'socialistic'. It could be obtained only by creating customer satisfaction. This realization meant radical innovations in business policy. It meant constant stress on dedication to service by all employees. It meant emphasis on research and technological leadership. It required a financial policy which assumed that the company has to give service wherever there was a demand, and that it was management's job to find the necessary capital and to earn a return on it. The United States would not have gone through the New Deal period without a serious attempt at telephone nationalization but for the careful analysis of its own business that the Telephone Company made between 1905 and 1915.

Vail's definition served his company for two-thirds of a century, up into the late 1960s; it may have been the longest-lived answer to the question 'What is our business?' That the American railroads never thought their way through to any definition of their business is surely a major reason for the perpetual crisis in which they have floundered since World War I, and for the almost complete lack of community support that is their greatest weakness.

The answer to the question 'What is our business ?' is the first responsibility of top management. Indeed, one sure way to tell whether a particular job is top management or not is to ask whether its holder is expected to be concerned with, and responsible for, answering this question. Only top management can make sure that this question receives the attention it deserves and that the answer makes sense and enables the business to plot its course and set its objectives.

But there are reasons that management shy away from asking the question. The question causes controversy, argument, and disagreement. To raise the question always reveals cleavages and differences within the top-management group itself. People who have worked side by side for many years and who think that they know each other's thoughts suddenly realize with a shock that they are in serious disagreement.

## The need for dissent

Most managements shrink from these disagreements as divisive and painful. But deciding 'What is our business ?' is a genuine decision; and a genuine decision must be based on divergent views to have a chance to be a right and effective decision. The answer to the question 'What is our business ?' is always a choice between alternatives, each of which rests on different assumptions regarding the reality of the business and its environment. It is always a high-risk decision. It always leads to changes in objectives, strategies, organization, and behaviour. The decision must be based on conscious choice of alternatives rather than on suppression of different and dissenting opinions and points of view.

The main reason that it is important to bring out dissent within the top-management group on the question 'What is our business ?' is that there is never one right answer. The answer never emerges as a logical conclusion from 'facts'. It requires judgement and considerable courage. The answer rarely follows what 'everybody knows'. It should never be made on plausibility alone: it should never be made quickly; it can never be made painlessly.

## Method rather than opinions

Another reason that managements fail to ask 'What is our business?' is their reluctance to listen to opinions. And everyone has an opinion on 'what our business is'. Managements, however, quite rightly dislike debating societies and bull sessions.

There must be a method for defining 'what our business is'. Opinions are, of course, needed – and anyhow are unavoidable. But they need to be focused on a specific, central issue to become productive.

With respect to the definition of business purpose and business mission, there is only one such focus, one starting point. It is the customer. The customer defines the business.

Management always, and understandably, considers its product or its service to be important. If it did not, it could not do a good job. Yet to the customer, no product or service, and certainly no company, is of much importance. The executives of a company always tend to believe that the customer spends hours discussing their products. But how many housewives, for instance, ever talk to each other about the whiteness of their laundry? If something is badly wrong with one brand of detergent, they switch to another. Customers only want to know what the product or service will do for them tomorrow. All they are interested in are their own values and wants. Any serious attempt to state 'what our business is' must start with these truths about the customers.

## Who is the customer?

'Who is the customer?' is the first and crucial question in defining business purpose and business mission. It is not an easy, let alone an obvious question. How it is answered determines, in large measure, how the business defines itself.

The power of the question 'Who is the customer ?' and the impact of a thoughtful answer to it are shown by the experience of the carpet industry in the United States since World War II.

The carpet industry is an old one, with little glamour and little sophisticated technology. Yet it has been a conspicuous marketing success in the American economy of the post-World War II period. Until well into the early 1950s the industry had, however, been in a steady, long-term, and apparently irreversible decline. Then, within a few years, the industry completely reversed the trend. Even 'good' houses built before the fifties had, as a rule, no more than a cheap rug in the living room. Today, even low-cost homes – including most mobile homes – have wall-to-wall carpeting of fair quality in all rooms, kitchen and bathrooms included. And the home buyer is spending an increasing share of the housing dollar on carpeting.

Floor covering is one of the very few means to alter the appearance and comfort of a home, especially of a cheap and small one. This message had been broadcast by the rug and carpet manufacturers for decades, without the slightest effect on actual customer behaviour. The rug and carpet industry achieved its success only when it stopped persuasion and hard-selling, and instead thought through the questions, 'Who is our customer ?' 'Who should our customer be ?'

Traditionally the rug and carpet manufacturers had defined their customers as the homeowner, and especially as the family buying its first home. But at that stage, the young couple has no money left over for luxuries. They postpone buying rugs – and this means they are not likely to buy them at all. As a result of asking 'Who is our customer, and who should he be ?' the industry realized that it must succeed in making the mass builder its customer. It therefore had to make it profitable for the mass builder to incorporate rugs and carpets into the new home at the time of building. This meant switching from selling individual rugs and carpets to selling wall-to-wall carpeting. In the traditional home the builder had to lay expensive and fully finished floors. Wall-

to-wall carpeting can be put over cheap and unfinished flooring –
resulting in a better house at lower cost to the builder.

The industry further realized that it must enable new homeowners to pay for floor covering as part of the monthly payment
on the mortgage, rather than expecting them to pay a substantial
sum at a time when cash is already short. It therefore worked
hard at getting the lending agencies, and especially the government agencies insuring home mortgages (such as the Federal
Housing Administration), to accept floor covering as part of the
capital investment in the house and thus as part of the mortgage
value. Finally, the industry redesigned its product to enable
building contractors to act as the informed buyer for customers,
the homeowners. Today home buyers are offered a great variety
of patterns and colours, but essentially only three qualities:
'Good', 'better', and 'best'. The difference among them amounts
to very little in the monthly mortgage payment, with the result
that most homeowners order at least the 'better' carpeting.

As this story shows, the right answer to 'Who is the customer ?'
is usually that there are several customers.

Most businesses have at least two. The rug and carpet industry
has both the contractor and the homeowner for its customers.
Both have to buy if there is to be a sale. The manufacturers of
brand-name consumer goods always have two customers at the
very least: the shopper and the grocer. It does not do much good
to have the shopper eager to buy if the grocer does not stock the
brand; conversely, it does not do much good to have the grocer
display merchandise advantageously and give it shelf space if the
shopper does not buy.

One of the great strengths of Vail's definition of Bell Telephone's business was the recognition of two separate customers:
the telephone subscriber and the government regulating agency.
Both had to be given service. Both had to be satisfied. Yet, they
had widely different concepts of value, wanted and needed different things, and behaved quite differently.

There are also businesses in which economically there is only
one customer while strategically – in terms of buying decision –
there are two or more.

One of the reasons that IBM has been so successful in the computer business is that it realized early that many different people in a company have to buy a computer if there is to be a sale. The people who use the computer (which largely means accounting and financial people) have to buy it. But top management also has to buy. And so do the people who are to use the computer as their information tool, that is, operating managers. From the beginning, IBM has sold all these groups and has thought through what each looks for, needs to know and considers value; and how each can be reached.

It is also important to ask 'Where is the customer?' One of the secrets of Sears' success in the 1920s was the discovery that its old customer was now in a different place: the farmer had become mobile and was beginning to buy in town. This made Sears realize early – almost two decades before most other American retailers – that store location is a major business decision and a major element in answering the question 'What is our business?'

The next question is, 'What does the customer buy?'

The Cadillac people say that they make an automobile, and their business is called the Cadillac Motor Division of General Motors. But do people who spend $15,000 on a new Cadillac buy transportation or do they buy primarily prestige? Does the Cadillac compete with Chevrolet, Ford, and Volkswagen? Nicholas Dreystadt, the German-born service mechanic who took over Cadillac in the Depression years of the thirties, answered: 'Cadillac competes with diamonds and mink coats. The Cadillac customer does not buy "transportation" but "status".' This answer saved Cadillac, which was about to go under. Within two years or so, it became a major growth business, despite the Depression.

## What is value to the customer?

The final question that must be answered if management is to come to grips with business purpose and business mission is 'What is value to the customer?' It may be the most important question. Yet it is the one least often asked.

One reason is that managers are quite sure that they know the answer. Value is what they, in their business, define as quality. But this is almost always the wrong definition.

For the teenage girl, for instance, value in a shoe is high fashion. It has to be 'in'. Price is a secondary consideration, and durability is not value at all. For the same girl a few years later, high fashion becomes not a necessity but a restraint. She will not buy something that is quite unfashionable, but she is more interested in durability, price, comfort, and fit. The same shoe that represents the best buy for the teenager is a very poor value for her older sister.

The customer never buys a product. By definition the customer buys the satisfaction of a want. The customer buys value. Yet the manufacturer, by definition, cannot produce a value, but can only make and sell a product. What the manufacturer considers quality may, therefore, be irrelevant and nothing but waste and useless expense.

Another reason why the question 'What is value to the customer?' is rarely asked is that the economists think they know the answer: value is price. This is misleading, if not actually the wrong answer.

To begin with, price is anything but a simple concept. Then there are other value concepts which may determine what price really means. And in many cases price is secondary, a limiting factor rather than the essence of value.

Here are some examples to illustrate what price might mean to different customers:

Electrical equipment such as fuse boxes or circuit breakers are paid for by the homeowner but selected and bought by the electrical contractor. What is price to the electrical contractor is not the manufacturer's price for the product. It is the price of the manufacturer plus the cost of installation – for that, of course, is price to the customer, the homeowner. Contractors are notoriously price-conscious. Yet, a high-priced make of fuse boxes and circuit breakers is the market leader in the US. To the contractor this line is actually low-priced because it is engineered to be installed fast and by relatively unskilled labour.

Xerox owes its success, to a large extent, to defining price as what the customer pays for a copy rather than what he or she pays for the machine. Xerox, accordingly, has priced its machines in terms of the copies used. In other words, the customer pays for the copy rather than for the machine – and, of course, what the customer wants are copies rather than a machine.

For products and services – as distinct from undifferentiated commodities such as copper of a certain purity – price can be determined only by understanding what is value to the customer. As the example shows it is up to the manufacturer or supplier to design a pricing structure that fits the customer's value concept.

But price is also only a part of value. There is a whole range of quality considerations that are not expressed in price: durability, freedom from breakdown, the maker's standing, service, etc. High price itself may actually be value – as in fashionable perfumes, expensive furs, or exclusive gowns.

Here is an example:

In the early days of the Common Market, two young European engineers opened a small office with a few hundred dollars, a telephone, and a shelf full of manufacturers' catalogues of electronic components. Within ten years they had built a large and highly profitable wholesale business. Their customers are the industrial users of electronic equipment such as relays and machine controls. The young engineers manufacture nothing. The components which they supply can be obtained, often at a lower price, directly from the manufacturer. But these young engineers relieve the customer of the tedious chore of finding the right component part. They need only be told the equipment, the manufacturer, the model number, and the part that needs replacement – a condenser, for instance, or a microswitch. They then immediately identify the specific part needed. They also know what parts made by other manufacturers can be used for a job. They therefore can tell the customer what he or she needs, give immediate service, often on the same day, and yet keep their inventory very low. Expertise and speedy service is value to the customers, for which they are perfectly willing to pay a substantial premium. 'Our business is not electronic parts,' said one of the young men, 'it is information.'

What about such concepts of value on the part of the customer as the service received? There is little doubt, for instance, that the American housewife today buys appliances largely on the basis of the service experience she or her friends and neighbours have had with other appliances of the same brand. The speed with which she can obtain service if something goes wrong, the quality of the service, and its cost have become major determinants in the buyer's decision.

The marketing approach outlined here will not, by itself, result in a definition of the purpose and mission of a business. For many businesses the approach will raise more questions than it answers. This is true of the business which has as its basic unity a common technology rather than a common market. Examples are chemical companies but also commercial banks. Similarly, process businesses – e.g. steel companies or aluminium refiners – need much more than one market definition for their business. Of necessity, their products go into an infinity of markets, serve a multitude of customers, and have to satisfy a great variety of value concepts and value expectations.

Yet even such businesses should start their attempt to ask 'What is our business ?' by first asking, 'Who are our customers ? Where are they ? What do they consider value ?' A business – and for that matter any institution – is defined by its contribution; everything else is effort rather than result. What the customer pays is revenue; everything else is cost. The approach from the outside, that is, from the market, is only one step. But it is the step that comes before all others. It alone can give understanding and thereby replace opinions as the foundation for the most fundamental decision that faces every management.

## When to ask 'what is our business?'

Most managements, if they ask the question at all, ask 'What is our business ?' when the company is in trouble. Of course, then it must be asked. And then asking the question may, indeed, have spectacular results and may even reverse what appears irreversible decline – as shown by the example of Vail's work at Bell Telephone and of the reversal of the carpet industry's long-term downward trend.

But to wait until a business – or an industry – is in trouble is playing Russian roulette. It is irresponsible management. The question should be asked at the start of a business – and particularly for a business that has ambitions to grow. Such a business had better start with a clear entrepreneurial concept.

One successful example is a Wall Street firm which in the 1960s rose to leadership in the American securities market. Donaldson, Lufkin, and Jenrette (DLJ) was founded by three young men right out of business school. They had little except an idea. Yet the firm rose within five or six years to seventh place among Wall Street houses. DLJ then became the first Wall Street firm to sell its shares to the public and started the long over-due change of the New York Stock Exchange from a private club to a service institution. It was the first firm to do something about Wall Street's need to broaden its capital base, which thoughtful people had seen for thirty years. 'Our business,' the founders of DLJ said, 'is to provide financial services, financial advice, and financial management to the new "capitalists", the institutional investors such as pension funds and mutual funds.' In retrospect, this definition was obvious: right answers always are. By 1960 it had become quite clear that these new institutional investors were rapidly becoming the dominant force in the American capital market and the main channel through which individuals were directing their savings into the capital market. Yet at the time at which this answer was given, it went counter to everything the rest of Wall Street knew.

Yet the most important time to ask seriously 'What is our business?' is when a company has been successful. To understand this has been a great strength of Sears, Roebuck. It is also one of the secrets of the success of Marks and Spencer in Great Britain. (See the next chapter.) And not to have understood this is a major reason for the present crisis of American schools and universities.

Success always outdates the very behaviour that achieved it. It always creates new realities. It always creates, above all, its own different problems. Only the fairy story ends 'They lived happily ever after'.

It is not easy for the management of a successful company to ask, 'What is our business ?' Everybody in the company thinks that the answer is so obvious that it is not worth discussion. It is never popular to argue with success.

Above all: when a management attains the company's objectives, it should always ask seriously, 'What is our business ?' This requires self-discipline and responsibility. The alternative is decline.

## 'What will our business be?'

Sooner or later, even the most successful answer to the question 'What is our business ?' becomes obsolete.

Theodore Vail's answer was good for almost two-thirds of a century. But by the late 1960s it became apparent that it was no longer adequate. The telephone system was no longer, as in Vail's days, a natural monopoly. Alternative ways of telecommunication were rapidly becoming possible. It had also become apparent that the traditional definition of the telephone as an instrument to transmit voice messages had become inadequate, both because of the rapid growth in data transmission over telephone wires and because of the increasing possibility of transmitting visual images together with the voice. Vail's simple and elegant definition of the business of the Bell Telephone System was in need of re-examination.

Very few definitions of the purpose and mission of a business have a life expectancy of thirty, let alone fifty, years. To be good for ten years is probably all one can normally expect.

In asking 'What is our business ?' management therefore also needs to add, 'And what will it be ? What changes in the environment are likely to have high impact on the characteristics, mission, and purpose of our business ?' and 'How do we now build these anticipations into our theory of the business, into its objectives, strategies, and work assignments ?'

Again the market, its potential and trends, is the starting point. How large a market can we project for our business in five or ten years – assuming no basic changes in customers, in market structure, or in technology ? And what factors could validate or disprove these projections ?

The most important of these trends is one to which few businesses pay much attention: changes in population structure and population dynamics. Businesspeople, following the economists, have traditionally assumed that demographics are a constant. Historically this has been a sound assumption. Populations used to change very slowly except as a result of catastrophic events, such as major war or famine. This is no longer true, however. Populations nowadays can and do change drastically, in developed as well as in developing countries.

The importance of demographics does not lie only in the impact population structure has on buying power and buying habits, and on the size and structure of the work force. Population shifts are the only events regarding the future for which true prediction is possible. People do not enter the labour force until they are in their teens – and in the developed countries, increasingly not until they are twenty. They do not form households until then, nor become primary customers in their own right. Therefore, major trends in markets, buying power and buying behaviour, customer needs, and employment can be predicted with near-certainty by analysing what has already happened in population dynamics and population structure.

Any attempt to anticipate tomorrow – and this is, of course, what we are trying to do by asking 'What will our business be'? – has to start with demographic analysis as the sturdiest and most reliable foundation.

The massive impact of even fairly minor demographic changes is illustrated by the sharp shift in the American magazine industry.

As late as 1950, the mass-circulation magazine was America's most successful and most profitable communications medium. But the leaders of those days – *Collier's*, *The Saturday Evening Post*, *Look*, and *Life* – have disappeared. The development is often blamed on television. But magazines as a whole have not suffered from television – just as they did not earlier suffer from radio. On the contrary, total magazine circulation as well as magazine advertising have gone up faster since television appeared than they did before, and they are still going up fast. What has happened is that population has changed – partly because of the change in age structure, but primarily because of the change in educational levels. The undifferentiated mass audience is gone. Its place has been taken by a large number of speciality mass markets, that is, groups of substantial but still limited size, of much higher education and purchasing power, and of sharply defined and specialized interests. These groups read more magazines than the earlier generation – for the simple reason that they read more. They are a better market for magazine advertisers – for the simple reason that they buy more. Each of these better-educated and affluent audience segments is, in itself, a mass audience – but a specialized one.

This change in audience could easily have been anticipated by 1950, for the demographic development had already happened. It was seen clearly by a number of publishers. On this understanding are based all the American magazine successes of the last twenty or thirty years, from *Business Week* to *Modern Bride*, from *Sports Illustrated* to *Playboy*, from *Scientific American* to *Psychology Today* or *TV Guide*. All these magazines of the post-war generation apply basic editorial, circulation, and advertising concepts which the mass-circulation magazines first developed. But they apply them in accordance with the new population structure, to a demographic segment characterized by a common interest. All of them have circulations well above half a million, if not larger; but they deliberately do not appeal to a general audience.

Management needs to anticipate changes in market structure resulting from changes in the economy; from changes in fashion or taste; from moves by competition. And competition must always be defined according to the customer's concept of the product or service he or she buys, and thus must include indirect as well as direct competition.

## The unsatisfied wants of the customer

Finally, management has to ask which of the consumer's wants are not adequately satisfied by the products or services offered today. The ability to ask this question and to answer it correctly usually makes the difference between a growth company and one that depends for its development on the rising tide of the economy or of the industry. But those content to rise with the tide will also fall with it.

Sony asked the question 'What are the customer's unsatisfied wants?' when it first decided to move into the American consumer market in the mid-1950s. Sony had been founded right after the end of World War II as a manufacturer of tape recorders and had achieved modest success with its products in the Japanese market. It had entered the US as a small but reliable supplier of high-priced professional tape-recording equipment for broadcasting studios. Yet the product with which it first established itself in the American mass-consumer market was a product it had never made before – portable transistor radios. Young people, Sony's analysis of the market showed, were taking the existing heavy, clumsy, and expensive equipment – phonographs weighing many pounds, or battery-powered radios with audio tubes – on picnics, camping trips, and other excursions. Surely here was an unsatisfied want for a light, cheap, and yet dependable instrument. Sony did not develop the transistor – Bell Laboratories had done that, in America. But the Bell Laboratories people and all electronic manufacturers in America had decided that the customer was not yet ready for transistorized equipment. They looked at the wants of the customer that were satisfied by the existing equipment, wants for equipment that was to be kept in one place. Sony, by asking, 'What are the unsatisfied wants?' identified a new growth market – and within an incredibly short period established itself worldwide as the leader and the pacesetter.

### 'What should our business be?'

'What will our business be?' aims at adaptation to anticipated changes. It aims at modifying, extending, developing the existing, ongoing business.

But there is need also to ask 'What should our business be?' What opportunities are opening up or can be created to fulfill the purpose and mission of the business by making it into a different business?

IBM had long defined its business as data processing. Prior to

1950, this meant punch cards and equipment for sorting them. When the computer came, and with it a new technology in which IBM had not the slightest expertise, IBM asked 'What should our business be?' Management realized that in the future data processing would have to mean computers rather than punch cards.

Changes in society, economy, and market demand consideration in answering 'What should our business be?' So too does innovation, one's own and that of others.

Changes in the nature of the business arising out of innovation are too well known to require much documentation. All major enterprises in the engineering and chemical fields have largely grown by converting innovation into new business. The 'Eurodollar' (that is, a bank deposit or bank loan outside the US but calculated in US dollars) which is financing an increasing share of world trade was not invented by the large commercial American banks. (It was actually invented by Soviet Russia's trade bank.) But the American banks immediately saw the significance of this new monetary unit, and their success in making the Eurodollar into an international currency explains, in large measure, their rapid growth in multinational banking.

## The need for planned abandonment

The decision on what new and different things to do is important; just as important is planned, systematic abandonment of the old that no longer fits the purpose and mission of the business, no longer conveys satisfaction to the customer or customers, no longer makes a superior contribution.

An essential step in deciding what our business is, what it will be, and what it should be is systematic analysis of all existing products, services, processes, markets, end uses, and distribution channels. Are they still viable? Are they likely to remain viable? Do they still give value to the customer? And are they likely to do so tomorrow? Do they still fit the realities of population and markets, of technology and economy? And if not, how can we best abandon them – or at least stop pouring in further resources and efforts ? Unless these questions are being asked seriously and systematically, and unless managements are willing to act on the answers to them, energy will be used up in defending yesterday. No one will have the time, resources, or will to work on exploiting today, let alone to work on making tomorrow.

Defining the purpose and mission of the business is difficult, painful, and risky. But it alone enables a business to set objectives, to develop strategies, to concentrate its resources, and to go to work. It alone enables a business to be managed for performance.

## Summary

Every successful enterprise has been based on a clear and simple theory of the business, and on clear objectives derived therefrom. Yet it is never obvious what 'our business' is. To arrive at the right answer, one has to start out with the question: who is our customer ? – and there will always be more than one customer. One must also ask: what should our business be ? And finally one must ask: which of our products, services, and activities no longer serve the customer and should be abandoned ?

# 6 The Power and Purpose of Objectives

## The Marks & Spencer story and its lessons

One company in the Western world can be compared with Sears, Roebuck: Marks & Spencer in England.

Like Sears, Marks & Spencer is a retail chain. It opened its first 'penny bazaar' in 1884, in Manchester, at about the time Richard Sears made his first mail order offer of cheap but reliable watches to the Midwestern farmer. By 1915 the company was building

variety stores. It has been growing fast ever since. Its most spectacular growth period, however, was the ten years between 1963
and 1972 – a period in Britain's economic history which was characterized by 'stagflation', i.e. inflationary stagnation, rather than
growth. During this difficult period, Marks & Spencer more than
doubled its sales volume (from £184 million to £462 million).
Profits went up just as fast, from £22 million to £54 million.
Equally remarkable was the profit margin – almost 12 per cent
on sales before taxes – which is double what any other retail
merchant (except Sears) would consider fully satisfactory.

## Social revolution as a business mission

By the mid-1920s the four brothers-in-law (Simon Marks, Israel
Sieff, Harry Sacher, and Norman Laski) who had built the penny
bazaars of 1915 into a major chain of variety stores owned a successful business. They might have been satisfied to rest on their
laurels and to enjoy their considerable wealth. Instead they decided – following a trip to America by Simon Marks in 1924 in
the course of which he carefully studied Sears, Roebuck – to re-
think the purpose and mission of their business. The business of
Marks & Spencer, they decided, was not retailing. It was social
revolution.

Marks & Spencer redefined its business as the subversion of
the class structure of nineteenth-century England by making
available to the working and lower middle classes goods of upper-
class quality, at prices the working and lower-middle-class customer could well afford.

Marks & Spencer was by no means alone in the England of that
time in seeking a major opportunity in the rapid social changes of
the Post-World War I period. What made Marks & Spencer unique and successful, however, was its conversion of the definition
of 'what our business is, and should be' into a number of clear,
specific, operationally effective objectives.

This required first a decision as to what to concentrate on, that
is, a basic strategy objective.

Marks & Spencer had been a variety store chain like many

others, offering a large assortment of products which had nothing in common except low price. Now the company decided to concentrate on wearing apparel (to which it soon added household textiles such as towels and draperies).

This was a rational decision. In the England of that time dress was still highly class-determined and the most visible of all class distinctions. Yet all of Europe, after World War I, had become fashion conscious. At the same time mass-production facilities for good-quality but inexpensive fabrics and clothes had come into being, in large part as a result of the huge demand for uniforms during World War I. New textile fibres, such as rayon and acetate, were coming on the market. There was still, however, no mass-distribution system in England for well-designed, up-to-date, and inexpensive clothing for the masses.

Within a few years the new Marks & Spencer had become the leading clothing and textile distributor in England, a position it has held ever since. By 1972 clothing sales accounted for £327 million, (then roughly $800 million), a full three quarters of the total Marks & Spencer volume.

After World War II the same thinking was applied to a new major product category: food. During World War II the English people, formerly known for their dogged resistance to any innovation in eating, learned to accept new foods. Marks & Spencer's food business accounted, in 1972, for the remaining one-fourth of its sales.

From having been a successful variety chain in the early 1920s, and even in the early 1930s, Marks & Spencer purposefully changed itself into a highly distinct 'specialty' marketer – maybe the largest in the world.

The concentration decision enabled the company next to set specific marketing objectives. The decision enabled it to decide who its customer was and should be; what kind of store it needed and where; what pricing policy to follow; and what market penetration to aim at.

The next area which Marks & Spencer tackled was that of innovation objectives. The clothing and textiles Marks & Spencer needed did not exist at the time. Marks & Spencer had been using quality control, like any other large retailer. But it rapidly built its quality-control laboratories into research, design, and development centres. It developed new fabrics, new dyestuffs, new processes, new blends, and so on. It developed designs and fashions. Finally, it went out and looked for the right manufacturer, whom it often had to help get started – for the existing old-line manufacturers were for obvious reasons none too eager to throw in their lot with the brash upstart who tried to tell them how to run their business. And when, after World War II, the company moved into prepared and processed foods, bakery goods, and dairy products, it applied the same innovative approach to a new industry.

Marks & Spencer set innovation goals in marketing. It pioneered, for instance, in consumer research in the early 1930s, when such work was still so new that Marks & Spencer had to develop the needed techniques.

Marks & Spencer set objectives for the supply and development of key resources. It copied and adapted the Sears programme for recruiting, training, and developing managers. It set objectives for the systematic development of financial resources, and measurements to control the utilization of these resources. And it set objectives for the development of its physical facilities, the retail stores.

Hand in hand with these objectives for resources went objectives for their productivity. Marks & Spencer had originally taken its measurements and controls from America. In the 1920s and early 1930s, it began to set its own objectives for continuously improving the productivity of key resources.

As a result, Marks & Spencer has a singularly high productivity of capital – surely one of the keys to its success. The productivity of the Marks & Spencer retail store exceeds, to my knowledge, anything to be found anyplace else, including even Sears, Roebuck or Kresge's K-Marts.

Until the late twenties, the expansion of Marks & Spencer had been achieved primarily by opening new stores. Since the thirties, Marks & Spencer's expansion has been achieved primarily by making each store more productive and by raising sales per square foot of selling space. Measured by the number of its stores, Marks & Spencer is still a small chain; there are only 250 stores. The stores themselves are not large, even by English standards; the average selling area is only 20,000 square feet per store. (The large American supermarket, by comparison, goes up to 100,000 square feet.) Yet these small stores sell something like $4 million a piece a year, which is many times what even highly successful retail stores of other companies do. The only explanation is continual upgrading of merchandise, display, and sales per customer, in each store. Selling space is the limiting resource of a retail merchant; Marks & Spencer's success in getting more sales out of its limited space was central to its performance.

Marks & Spencer set objectives for its social responsibilities, especially in areas of major impact: its own work force and its suppliers. It introduced 'staff manageresses' into its stores to look after the employees, to take care of personal problems, and to make sure employees were treated with intelligence and compassion. Personnel management remains the job of the store manager. The staff manageress was set up to be the 'people conscience' of the company.

Marks & Spencer also developed objectives for its relations with its suppliers. The more successfully a supplier works with Marks & Spencer, the more dependent upon the company he will be. Safeguarding the supplier against exploitation by the company became a concern of the company's management. It set out to develop a system that would enrich the supplier and give it security.

But what about a profit objective? The answer is that there has never been one. Profit goals are being shunned at Marks & Spencer. But it sees profit not as an objective but as a requirement of the business, not as a goal but a need. Profit, in the Marks & Spencer view, is the result of doing things right, rather than the purpose of business activity. It is, above all, determined by what is necessary to attain company objectives. Profitability is a measurement of how well the business discharges its functions in serving market and customer. Above all, it is a restraint; unless profit is adequate to cover the risks, a company will not be able to attain its objectives.

Marks & Spencer from the start converted objectives into

work assignments. It thought through what results and contributions were needed in each objectives area. It assigned responsibility for these results to someone and held him or her accountable. And it measured performance and contribution against the objectives.

## The lessons

The Marks & Spencer story reaffirms the central importance of thinking through 'what our business is and what it should be.' But it also shows that this, by itself, is not enough. The basic definition of the business and its purpose and mission have to be translated into objectives. Otherwise, they remain brilliant insights and good intentions that never become achievement.

The Marks & Spencer story brings out the specifications for objectives. Each of them will be discussed in some detail in the next chapter. But here is the list:

1 Objectives must be derived from 'what our business is, what it will be, and what it should be.' They are not abstractions. They are the action commitments through which the mission of a business is to be carried out, and the standards against which performance is to be measured. Objectives, in other words, are the fundamental strategy of a business.

2 Objectives must be operational. They must be capable of being converted into specific targets and specific assignments. They must be capable of becoming the basis, as well as the motivation, for work and achievement.

3 Objectives must enable the concentration of resources and efforts. They must select the fundamentals among the goals of a business so that the key resources of people, money, and physical facilities can be concentrated. They must, therefore, be selective.

4 There must be multiple objectives rather than a single objective. Much of today's lively discussion of management by objectives is concerned with the search for the 'one right objective.' This search is not only likely to be unproductive; it does harm and misdirects. To manage a business is to balance a variety of

needs and goals. And this requires multiple objectives.

5 Objectives are needed in all areas on which the survival of the business depends. The specific targets, the goals in any object-ive area, depend on the strategy of the individual business. But the areas in which objectives are needed are the same for all busi-nesses, for all businesses depend on the same factors for their survival.

A business must first be able to create a customer. There is, there-fore, need for a marketing objective. Businesses must be able to innovate, or else their competitors will make them obsolete. There is need for an innovation objective. All businesses depend on the three factors of production – human resources, capital re-sources, and physical resources. There must be objectives for their supply, their employment, and their development. The resources must be employed productively and their productivity has to grow if the business is to survive. There is need, therefore, for productivity objectives. Business exists in society and com-munity, and, therefore, has to take responsibility for its impact on the environment. Therefore objectives in respect to the social dimensions of business are needed.

Finally, there is need for profit – otherwise none of the object-ives can be attained. They all require cost. And they can be finan-ced only out of the profits of a business. They all entail risks; they all, therefore, require a profit to cover the risk of potential losses. Profit is not an objective but it is a requirement that has to be ob-jectively determined in respect to the individual business, its strategy, its needs, and risks.

Objectives, therefore, have to be set in these eight key areas:

—marketing
—innovation
—human organization
—financial resources
—physical resources
—productivity
—social responsibility
—profit requirements

Objectives in these key areas enable us to do five things: to organize and explain the whole range of business phenomena in a small number of general statements; to test these statements in actual experience; to predict behaviour; to test the soundness of decisions while they are still being made; and to let managers on all levels analyse their own experience and improve their performance.

## The basis for work and assignments

Objectives are the basis for work and assignments.

They determine the structure of the business, the key activities which must be discharged, and, above all, the allocation of people to tasks. Objectives are the foundation for designing both the structure of the business and the work of individual units and individual managers.

Objectives are always needed in all eight key areas. The area without specific objectives will be neglected. Unless we determine what shall be measured and what the yardstick of measurement in an area will be, the area itself will not be seen.

The measurements available for the key areas of a business enterprise are still haphazard. We do not even have adequate concepts, let alone measurements. For something as central as profitability we have only a rubber yardstick; and we have no reliable tools at all to determine how much profitability is necessary. In respect to innovation and, even more, to productivity, we hardly know more than that something ought to be done. In the other areas – including physical and financial resources – we are reduced to statements of intentions; we do not possess goals and measurements for their attainment.

However, enough is known about each area to give a progress report at least. Enough is known for each business to go to work on objectives.

## How to use objectives

We know one more thing about objectives: how to use them.

If objectives are only good intentions, they are worthless. They must carry over into work. And work is always specific, always has – or should have – clear, unambiguous, measurable results, a deadline and a specific assignment of accountability.

But objectives that become a straitjacket do harm. Objectives are always based on expectations. And expectations are, at best, informed guesses. Objectives express a judgement of factors that are largely outside the business and not under its control. The world does not stand still.

The proper way to use objectives is the way an airline uses schedules and flight plans. The schedule provides for the 9 a.m. flight from Los Angeles to get to Boston by 5 p.m. But if there is a blizzard in Boston that day, the plane will land in Pittsburgh instead and wait out the storm. The flight plan provides for flying at 30,000 feet and for flying over Denver and Chicago. But if the pilot encounters turbulence or strong headwinds, he will ask flight control for permission to go up another 5,000 feet and take the Minneapolis-Montreal route. Yet no flight is ever operated without a schedule and flight plan. Any change is immediately fed back to produce a new schedule and flight plan. And unless most flights stay within the original schedules – or within a very limited range of deviation from them – a well-run airline gets another operations manager who knows his job.

Objectives are not fate; they are direction. They are not commands; they are commitments. They do not determine the future; they are means to mobilize the resources and energies of the business for the making of the future.

## Summary

What Sears represents in the US, Marks & Spencer (though much smaller) represents in England. Starting with 'penny bazaars' in 1916, it has become the world's largest and most successful specialty retailer for the mass market, concentrating on textiles and clothing, and on foods. The company maintained its ability to grow in sales volume and profits during the long years of English economic stagnation and decline in the 1960s and 1970s. Its success is founded on a 'theory of the business' formulated in the 1920s: the mission of Marks & Spencer was not to be retailing; it was to subvert the class structure of nineteenth-century England by making available to working and lower-middle-class customers upper-class goods in superior quality but at a price the customers could afford. From this definition of what 'our business' is, Marks & Spencer then derived a strategy of concentration on clothing and textiles – foods were added after World War II. This then yielded specific marketing and innovation objectives, and also objectives in respect to productivity, to people and to social responsibilities. Altogether the Marks & Spencer story shows that there are eight key areas in each of which objectives have to be thought through and established to ensure the survival and success of a business. It further shows that each of these objectives needs to be made the basis for work and for clear work assignments.

# 7 Strategies, Objectives, Priorities and Work Assignments

Marketing and innovation are the foundation areas in objective setting. It is in these two areas that a business obtains its results. It is performance and contribution in these areas for which a customer pays. All objectives must be performance objectives, aimed at doing rather than at good intentions. In all other objective areas the purpose of doing is to make possible the attainment of the objectives in the areas of marketing and innovation.

It is somewhat misleading to speak of a marketing objective. Marketing performance requires a number of objectives:

—for existing products and services in existing and present markets;

—for abandonment of 'yesterday' in product, services, and markets;
—for new products and services for existing markets;
—for new markets;
—for the distributive organization;
—for service standards and service performance;
—for credit standards and credit performance, and so on.

Many books have been written on every one of these areas. But it is almost never stressed that objectives in these areas can be set only after two key decisions have been made: the decision on concentration, and the decision on market standing.

## The concentration decision

Whereas objectives are 'strategy', the concentration decision is 'policy'. It is, so to speak, the decision in what theatre to fight a war. Without such a policy decision, there can be rules of warfare but no strategy, that is, no purposeful action.

At about the same time at which Marks & Spencer chose to concentrate on wearing apparel and textiles, Sears faced up to the concentration decision. The area of concentration it decided on was household appliances. This was a very different decision from that of Marks & Spencer but it was the right decision, considering both Sears' basically different theory of its business and the conditions prevailing in the American market in the late twenties. Sears did not drop textiles from its stores. But until World War II it paid little attention to them and did not aggressively compete in the apparel market. The Sears concentration decision led the company into different directions from those Marks & Spencer took. Among the results were very large stores; heavy emphasis on a service organization, which eventually led into the automotive field as a second concentration area; and heavy investment in the ownership of appliance makers.

Wherever we find a business that is outstandingly successful, we will find that it has thought through the alternatives and has made a concentration decision.

During the first fifteen years of the computer, that is, until the mid-1960s, only two companies out of the fifty or so who had entered the field managed to make any profit on computers and obtain any kind of market position: IBM and the much smaller Control Data Corporation. Both owed their success largely to facing up to the concentration decision. IBM, in the very infancy of computers, decided to concentrate on the business market and to offer the computer essentially as an accounting machine for large-scale, repetitive handling of conventional data, such as accounting and payroll. Control Data, at almost the same time, made the radically opposite decision to concentrate on large-scale scientific applications. Both companies did very well. The other computer companies all tried to 'cover the market'; none succeeded.

This is big-company stuff, many might say. But neither IBM nor Control Data was a big company when it made its concentration decision. In fact, a small company needs concentration even more than a big one. Its resources are limited and will produce no results unless concentrated.

The concentration decision is highly risky. It is a genuine decision. It has to be tested again and again against the market, its dynamics, its trends, and its changes. Without concentration, marketing objectives – but also innovation objectives – are promises and good intentions rather than true goals. Without them, the resources of the business will not be allocated to performance.

## The market-standing decision

The other major decision underlying marketing objectives is that on market standing. One common approach is to say, 'We want to be the leader.' The other is to say, 'We don't care what share of the market we have as long as sales go up.' Both sound plausible, but both are wrong.

Obviously, not everybody can be the leader. One has to decide in which segment of the market, with what product, what services, what values, one should be the leader. It does not do much good for a company's sales to go up if it loses market share, that is, if the market expands much faster than the company's sales do.

A company with a small share of the market will eventually become marginal in the marketplace, and thereby exceedingly vulnerable. In the slightest economic setback, its customers are likely to concentrate their buying – and then they will concentrate on suppliers that have a substantial share. Distributors and retailers will try to cut inventory by eliminating the marginal supplier. The sales volume of the marginal supplier may become too small to give the needed service – one of the main reasons that marginal appliance manufacturers, no matter how good their product or how well known their brand name, usually do not survive long.

Market standing, regardless of the sales curve, is therefore essential. The point at which the supplier becomes marginal varies from industry to industry. But to be a marginal producer is dangerous for long-term survival. And this is just as true for a department store, a bank, an airline, or an insurance company as it is for a manufacturer.

There is also a maximum market standing above which it may be strategically unwise to go (even if there were no antitrust laws). Market domination tends to lull the leader to sleep; monopolists flounder in their own complacency rather than on public opposition. Market domination produces tremendous internal resistance against any innovation and thus makes adaptation to change dangerously difficult. Also, it usually means that the enterprise has too many of its eggs in one basket and is too vulnerable to economic fluctuations.

Finally, the dominant supplier in a new market is likely to do less well than if it shared that market with one or two other major and competing suppliers. This may seem paradoxical – and most businesspeople find it difficult to accept. But the fact is that a new market, especially a new major market, tends to expand much more rapidly when there are several suppliers rather than only one. It may be very flattering to a supplier's ego to have 80 per cent of a market. But if as a result of domination by a single source, the market does not expand as it otherwise might, the supplier's revenues and profits are likely to be considerably lower than they would be if two suppliers shared a fast-expanding market. Eighty per cent of 100 is considerably less than 50 per cent of 250. A new market which has only one supplier is likely to become static at 100. It will be limited by the imagination of the one supplier who always knows what the product or service cannot or should not be used for. If there are several suppliers, they are likely to un-cover and promote markets and end uses the single supplier never dreams of. And the market might grow rapidly to 250.

Du Pont seems to have grasped this. In its most successful in-novations Du Pont retains a sole-supplier position only until the new product has paid for the original investment. Then Du Pont licenses the innovation and launches competitors deliberately. As a result, a number of aggressive companies start developing new markets and new uses for the product. Nylon would surely have grown much more slowly without Du Pont-sponsored com-petition. Its markets are still growing, but without competition it would probably have begun to decline in the early 1950s, when newer synthetic fibres were brought on the market by other companies.

The market standing to aim at is not the maximum but the *op-timum*. This requires careful analysis of customers, of products or services, of market segments, and distribution channels. It requires a market strategy, and it requires a decision of high risk.

## Innovation objective

The innovation objective is the objective through which a com-pany makes operational its definition of 'what our business should be'.

There are essentially three kinds of innovation in every busi-ness: innovation in product or service; innovation in market-place and consumer behaviour and values; and innovation in the various skills and activities needed to make the products and ser-vices and to bring them to market. They might be called respect-ively product innovation, social innovation and managerial innovation.

Innovation may arise out of the needs of market and customer; necessity may be the mother of innovation. Or innovation may come out of the advancement of skill and knowledge.

The problem in setting innovation objectives is the difficulty of measuring the relative impact and importance of various innovations. Technological leadership is clearly desirable, especially if the term technology is used in its rightful sense as applying to the art, craft, or science of any organized human activity. But how are we to determine which weighs more: a hundred minor but immediately applicable improvements in packaging a product, or one fundamental chemical discovery which after ten more years of hard work may change the character of the business altogether? A department store and a pharmaceutical company will answer this question differently; but so may two different pharmaceutical companies.

Innovating objectives can, therefore, never be as clear and as sharply focused as marketing objectives. To set them, management must first anticipate the innovations needed to reach marketing goals – according to product lines, existing markets, new markets, and service requirements. Second, it must appraise developments arising or likely to arise out of technological advancement in all areas of the business and in all of its activities. These forecasts are best organized in two parts: one for the immediate future, projecting fairly concrete developments which utilize innovations that have already been made; another for the more distant future, aiming at what might be.

Deliberate emphasis on innovation may be needed most where technological changes are least spectacular. No one in a pharmaceutical company or in a company making synthetic organic chemicals needs to be told that survival depends on the ability to replace three-quarters of the company's products by entirely new ones every ten years. But how many people in an insurance company realize that the company's growth – perhaps even its survival – depends on the development of new forms of insurance, the modification of existing policies, and the constant search for new, better, and cheaper ways of selling policies and settling claims? The less visible or prominent that technological change is in a business, the greater the danger that the whole organization will ossify. Hence, the emphasis on innovation is doubly important.

## Resources, their supply, utilization and productivity

A group of objectives deals with the resources a business needs to be able to perform – their supply, utilization, and productivity.

All economic activity, economists have told us for two hundred years, requires three kinds of resources: land, that is products of nature; labour, that is, human resources; and capital, that is, the means to invest in tomorrow. The business must be able to attract all three and to put them to productive use. In these three areas, therefore, every business needs objectives. In addition, it needs an objective for the productivity of these resources. Again, each of these areas will require a plurality of objectives rather than a single one.

In respect to human resources, for instance, it is highly desirable to have specific objectives for manager supply, development, and performance, but also specific objectives for major groups within the nonmanagerial work force, and for relations with unions. There is need for objectives on employee attitudes as well as on employee skills.

Similarly a business needs physical facilities; manufacturing businesses also need raw-material resources. Retail chains, such as Sears, Roebuck and Marks & Spencer, need an objective for the development of stores and the utilization of shelf space, but also for the development of sources of supply for the merchandise they plan to sell.

The capital area is equally crucial – and very few businesses have yet tackled it. Again, objectives are needed for the supply of capital, as well as for its utilization.

The first sign of decline of an industry is loss of appeal to qualified, able, and ambitious people. The American railroads, for instance, did not begin their decline after World War II; it only became obvious and irreversible then. The decline actually set in around the time of World War I. Before World War I, able graduates of American engineering schools looked for a railroad career. From the end of World War I on – for whatever reason – the railroads no longer appealed to young engineering graduates, or to any educated young people. As a result there was nobody in management capable and competent to cope with new problems when the railroads ran into heavy weather twenty years later, around the time of World War II.

In the two areas of people and capital supply, genuine marketing objectives are therefore required. 'What do our jobs have to be to attract and hold the kind of people we need and want? What is the supply available on the job market? And, what do we have to do to attract it?' Similarly, 'What does the investment in our business have to be, in the form of bank loans, long-term debts or equity, to attract and hold the capital we need?'

One American company that for many years has systematically applied market planning to the supply of capital is AT&T. A telephone business is highly capital-intensive; it depends on continuing heavy investment. The customer is, in effect, prefinanced to the tune of three years of future revenues from him. As one of his last contributions – and one of his most important ones – Theodore Vail thought through the problem. He realized, at the end of World War I, that the American capital market was changing and that Bell no longer could expect to obtain its capital from the traditional sources, such as the estates of wealthy Bostonians. Instead, a mass-capital market was coming into being. As a result of his analysis, Vail designed a brand-new security, unknown up to this time, and unparalleled ever since: an AT&T common share with an almost-guaranteed dividend, which was both an equity investment with a promise of long-term capital gains and, in large measure, a fixed-income-producing investment. It thus appealed to a new middle class which could not afford to risk much, but still had some savings available for investment after paying for life insurance or home mortgage.

Forty years later, in the early 1960s, the company's top management realized that this investment instrument had ceased to be appropriate. It drastically changed the nature of the AT&T common share to make it attractive to the new capitalists – the

large investment institutions, such as pension funds and investment trusts.

Setting objectives also applies to objectives concerning union
relations or workers' attitudes. Union relations, most executives
will argue, are beyond their control. For short periods of time this
is indeed true. Circumstances beyond any management's control, such as governmental policies or inflation, strongly mould
union attitudes and demands, as well as union strength. But this
is all the more reason for setting long-range objectives for the relationship with the union.

One may criticize the labour relations policies of General
Motors and General Electric. But these two companies, alone
perhaps among major American businesses, thought through
their union relations, developed objectives for them, and based
their policies on them. The policies, while basically different in
strategy and in tactics, are both very 'tough' ones. Both aim at
maintenance of the company's initiative in labour relations and of
the company's control of worker assignment and worker productivity. Both companies are willing to take a strike over matters of
principle and refuse to buy short-term union concessions on
money issues by yielding on long-term fundamentals. Both policies have been remarkably successful in maintaining productivity and competitive positions for the two companies. Though
labour bitterly criticizes the two companies and has never ceased
to attack their policies, their labour negotiators are among the
few whom labour respects. Indeed, GM and GE lose fewer work-
hours to strike and slowdowns than companies enjoying a much
'better' relationship but relying on short-term expediency.

Resource objectives have to be set in a double process. One
starting point is the anticipated needs of the business, which then
have to be projected on the market for land, labour, and capital.
But the other starting points are these 'markets' themselves,
which then have to be projected onto the structure, the direction, the plans of the business. It is no longer adequate, as most
managers still seem to think, to say, 'This is what we need: how
much do we have to pay for it ?' One also has to say, 'This is what
is available; what do we have to be, how do we have to behave,
to get the fullest benefit ?'

## Productivity: the first test of management's competence

Attracting resources and putting them to work is only the beginning. The task of business is to make resources productive. Every business, therefore, needs productivity objectives with respect to each of the three major resources (land, labour, and capital) and with respect to overall productivity itself.

A productivity measurement is the best yardstick for comparing managements of different units within an enterprise, and for comparing managements of different enterprises. For productivity includes all the efforts the enterprise contributes; it excludes everything it does not control. Productivity is the first test of management's competence.

The continuous improvement of productivity is one of management's most important jobs. It is also one of the most difficult; for productivity is a balance between a diversity of factors, few of which are easily definable or clearly measurable.

The goal is not to try to find the one perfect productivity measurement, but to use a number of measurements – at least one gains insights that way. Output per workhour, for instance, is by itself almost meaningless, even though governmental statistics in most countries are based on it. It does not even measure labour productivity. It becomes meaningful only if the figures show output and profit in both units and dollars per workhour.

Labour is only one of the three factors of production. We also need to measure productivity in other areas by a number of yardsticks to gain insight and judgement. If productivity of labour is accomplished by making the other resources less productive, there is actually loss of productivity.

A telling example is the paper industry. Very few industries have enjoyed as much of a rise in demand and sales. Few industries can match the technical advances of the paper industry, for instance, the stepup in the speed of paper machines. Since World War II the industry has been enjoying a boom in sales and output. Yet it has been unable, in most years, to produce any but marginal profits – well below what money earns in a savings bank. The break-even point of most up-to-date paper mills is just barely below 100 per cent of capacity operations. The explanation for this puzzling phenomenon is a long decline in the productivity of capital in the industry. Paper prices have risen faster than the prices for papermaking equipment. Yet, where it took 80 cents of capital investment to build productive capacity for a dollar of paper sales forty years ago, today it takes two to three dollars of capital investment to produce one dollar's worth of paper sales. Labour productivity in the paper industry has gone up much faster than in most other industries. The paper industry, in other words, has substituted capital for labour on a massive scale. But the trade-off was a thoroughly uneconomical one. In fact, the paper industry represents a massive triumph of engineering over economics and common sense.

A century ago, Karl Marx based his confident prediction of the coming decline of capitalism on the premise that the productivity of capital is bound to go down. This decline was to Marx the basic 'contradiction of capitalism.' That the prophecy has not been fulfilled so far is the result of our ability to innovate, that is, to develop new processes and new industries with higher productivity of capital. But Marx was right in his basic premise: the key to the survival of a business, a company, or an economy is, in the last analysis, productivity of capital. Productivity of capital is the area most companies pay least attention to – if only because so many people mistakenly think that profitability by itself measures it.

But as the Marks & Spencer example shows, the productivity of physical resources needs to be measured fully as much, and objectives for each category need to be set. For productivity includes all three factors of production. The wrong trade-off, that is, an increase in the productivity of one factor of production paid for by a disproportionate drop in another factor results, as the paper industry shows, in a loss of overall productivity.

## Contributed value

We do not have one single yardstick. But at least we have a basic concept that enables us to define productivity for the whole business. The economist calls this concept 'contributed value.'

Contributed value is the difference between the gross revenue received by a company from the sale of its products or services and the amount paid out for the purchase of raw materials and for services rendered by outside suppliers. Contributed value, in other words, includes all the costs of all the efforts of the business and the entire reward received for these efforts. It accounts for all the resources the business itself contributes to the final product and the appraisal of their efforts by the market.

Contributed value can be used to analyse productivity only if the allocation of costs is economically meaningful. The movement in accounting during the last twenty years from financial accounting and tax accounting to management accounting, while still only in its early stages, is thus a major step towards making business manageable and managed.

Contributed value will not measure productivity resulting from qualitative, rather than quantitative, factors. Contributed value is strictly a quantitative tool. Yet qualitative factors have major impact on productivity. Organization structure, the utilization of knowledge in the business, or the quality of tommorrow's management are fundamental factors in productivity, over the short or the long range. However, they elude our existing measurements.

Finally, contributed value can be used, by and large, only in businesses that make something, that is, in manufacturing businesses.

Within these limitations, contributed value makes possible the rational analysis of productivity and the setting of goals for its improvement. In particular, it makes it possible to apply such tools as Operations Research to the systematic study of productivity. For these tools aim at working out alternative courses of action and their predictable consequences. The productivity problem is always one of seeing the range of alternative combinations of the various resources, and of finding the combination that gives the optimal ratio of output to cost and effort and risk.

Productivity is a difficult concept, but it is central. Without productivity objectives, a business does not have direction. Without productivity measurements, it does not have control.

## The social dimension

Only a few years ago managers as well as economists considered the social dimension so intangible that performance objectives could not be set. We have now learned that the intangible can become very tangible indeed. Such lessons as consumerism, or the attacks on industry for the destruction of the environment, are expensive ways to learn that business needs to think through its impacts and its responsibilities, and to set objectives for both.

The social dimension is a survival dimension. The enterprise exists in society and economy. Inside an institution one always tends to assume that the institution exists by itself in a vacuum. And managers inevitably look at their business from the inside. But the business enterprise is a creature of society and economy. Society or the economy can put any business out of existence overnight. The enterprise exists only as long as society and economy believe that it does a necessary, useful, and productive job.

Again, many managers will say, 'This is big-company stuff.' But the small company is also an employer, also exists in a community, and also depends on support or at least on acceptance by community and society. It needs social objectives fully as much as the big business – though it may need very different ones.

What such objectives might be will be discussed further on (in Part Four). But that such objectives need to be built into the strategy of a business, rather than stated as good intentions, needs to be stressed here. These objectives are needed not because the manager has a responsibility to society; they are needed because the manager has a responsibility to the enterprise.

## Profit as a need and a limitation

Only after the objectives in the seven key areas have been thought through and established can a business tackle the question 'How much profitability do we need?' To attain any of the objectives entails high risks. It requires effort, and that means cost. Profit is, therefore, needed to pay for attainment of the objectives of the business. Profit is a condition of survival. It is the cost of the future, the cost of staying in business.

A business that obtains enough profit to satisfy its objectives in the key areas is a business that has the means of survival. A business that falls short of the profitability demands made by its key objectives is a marginal and endangered business.

The profitability needed to support the objectives of the business in the seven key areas discussed so far is also the quantitative expression of the profitability needed to fulfil the social and economic function of profit:

—as the 'risk premium' covering the costs of staying in business;
—as the source of capital to finance the jobs of tomorrow;
—as the source of capital for innovation and for growth of the
 economy.

Profit planning is necessary. But it is planning for a needed minimum profitability rather than for that meaningless phrase 'profit maximization'. The minimum needed may well turn out to be a good deal higher than the profit goals of many companies, let alone their actual profit results.

## The Japanese example

By historical accident the only economy which understands that profit is a minimum rather than a maximum concept is the Japanese economy.

There has been heated discussion wheter Japan has a lower cost of capital or a higher cost of capital than the West – the Westerners contending that Japan's cost of capital is lower, the Japanese that it is higher. Both are wrong. The cost of capital of a Japanese business is pretty much the same as that of a Western business. Only the method of computation differs.

Japan finances its businesses mostly by bank loans. Legally these are short-term credits. Economically, they are permanent equity investments by the bank. The reason for this is that Japan in the nineteenth century did not have a capital market; the banks were created largely by the industrial groups to be their suppliers of capital. In the West the situation is the reverse, the result of the fact that a capital market existed in England and America before industry started to grow.

A Japanese company typically carries 70 per cent debt capital and 30 per cent equity capital. The typical American company has the reverse ratio. We can compute the costs of capital for the two companies. On the 70 per cent debt capital, the Japanese company has to pay at least 10 per cent interest; this requires a 7 per cent return. On the 30 per cent equity, it is expected to earn after taxes about 8 per cent, or 2.4 per cent on its total capital. This adds up to a 9.4 per cent rate of return on total capital employed. The American company has to earn 7 per cent (the average for interest rates in the twenty-five years after World War II) on its 30 per cent debt, amounting to 2.1 per cent on its total invested capital. It has to earn 10 per cent after taxes on its equity capital, which, at a rate of equity capital of 70 per cent of the total, amounts to 7 per cent. This adds up to a total return of 9.4 per cent.

Both come out, in other words, at the same overall cost of capital. (The Japanese carry a much lower tax burden, since interest on loans in Japan is considered, as in the West, a deductible business expense. The tax burden is much higher in the West – but whether this is to be considered as being borne by the business, by the consumer, or by the investor is a point on which economists cannot agree.)

The profitability needed by a Japanese company is what the bank needs to attract deposits to pay its own operating expenses and to cover its risks. It is the margin between the cost of capital to the bank – maybe 6 per cent – and the interest income the bank charges for what, in effect, are equity investments in the businesses it finances. For the Japanese business manager the central fact of life is that he has to earn at least enough to carry the interest on the money he owes to the banks with a margin adequate to maintain his credit standing.

The Japanese manager, therefore, starts out with the clear aim to *minimize* the capital he needs to operate. He sees profit as a need, rather than as something desirable and nice to have. He knows that he will go out of business if he does not produce the minimum profit needed to obtain the capital required. He is no less profit-conscious than the Westerner, but, by historical accident, he is in a position where he understands the function of profit, and where, therefore, he tends to plan more rationally and more purposefully to obtain the profitability on which the survival and growth of his business depends.

The Japanese illustration shows clearly that the *minimum* rate of profitability adequate to the needs of business is the cost of capital. The minimum rate is the capital market rate needed to obtain the financial resources the business needs to attain its objectives.

The cost of capital is never higher than the minimum profitability needed – at least not when there is a capital market rather than government allocation of capital. But it might well be lower than the minimum. It is, however, the best starting point for profit planning.

Whether the business is large or small, complex or simple, profitability should be computed as an average of the profits of both good and bad years. Let us assume that business needs a profitability of 20 per cent before taxes on its invested capital. If the 20 per cent is being earned in a good year, it is unlikely to be earned over the lifetime of the investment. We may need a 40 per cent return in good years to average 20 per cent over a dozen years. And we have to calculate how much we actually need to get the desired average.

**How to measure profitability**

How to measure profitability is a much debated question. No one yardstick will do. Profit on sales (the profit margin) is clearly not adequate by itself. For profit is profit margin multiplied by the rate of turnover of capital. Profit margin is a meaningful figure, only insofar as it shows where the opportunities for profit improvement lie. Return on invested capital makes sense; but in practice it is the worst of all yardsticks – rubber of almost infinite elasticity. What is 'invested capital'? Is a dollar invested in 1950 the same thing as a dollar invested in 1970? Is 'capital' to be defined with the accountant as original cash put in less subsequent depreciation? Or is it to be defined as the economist defines it, as future wealth-producing capacity, discounted at capital-market interest rates to current cash value? The search for a perfect yardstick for measuring profitability is likely to be frustrating and futile. It is far sounder to use a number of yardsticks simultaneously and look at them for what they tell us about the business.

## A note on inflation

One additional aspect of profitability should be mentioned: the impact of inflation on profits. Traditionally it has been held that productive assets are a hedge against inflation. In a sense, this is true. A steel mill will still be standing, capable of producing steel, even when the currency has gone to rack and ruin. The original cost of the mill will have become negligible or zero, so that a larger share of its revenue becomes available to the equity owners. Yet this is a simplistic view; inflation also destroys assets. It creates false profits, profits which in effect represent destruction of capital. In an inflation, even in very rapid inflations at the rate of 40 or 60 per cent a year, such as many South American countries have been experiencing, asset values are not adjusted in the books. In fact, in most countries this is forbidden. Depreciation charges are, therefore, based on yesterday's currency value; and, with a shrinking currency, depreciation rapidly becomes inadequate. Sooner or later, the asset will have to be replaced, and then the costs in depreciated currency will be many times greater than the book value. If this loss is not recognized – and few managements are even aware of it – profits will be shown which, in effect, are underdepreciation, and dividends will be paid out which are in effect distributions of capital. The Securities and Exchange Commission (SEC) in the United States long ago recognized this with respect to the investments of American companies overseas. It demands that the asset value of such investments – in a subsidiary in Brazil, for instance – be adjusted each year to reflect the hidden loss. (Paradoxically, the American tax authorities refuse to accept this adjustment. They make a business pay taxes on a profit which the SEC has forced it to show as a loss in its published accounts.)

In an inflationary situation – and that means in most countries at the present time – inflation should be considered a genuine cost. There is good reason to adopt, at least for internal purposes, a method of accounting in 'constant dollars' or 'constant yen' or 'constant marks.' At least it forces management to realize that inflation rather than its own performance underlies a good profit showing.

If American companies had used accounting in constant dollars during the late sixties, most of them would have realized that they produced no profits, let alone the reported 'record profits' of these inflation years. Few of them showed after-tax profits of more than 8 per cent on their assets – yet the US then had an annual 8 per cent inflation rate. Had managers realized this, they would not have been so surprised at the collapse of the stock market prices of the growth companies in 1969–1970.

## Profitability as a limitation

Profitability is not only a need, it is also a limitation. The object-ives of a business must not exceed the profitability with which it can expect to operate. The minimum profitability must not be so high that one cannot prudently expect to attain it. The profit-ability need, therefore, has to be projected back on the objectives. If profitability is inadequate to the objectives, the objectives have to be pruned. The company's eyes ought not be bigger than its stomach.

Almost any business, in setting objectives in key areas, will come up with greater efforts and higher risks than it is likely to be able to support in terms of profitability. Any business, there-fore, will have to balance objectives.

## Balancing objectives

There are three kinds of balance needed in setting objectives. Objectives have to be balanced against attainable profitability. Objectives have to be balanced as to the demands of the immedi-ate and the distant future. They have to be balanced against each other, and trade-offs have to be established between desired performance in one area and desired performance in others.

In setting objectives, management always has to balance the immediate future against the long range. If it does not provide for the immediate future, there will be no long-range future. But if it sacrifices the long-range needs of 'what our business *will* be' and 'what our business *should* be' to immediate results, there will also be no business fairly soon.

Setting objectives always requires a decision on where to take the risks, a decision as to how much immediate results should be sacrificed for the sake of long-range growth, or how much long-range growth should be jeopardized for the sake of short-run performance. There is no formula for these decisions. They are risky, entrepreneurial, uncertain – but they must be made.

The growth companies of the 1950s and 1960s promised both more sales and higher profits indefinitely. This alone was reason to distrust them. Every experienced manager should have known that these two objectives are not normally compatible. To produce more sales almost always means to sacrifice immediate profit. To produce higher profit almost always means to sacrifice long-range sales. In almost every case, this irrational promise and the resulting refusal to make balancing decisions between growth and profitability objectives was the direct cause of the large losses and the equally large write-offs of the growth companies in the late sixties and early seventies.

There are few things that distinguish competent from incompetent management quite as sharply as performance in balancing objectives. There is no formula for doing the job. Each business requires its own balance – and it may require a different balance at different times. Balancing is not a mechanical job. It is risk-taking decision. (For further discussion of these strategic decisions, see the next chapter.)

## The role of budgeting

Setting and balancing objectives does require a mechanical expression. The budget is the instrument, and especially the budget for managed and capital expenditures.

Budgeting is commonly thought to be a financial process. But only the notation is financial; the decisions are entrepreneurial. Today the so-called managed expenditures, e.g. research or advertising, and the capital expenditures, e.g. a new factory, are usually considered to be quite separate. But the distinction is an accounting (and tax) fiction and misleading. Both expenditures commit scarce resources to an uncertain future; both are, economically speaking, expenditures of capital that are investments in the future. If the company is to succeed, the expenditures have to express the same basic decisions on survival objectives. Today, most of our attention in budgets is usually given to other than the managed expenses, especially to the so-called variable expenses, e.g., wages. Historically that is where the most money was being spent. But no matter how large or small the sums, decisions on the managed expenses determine the future of the enterprise.

We have little control over what the accountant calls variable expenses, those which relate directly to units or production and are fixed by a certain way of doing things. We can change them, but slowly. We can change a relationship between units of production and labour costs (which we, with a certain irony, still consider variable expenses despite the largely fixed fringe benefits). But within any time period these expenses cannot be changed. This is, of course, even more true for expenses with respect to past decisions, the fixed expenses. We cannot undo them at all, whether they are the cost of past capital investment, local taxes, or insurance premiums to protect assets. They are beyond management's control.

The expenses under management's control are the expenses for the future. The capital expenses and the managed expenses express management's risk-taking decisions. These include expenses on facilities and equipment, on research and merchandising, on product development and people development, on management and organization, on customer service, and on advertising. The capital budget and the managed expense budget are the areas in which a business makes its real decisions on its objectives.

## Setting priorities

The two budgets regarding the future: capital expenditures and managed expenditures, also express the priorities which management sets.

No business can do everything. Even if it has the money, it will never have enough good people. It has to set priorities. The worst thing is to try to do a little bit of everything. This makes sure that nothing is being accomplished. It is better to pick the wrong priority than none at all.

Setting priorities is risky. For whatever does not receive priority is, in effect, abandoned. There is no formula for making the decision, but it has to be made, and the mechanism for making it are the budgets for capital and managed expenditures.

## From objectives to doing

One final step remains: to convert objectives into doing. Action rather than knowledge is the purpose of asking, 'What *is* our business, what *will* it be, what *should* it be?' and of thinking through objectives. The aim is to focus the energies and resources of the organization on the right results. The end product of business analysis, therefore, are work programmes, and specific and concrete work assignments with defined goals, with deadlines, and with clear accountability. Unless objectives are converted into action, they are not objectives; they are dreams.

## Summary

Marketing and innovation are the two result areas with which the setting of objectives has to begin. Both are likely to require a range of objectives rather than one target figure. Both also require prior decisions of high risk: on concentration and on market standing. And then there is need for objectives in respect to all resources – people, capital, facilities, and key physical resources – their supply, their utilization, and their productivity. There is need for objectives in respect to the social dimension of business, its social responsibilities and social impacts. In all these areas, the small business needs clear objectives just as much as the big one. Profit and profitability come at the end; they are survival needs of a business and therefore require objectives. But the needed profitability also establishes limitations on all other objectives. Objectives have to be balanced – with each other, in terms of the different requirements of the short and the long term, and against available resources. Finally, action priorities have to be set.

# 8 Strategic Planning: The Entrepreneurial Skill

Practically every basic management decision is a long-range decision – ten years is a rather short time span these days. Whether concerned with research or with building a new plant, designing a new marketing organization or a new product, every major management decision takes years before it is really effective. And it has to be productive for years thereafter to pay off the investment of people and money. Managers, therefore, need to be skilled in making decisions with long futurity on a systematic basis.

Management has no choice but to anticipate the future, to attempt to mould it, and to balance short-range and long-range goals. It is not given to mortals to do well any of these things. But lacking divine guidance, management must make sure that these difficult responsibilities are not overlooked or neglected.

The idea of long-range planning – and much of its reality – rests on a number of misunderstandings. The present and the immediate short range require strategic decisions fully as much as the long range. The long range is largely made by short-run decisions. Unless the long range is built into, and based on, short-range plans and decisions, the most elaborate long-range plan will be an exercise in futility. And conversely, unless the short-range plans, that is, the decisions on the here and now, are integrated into one unified plan of action, they will be expedients, guesses, and misdirections.

'Short range' and 'long range' are not determined by any given time span. A decision is not short range because it takes only a few months to carry it out. What matters is the time span over which it has to be effective. A decision is not long range because in the early 1970s we resolve on making it in 1985; this is not a decision but an idle diversion. It has as much reality as the eight-year-old boy's plan to be a fireman when he grows up.

The idea behind long-range planning is that 'What *should* our business be ?' can and should be worked on and decided by itself, independent of the thinking on 'What *is* our business ?' and 'What *will* it be ?' There is some sense to this. It is necessary in strategic planning to *start* separately with all three questions: What *is* the business ? What *will* it be ? What *should* it be ? These are, and should be, separate conceptual approaches. With respect to 'What *should* the business be ?' the first assumption must be that it will be different.

Long-range planning should prevent managers from uncritically extending present trends into the future, from assuming that today's products, services, markets, and technologies will be the products, services, markets, and technologies of tomorrow, and, above all, from dedicating their resources and energies to the defence of yesterday.

Planning what *is* our business, planning what *will* it be, and planning what *should* it be have to be integrated. What is short range and what is long range is then decided by the time span and futurity of the decision. Everything that is 'planned' becomes immediate work and commitment.

The skill we need is not long-range planning. It is strategic decision making, or perhaps strategic planning.

General Electric calls this work 'strategic business planning'. The ultimate objective of the activity is to identify the new and different businesses, technologies, and markets which the company should try to create long range. But the work starts with the question, 'What *is* our present business ?' Indeed, it starts with the questions, 'Which of our present businesses should we abandon ? Which should we play down ? Which should be push and supply new resources to ?'

## What strategic planning is not

It is important for the manager to know what strategic planning is *not*:

1 *It is not a box of tricks, a bundle of techniques*. It is analytical thinking and commitment of resources to action.

Many techniques may be used in the process – but, then again, none may be needed. Strategic planning may require a computer, but the most important questions – 'What *is* our business ?' or 'What *should* it be ?' – cannot be quantified and programmed for the computer. Model building or simulation may be helpful, but they are not strategic planning; they are tools for specific purposes and may or may not apply in a given case.

Quantification is not planning. To be sure, one uses rigorous logical methods as far as possible – if only to make sure that one does not deceive oneself. But some of the most important questions in strategic planning can be phrased only in terms such as 'larger' or 'smaller,' 'sooner' or 'later'. These terms cannot easily be manipulated by quantitative techniques. And some equally important areas; such as those of political climate, social responsibilities, or human (including managerial) resources, cannot be quantified at all. They can be handled only as restraints, or boundaries but not as factors in the equation itself.

Strategic planning is *not* the 'application of scientific methods to business decision' (as one well-known text on planning defines it). It is the application of thought, analysis, imagination, and judgement. It is responsibility, rather than technique.

2 *Strategic planning is not forecasting*. It is not masterminding the future. Any attempt to do so is foolish; the future is unpre-

dictable. We can only discredit what we are doing by attempting it.

If anyone suffers from the delusion that the human being is able to forecast beyond a very short time span, look at the headlines in yesterday's paper, and ask which of them anyone could possibly have predicted a decade or so ago. For example, could we, in 1960, in the waning days of the Eisenhower Administration, have forecast the almost explosive growth of the black middle class in America, which by 1970, had raised two-thirds of black families above the poverty line and had given the American Negro family an average income well above the average income of affluent Great Britain? But could we also have predicted that this unprecedented achievement could only have made more acute and pressing the problem of the one-third of American blacks remaining in poverty?

We must start out with the premise that forecasting is not a respectable human activity and not worthwhile beyond the shortest of periods. *Strategic planning is necessary precisely because we cannot forecast.*

Another, even more compelling, reason why forecasting is not strategic planning is that forecasting attempts to find the most probable course of events or, at best, a range of probabilities. But the entrepreneurial problem is the unique event that will change the possibilities; the entrepreneurial universe is not a physical but a social universe. Indeed, the central entrepreneurial contribution, which alone is rewarded with a profit, is to bring about the unique event or innovation that changes the economic, social, or political situation.

This was what Xerox Corporation did in the 1950s when it developed and marketed photocopying machines. This is what the entrepreneurs in mobile housing did in the 1960s, when the trailer became the new, permanent, and immobile home and took over practically the entire US low-cost housing market. The unique event of Rachel Carson's book *Silent Spring*, in the 1950s, changed the attitude of a whole civilization towards the environment. On the social and political scene, this is what the leaders of the civil rights movement did in the 1960s, and what the leaders in women's rights were doing at the start of the 1970s.

Since the entrepreneur upsets the probabilities on which predictions are based, forecasting does not serve the purposes of planners who seek to direct their organizations to the future. It certainly is of little use to planners who would innovate and change the ways in which people work and live.

3 *Strategic planning does not deal with future decisions. It deals with the futurity of present decisions.* Decisions exist only in the present. The question that faces the strategic decision-maker is not what the organization should do tomorrow. It is, 'What do we have to do today to be ready for an uncertain tomorrow?' The question is not what will happen in the future. It is, 'What futurity do we have to build into our present thinking and doing, what time spans do we have to consider, and how do we use this information to make a rational decision now?'

Decision-making is a time machine which synchronizes into a single time – the present – a great number of divergent time spans. We are only learning this now. Our approach still tends towards making plans for something we will decide to do in the future, which may be entertaining but is futile. We can make decisions only in the present and yet we cannot make decisions *for* the present alone; the most expedient, most opportunistic decision – let alone the decision not to decide at all – may commit us for a long time, if not permanently and irrevocably.

4 *Strategic planning is not an attempt to eliminate risk.* It is not even an attempt to minimize risk. Such an attempt can lead only to irrational and unlimited risks and to certain disaster.

Economic activity, by definition, commits present resources to the future, i.e., to highly uncertain expectations. To take risks is the essence of economic activity. An important principle of economics (Boehm-Bawerk's Law) proves that existing means of production will yield greater economic performance only through greater uncertainty, that is, through greater risk.

While it is futile to try to eliminate risk, and questionable to try to minimize it, it is essential that the risks taken be the right risks. The end result of successful strategic planning must be capacity to take a greater risk, for this is the only way to improve *entrepreneurial* performance. To extend this capacity, however, we must understand the risks we take. We must be able to choose rationally among risk-taking courses of action rather than plunge into uncertainty on the basis of hunch, hearsay, or experience, no matter how carefully quantified.

## What strategic planning is

We can now attempt to define what strategic planning is. It is the continuous process of making present risk-taking *decisions* systematically and with the greatest knowledge of their futurity; organizing systematically the *efforts* needed to carry out these decisions; and measuring the results of these decisions against the expectations through organized, *systematic feedback.*

## Sloughing off yesterday

Planning starts with the objectives of the business. In each area of objectives, the question needs to be asked, '*What do we have to do now* to attain our objectives *tomorrow* ?' The first thing to do to attain tomorrow is to slough off yesterday. Most plans concern themselves only with the new and additional things that have to be done – new products, new processes, new markets, and so on. But the key to doing something different tomorrow is getting rid of the no-longer-productive, the obsolescent, the obsolete.

The first step in planning is to ask of any activity, any product, any process or market, 'If we are not committed to this today, would we go into it ?' If the answer is no, one says, 'How can we get out – fast ?'

Systematic sloughing off of yesterday is a plan by itself – and adequate in many businesses. It will force thinking and action. It will make available people and money for new things. It will create willingness to act.

Conversely, the plan that provides only for doing additional and new things without provision for sloughing off old and tired ones is unlikely to have results. It will remain plan and never become reality. Yet getting rid of yesterday is the decision that most long-range plans in business (and even more in government) never tackle – maybe the main reason for their futility.

## What new things do we have to do - when?

The next step in the planning process is to ask, 'What *new* and different things do we have to do, and when ?'

In every plan there will be areas where all that is needed – or appears to be needed – is to do more of what we already do. It is prudent, however, to assume that what we already do is never adequate to the needs of the future. But, 'What do we need ?' is only half the question. Equally important is 'When do we need it ?' for it fixes the time for beginning work on the new tasks.

There is indeed a 'short' range and a 'long' range to every decision. The five years between the commitment to a course (building a steel mill) and the earliest possible moment for results (getting finished steel) is the short range of a decision. And the twenty years or more it takes before we get back with compound interest the money invested in the steel mill is the long range. The long range is the time during which the initial decision must remain reasonably valid – as to markets, process, technology, plant location, etc – to have been the right decision originally.

But it is meaningless to speak of short-range and long-range plans. There are plans that lead to *action today* – and they are true plans, true strategic decisions. And there are plans that talk about action tomorrow – they are dreams, if not pretexts for non-thinking, nonplanning, nondoing. The essence of planning is to make present decisions with knowledge of their futurity. It is the *futurity* that determines the time span, and not vice versa.

Results that require a long gestation period will be obtained only if initiated early enough. Hence, long-range planning requires knowledge of futurity: 'What do we have to do today if we want to be in some particular place in the future ? What will not get done at all if we do not commit resources to it today ?'

To repeat an oft-used illustration: if we know that it takes ninety-nine years to grow Douglas firs in the Northwest to pulp-

ing size, planting seedlings today is the only way we can provide
for pulp supply in ninety-nine years. Someone may well develop
a speeding-up hormone; but we cannot bank on it if we are in the
paper industry. It is quite conceivable – perhaps highly probable – that we will use wood primarily as a source of chemicals
long before the trees grow to maturity. The paper supply thirty
years hence may depend on less precious, less highly structured
sources of cellulose than a tree, which is the most advanced chemical factory in the plant kingdom. This simply means, however,
that forests may put their proprietors into the chemical industry
sometime within the next thirty years and they had better learn
now something about chemistry. If, however, paper plants depend on Douglas fir, planning cannot confine itself to twenty
years, but must consider ninety-nine years.

For other decisions, even five years would be absurdly long. If
our business is buying up distress merchandise and selling it at
auction, next week's clearance sale is long-range future; anything beyond is largely irrelevant to us. Thus, the nature of the
business and the nature of the decision determine the time
spans of planning.

Time spans are neither fixed nor 'given'. The time decision itself is a risk-taking decision in the planning process. It largely
determines the allocation of resources and efforts. It largely determines the risks taken. One cannot repeat too often that to
postpone a decision is in itself a risk-taking and often irrevocable
decision. The time decision largely determines the character
and nature of the business.

To sum up: What is crucial in strategic planning is, first, that
systematic and purposeful *work* on attaining objectives be done;
second, that planning start out with sloughing off yesterday, and
that abandonment be planned as part of the systematic attempt
to attain tomorrow; third, that we look for new and different
ways to attain objectives rather than believe that doing more of
the same will suffice; and finally, that we think through the time
dimensions and ask, 'When do we have to start work to get results when we need them?'

## Everything degenerates into work

The best plan is *only* good intentions unless it leads *into work*. What makes a plan capable of producing results is the commitment of key people to work on specific tasks. The test of a plan is whether management actually commits resources to action which will bring results in the future. Unless such commitment is made, there are only promises and hopes, but no plan.

A plan needs to be tested by asking managers, 'Which of your best people have you put on this work today ?' The manager who comes back (as most of them do) and says, 'But I can't spare my best people now. They have to finish what they are doing now before I can put them to work on tomorrow' – this manager simply admits that he or she does not have a plan. But the manager also proves that a plan is needed for it is precisely the purpose of a plan to show where scarce resources – and the scarcest is good people – should be working.

Work implies not only that somebody is supposed to do the job, but also accountability, a deadline, and finally the measurement of results, that is, feedback from results on the work and on the planning process itself.

In strategic planning, measurements present very real problems, especially conceptual ones. Yet precisely because what we measure and how we measure determine what will be considered relevant, and determine thereby not just what we see, but what we – and others – do, measurements are all-important in the planning process. Above all, unless we build expectations into the planning decision in such a way that we can find out early whether they are actually fulfilled or not – including a fair understanding of what are significant deviations both in time and in scale – we cannot plan. We have no feedback, no way of self-control from events back to the planning process.

The manager cannot decide whether he or she wants to make risk-taking decisions with long futurity; making them defines the role of manager. All that is within a manager's power is to decide whether he or she wants to make them responsibly or irresponsibly, with a rational chance of effectiveness and success, or as a blind gamble against all odds. And both because the decision-making process is essentially a rational process and because the effectiveness of the entrepreneurial decisions depends on the understanding and voluntary efforts of others, the approach will be more responsible and more likely to be effective if it is rational, organized, and based on knowledge, not prophecy. The end result, however, is not knowledge but strategy. *Its aim is action now.*

Strategic planning does not substitute facts for judgement, does not substitute science for the manager. It does not even lessen the importance and role of managerial ability, courage, experience, intuition, or even hunch – just as scientific biology and systematic medicine have not lessened the importance of these qualities in the individual physician. On the contrary, the systematic organization of the planning job and the supply of knowledge to it strengthen the manager's judgement, leadership, and vision.

## Summary

Strategic planning prepares today's business for the future. It asks: what *should* our business be? It asks: what do we have to do today to deserve the future? Strategic planning requires risk-taking decisions. It requires an organized process of abandoning yesterday. It requires that the work to be done to produce the desired future be clearly defined and clearly assigned. The aim of strategic planning is *action now.*

# Part Two
# Performance in the
# Service Institution

The public-service institutions – government agency and
hospital, school, college and university, armed service and
professional association – have been growing much faster than
business in this century. They are the growth sector of a
modern society. And within business, the service staffs have
been growing much faster than the operating units. Yet
performance has not kept up with growth or importance.
What explains the lag in performance in the service institutions ?
How can service institutions be managed for performance ?

# 9 The Multi-Institutional Society

Business enterprise is only one of the institutions of modern society, and business managers are by no means our only managers. Service institutions are equally institutions and, therefore, equally in need of management. Some of the most familiar of these service institutions are government agencies, the armed services, schools, colleges and universities, research laboratories, hospitals and other health-care institutions, unions, professional practices such as the large law firm, and professional, industry, and trade associations. They all have people who are paid for doing the management job, even though they may be called administrators, commanders, directors, or executives rather than managers.

We are a multi-institutional society rather than a business society. And the public-service institutions – to give them a generic name – are the real growth sector of modern society.

## Service institutions within Business

Within business enterprises, the growth sector also includes 'service institutions.' In every large business – and in many fairly small businesses – there has been rapid increase in service groups and service functions. Such units as research departments, planning groups, coordinators, management information systems, and so on, are all service institutions rather than operating units. While they operate within an economic institution, none of them produces economic results directly or performs economically by itself. They have no direct relationship to the economic performance and the results of the business.

All service institutions are supported by the economic surplus produced by economic activity. They are overhead – either social overhead or business overhead. The growth of the service institutions in this century is the best testimonial to the success of business in discharging its economic task, producing economic surplus.

Yet – unlike the early nineteenth-century university – the service institutions are not luxury or ornament. They are essentials of a modern society. They *have* to perform if society and business are to function. These service institutions are the main expense of a modern society. Half of the gross national product of the US (and of most of the other developed countries) is spent on public-service institutions. Every citizen in the developed, industrialized, urbanized societies depends for survival on the performance of the public-service institutions. These institutions also embody the values of developed societies. Education, health care, knowledge, and mobility – not just more food, clothing, and shelter – are the fruits of our society's increased economic capacities and productivity.

The service institutions within business should also be load-bearing members of the structure. It is not just their steadily increasing cost that requires that they be managed for contribution and performance. Business enterprise depends on the performance of its service staffs, its planners, researchers, information specialists, analysts, and accountants.

Yet the evidence for performance in the service institutions is not impressive, let alone overwhelming. Colleges, hospitals, and universities have grown larger than an earlier generation would have dreamed possible. Their budgets have grown even faster. Yet everywhere they are in crisis. A generation or two ago their performance was taken for granted. Today they are attacked on all sides for lack of performance. Services which the nineteenth century managed successfully with little apparent effort – the postal service, for instance, or the railroads – are today deep in the red, require enormous subsidies, and give poorer service than they did a century ago. National and local government agencies are constantly being reorganized for efficiency. Yet in every country citizens complain loudly of growing bureaucracy in government. What they mean is that the government agency is being run more for the convenience of its employees than for contribution and performance. This is mismanagement.

The most persistent critics of bureaucracy in government and in the public-service institutions tend to be business executives. But it is by no means certain that business's own service institutions are any more effective than the public service bureaucracies.

In the last twenty years, staff activities, planning departments, coordinators, and management information systems have snowballed in all large (and in many small) corporations. Judged by their ability to get their budgets funded, they are tremendous successes. Many also have employees of great ability and competence with impressive functional knowledge, and produce a rapidly growing literature. But do they all make a contribution? Worse still, who can judge their performance or measure their results? And by what standard? The inability to measure their contribution is one factor in the growing disenchantment with many service departments within business.

Research activity in business has grown as fast as service staffs. So has government-sponsored research in the universities and in separate research institutes. With research, too, disenchantment has set in. Far too many companies have little except beautiful buildings to show for all the research money they spent. It is still the rare research department that can answer the question, 'And what have you *contributed*?' – and it still is uncommon to find a research department that asks this question of itself.

## Are service institutions managed?

The service institutions themselves have become 'management conscious.' Increasingly they turn to business to learn management. In all service institutions, manager development, management by objectives, and many other concepts and tools of business management are now common.

This is a healthy sign, but it does not mean that the service institutions understand the problems of managing themselves. It only means that they begin to realize that at present they are not being managed.

## But are they manageable?

There is another and very different response to the performance crisis of the service institutions. A growing number of critics have come to the conclusion that service institutions are inherently unmanageable and incapable of performance. Some go so far as to suggest that they should therefore be dissolved. But there is not the slightest evidence that today's society is willing to do without the contributions the service institutions provide. The people who most vocally attack the shortcomings of the hospitals want more and better health care. Those who preach 'deschooling' society, want better, not less, education. The voters most bitter about government bureaucracy vote for more government programmes. Similarly, business is not going to do without the contribution of knowledge, expertise, and systematic thinking which service staffs and research departments are intended to furnish.

We have no choice but to learn to manage the service institutions for performance.

*And they can be managed for performance.*


## The importance of the exceptions

Performance in a service institution – whether public service or service staff in business – is the exception rather than the rule. But the exceptions prove that service institutions can perform.

Several examples of performing service institutions will be discussed in Chapter 11, 'The Exceptions and Their Lessons,' but a few might be mentioned here. Among government agencies of the last forty years, two performers stand out: the Tennessee Valley Authority (TVA), the big regional electric-power and irrigation project in the Southeastern United States; and in the sixties, the National Aeronautics and Space Agency (NASA), which managed the American space programme. Among universities attempting mass higher education some of the new English universities have been notably effective. While a great many – perhaps most – schools in the inner-city, black ghettos of America deserve the harshest criticism, a few schools in the very worst ghettos have shown high capacity to teach the most disadvantaged children the basic skills of literacy.

What is it then that hinders the typical service institutions from performing? And what is it that the few performing service institutions do – or avoid doing – that makes them capable of performance? These are the questions to ask, and they are management questions.

## Making the service institutions perform

The service institution does not differ much from a business enterprise in any area other than its specific mission. It faces very similar challenges to make work productive and the workers achieving. It does not differ significantly from a business in its social responsibility. Recent events have shown that the service institutions face the same problems in their relationship with the environment and with society as do businesses. The worst polluters today are, after all, governments – local governments with inadequate sewer plants. The discussion of social impacts and social responsibilities in Part IV of this book applies with little modification to all institutions, public or private.

But the service institution is fundamentally different from business in its 'business'. It is different in its purpose. It has different values. It needs different objectives, and it makes a different contribution to society. Performance and results are quite different in a service institution from what they are in business. Managing for performance is the one area in which the service institution differs significantly from a business.

We have no coherent theory of institutions and their management that encompasses the service institutions. Compared to the work done in business management over the last seventy years, little has been done on the management of the service institution. All we can attempt so far is a first sketch. We do understand why the service institution has difficulty performing. And we can outline what is needed to offset the built-in obstacles to performance and results in service institutions.

Managing the service institutions for performance will increasingly be seen as the central managerial challenge of a developed society and as its greatest managerial need.

## Summary

Our society has become a multi-institutional society. And the public-service institutions – government agency and armed service, school, college and university, hospital, professional practice, and professional or trade association – have grown faster in this century than business. Altogether some fifty per cent of the country's national income now goes to or through such public-service institutions. And within business, service staffs – the research lab, the personnel department, the planning department or the management information staff – have also grown faster than business itself. Every one of these service institutions and service staffs needs to be managed. On the performance of service institutions our society – and every citizen – increasingly depends. Although these service institutions are increasingly becoming 'management conscious', few are actually being managed for performance. Many critics maintain indeed that they are inherently unmanageable, if not altogether incapable of performance. Yet there is enough evidence to show that service institutions can be managed for performance.

# 10 Why Service Institutions Do Not Perform

There are three popular explanations for the common failure of service institutions to perform:

—their managers aren't businesslike;
—they need better people;
—their objectives and results are intangible.

All three are alibis rather than explanations.

## How businesslike are they?

The service institution will perform, it is said again and again, if only it is managed in a businesslike manner.

The service institution has performance trouble precisely because it is not a business. What characterizes a business is control by performance and what 'businesslike' means in a service institution is control of cost, a measure of efficiency. But it is *effectiveness and not efficiency which the service institution lacks*. Effectiveness cannot be obtained by businesslike behaviour as the term is understood – that is, by greater efficiency.

To be sure, efficiency is necessary in all institutions. Because there is usually no competition in the service field, there is no outward and imposed cost control on service institutions as there is for business in a competitive market. But the basic problem of service institutions is not high cost but lack of effectiveness. Some are very efficient, but they tend not to do the right things.

## The need for better people

The cry for better people is probably even older than the belief that being businesslike will save the service institution. It can be found in the earliest Chinese texts on government. It has been the constant demand of all American reformers, from Henry Adams, shortly after the Civil War, to Ralph Nader today. They have all believed that the one thing lacking in the government agency is better people.

Service institutions can no more depend on supermen or lion tamers to staff their managerial and executive positions than can businesses. There are far too many institutions to be staffed. It is absurd to expect that the administrator of every hospital in the world be a genius or even great. If service institutions cannot be run and managed by administrators of normal capability, they are indeed unmanageable. If, in other words, we cannot organize the task so that it will be done adequately by men and women who only try hard, it cannot be done at all.

There is no reason to believe that the people who staff the managerial and professional positions in our service institutions are any less qualified, any less competent or honest, or any less hard-working than those who manage businesses. On the other hand, there is also no reason to believe that business managers, put in control of service institutions, would do better than the 'bureaucrats'. Indeed, we know that they immediately become bureaucrats themselves.

In World War II large numbers of American business executives who had performed very well in their own companies moved into government positions. Many of them rapidly became bureaucrats. The individuals did not change, but whereas they had been capable of obtaining performance and results in a business, in government they found themselves producing mainly procedures and red tape – and deeply frustrated.

## The tangibility of goals

The most sophisticated and, at first glance, the most plausible explanation for the failure of service institutions to perform is the last one: the objectives of service institutions are 'intangible' and so are their results. This is at best a half-truth.

The definition of what 'our business is' is always intangible, for a business as well as for a service institution. To say, as Sears, Roebuck does, 'Our business is to be the informed buyer for the American family' is intangible. To say, as Vail did at Bell Telephone, 'Our business is service to the customer' may sound like a public relations slogan. At first glance these statements seem to defy any attempt at translation into operational terms, let alone quantitative ones. To say, 'Our business is electronic information', as Sony of Japan does, is equally intangible; so is IBM's definition of its business as data processing. Yet as these businesses have shown, it is not too difficult to derive measurable goals and targets from such intangible definitions.

Specific targets can also be derived from the apparently even less tangible goals of service institutions.

'Saving souls' as the definition of the objectives of a church is intangible. At least the bookkeeping is not of this world. But church attendance is measurable. And so is 'getting the young people back into the church'.

'The development of the whole personality' as the objective of the school is, indeed, intangible. But 'teaching a child to read by the time he has finished third grade' is by no means intangible. It can be measured easily and precisely.

Achievement is only possible against specific, limited, clearly defined targets, in business as well as in a service institution. Only if targets are defined can resources be allocated to attain them. Only then can priorities and deadlines be set, and somebody be held accountable for results. But the starting point for effective work is the definition of purpose and mission of the institution, which is almost always intangible.

'What is our business ?' is as ambiguous and as controversial a question for a service institution as it is for a business. There will surely be dissent and controversy before a workable definition is found. Service institutions have many constituents. The school is of vital concern not only to children and their parents, but to teachers, to taxpayers, to the community at large. Similarly the hospital has to satisfy the patient, but also the doctors, the nurses, the technicians, the patient's family – and again taxpayers or, as in the United States, employers and unions who together provide the bulk of the support of most hospitals through their insurance contributions.

## Misdirection by budget

The one basic difference between a service institution and a business is the way the service institution is paid.

Businesses (other than monopolies) are paid for satisfying the customer. They are paid only when they produce what customers want and what they are willing to exchange purchasing power for. Satisfaction of the customer is, therefore, the basis for assuring performance and results in a business.

Service institutions, by contrast, are typically paid out of a budget allocation. This means that they are not paid for what taxpayer and customer mean by results and performance. Their revenues flow from a general revenue stream that depends not on what they are doing but on some sort of tax.

This is as true for the service institution within a business as it is, for instance, for the state school. The typical staff department is not paid for its results. It is, as a rule, not even paid according to the extent to which its customers, that is, the managers, use it. It is paid out of an overhead allocation, that is, out of a budget. The fact that the service institution within a business tends to exhibit the same characteristics and to indulge in the same behaviour as service institutions in the public sector indicates that it is not business that makes the difference. It is the method of payment.

The typical service institution – including most service staffs in business – also has monopoly powers. The intended beneficiary has no choice. Most service institutions have power beyond what the most monopolistic business enjoys.

If I am dissatisfied with the service of the local power company or of the telephone company, I have no other place to go for electric power or telephone service. But if I choose to do without either power or telephone, I do not have to pay for it. This option is not available, however, to customers dissatisfied with a service institution. There the customers pay whether they want to use the service or not.

The American household pays school taxes whether it has children of school age or not. Parents may choose to send their children to a private or a parochial school but they still pay taxes for the state school, even though they do not use it and consider it inappropriate or unsatisfactory for their own children. Behind the school, or any government service institution, stands the police power of the state, which exacts payment, not for services rendered but for the support of a governmental agency.

Most service staffs in business have this monopoly power too. Operating managers know that they are judged in some measure by how well they cooperate with the staff services; and only rarely are they permitted to go outside their own company for advice or expertise in a staff service's area.

Being paid out of a budget allocation rather than for results changes what is meant by performance. Results in the budget-based institution are measured by the budget size. Performance is the ability to maintain or to increase one's budget. Results in the usual sense, that is, contributions to the market or achievement towards a goal and objectives, are secondary. The first test of a budget-based institution and the first requirement for its survival is to obtain the budget. And the budget is not, by definition, related so much to contribution as to good intentions.

## When efficiency is a sin

Efficiency and cost control, however much they are preached, are not really virtues in the budget-based institution. The importance of a budget-based institution is measured essentially by the size of its budget and the size of its staff. To achieve results with a smaller budget or a smaller staff is, therefore, not performance. It might actually endanger the institution. Not to spend the entire budget will only convince the budget maker – whether legislature or the budget committee of a company – that the budget for the next fiscal period can safely be cut.

Thirty or forty years ago it was considered characteristic of Russian planning that Soviet managers, towards the end of the plan period, engaged in a frantic effort to spend all the money allocated to them. This usually resulted in total waste. Today the disease has become universal as budget-based institutions have become dominant everywhere. End-of-year pressure on the executive of a budget-based institution certainly accounts for a good deal of waste in the American defence effort. The practice of 'buying-in', that is, getting approval for a new project by grossly underestimating its total cost, is also built into the budget-based institution.

Efficiency loses out when the acid test of performance is budget size. This standard of success subtly discourages administrators from trying to do a job cheaply and efficiently and may even penalize them for doing so.

## A confusion of goals

But effectiveness even more than efficiency is endangered by reliance on the budget allocation. It becomes dangerous to raise the question as to what the business of the institution should be. The question is always controversial. The controversy is likely to alienate support and is therefore shunned by the budget-based institution. At best the institution may achieve effectiveness by deceiving the public and itself.

The US Department of Agriculture, for instance, has never been willing to ask whether its goal should be farm productivity or support of the small family farm. It has known for decades that these two objectives are not identical, as had originally been assumed. In fact, they are becoming increasingly incompatible. To admit this, however, would have created controversy that might have endangered the Department's budget. As a result, American farm policy has frittered away an enormous amount of money and human resources on what might be called a public relations campaign, that is, on a show of support for the small family farmer. Its effective activities, however – and they have been very effective indeed – have been directed towards eliminating the small family farmer and replacing him by the far more productive 'agribusiness'. These large, highly capitalized and mechanized farms are run as businesses, not as a 'way of life'. Favouring agribusiness may have been right, but it was not what the Department was founded to do, nor what the legislators, in approving the Department's budget, expected it to do.

The American community hospital is not governmental but private, though nonprofit. Yet, like hospitals everywhere, it presents the same confusion of missions and objectives, with the resulting impairment of effectiveness and performance. Should a hospital be, in effect, a physician's plant facility, as most older American physicians maintain ? Should it be a community health centre ? Should it focus on the major health needs of a community or try to do everything and be abreast of every medical advance, no matter how costly and how rarely used the facility will be ? Should it focus on preventive medicine and on health education for the community ? Or should it concentrate on the repair of health damage that has already been done ?

Each of these definitions of the mission of the hospital can be defended. Each deserves a hearing. The effective hospital is a multi-purpose institution that strikes a balance between various objectives. What most hospitals do, however, is pretend that there are no basic questions to be decided. The result, predictably, is confusion and impairment of the capacity of the hospital to serve any function and to carry out any mission.

A service organization within a business has the same tendency to avoid controversy over function, mission, and objectives. What, for example, is the first function of the personnel department ? Is it to obtain the most effective utilization of the company's human resources ? Or is the personnel department a welfare department and babysitter ? Is the purpose of the personnel department to make employees accept the policies, rules, and regulations of the company ? Or is the purpose to help develop the organization structure and job structure that makes sense for the employees and will enable them to develop and achieve ? All these are legitimate definitions of the personnel job. Each could be the foundation of a truly effective personnel department. But practically no personnel department I know will face up to these questions. They are controversial. As a result, the personnel department says different things to different constituents. It is likely to end up ineffectual and frustrated.

Being dependent on a budget allocation discourages an institution from setting priorities and concentrating efforts, yet nothing is ever accomplished unless scarce resources are concentrated on a small number of priorities.

A shoe manufacturer that has 22 per cent of the market for work shoes may be a profitable business. If the business succeeds in raising its market share to 30 per cent, especially if the market for work shoes is expanding, the company is doing very well indeed. It need not be concerned too much with the 70 per cent of the users of work shoes who buy from somebody else. And the customers for ladies' fashion shoes are of no concern at all.

Contrast this with the situation of an institution on a budget. To obtain its budget, it needs the approval, or at least the acquiescence, of practically everybody who could possibly be considered a constituent. Where a market share of 22 per cent might be perfectly satisfactory to a business, rejection by 78 per cent of the constituents – or even by a much smaller proportion – would be absolutely fatal to a budget-based institution. It might survive without the active support of 22 per cent of its constituents but it certainly should consider itself in serious danger. And this means that the service institution cannot concentrate; it must instead try to please everyone and offend none.

Finally, being budget-based makes it even more difficult to abandon the wrong things, the old, the obsolete. As a result, service institutions are even more encrusted than businesses with the barnacles of unproductive efforts. No institution likes to abandon anything it does. Business is no exception. An institution paid for its performance and results stands, however, under a performance test. The unproductive, the obsolete, is sooner or later killed off by the customers. In a budget-based institution, no such discipline is enforced. On the contrary, what a service institution does is always virtuous and likely to be considered in the public interest.

The temptation is great, therefore, to respond to lack of results by redoubling efforts. The temptation is great to double the budget, precisely because there is no performance. The temptation, above all, is to blame the outside world for its stupidity or its reactionary resistance, and to consider lack of results a proof of one's own righteousness and a reason in itself for keeping on with the good work.

The tendency to continue unproductive efforts is not confined to service institutions in the public sector. It is just as common in staff services within large business enterprise. The organization planner, the computer specialist, or the operations researcher all tend to argue that the resistance of operating managers to their wares is itself evidence of the need for their services and reason for doubling the 'missionary effort'. Sometimes this argument is, of course, valid. But more often it makes impossible concentration of efforts on important areas where results are attainable.

All service institutions are threatened by the tendency to cling to yesterday and to put their best and ablest people on defending what no longer makes sense or serves a purpose. Government is particularly prone to this disease, believing that present policies and projects will be equally valid forever. It might better realize that conditions and needs change and that every programme should be reviewed often.

## Earned revenue or deserved

Human beings will behave as they are rewarded – whether the reward is money and promotion, a medal, an autographed picture of the boss, or a pat on the back. This is a lesson the behavioural psychologist has taught us. A business or any institution that is rewarded for its performance in such a way that the dissatisfied or disinterested customer need not pay has to earn its income. An institution which is financed by a budget – or which enjoys a monopoly that the customer cannot escape – is rewarded with what it deserves rather than what it earns. It is paid for good intentions and for 'programmes'. It is paid for not alienating important constituents rather than for satisfying any one group. It is misdirected by the way it is paid into defining performance as what will produce the budget rather than as what will produce contribution.

This is a built-in characteristic of budget-based institutions. Amazingly enough, it has escaped the attention of the economists – perhaps because few of them seem to be aware of the fact that more than half of the gross national product these days does not go to businesses, that is, to institutions paid for performance and results, but rather to service institutions paid for promises or, at best, for efforts.

Being budget-based is not necessarily bad or even undesirable. Self-supporting armies, for instance, such as the armies of the fifteenth century or the traditional armies of the Chinese warlords, had to engage in continual warfare, terrorize the citizens of their own nation, and depend on plunder for their support. Civilian control and defence budgets paid out of taxes were instituted precisely to stop free enterprise in warfare.

Similarly, most service staffs in business should be on a budget allocation. To pay a research laboratory for results, for instance, in the form of a royalty on the sales of the new products and processes it produces (as has been tried in several businesses) is almost certain to misdirect the research laboratory even more than the budget allocation does. It is likely to divert resources from research into gadgetry. But there is also no question that budget allocation induces research directors to inflate the research staff, to come up with an impossible list of projects, and to hang on to projects that are unlikely to produce results.

## Summary

There are three common explanations for the lack of performance in service institutions: their managers aren't businesslike; the people are not as good as they should be; results are intangible and incapable of definition or measurement. All three are invalid and are pure alibi. The basic problem of the service institution is that it is paid for promises rather than for performance. It is paid out of a budget rather than for (and out of) results.

# 11 The Exceptions and Their Lessons

The exception, the comparatively rare service institution that is effective, matters as much as the great majority, which achieve mostly procedures. The exception provides the lessons. It shows that effectiveness in the service institution is achievable – though by no means easy. It shows what different service institutions can do and need to do. It shows limitations and pitfalls. But it also shows that the service-institution managers can do unpopular and highly controversial things if only they face up to the risk-taking decision as to what the business of the institution is, will be, and should be.

## Bell telephone

The first and perhaps simplest example is that of the Bell Telephone System. A telephone system is a natural monopoly. The one thing any subscriber to a public telephone service requires is access to all other subscribers. This means that within a given area one supplier of telephone service must have exclusive rights. As a whole country or continent becomes in effect one telephone system, this monopoly has to be extended over larger and larger areas.

An individual may be able to do without a telephone – though in today's society only at great inconvenience. But a professional, a shopkeeper, an office, or a business must have a telephone. Residential phone service may still be an option. Business phone service is compulsory.

Theodore Vail saw this in the early years of this century. He also saw that the American Telephone Company, like the telephone systems in all other industrially developed nations, could easily be taken over by government. To prevent this, Vail thought through what the telephone company's business was and should be, and came up with his famous definition: 'Our business is service'.

This statement of the Telephone Company's business enabled Vail to set specific goals and objectives. He could then develop measurements of performance and results in terms of his definition of the business. His customer-satisfaction standards and service-satisfaction standards created, in effect, nationwide competition among telephone managers in various areas. The standards became the measurements by which the managers were judged and rewarded. As a result, the Telephone Company's managers were directed, despite the monopolistic nature of their company, towards performance and results.

Vail did something even more radical for his day (and, by and large, even for this day). He identified Bell's constituencies as the regulatory agencies, the public utility commissions of the various states. The regulatory agencies are supposed to make private enterprise function in the public interest under conditions of natural monopoly where competition cannot effectively do the job. These agencies, by and large, have three functions: to maintain competition in a service area as far as feasible; to protect the public against exploitation by natural monopolies through control of prices and service standards; and to limit the earnings of natural monopolies to a 'fair return' on their investments. Any right-thinking businessman of Vail's day considered the regulatory agencies 'pernicious socialism' and the 'enemy'. Vail, however, decided that the public was, indeed a legitimate constituency. It, therefore, was the job of the telephone company to make the regulatory agencies function. He tried to think through what their objectives were and should be. The Bell System would almost certainly have been nationalized long ago if the American public did not feel that the regulatory agencies had been doing their job with only occasional lapses. Vail's recognition of the regulatory agencies as a distinct constituency enabled the public utility commissions to function and to understand their own work.

## The American university

The building of the modern American university from 1860 to World War I also illustrates how service institutions can be made to perform. The American university as it emerged during that period is primarily the work of a small number of men: Andrew W. White (president of Cornell from 1868 to 1885); Charles W. Eliot (president of Harvard, 1869–1909); Daniel Coit Gilman (president of Johns Hopkins, 1876–1901); David Starr Jordan (president of Stanford, 1891–1913); William Rainey Harper (president of Chicago, 1892–1904); and Nicholas Murray Butler (president of Columbia, 1902–1945).

These men all had one basic insight in common; the traditional college – essentially an eighteenth-century seminary to train preachers – had become totally obsolete, sterile, and unproductive. It was dying fast; America in 1860 had far fewer college students than it had had forty years earlier for a much smaller population. The men who built the new universities shared a common objective: to create a new institution, a true university. They all realized that while European universities had much to offer as examples, these new universities had to be *American* institutions.

Beyond these shared beliefs, however, they differed sharply on what a university should be and what its purpose and mission were.

Eliot, at Harvard, saw the purpose of the university in educating a leadership group with a distinct style. His Harvard was to be a national institution rather than the preserve of the 'proper Bostonian', for whom Harvard College had been founded. But its function was also to restore to New England the leadership of a moral elite, such as had been held by the Federalist leaders in the early days of the Republic. Butler at Columbia – and to a lesser degree Harper at Chicago – saw the function of the university as the systematic application of rational thought and analysis to the basic problems of a modern society – education, economics, government, foreign affairs. Gilman at Johns Hopkins saw the university as the producer of advanced knowledge. Originally Johns Hopkins was to confine itself to advanced research and was to give no undergraduate instruction. White at Cornell aimed at producing an educated public, and so on.

Each of these men knew that he had to make compromises. Each knew that he had to satisfy a number of constituencies and publics, each of whom saw the university differently. Eliot and Butler, for instance, had to build their new universities on existing, old foundations without alienating existing alumni and existing faculty. The others could build from the ground up. They all had to be exceedingly conscious of the need to attract and hold financial support.

It was Eliot, with all his insistence on 'moral leadership', who invented the first placement office and set out to find for Harvard graduates well-paid jobs, especially in business. Butler, conscious that Columbia was a latecomer and that the millionaire philanthropists of his day had already been snared by his competitors, invented the first public relations office in a university. It was designed – and most successfully – to reach the merely well-to-do and get their money.

Each of these men gave priority to his definition of the university's purpose and mission. These definitions did not outlive the founders. Even during the lifetimes of Eliot and Butler, for instance, their institutions escaped their control, began to diffuse objectives and to confuse priorities. In this century all these universities – and many others like California and other major state universities – have converged towards a common type.

Today it is hard to tell one 'multiversity' from another. Yet the imprint of the founders has still not been totally erased. It is hardly an accident that Roosevelt's New Deal chose primarily faculty members from Columbia and Chicago as high-level advisers and policy-makers. The New Deal, like these universities, was committed to the application of rational thought and analysis to public policies and problems. Thirty years later when the Kennedy Administration came in with an underlying belief in the 'style' of an elite, it naturally turned to Harvard. The original clear commitment to purpose and to mission that made these institutions effective is still visible – though only faintly – in their faculty and graduates.

## Lilienthal and the TVA

A different but equally instructive example is that of the Tennessee Valley Authority, the public utility and public works complex in the southcentral United States. Built mainly in New Deal days, the TVA today is no longer controversial. It is just another large power company, but one owned by the government rather than by private investors. But in its early days, forty years ago, the TVA was more: a slogan, a battle cry, a symbol. Some, friends and enemies alike, saw government ownership of the TVA as the opening wedge for the nationalization of electric energy in the United States. Others saw it as a boon to the Tennessee Valley region, providing cheap power and free fertilizer to a largely agricultural area. Others still were primarily interested in flood control and navigation. There was such a conflict in expectations that TVA's first head, Arthur Morgan, floundered completely. Unable to think through what the business of the TVA should be and how varying objectives might be balanced, he accomplished nothing. Finally, President Roosevelt replaced him with an almost totally unknown young lawyer with little previous experience as an administrator, David Lilienthal.

Lilienthal faced up to the need to define TVA's business. He concluded that the first objective was to build truly efficient electric plants and to supply an energy-starved region with plentiful and cheap power. All the rest, he decided, hinged on attaining this first need. Today TVA has accomplished many other objectives as well: flood control, navigable waterways, fertilizer production, and even balanced community development. But it was Lilienthal's insistence on a clear definition of TVA's business and on setting priorities that explains why TVA is now taken for granted, even by those who, forty years ago, were its enemies.

## Market approach and 'socialist competition'

Our examples illustrate, first, that service institutions can be managed for performance, but also that the task cannot be accomplished by either of the traditional approaches. Neither the approach that says 'Let the market do the job' nor the one that says 'Let public interest prevail and drive the money-changers out' works for the budget-based service institution.

The market approach is commonly considered 'capitalist', but this is a misunderstanding. The market approach can equally be 'socialist'. Whether ownership is in capitalist hands or not is no longer primary. What matters is managerial independence and accountability. What matters is whether resources are allocated to produce results and on the basis of results.

The prevailing idea that the US economy is capitalistic because ownership is private is a misunderstanding. Big business in the US has not been nationalized, but it *has* largely been socialized. Ownership of American big business is in the hands of the people – that is, in the hands of the mutual funds and the pension funds who are the agents of the middle class and the workers. In terms of the classical definition, the US is at least a mixed and may steadily be approaching a socialist economy in which the public owns the means of production. But enterprise in the US is largely self-governing. Resources are allocated on the basis of results. It is still a market economy.

Labelling the Japanese economy capitalistic or socialistic according to the ownership of industry is still more misleading. If anyone in Japan can be said to own the big companies, it is their employees and especially their managers. Since they cannot be dismissed but have lifetime employment, they are what the law calls the beneficial owners even though they have no legal title. Yet, Japan is clearly not a socialist economy.

The most searching discussion of market economics in the last fifty years has been conducted outside the free-enterprise countries. Its subject is *socialist competition*, that is, competition in an economy in which the means of production are not owned by private capitalists. The discussion was begun after World War I by a Polish socialist, Oscar Lange, who for many years taught at the University of Chicago. Lange proposed socialist competition as an alternative to the failures of government monopolies and the tendency of privately owned monopolies to exploit. Lange's model provided for public ownership of the means of production, thus eliminating the capitalist. But it also provided for individual businesses, under their own managements, competing in a market economy and getting paid for results. What Lange said, in other words, is that socialist doctrine demands that ownership be socialized. But the allocation of resources has to be done by performance and results (that is, on the basis of the market test) if an economy is to allocate its resources rationally and be capable of performance.

Lange's socialist competition underlies all proposals for liberalization in the Soviet Bloc. His ideas became reality in Yugoslavia in the late 1960s. There major businesses, while nominally owned by the government, are managed autonomously and must prove themselves in a market where there is a good deal of competition. Yugoslav businesses are largely financed directly by allocation on the basis of the expected return on the investment, that is, on a 'capitalist' and profit-making basis.

All attempts to inject performance into the economy in the Soviet Union are essentially attempts to introduce Lange's socialist competition, that is, managerial autonomy and accountability based on market performance and market result. There is little resistance any more to the argument of the reformers that socialist competition would yield vastly superior economic results; the resistance is to the risk of losing political control.

The debate over the morality of private ownership for profit is largely becoming irrelevant. The debate should be over the performance capacity of a system in which business is being paid for results and performance as against a system in which it is being financed out of budget allocations. On that score there is essentially no debate. *Wherever a market test is truly possible, it will result in performance and results* – not because of the greater 'virtue' of free enterprise or of autonomous managers but because being paid for performance and results directs towards performance and results.

## The limits of the market

But it is equally clear that the market is not capable of organizing all institutions.

Service institutions are a diverse lot. They include natural monopolies, which are obviously economic institutions – the telephone service, the electricity supply in a given area. Service institutions also include the administration of justice and defence, which, equally obviously, are not and should not be economic institutions. The one and only thing they all have in common is that, for one reason or another, they cannot be organized under a competitive market test.

## The limits of public policy

Capitalists and socialists agree that where the market cannot provide a performance test, 'public policy' will provide guidance and control. As our discussion of the impact of the budget basis shows, this is not nearly enough. To be sure, service institutions, including those within a business, must be controlled by policy. But they need more than programmes, promises, good intentions, and hard work, all underwritten by a budget. Whereever possible, they need a system and structure that directs them towards performance.

Service institutions also need the discipline of planned obsolescence and planned abandonment of their policies. In every one of our cases, effectiveness was obtained for a time – but not forever. Vail's solution worked for a half-century, but it is by no means sure that it works any longer. The American university has outgrown the structure its founders built a century ago. It now needs new thinking about its mission and function, its priorities and the criteria by which to measure its accomplishments and results. The TVA has performed so well as to make itself irrelevant. What it pioneered forty years ago is now commonplace; no one any longer expects salvation by electrification. Yet each of these impermanent, imperfect answers did a job that had to be done and did it well.

## Summary

The exceptional service institution that does perform shows not only that performance is possible in the service institution but also how it can be achieved. This lesson was taught by Bell Telephone for the 'natural monopoly'; by the American universities during their formative years in the late nineteenth century for such institutions as schools or hospitals; and by the TVA (Tennessee Valley Authority) in the 1930s for government agencies.

# 12 Managing Service Institutions for Performance

Different classes of service institutions need different structures. But all of them need first to impose on themselves discipline of the kind imposed by leaders of the institutions in the examples in the previous chapters.

1 They need to define 'what our business is and what it should be'. They need to bring alternative definitions into the open and consider them carefully. They should perhaps even work out (as did the presidents of the emerging American universities) some balance between the different and conflicting definitions of mission.

2 They must derive clear objectives and goals from their definition of function and mission.

3 They then must set priorities that enable them to select targets, to set standards of accomplishment and performance – that is, to define the minimum acceptable results; to set deadlines; to go to work on results, and to make someone accountable for results.

4 They must define measurements of performance – the customer satisfaction measurements of the Telephone Company, or the number of households supplied with electric power, a quantity much easier to measure.

5 They must use these measurements to feed back on their efforts. That is, they must build self-control by results into their system.

6 Finally, they need an organized review of objectives and results, to weed out those objectives that no longer serve a purpose or have proven unattainable. They need to identify unsatisfactory performance, and activities which are outdated or unproductive, or both. And, they need a mechanism for dropping such activities rather than wasting money and human energies where the results are poor.

The last requirement may be the most important one. Without a market test, the service institution lacks the discipline that forces a business eventually to abandon yesterday – or else go bankrupt. Assessing and abandoning low-performance activities in service institutions, outside and inside business, would be the most painful but also the most beneficial change.

As the examples show, no success is 'forever'. Yet it is even more difficult to abandon yesterday's success than it is to re-appraise a failure. A once successful project gains an air of success that outlasts the project's real usefulness and disguises its failings.

In a service institution particularly, yesterday's success becomes 'policy', 'virtue', 'conviction', if not holy writ. The institution must impose on itself the discipline of thinking through its mission, its objectives, and its priorities, and of building in feedback control from results and performance on policies, priorities, and action. Otherwise, it will gradually become less and less effective. We are in such a 'welfare mess' today in the United States largely because the welfare programme of the 1930s was such a success. We could not abandon it and, instead misapplied it to the radically different problem of the black immigrants in the cities in the fifties and sixties.

To make service institutions perform, it should by now be clear, does not require great leaders. It requires a system. The essentials of this system are not too different from the essentials of performance in a business enterprise, but the application will be quite different. The service institutions are not businesses; performance means something quite different in them.

The applications of the essentials differ greatly for different service institutions. As our examples showed, there are at least three different kinds of service institutions – institutions that are not paid for performance and results, but for efforts and programmes.

## The three kinds of service institutions

There is first the natural monopoly. It produces economic goods and services, or at least it is supposed to. Yet it cannot be paid for out of results and performance precisely because it is a monopoly.

The economist defines as natural monopolies those businesses which must have exclusive rights in a given area – the telephone service or the electric power service. But the research laboratory of a chemical company is also a natural monopoly within its business.

The next group of service institutions are those that have to be paid for out of a budget allocation. While all of these share a common character, their individual purpose and the specific way in which they try to accomplish it need not be uniform. Their priorities can – and indeed often should – be quite diverse.

The American university is one example. Each of the six university presidents was concerned with higher education. Each was out to build a university on the ruins of the old, decayed eighteenth-century seminary. They all saw alternative missions and functions. Each tried to structure his university to give different emphasis among these alternatives of 'what our business is or should be', and each set different priorities. They knowingly and deliberately built competing institutions with the same structure: trustees, an administration, faculty and students, and similar courses leading to the same degrees.

Finally, there are those service institutions in which means are as important as ends, and which, therefore, must be structured and operated uniformly. In this class belongs the administration of justice or defence.

## The institutions' specific need

What does each of these institutions need ?

The natural monopoly needs the least structure. Even though it is not directly paid for results, it is close to them. All it needs is to do what any business should be doing anyhow, but to do it more systematically.

This, incidentally, is a strong argument in favour of keeping natural monopolies under public regulation rather than under public ownership. An unregulated natural monopoly will inevitably exploit, in addition to being ineffective and inefficient. A government-owned monopoly may not exploit, but the customer has no redress against inefficiency, poor service, high rates, and disregard of his or her needs. An independently managed monopoly under public regulation is likely to be far more responsive to customer dissatisfactions and consumer needs than either the unregulated private or the government-owned monopoly. The regulated but independently managed monopoly stays in touch with its performance through the regulatory agencies. By their control of rates and profits, these agencies express, at least in theory, public opinion on the performance of the monopoly.

In the late 1960s, the operating efficiency of the American telephone system declined in some areas, notably New York City, and waiting periods for service or for repair grew from days to weeks or months. Customers could and did take effective action. They began immediately to oppose requests from the telephone company for rate increases – and a more effective means of disciplining a monopoly is hard to imagine. The French telephone customer, on the other hand, who enjoys about the worst telephone service in any developed country, can only grumble. Telephone service there is a government-owned monopoly, against which the consumer is powerless.

In addition, government regulatory agencies can provide the means for building into the structure of monopolies the self-discipline that leads to systematic performance. Both the Federal Communications Commission in its study of the long-distance service of the Bell system, and the Federal Power Commission in its study of electric-power supply in the Mid-Atlantic states, have moved towards demanding such self-discipline from the various companies.

With respect to the monopoly that the research laboratory represents in a business, top management can and should demand the discipline of thinking through objectives, setting goals and priorities, measuring performance, and sloughing off the unproductive. This is the only way to make the research laboratory productive and responsive to the company's needs.

One of the most effective research managers – himself a scientist of world renown – makes it his practice to ask, 'What have you in this research lab contributed to the company's vision, knowledge, and results during the last three to five years ?' And then he asks, 'And what do you expect to contribute to the company's vision, knowledge, and results during the next five years ?' He reports that he never gets an answer the first time he asks the question. But after asking the question for a few years, he begins to get answers; and a few years later he even gets research results.

### 'Socialist competition' in the service sector

The second kind of service institution is exemplified by schools, universities, and hospitals. Most of the service staffs within business organizations belong here too.

Service institutions of the second kind are characteristic of a developed society. Monopolies and institutions of government – the service institutions of the first and third categories – dominate undeveloped societies. But the service institution of the second category becomes central in the process of economic and social development. Its performance is crucial to modern developed society. And in developed societies – or developed businesses – it is this service institution that most closely touches the daily life of the citizen – or of the manager.

Customers of this kind of service institution are not really customers. They are more like taxpayers. They pay for the service institution whether they want to or not, out of taxes, levies such as compulsory insurance, or overhead allocations. The products of these institutions do not supply a want. They supply a need. School, hospital, and the typical service staff in business supply what everybody should have, ought to have, must have, because it is 'good for them', or good for society.

We talk of the 'right of every child to an education' and of the 'right of every citizen to decent health care'. Yet we already have *compulsory* education and are well on the way towards compulsory health care. In many companies, for instance, executives are required to have an annual physical checkup or else they lose their vacation or their salary. We have compulsory vaccination.

And when the focus shifts to preventive medicine for large numbers of people, as is likely to happen soon, we will demand that everybody avail themselves of health care facilities. In other words, we will make health care compulsory.

Utilization of the service staff is compulsory in many businesses. The marketing managers in the divisions of a decentralized company are not asked, as a rule, whether they want to attend the marketing seminars put on by the central marketing staff. They are told to come.

Service institutions of this second type need a system like Oskar Lange's socialist competition. The objective – the overall mission – must be general for this kind of service institution. There must be minimum standards of performance and results. But for the sake of performance, it is highly desirable that they should have managerial autonomy and not be run by government even if they are supervised and regulated by it. There should also be a fair amount of consumer choice between different ways of accomplishing the basic mission, between different priorities and different methods. There should be enough competition for these institutions to hold themselves to performance standards.

We talk today in the US about a voucher system for elementary and high school education under which the government would pay to whatever accredited school the child attends an amount equal to the cost of teaching a child in the public schools. No matter how much latitude schools were to be given under such a voucher plan, surely no school would be considered accredited under it unless it promised to teach at least the basic skills such as reading, writing, and arithmetic. We may leave it up to the school what method it uses – there is room for the traditional classroom, and for the open classroom, or some combination of both – but fundamental goals and minimum standards will, and should be, insisted upon. There will be no choice as to whether children of school age go to school or not – they will go whether they and their parents like it or not – but parents or child will exercise the consumer's option in choosing which school to attend.

The same approach is already being applied to service staffs in major businesses. One large multinational company, primarily producing and selling branded consumer goods, defines its business as 'marketing'. With such a definition, one would expect to find a large marketing services staff in the company. But the staff is remarkably small. The marketing services staff has a small budget that pays for such activities as training the marketing services personnel, research in the marketing field, the library, and so on, but not for marketing services to the company's businesses. Every one of the forty-five to fifty decentralized and autonomously managed businesses of the company located in more than thirty countries is held responsible for its marketing performance and marketing results. To help their businesses reach these results, the local general managers may use the marketing services staff but they are under no compulsion to do so. They are entitled to use outside consultants of their choice or they may act as their own marketing consultants. Only if a manager does use the marketing services staff does his or her unit pay for marketing services. The marketing staff, however, evaluates the marketing standards and marketing performance of every unit. When last heard of, eighteen or twenty of the divisional and territorial managers of the company used the marketing services staff. Eleven or twelve used outside consultants. Another dozen used no service staff inside or outside the company. The marketing results of these managers show no correlation to their methods. Among the best and among the poorest performers are divisions which use the company's marketing staff, divisions which use outside consultants, and divisions which do not use any marketing staff at all. Even the poor performers in this company have high standards and good marketing results. And the marketing services staff is among the best I know, in its effectiveness, in its performance, and in its spirit and enthusiasm.

## The institutions of governance

Service institutions of the third category are by and large, the traditional government activities – the administration of justice and defence and all the activities concerned with policy-making. These institutions do not provide public goods in the economist's sense of the term; they govern.

Here managerial autonomy is not possible. Competition, if possible at all, would be most undesirable. These institutions have to be under direct government control and directly government-operated, yet their activities require the discipline of objectives, priorities, and measurement of results.

Such institutions require, therefore, an organized, independent review of their promises, the assumptions on which they base themselves, and their performance. There is no way of building feedback from results into these institutions. The only discipline, therefore, to which they can be subjected is analysis and review.

Now that service institutions have become so central, so important, and so costly, we need an auditor-general of objectives and performance. We need to force ourselves to look at proposed government policies, laws, and programmes – but also at the policies, programmes, and activities of service staffs – and ask, 'Are the objectives realistic ? Are they attainable or just slogans ? How do they relate to the needs they are supposed to satisfy ? Have the right targets been set ? Have priorities been thought through ? And, do results relate to promises and expectations ?'

We need to go further and accept as a basic premise that every governmental agency and every act of the legislature be considered impermanent. A new activity, a new agency, a new programme should be enacted for a specific time, to be extended only if results prove the soundness of the objective and of the means chosen. Outside of government, in other service institutions – including those that should be autonomous even though public (school or hospital, for example) – this way of thinking will also have to become standard. Society is becoming too dependent on the performance and results of service institutions to tolerate the traditional system forever.

Failure to drop nonperforming programmes accounts for many of our worst problems. It underlies the failure of the US and the Common Market farm programmes; it underlies the 'welfare mess' that threatens to destroy our cities; it underlies the frustration of our international development programmes which threatens to bring about worldwide race war of poor non-white against rich white countries.

Without feedback from results, our efforts to protect the environment are unlikely to succeed. Results are badly needed, but so far we have neither thought through what we are after nor set priorities. Nor have we organized a feedback from results on the direction, the priorities, and the efforts of the environmental crusade. Predictably, this can only mean no results and rapid disenchantment.

What the service institutions need is not to be more business-like. They need to be subjected to performance tests – if only to that of 'socialist competition' – as much as possible. They need to be more hospital-like, university-like, government-like, and so on. In other words, they need to think through their own specific functions, purposes, and missions.

What the service institutions need is not better people. They need people who do the management job systematically and who focus themselves and their institution purposefully on performance and results. They do need efficiency – that is, control of costs – but above all they need effectiveness – emphasis on the right results.

Few service institutions today suffer from having too few administrators. Most of them are overadministered and suffer from a surplus of procedures, organization charts, and management techniques. What we have to learn is to manage service institutions for performance. This may well be the most important management task in this century.

## Summary

To make service institutions and service staffs perform does not require genius. It requires first clear objectives and goals. Next it demands priorities on which the resources can be concentrated. It requires further clear measurements of accomplishment. And finally it demands organized abandonment of the obsolete. And these four requirements are just as important for the service staff of a business as for the service institution in society.

# Part Three
# Productive Work and
# Achieving Worker

Making work productive and the worker achieving is the second major aspect of the management task. We do not know enough about it. Folklore and old wives' tales abound, but solid, tested knowledge is scarce. We do know that work and the work force are undergoing greater changes today than at any time since the beginning of the industrial revolution two centuries ago. We do know that, at least in the developed countries, radically new approaches are needed – to analysis, synthesis, and control of work and production; to job structure, work relationships, and the structure of economic rewards and power relations; to making workers responsible. We do know that we have to move from managing 'personnel' as a 'cost centre' and a 'problem' to the leadership of people.

# 13 The New Realities

Few words in the language are as ambivalent as 'work', or as emotion-laden. In the pairing 'work and rest,' 'rest' is clearly good. But whether 'retirement' is better than 'work' is already questionable. And work is definitely preferable to 'idleness'. Being 'out of work' is far from good – is, indeed, a catastrophe.

In 'work and play,' 'play' carries a favourable connotation. But 'playing at being a surgeon' is not good at all. Work can be high achievement, as in the phrase 'an artist's life work.' Or it can be sheer drudgery, backbreaking, and utter boredom.

There is 'work', and there is 'working'. They are totally dependent on each other. Unless someone is working, no work gets done. And where there is no work, there is also no working.

Yet work and working are quite different. Work is impersonal, and objective. It is 'something'. Not all work can be weighed or measured. But even the most intangible piece of work is outside and independent of the worker.

What distinguishes work from play is an old question that has never been answered satisfactorily. Work and play may be the very same activity, down to the smallest detail – woodfinishing is work when done by a furniture factory worker and play when done by a weekend hobbyist. Psychologically and socially, the two are quite different. The distinction may well be that work, unlike play, is impersonal and objective. The purpose of play lies in the player; the purpose of work lies with the user of the end product. Where the end product is not determined by the player but by others, we do not speak of play, we speak of work.

Working is done by a human being, a worker. It is a uniquely human activity. Working, therefore, is physiology and psychology, society and community, personality, economics, and power. As the old human relations tag has it, 'One cannot hire a hand; the whole man always comes with it.'

Work and working, therefore, follow different rules. Work belongs to the realm of objects. It has its own impersonal logic. But working belongs to the realm of human beings. It has dynamics. Managers always have to manage both work and working. They have to make work productive and the worker achieving. They have to integrate work and working.

## Work and worker in rapid change

Both work and worker are in a period of rapid change. The changes that will dominate the rest of this century – and probably most of the next century as well – are the most radical changes since the beginning of the industrial revolution more than two hundred years ago.

Over the last two centuries, work has shifted away from the home and from people working alone to a society of employees, working in organizations. At the same time the centre of gravity of the work force is shifting from the manual worker to the knowledge worker. A larger and larger proportion of the labour force in all developed countries does not work with its hands but with ideas, concepts, theories. The output of these workers is not physical objects, but knowledge and information. Half a century ago knowledge work was performed by a few independent professionals working either alone or in very small groups. The bulk of the labour force was manual workers.

Knowledge work need not be highly skilled or highly schooled. Filing, after all, requires neither mental capacity nor advanced schooling. But the tool of the file clerk is not hammer or sickle, but the alphabet, an abstraction concept and a symbol rather than a thing. One does not learn the alphabet through experience but through formal education.

## The crisis of the manual worker

These changes have produced a crisis with respect to manual workers and to their specific organization, the union.

For two hundred years the manual worker in industry, the child of the industrial revolution, has been struggling to gain economic security, status, and power in industrial society. During the last fifty years, since the end of World War I, the workers' progress has been dazzling. In most developed countries the manual worker, only yesterday a 'proletarian' scratching a bare living at the margin of subsistence, has acquired substantial economic security, an income level higher than that of the upper middle class of yesterday, and increasing political power.

With the rise of the knowledge worker, the manual workers are endangered again. Their economic security is not threatened – on the contrary, it is likely to become even more firmly established. But their social position and status are rapidly diminishing. In the developed countries industrial workers see themselves severely deprived. They are defeated, losers, before they even start. This is not a result of managerial actions, but of social developments and of the pressures they generate.

Increasingly in all developed societies the able, intelligent, and ambitious members of the working class stay in school beyond the point at which they are eligible for manual work. All the pressures of society, family and neighbours, community and school, push youngsters towards more schooling. The ones who leave school at the age at which they once would have graduated into the manual work force – fifteen or so – are dropouts, failures, rejects.

The manual workers in the developed countries today have little self-respect. This inevitably makes them bitter, suspicious, distrustful of themselves as well as of organization and management, and resentful. They are not revolutionaries, like their parents and grandparents, for it is obvious to them that revolution cannot alter the fundamental conditions. But they are militant and likely to become more militant as the centre of social gravity keeps shifting towards knowledge work and knowledge worker.

The rhetoric of workers' parties and movements still talks of the wicked capitalists and attacks the profit system. But the true class war is increasingly being fought between the hard hats – manual workers – and the liberals – the middle-class knowledge workers. During most of this century it has been the coalition of manual and knowledge workers that has dominated politics in the developed world – in America's New Deal as well as in the social democratic and labour parties of Europe. The major political event for the remainder of this century may well be the growing split between these two groups.

## The crisis of the union

The status changes of the manual worker that attend the shift in emphasis to knowledge work and knowledge worker not only create a new class distinction, but also create severe difficulties for the manual worker's own institution, the union.

Perhaps the most visible sign of this is the sharp drop in the quality of trade-union leadership – a change that is largely the result of the educational explosion. Yesterday, union leadership was the career opportunity for the able and ambitious young worker forced out of school early by a lack of money. In the developed countries today almost any able and ambitious youngster can stay in school – and may go on to a graduate degree. As a result, he moves into the professional and managerial ranks. His sympathies may still be with labour, but his leadership qualities are lost to the working class. The leaders who are moving into the vacuum this creates are likely to be men and women driven by resentment rather than by ambition, of far lower ability, and above all, without self-confidence. They are weak leaders – and the worst situation for an industry to be in is to have to deal with weak union leadership.

At the same time, the fact that young workers see themselves as 'losers' makes them resist and resent the very union leaders they put into office. The moment a worker gains an important leadership position in the trade union, he or she automatically becomes 'establishment'. Union leaders consort with the mighty, whether in government or in business. They exercise power. They have the trappings of power – the big office, the retinue of aides and assistants, the four telephones on the desk, and so on. In order to be effective, the union leader has to become one of 'them' and ceases to be one of 'us'. Yesterday's workers looked upon union power as representing them. They were proud of the fact that the union leader had become a person of authority. To-day's young workers, feeling keenly that they are losers and rejects, resist the union leader's authority even more than they resist the rest of the bosses. As a result, union leaders are increasingly losing control over their own members, are repudiated by them, resisted by them, disavowed by them. This, in turn, makes the union increasingly weak. For a union is power-less if it cannot deliver the union member's vote and behaviour, cannot guarantee observance of a contract agreement, and cannot count on the members' support for the leader's position and actions.

There is little doubt that collective bargaining, whether between an individual company and a trade union, or – as in West-ern Europe and Japan – between an industry and industry-wide union, is in trouble. Whether the civilized industrial warfare of collective bargaining – a major achievement of the early years of the twentieth century – can even survive is questionable. If it doesn't, there is no hint of what might be an effective replace-ment. And a replacement would be essential if we are to avoid all-out industrial warfare or spiralling labour costs and inflation.

## Unions and the knowledge workers

An organ for the representation of workers in their dealings with management is needed – by the workers, but also by society. Management is and has to be a power. Any power needs restraint and control – or else it becomes tyranny. The union is a very pe-culiar, an almost unprecedented, organ of restraint on the power of management. It is an opposition party that can never become the governing party. Yet within its limited scope it serves an essential function in industrial society. Unfortunately it is in-creasingly becoming incapable of discharging this function.

The opposition function of the union will be needed more in the future than it ever was in the past. Manual workers are be-ginning to feel – rightly – that they can no longer depend on a political party and its appeal to a majority. That is the conse-quence of the gradual failure of the New Deal marriage between worker and liberal. Increasingly, also, the power that needs restraint is not that of the bosses or the capitalists but of the educated managerial middle class of knowledge workers. They are not greatly interested in profits, but they are interested in power. The most bitter power conflicts are not those that erupt in private enterprise or in business; they are conflicts between janitors and school boards, medical orderlies and hospital administrators, teaching assistants and graduate faculties, or, as in the Swedish steel industry, between workers and their staunchly socialist bosses in a nationalized industry. They are conflicts between workers and the public interest (at least as defined by the liberals). In such conflicts political parties, which aim at mass support and at attracting a majority of the voters, are almost bound to side with the bosses, if only because no amount of rhetoric can conceal that the price of a settlement will not be paid out of profits but surely out of prices or taxes.

Public-service institutions may face a much more difficult industrial relations problem than business and are much less prepared for it. Hospitals, schools, government agencies, and so on have all become increasingly unionized. In these institutions the manual worker – or the lower ranking clerical worker – feels even more 'dispossessed', and even more confined to second-class citizenship than the manual worker does in manufacturing or service industries.

The unions themselves are incapable of thinking through their own future role and developing new approaches to their own structure and function. One reason is that the new leaders who replace the dying or retiring pioneers are so often individuals of lesser ability, lesser maturity, and lesser competence. But as important is the fact that the new leaders can keep their slender grip on the membership only by opposing everything. The new leaders dare not even ask questions, let alone come up with answers. They dare not lead but must fight hard even to stay in place.

We need new policy in industrial relations. In all developed and developing countries, managers in business and in public-service insitutions will have to think through the future of the union, its role, its function, and its position, both within the institution and in society. This is a major social responsibility of management. It is also a business responsibility of management.

The future of business, of the economy, and of society will be influenced greatly by the way we solve or fail to solve the growing crisis of the unions.

To think through the role and function of the union is also self-interest for management. To believe that union weakness means management strength is sheer self-delusion. Unionization is a fact of life in all developed noncommunist countries. And a weak union – that is, one without established role, function, and authority, and without strong, secure, and effective leadership – means strife, irresponsible demands, and increasing bitterness and tension. It does not mean management strength; it means management frustration.

## Managing the knowledge worker: the new challenge

Managing knowledge work and knowledge workers is essentially a new task. We know even less about it than we know about the management (or mismanagement) of the manual worker. It is, therefore, going to be the more difficult task. But because it is new, it is not burdened with a long history of bitterness, of mutual suspicion, and of outdated restrictions, rules, and regulations. Managing knowledge work and knowledge worker therefore can focus on developing the right policies and practices. It can focus on the future rather than on undoing the past, on the opportunities rather than on 'problems'.

Managing knowledge work and knowledge worker will require exceptional imagination, exceptional courage, and leadership of a high order. In some ways it will be a far more demanding task than managing the manual worker was until very recently. The weapon of fear – fear of economic suffering, fear of job security, physical fear of company guards or of the state's police power – which for so long substituted for managing manual work and the manual worker, simply doesn't work at all for knowledge work and knowledge workers. Knowledge workers, except at the very lowest levels, are not productive under the spur of fear; only self-motivation and self-direction make them productive. They have to be achieving in order to produce at all.

The productivity of every developed society depends increasingly on making knowledge work productive and the knowledge worker achieving. This is a central social problem of the new, the knowledge society. There are no precedents for the management of knowledge work. Knowledge work traditionally has been carried out by individuals working by themselves or in small groups. Now knowledge work is carried out in large, complex, managed institutions. The knowledge workers are not even the successor to yesterday's 'knowledge professionals'. They are the successors to yesterday's skilled workers. The status, function, contribution, position in the organization of each knowledge worker, therefore, still have to be defined.

Worse, we cannot truly define, let alone measure, productivity for most knowledge work. One can define and measure it for the file clerk or the salesclerk in the variety store. But productivity is already a murky term with respect to the field salesperson of a manufacturing business. Is it total sales ? Or is it the profit contribution from sales, which might vary tremendously with the product mix an individual salesperson sells ? Or is it sales (or profit contribution) related to the potential of a sales territory ? Perhaps a salesman's ability to hold old customers should be considered central to his productivity. Or perhaps it should be the ability to generate new accounts. These problems are far more complex than the definition and measurement of the productivity of even the highly skilled manual worker. There one can almost always define and measure productivity in terms of the quantity of output – for example, the number of pairs of shoes produced per hour, per day, or per week, subject only to a minimum quality standard.

Achievement for knowledge workers is even harder to define. No one but the knowledge workers themselves can come to grips with the question of what in work, job performance, social status, and pride constitutes the personal satisfaction that makes a knowledge worker feel that he contributes, that he performs, that he serves his values, and that he fulfils himself.

## The segmentation of the work force

Manual workers and knowledge workers are not the only work-

force segments, however. For example, the clerical worker who is a production worker without being a machine worker is a distinct and important group. Equally important is the fact that the work force in all developed countries is segmenting itself according to sex.

Until fairly recently, women employees were essentially either temporary, working in the interlude between school and marriage, or distinctly lower class. Wives of 'respectable' workers did not work outside the home. Such upper-class women as worked were largely independent professionals, doctors, lawyers, and university teachers. The rest were schoolteachers and hospital nurses, and they either stayed unmarried or had to quit.

In all developed countries – the one exception so far being Japan – this is changing drastically. It might well be the sign of a developed country that a large portion of its women work as employees. The married middle-class woman is increasingly becoming the typical woman employee. With family size decreasing and with housework greatly reduced, more and more middle and upper-class women are joining the work force. The trend is likely to continue. The driving forces are economic, social, and psychological.

The working woman may require a different job structure appropriate to her realities and conditions. She may require different treatment from the male worker with respect to job, economic rewards, and social status in the plant community. Women with children, for example, often need part-time work of flexible hours. And for married women, retirement pensions are often of little interest compared with higher cash incomes.

Various segments of the work force also have different needs with respect to benefits. When it comes to cash wages the standard of value is about the same for all. But when it comes to retirement pay, housing or educational allowances, health and other benefits, their needs and expectations vary greatly with sex, age, and family responsibilities, with the stage in their own life cycle and that of their families, and so on.

Traditionally an employer, whether in a business or any other institution, has had a single personnel policy. In the future there will be need for as many personnel policies as there are segments of the work force. Increasingly the segmentation of the work force will require differentiated approaches to the task of making work productive, and especially to the task of making the worker achieving.

The three main challenges to managing work and working are *the arrival of the employee society*; the changed psychological and social *position of the manual worker*: better educated and better paid, he still sees himself moving down from yesterday's self-respecting working class into second-class citizenship; and *the emergence of knowledge work and the knowledge worker* as the economic and social centre of what some people now call post-industrial society.

## The new breed

It is these changes that explain the arrival of a new breed of workers. These are the young people, and especially the well educated young people, who are challenging the traditional economic and power relationships as well.

This challenge to the old wisdom is often attributed to affluence, as the result of which, we are being told, the old Protestant ethic extolling the value of work is crumbling. This is far too simple an explanation. To be sure, affluence is new. Throughout all of human history the great majority of people have always lived at the margin of subsistence. The great majority never knew where their next meal was going to come from. Now, in the developed countries, the great majority are economically secure, at least in traditional terms. But there is no sign that the great majority – or any but the tiniest of minorities – have lost their appetite for economic rewards, whether material or immaterial. On the contrary, the great majority, now that they have tasted some of the fruits of productivity, are clearly eager for more – much more than the economy can produce so far, and possibly more than the limited resources of our planet could produce.

The shifting structure and character of work has created a demand that work produce more than purely economic benefits.

Making a living is no longer enough. Work also has to make a life. This means that it will be more important than ever to make work productive. At the same time, both manual workers with their deep psychological insecurity and knowledge workers with their new and ill-defined status expect work to provide nonmaterial psychological and social satisfactions. They do not necessarily expect work to be enjoyable but they do expect it to be achieving.

## Summary

The main challenges to managing work and working are the arrival of the employee society; the changed psychological and social position of the manual worker; the crisis of the traditional role and function of the union as a result of its success; and the emergence of knowledge work as the economic and social centre of what some people call post-industrial society. Work is changing – but so is the work force, especially as more and more married women of all classes are working in the developed countries.

# 14 What We Know (and Don't Know) About Work, Working and Worker

Work has been central to human consciousness for untold ages. *Homo Sapiens* is not fully defined as the toolmaker; but making tools, the systematic, purposeful, and organized approach to work, is specific and unique human activity. Work has, therefore, been a profound concern for thousands of years.

What was always a deep concern became a central issue with the industrial revolution. The economic and social theories of the last two hundred years centre on work. This is true not only of Marxism but of most other economic and sociological theories of the last two centuries.

However central work has been to human existence all along, organized study of work did not begin until the closing decades of the nineteenth century. Frederick W. Taylor was the first man in recorded history systematically to study and describe work. Taylor's 'scientific management' is a key factor in the tremendous surge of affluence in the last seventy-five years. This extraordinary change has lifted the standard of living of the working masses in the developed countries well above any level recorded before, even for the well-to-do. Taylor, though founding father of the science of work, really laid only first foundations. Not much, however, has been added to them since his death in 1915.

The worker has been given even less attention – and the knowledge worker so far received almost none. Serious, systematic study has been confined to a few aspects of working.

There is *industrial physiology*, dealing with the relationship of such things as lighting, tool and machine speeds, design of the work place, and so on, to the human being who is the worker. The fundamental work in this field was done in the early years of this century, for example, in the fatigue and vision studies of the German-born Harvard psychologist Hugo Muensterberg. Cyril Burt, an Englishman, might be called the father of *industrial psychology*. During World War I he studied aptitudes, that is, the relationship between the demands of specific manual work and the physical skill, motor coordination and reactions of individual workers. Finally, in the early twentieth century, Australian-born Elton Mayo, working primarily at Harvard, developed *human relations*, that is, the study of the relationship between people working together – though in human relations work itself, the task to be done, received almost no attention.

Managers cannot wait till the scientists and scholars have done their work. Nor can the worker. Managers have to manage today. They have to put to work the little we know, inadequate though it is. They have to try to make work productive and the worker achieving. It is, therefore, appropriate to put down what we know about work and working.

The most important thing we know is that work and working are fundamentally different. What is needed to make work productive is quite different from what is needed to make the worker achieving. The worker must, therefore, be managed according to both the logic of the work and the dynamics of working. Personal satisfaction of the worker without productive work is failure; but so is productive work that destroys the worker's achievement. Neither alone can be sustained for very long.

## Analysis, synthesis, and control

Work, as has been said in Chapter 13, is impersonal and objective. Work is a task. It is a 'something'. Work has a logic. It requires analysis, synthesis, and control.

As with every phenomenon of the material world, the first step towards understanding work is to *analyse it*. This, as Taylor realized a century ago, means identifying the basic operations, analysing each of them, and arranging them in logical, balanced, and rational sequence.

Taylor worked on manual operations; his analysis applies just as well to mental and even to totally intangible work. The 'outline' that the budding writer is told to work out before he starts to write is in effect scientific management. And the most advanced, most perfect example of scientific management was not developed by industrial engineers during the last hundred years. It is the alphabet, which enables all words in a language to be written with a very small number of simple symbols.

But after it is analysed, work has to be *synthesized* again – something Taylor did not realize. Work has to be put back together into a process. This is true for the individual job. It is even more true for the work of a group, that is, for a work process. We need *principles of production* that enable us to know how to put together individual operations into individual jobs and individual jobs into 'production'.

Because work is a process rather than an individual operation, it needs a built-in control. It needs a *feedback mechanism* to sense unexpected deviations that call for change in the process and to maintain the process at the level needed to obtain the desired results.

Those three elements, analysis, synthesis into a process of production, and feedback control, are particularly important in knowledge work. Knowledge work by definition does not yield a product. It yields a contribution of knowledge to somebody else. The output of the knowledge worker is always somebody else's input. It is, therefore, not self-evident in knowledge work, as it is in making a pair of shoes, whether the work has results or not. This can be seen only by projecting backward from the needed results. At the same time, knowledge work, being intangible, is not controlled by its own progress. We do not know the sequence of knowledge work in the way we have known since Taylor's work the sequence of manual operations. Knowledge work, therefore, needs far better design, precisely because it cannot be designed *for* the worker. It can be designed only *by* the worker.

### The five dimensions of working

Working is the activity of the worker; it is a human being's activity and an essential part of his or her humanity. It does not have a logic. It has dynamics and dimensions.

Working has at least *five dimensions*. The worker has to be achieving in each of them in order to be productive.

### Machine design and human design, the physiological dimension

There is, first, a *physiological* dimension. The human being is not a machine and does not work like a machine.

Machines work best if they do only one task, if they do it repetitively, and if they do the simplest possible task. Complex tasks are done best as a step-by-step series of simple tasks in which the work shifts from machine to machine. This may be done either by moving the work itself physically, as on the assembly line, or, as in modern computer-controlled machine tools, by bringing machines and tools in pre-arranged sequence to the work, with the tool changing with each step of the process. Machines work best if run at a constant speed and rhythm, with a minimum of moving parts.

The human being is engineered quite differently. For any one task and any one operation, the human being is ill-suited. He lacks strength. He lacks stamina. He gets fatigued. Altogether he is a very poorly designed machine tool. The human being excels, however, in coordination. He excels in relating perception to action. He works best if the entire human being, muscles, senses, and mind, is engaged by the work.

If confined to an individual motion or operation, the human being tires fast. The fatigue is not just boredom, which is psychological; it is genuine physiological fatigue as well. Lactic acid builds up in the muscles, vision dims, reaction speed slows and becomes erratic.

The human being works best at a group of operations rather than at a single operation. But also – and this may be even more important – the human being is very poorly equipped to work at an unvarying speed and a standard rhythm. He works best if capable of varying both speed and rhythm fairly frequently.

There is no one 'right' speed and no one 'right' rhythm for human beings. Speed, rhythm, and attention span vary greatly among individuals. To be productive the individual has to have a good deal of control over the speed, rhythm, and attention spans with which he is working.

Whereas *work* is best laid out as uniform, *working* is best organized with a considerable degree of diversity. Working requires freedom to change speed, rhythm, and attention fairly often. It requires fairly frequent changes in operating routines as well. What is good industrial engineering for work is exceedingly poor human engineering for the worker.

## Work as curse and blessing: The psychological dimension

The next dimension of working is *psychological*. Work, we know, is both a burden and a need, both a curse and a blessing. Whether this is in-born or learned, we do not know – and it does not greatly matter. By the time a human being reaches the age of four or five, she has been conditioned to work. To be sure, child labour is outlawed in most countries, but learning the fundamentals of being a person, especially learning to talk, is work and creates the habit of work. We long ago learned that unemployment creates severe psychological disturbances, not because of economic deprivation, but primarily because it undermines self-respect. Work is an extension of personality. It is achievement. It is one of the ways in which a person defines himself, measures his worth, and his humanity.

The peculiar characteristic of the work ethic of the West is not that it glorified work. That was neither new nor particularly Western. It sanctified the 'calling'; it preached that *all* work was service and contribution and equally deserving of respect.

The commercial and industrial revolutions of the eighteenth and nineteenth centuries brought a sharp stepup in the hours worked by farmers, machine tenders, merchants, and industrialists alike.

In large measure this reflected a great improvement in living conditions and nutrition. This greatly increased the physical energy available for work. No matter how horrible living conditions were in the nineteenth-century slums of industrial towns – or are today in the slums that ring Latin America's cities – they were better, especially with respect to food, than the living conditions under which the landless labourer or the weavers and spinners in the cottage industries subsisted. Anyone who doubts this need only to note the starvation rations of wormy biscuits on which seamen in the sailing vessels were supposed to live and work; there are abundant records in such literary classics as Dana's *Two Years Before the Mast*, Melville's *Typee* and *Moby Dick*. Yet sailors, by all reports, were the best-fed workers, both because the work was hard and made great physical demands and because of the ever-present danger of mutiny.

The great increase in working in these recent centuries also represented a shift in values. Economic rewards became more meaningful – mostly, perhaps, because economic satisfactions became more generally available. The worker in the English slums of eighteenth-century Liverpool or Manchester could not buy much; he lacked purchasing power. But even purchasing power would not have helped his grandfather, the landless labourer; in his day, there wasn't anything around to buy.

Rejection of the work ethic – if there is such a phenomenon outside the headlines – therefore does not represent simple pleasure-seeking. In part it represents a reaction against long decades of overworking, and a righting of the balance between work and leisure. In larger part it may, however, represent a return to earlier elitist work concepts which relate certain kinds of work to the nobility or baseness of the person. What lends support to this hypothesis is the strong, positive value that the educated young people who supposedly repudiate the work ethic give to the work of teacher and artist. Teaching and art, however, are far more demanding taskmasters than tending machines or selling soap.

The workless society of the futurist utopia may, indeed, be ahead. Should it come, it would, however, produce a major personality crisis for most people. It is perhaps fortunate that so far there is not the slightest sign of the end of work in the near future. So far the task is still to make work serve the psychological need of workers.

## Work as social and community bond

Work is a *social bond* and a *community bond*. In the employee society it becomes the primary access to society and community. It largely determines status. Saying, 'I am a doctor' or 'I am a plumber' makes a meaningful statement about the speaker, about her or his position in society and role in the community.

Perhaps more important, work, since time immemorial, has been the means to satisfy human beings' need for belonging to a group and for a meaningful relationship to others. When Aristotle said that man is a social animal, he said in effect that human beings need work to satisfy their need for community.

Work is for most people the *one* bond outside of their own family – and often more important than the family especially for the young not-yet married and for older people whose children have grown up. This is exemplified strongly by the experience of companies who hire mature women for part-time work. They make the most loyal employees. The work place becomes their community, their social club, their escape from loneliness.

Every company that has polled its retired employees has found the same reaction: 'What we miss isn't the work; it's our colleagues and friends. What we want to know isn't how the company is doing but what the people do with whom we worked, where they are, how they are coming along.' 'Don't, please, send me the annual report,' a retired senior vice-president of a big company once said in a burst of candour, 'I'm no longer interested in sales. Send me the gossip. I miss even the people I couldn't stand.'

This last comment puts the finger on the greatest strength of the work bond and its special advantage compared to all other bonds of community. It is not built on personal likes or dislikes. It can function without making emotional demands. A woman can work very well with somebody whom she never sees away from the job, and for whom she feels neither friendship nor warmth nor liking. She can even function well in a work relationship with somebody whom she dislikes – if only she respects the other person's workmanship. But the fellow worker can also be a close friend with whom one spends as many hours away from work as possible, with whom one plays tennis or golf, spends one's vacation, spends one's evenings, and shares much of one's life. The work relationship has an objective, outside focus, the work itself, but it makes possible strong social and community bonds that are as personal or as impersonal as one desires.

## The economic dimension

Work is a '*living*'. It has an economic component the moment a society adopts even the most rudimentary division of labour. The moment people cease to be self-sufficient and begin to exchange the fruits of their labour, work creates both an economic link and an economic conflict.

There is no resolution to this conflict. One has to live with it.

Work is a living for the workers. It is the foundation of their economic existence. But work also produces the capital for the economy. It produces the means by which an economy perpetuates itself, provides for the risks of economic activity and the resources to create tomorrow's jobs and the livelihood for tomorrow's workers. There is need in any economy for a wage fund and for a capital fund.

But the capital fund is in direct competition with the workers' need for a livelihood here and now. Whatever surplus goes to capital isn't available to pay the workers. Marx tried to deny the need for a capital fund. The great appeal of Marxism to workers was precisely that it presented capital accumulation as exploitation and as unnecessary. The great appeal of Marxism was its prophecy that the capital fund would disappear once the workers owned the means of production. This very soon was seen as a total misunderstanding. The capital fund is an objective necessity and not founded in social or power structure. All communist regimes, most of all the Soviet Union, now put the capital fund at the centre of their economic planning. In other words, they have all realized that profit is not simply a result of power, let alone exploitation, but that it is a genuine economic necessity.

Still, it does little good to argue, as the classical economists did, that there is no conflict between the demands of the capital fund, that is, the demands for a surplus, and the demands of the wage fund. The classical economists argued that, in the long run, these two harmonize. The workers need the capital fund fully as much as they need the wage fund. They need to be protected against the risks of uncertainty. They needs the jobs of tomorrow. The rapid improvement in wages and living standards of the American worker has been largely the result of steadily increasing capital investment – that is, the capital fund.

But 'the worker' is an abstraction. The beneficiary of the capital fund is rarely the same worker who has made the contributions to the fund. The capital accumulated in one industry, such as the American textile industry in the 1890s, went to finance a new industry, such as the chemical industry, rather than to create new jobs in the textile industry. Also, the capital fund creates jobs and incomes tomorrow, whereas the contribution to it has to be made today.

In other words, it is true that there is no ultimate conflict between wage fund and capital fund, but this is largely irrelevant for the individual. For him there is a real and immediate conflict.

## Wage as living and wage as cost

There is an even more basic conflict between wage as living and wage as cost. As 'living', wage needs to be predictable, continuous, and adequate to the expenditures of a family, its aspirations, and its position in society and community. Looked at from the opposite angle, as 'cost', wage needs to be appropriate to the productivity of a given employment or industry. It needs to be flexible and to adjust easily to even minor changes in supply and demand in the market. It needs to make a product or service competitive. It is determined, in the last result, by the consumer, without regard to the needs or expectations of the worker. Again, here is conflict which cannot easily be resolved and can at best be minimized.

Worker ownership has long been considered the alternative to both capitalism (ownership by the providers of capital) and nationalization (ownership by the government). It may be desirable that workers have a financial stake in the business. But wherever tried – and we have been trying worker ownership for well over a century – it has worked only as long as the enterprise is doing well. It works only in highly profitable businesses. And so do all the variants of workers' participation in profits, such as profit and productivity bonus plans. As soon as business profits drop, the conflict between wage as living and wage as cost (or that between the wage fund and the capital fund) becomes an issue again.

A financial stake in the business must always remain a secondary interest to the worker, compared to the job. Even in the most prosperous business, profit, that is, the contribution to the capital fund, is never more than a small fraction of wages. In manufacturing industries, wage costs typically are 40 per cent or so of gross sales. Profits after taxes are rarely more than 5 or 6 per cent, that is, one-eighth of wage costs. In the total economy, the wage and salary bill runs around 65–75 per cent of gross national product. Profits fluctuate from zero to 7 per cent or so – they are at most one-tenth of the wage bill. Most of the remainder is income of small proprietors, farmers, shopkeepers, professionals, that is, in effect, another compensation for labour rather than profits.

It is also debatable whether worker ownership is in the worker's own *financial* interest. No enterprise is profitable forever. And if the workers then, as in the typical worker-ownership plan, are dependent for retirement benefits, say, on investment in the company they work for, they are exceedingly vulnerable. The worker should no more than any other investor have all financial eggs in one basket. In that respect, the approach to pensions adopted in the United States in the last twenty-five years – development of a pension fund which invests broadly, and typically does not invest at all in the business that employs the future beneficiaries – is financially far sounder and far more in the worker's own financial interest than worker ownership in the enterprise he or she works for.

From a theoretical point of view, the developments in the United States during the last twenty or thirty years would seem to represent the best approach to assuage these conflicts. The employees of American business are gradually becoming the true 'owners' through their pension funds and mutual funds, which have become the dominant investors in the American economy. By now these institutional investors, who represent the employees and their savings, own control of the large publicly owned American corporations. America, in other words, has socialized ownership without nationalizing it. Yet this has by no means resolved – or even lessened – the conflict between wage fund and capital fund and between wage as living and wage as cost.

## The power dimension of working

There is always a *power relationship* implicit in working within a group, and especially in working within an organization.

The imposition on a worker's life of the clock that forces him or her to come to work at a given hour may appear a trivial exercise of power, and one that affects everybody equally. But it came as a tremendous shock to preindustrial people, whether peasants in developing countries, the former craftsmen in the mills of England in the early years of the industrial revolution, or blacks from the ghettos of the American city today. In an organization jobs have to be designed, structured, and assigned. Work has to be done on schedule and in a prearranged sequence. People are promoted or not promoted. In short, authority has to be exercised by someone.

Anarchists are right in their assertion that 'organization is alienation'. What they mean is that the more work is organized, the more the workers themselves are removed from control over it. Modern society is an employee society and will remain one. This implies power relationships that affect all of us directly and in our capacity as workers. Authority is an essential dimension of work. It has little to do with ownership of the means of production, democracy at the work place, worker representation at the board of directors, or any other way of structuring the 'system'. It is inherent in the fact of organization.

## The sixth dimension: the power dimension of economics

In all modern organizations there is what might be called a sixth dimension of working: a need for authority with respect to *economic shares*.

Power and economics are closely linked in the modern organization, whether business enterprise, government agency, university, or hospital. Dividing the economic rewards among the members of the institution demands a central organ of authority with power to make the decision. The reason is not capitalism or any other 'ism'. It is the fundamental fact that the modern institution is an organ of society, existing to provide satisfactions outside of itself. It, therefore, obtains its revenue from the outside – either from a customer, from the taxpayers through a budget-making authority, or from preset fees paid by users such as patients in a hospital or students in a college. At the same time, the contribution of the individual member of the institution cannot be directly related to the revenue. It is impossible to say even approximately, how much any individual employee, whether chief executive or lowliest sweeper, contributes to the business' sales. The same is true of hospital or university. Does the great scholar in ancient Chinese with six graduate students contribute more or less than the graduate assistant teaching English composition to a freshman class of 150? And what about the dean? All one can say is that everybody's contribution is, in theory, indispensable, although not everybody's contribution enters into every single product or performance, nor is everybody's contribution in any way equal in importance, skill, or difficulty.

An authority is, therefore, needed which apportions the available revenue among the members. The institution itself, whether business enterprise or hospital, is necessarily a *redistributive system*, a system for redistributing revenue among its members.

Where the contributions are simple, similar, and few in number, redistribution on the basis of complete equality is possible. That is, for instance, the case in the Israeli kibbutz, where all work on the farm, producing a very few products, most of them for their own use. But the moment the kibbutz went into industrial production, as a good many did, it had to abandon the principle of primitive socialism on which it had been founded and under which everybody received exactly the same. The kibbutzim became employers. In Israel the Trade Union Federation owns most of industry and is the country's leading employer. Most of Israel's industry is, in effect, 'socialized', but that has not in any way changed the power position of the 'employer'. Nor has it eliminated the problems of labour relations.

The simple fact that the results of a modern institution always lie outside itself and that, therefore, the economic rewards for its members always come from the outside and are not determined internally, leads inescapably to power and authority. It creates two power relationships. The first is a power relationship between management and labour. The second is among the various groups within the work force. While they are in a common power relationship to management, these groups stand in sharp and intense competition with respect to their relative shares in the total 'product' available for internal distribution.

If the last hundred years have taught us anything, it is that the distribution problem is built into every institution. It is not a feature of one form of ownership or another. It cannot be manipulated away. There has to be a decision on dividing the revenue available from the outside among the members inside the enterprise. The moment the institution, business, hospital, or other, produces more than a very few simple commodities, meant mostly for consumption within the group, the relationship between the individual input and the institution's output can no longer be determined 'impersonally' or 'scientifically'. At this moment also, the completely equal distribution of rewards becomes impossible – as the Russians learned in the 1920s, and as all other socialist experimenters have learned since.

There has then to be a redistribution and an authority to make the redistribution decisions. Redistribution, however, is, in effect, a political rather than an economic decision. It is influenced and restrained by a great number of forces: supply and demand, social convention, traditions, and so on. But in the last analysis, a decision by authority and a decision based on power structure and power relationships has to be made somehow by somebody. And this decision, no modern institution – and least of all, the business enterprise – can escape.

**The fallacy of the dominant dimension**

These dimensions of working – the physiological, the psychological, the social, the economic, and the power dimensions – are separate. Each can – and, indeed, should – be analysed separately and independently. But they always exist together in the worker's situation and in her or his relationship to work and job, fellow workers and management. They have to be managed together. Yet they do not pull in the same direction. The demands of one dimension are quite different from those of another.

The basic error of our traditional approaches to working has been to proclaim one of these dimensions to be *the* dimension.

Marx – and most other economists – saw the economic dimension as dominating everything else. If only economic relationships could be changed, there would be no more alienation. Marxism became bankrupt when it became clear that the transfer of ownership from the 'exploiters' to the workers did not fundamentally change the worker's situation because it did not change in any way any of the other dimensions (and did not indeed even change the economic problem).

Elton Mayo, to give another ınd radically different example, saw the dominant dimension as the interpersonal relations within the work group, that is, psychological and social aspects. And yet while it is true that one cannot 'hire a hand; the whole man always comes with it,' the work, too, matters and affects group relations. And neither the economic nor the power dimension was seen by Mayo and his associates.

The late Abraham H. Maslow, the father of the view of behaviour known as humanist psychology, argued that human wants are ranked on different levels. As a want of a lower order is satisfied, it becomes less and less important, with a want of the next-higher order becoming more and more important. Maslow put economic want at the bottom and the need for self-fulfilment at the top. But more important than the specific order is the insight that wants are not absolute; the more one want is being satisfied, the less its satisfaction matters.

But what Maslow did not realize is that a want changes in the act of being satisfied. As the economic want is satisfied, that is, as people no longer have to subordinate every other human need and human value to getting the next meal, it becomes less and less satisfying to obtain more economic rewards. But economic rewards do not become any less important. On the contrary, while the impact of an economic reward as a positive incentive decreases, its capacity to create dissatisfaction, if disappointed, rapidly increases. Economic rewards cease to be 'incentives' and become 'entitlements'. If not properly taken care of – that is, if there is dissatisfaction with the economic rewards – they become deterrents.

This is, we now know, true of each of Maslow's wants. As a want is satisfied, its capacity to reward, its power as an incentive, diminishes fast. But its capacity to deter, to create dissatisfaction, and to act as a disincentive rapidly increases.

Two vice-presidents in the same company whose salaries are only a few hundred dollars apart are equals economically. At that salary level, the income tax is so high as to make the difference meaningless. Yet the vice-president with the lower salary may be eaten up by frustration and envy. No matter how good his income, it will be a thorn in his side. The same applies all the way down the organization. Every trade-union leader knows that his biggest problem today is not absolute pay scales. It is the pay differences among various kinds of workers within his union. If the skilled worker receives 20 per cent more than a semi-skilled one, neither will be happy. They are equally dissatisfied. If the pay differential is narrowed, the skilled worker will feel that he has been deprived. And if the differential is not narrowed, the semi-skilled worker will feel deprived.

But also, contrary to what Maslow seemed to imply, the various dimensions of human beings at work change their character as they approach being satisfied. Pay, as we have just seen, becomes part of the social or psychological dimension rather than the economic one.

The opposite can also happen; power and status can become the basis for economic demands. In Yugoslav industry, for instance, the worker representatives on the workers' council, who hold positions of great social prestige and considerable power, almost immediately want more money as well. At the least, they want dvantages – housing, an office, a secretary, preferential prices at the company store, and .o on – which are, as they see it, economic rewards befitting their new rank.

We need to know much more than we now know about the dimensions of working and about their relationships. We are dealing with a combination of factors that seems likely to defy analysis. Nevertheless, managers have to manage now. They have to find solutions – or at least compromises – that will enable them to make work productive and the worker achieving. They must understand what the demands are. They cannot expect to succeed by continuing the practices of the last two hundred years. They will have to develop new approaches, new principles, and new methods – and fast.

## Summary

Although work has been around as long as humanity, the study of working is barely a hundred years old. And 'working', that is, the human being at work, has so far been given little systematic attention. Yet we know that work and working are different. Work is a 'something', an object – and as such outside ourselves and in need of systematic analysis and synthesis. 'Working' is a human activity, and as such endowed with personality, with distinct physiological, psychological and social needs and characteristics. And working has economic as well as power dimensions. Yet work and working have always to be together and have to be managed together.

# 15 Making Work Productive: Work and Process

We speak of unskilled work, skilled work, and knowledge work, but this is misleading. It is not the work that is unskilled, skilled, or knowledgeable; it is the worker. Skill and knowledge are aspects of working. The work itself is the same whether it requires no skill or high skill, a lot of knowledge or very little.

To make a pair of shoes one used to have to be 'highly skilled'. For almost a century now, we have been able to make shoes practically without skill. It would be no great trick (though probably uneconomical) to automate shoemaking fully so that it requires no manual work. Yet the shoe itself has hardly changed. Nor has the process. It requires the same steps, from preparing leather, to cutting, forming, stitching, and gluing. The steps are being carried out in the same sequence, to the same requirements and standards, and thus yield the same finished product. The work of shoe-making remains the same, even though tools and skill requirements have changed drastically. Only an expert could tell whether a shoe had been made entirely by hand and with great craft skill or in an entirely automated process.

This may seem to be quibbling. Yet the realization that skill and knowledge are in the working rather than in the work is the key to making work productive. The generic nature of work – certainly as far as manual or any other production work is concerned – implies that work can be worked on systematically, if not scientifically.

So far the study of work has been confined to manual work – for the simple reason that, until quite recently, this was the main work around. In describing what is known about making work productive, this book must, therefore, focus on manual work. But the same principles and approaches apply to any other production work, such as most service work. They apply to the processing of information, that is, to most clerical work. They even apply to most knowledge work. Only the applications and the tools vary. Precisely because work is general, there is essentially no difference among work of which the end product is a thing, work of which the end product is information, and work of which the end product is knowledge.

## The four requirements of productive work

Making work productive requires four separate activities, each with its own characteristics and demands.

First, making work productive requires *analysis*. We have to know the specific operations needed for work, their sequence, and their requirements.

But we also need *synthesis*. The individual operations have to be brought together into a *process* of production.

Third, we need to build into the process the *control* of direction, of quality and quantity, of standards, and of exceptions.

Fourth, the appropriate *tools* have to be provided.

One more basic point needs to be made. Because work is objective and impersonal and a 'something' – even if it is intangible, like information or knowledge – making work productive has to begin with the end product, the output of work. It cannot start with the input, whether craft skill or formal knowledge. Skills, information, knowledge, are tools; and what tool is to be applied when, and for what purpose, must always be determined by the desired end product. The end product determines what work is needed. It also determines the synthesis into a process, the design of the appropriate controls, and the specifications for the tools needed.

## The analysis of work

The analysis of work – known by such names as work study, scientific management, and industrial engineering – is by now almost a century old. As said earlier, it began with Frederick W. Taylor's work in the 1880s on individual manual operations, such as his famous study of shovelling sand in a steel mill. It was essentially completed in its present form shortly after Taylor died during World War I. In those war years and in the period immediately following, Taylor's most productive disciples, Frank Gilbreth and Henry Gantt, added to his scientific management what might be called the vocabulary and the grammar for the analysis of work.

Gilbreth studied, identified, and classified all the motions involved in manual work, such as 'lifting', 'moving', and 'putting down'. His *Therbligs* (Gilbreth spelled backwards) list the entire range of manual operations, specify how each can best be done, what motion it requires, and how much time it needs. They are not, as sometimes has been said, an alphabet. They are more like the characters of written Chinese, that is, symbols of a fundamental activity which in themselves contain all the information needed to engineer the activity they represent.

Gantt, at the same time, addressed himself to the order of operations in work. His Gantt Chart, which starts out with the desired end product and then outlines every step needed to attain it, with its place in the sequence and the time needed, created, in effect, a systematic arrangement for the steps of work.

Not only has the discipline of work analysis been with us for a long time; the practice has become general too. The industrial engineer is a common feature of production work, in the factory, in transportation, and increasingly in clerical work. Industrial engineering is a recognized academic discipline with a huge literature of its own. And its impact has been almost overwhelming.

Managers, therefore, tend to believe that they know all they need to know about industrial engineering. The analysis of work, they would tell a questioner, consists essentially of the following:

1 Identification of all operations necessary to produce a known end product, a known piece of work.
2 Rational organization of the sequence of operations to make possible the easiest, smoothest, and most economical flow of work.
3 Analysis of each individual operation and its redesign to make it as efficient as possible – including providing the appropriate tools, information, and materials where and when needed.
4 Integration of these operations into individual jobs.

And this is, in brief, what the books on industrial engineering say and what the courses on this subject teach. It is, however, not all that the analysis of work has to include to be effective.

In the first place, this standard answer omits the first crucial step in work analysis. Work analysis does not begin with identifying operations. It begins with defining the desired end product. As Gantt showed sixty years ago – and as far too few people have learned since – the analysis of the work has to start with the questions 'What do we want to produce? What is the work itself? How can the end product be designed to make possible the easiest, the most productive, the most effective work?'

To start out with the task rather than with the end product may result in beautiful engineering of work that should not be done at all. One cannot assume, as Taylor did, that the end product is rational, systematic, consistent. In most processes it represents little but untested assumptions, a lot of history, traditions and customs, and human errors. Those who start out to analyse the final product, the work itself, will soon find themselves asking the question 'Why do we do this, and why do we do that?' Usually there is no answer other than, 'We have always done it.' What proportion of inefficiency, that is, of lost productivity, can be attributed to the unquestioning acceptance of the final product as given, no one knows, but I have heard experienced industrial engineers put it as high as 30 per cent of total cost and total effort.

Managers, therefore, should realize that their work analysts have to participate in the design of product and process. Obviously the finish product cannot be engineered primarily to make work easier. Its basic specifications are set by the needs and values of the user and not by those of the producer. But within the restraints set by these basic specifications, there is usually considerable leeway to design a product or service that can be produced efficiently or inefficiently, simply or with unnecessary complications, with economy of work or wastefully.

The next – and much better known – weakness of the traditional definition of work analysis is that it includes something which does not belong in it. The fourth step that most managers – and most industrial engineers, at least in the West – include in their definition of industrial engineering is not truly part of the job. Laying out jobs is no longer analysis. Or rather, the analysis that it requires is not that of work, but that of working. While the industrial engineers have a role to play in this process, it is a totally different role from the one they play in the analysis of the work (as will be discussed in Chapter 18).

The inclusion of job design in work analysis is responsible in large measure for the traditional resistance to industrial engineering on the part of workers. It is largely responsible for the hostility of the intellectual to modern technology, and to modern industry and organization as well since work analysis is wrongly blamed for design of the assembly line and for the deadly boredom and 'dehumanization' of many jobs.

The manager needs to know that the logic of work analysis and the analysis of job structure are two different logics. The one is the logic of work; the other the logic of working.

The last and most common misunderstanding of the industrial engineer is the belief that work analysis is the whole job. It is only the first step in making work productive. Analysis identifies individual specific operations, their sequence, and their relationships. It deals with pieces. It is not concerned with the process of production as a whole, with its structures, its economy, or its performance.

## The principles of production

Production is not the application of tools to materials. It is the application of logic to work. The more clearly and rationally the right logic is applied, the less of a limitation and the more of an opportunity production becomes.

This definition implies that there must be principles of production. There must be a small number of basic models, each with its own rules, its own requirements, its own characteristics. The definition further implies that the more closely a process of production can be designed according to these principles, the smoother, the more effective, and the more productive it will be.

Each system of production makes its own demands on management – in all areas and on all levels. Each system requires different competence, skill, and performance. One set of demands is not necessarily 'higher' than another, but each is different. Unless management understands the demands of its system of production, it cannot truly make work productive.

There are four principles of production known to us so far. Each has been worked out for industrial production, that is, largely for traditional manual work. But each is equally applicable to producing and handling information, that is, to most clerical work. The principles apply also to knowledge work, at least to knowledge work concerned with learning and using knowledge already available and learnable.

The four systems are: (1) unique-product production; (2)

rigid mass production; (3) flexible mass production; and (4) process or 'flow' production. Each of these four has its own specifications; each makes specific demands on management.

There are two general rules for improving production performance and pushing back limitations: (1) The limitations on production are pushed back further and faster the more consistently and thoroughly the principles of the system in use are applied. (2) The systems themselves represent different degrees of complexity, with unique-product production the least complex, and process production the most complex. They represent different stages of control over physical limitations. This does not mean that opportunities for advance lie everywhere in moving from the unique-product system to the process-production system. Each system has its specific applications, requirements, and limitations. But by organizing parts of production on the principles of a more complex system and learning at the same time how to harmonize different systems within the same process, we advance the whole process.

There are two general rules concerning the demands on management competence made by each system:

1 The systems differ not just in the difficulty of their demands, but in the variety of skills they require and in the order and the sequence of performance. Management, in moving from one system to another, has to learn how to do new things rather than learn to do old things better.

2 The more we succeed in applying consistently the principles of each system, the easier it becomes for management to satisfy its demands. Each management has to meet the demands of the system it ought to have according to the nature of its products and process, rather than those of the system it actually uses. Failing to apply what would be the most appropriate system results only in lack of performance; it does not result in lower demands on management, but inevitably increases the difficulties of managing the business.

One industry that pays all the costs of a complex system without gaining its advantages is basic steelmaking. The basic steel industry is organized as a unique-product system though it makes all the demands of process production. The result, for reasons that will be clear when we have discussed the characteristics of all four systems, is that on the high investment of a process-production system, basic steelmaking earns only the relatively low revenue of a unique-product system.

A business using the wrong system has to satisfy all the demands that the appropriate and more complex system would make on management. Yet it does not have the wherewithal to pay for them, for this revenue can come only out of the increased ability to produce that the more complex system provides.

It is, in summary, important in managing a business to know which system applies; to carry its principles through as far as possible; to find out which parts of production can be organized in a more complex system and to organize them accordingly; and to know what demands each system makes on management.

All four principles of production provide the foundation for both production work *and* achieving worker. All are compatible with the dynamics of working or can be made so. When they fail, it is not the principle that is at fault; it is its misapplication.

Specifically, the failure of mass production to give the worker achievement is essentially poor engineering. It is either failure to understand the meaning of mechanization (see Chapter 16) or it is failure to understand the difference between work and working.

## Unique-product production

What, then, are these four systems of production and their principles?

In the first, the production of a unique product, each product is distinct. Of course, strictly speaking, there is no such thing as manufacturing unique products – they are produced only by the artist. But building a battleship, a big turbine, or a skyscraper comes close to turning out a unique product. So does the traditional way of building houses, one at a time, and, in most cases, batch production in a job shop.

What is unique in unique-product production is the product. In fact, unique-product production is always organized around standardized tools, and it typically works with standardized materials.

In unique-product production the basic organization is by homogeneous stages. In the building of the traditional single-family house – one of the oldest examples of unique-product production – we can distinguish four such stages. First, digging the foundation and pouring concrete for the foundation walls and the basement floor. Second, erecting frame and roof. Third, installing plumbing and wiring in the walls. Finally, interior finishing. Each stage can be varied from house to house without too much trouble or adjustment and without delaying the next stage. Each of these stages by the inner logic of the product, that is, the house, is an entity in itself.

Unique-product production, with its organization of the work by homogeneous stages, is radically different from craft organization, in which a carpenter does all the carpentry, a plumber all the plumbing, etc. Properly organized, unique-product production does not go by craft skills but by stage skills.

The US success in building ships at such a tremendous rate during World War II is an example of the unique-product system. It was not mass production that resulted in the unprecedented output of ships. It was the division of the work into homogenerous stages; the systematic organization of the work group for the specific requirements of each stage; and the systematic training of a large number of people to do all the work required within one stage. This in turn made possible the progressive scheduling of the work flow, which was the greatest time-saver.

## Rigid and flexible mass production

Most people when they hear the term 'mass production' think immediately of the assembly line. But this is misunderstanding. Very little mass production work is assembly line work. The assembly line is the rare exception even in true mass production of the most rigid kind.

A good example is the assembly of electronic appliances such as radios, TV sets and telephones. It is true mass production, but it is not assembly line production. One worker does the entire operation from start to finish. The operations are indeed in sequence. In that sense there is a line which goes from putting in the first rivet to soldering all wiring connections, and then to final inspection. But there is no line in the traditional sense. The work itself never moves but stays at the individual work place.

Altogether the assembly line is quite rare in reality. Only one out of every fifty workers in America in 1970 worked on an assembly line. Even in manufacturing employment assembly lines are rare – with fewer than 6 per cent of American manufacturing workers doing assembly-line work. Assembly-line work is even the exception in the automobile industry; of General Motors' 550,000 employees, only one-third do assembly-line work.

The traditional picture of the assembly line assumes, moreover, that there is only rigid mass production. The principle of production that is becoming more and more widely used is 'flexible' mass production.

What rigid and flexible mass production have in common is that the final product is assembled out of *standardized parts*. In unique-product production, tools and materials are standardized. In mass production, the parts are also standardized. And these parts, in turn, are usually built of standardized smaller parts. Mass production, in other words, assembles rather than makes.

Modern mass production goes back to the making of rifles for the American infantryman in the War of 1812. By 1880, long before Henry Ford, mass-production methods were actually in wide use throughout American industry, and also in such plants as the German Zeiss Optical Works and the Ericsson telephone plant in Sweden.

It may be the origin in gun manufacture which explains why for long years 'rigid' mass production was considered to be the only available mass-production technology. In making guns for soldiers it is important to have a completely uniform end product. Each rifle must be like any other, use exactly the same ammunition, require exactly the same cleaning, and be repaired easily with parts taken from any rifle.

In rigid mass production, therefore, the end product as well as the tools, materials, and parts is standardized and uniform. Flexible mass production, however, uses standardization of parts to make possible diversity of end products.

Historically, flexible mass production preceded rigid mass production by many hundreds of years. It was developed long before industrialization. We know far too little about the building methods of the ancients to know what production processes they applied, though it is likely that the great number of Greek and Roman temples in Europe and the Near East could have been built only on the basis of flexible mass production. For the Gothic cathedral, and for all the thousands of Gothic churches built in Northern and Western Europe between 1100 and 1300 AD, the evidence is clear. These were the product of flexible mass production. The basic parts, building blocks, roofing, and so on, were fully standardized. But their assembly varied with the architect's plan. Only windows, ornaments, doors, i.e., the features that make one church look different, were produced by unique-product production methods. But – and this is vitally important – all these are features that are added on to the almost finished building. The basic process itself was standardized, though it resulted in a very large diversity of finished products.

When the principle of mass production was rediscovered in the nineteenth century, uniform standardized end products were taken for granted. Henry Ford illustrates this perfectly. When he said, 'The customer can have a car in any colour as long as it's black,' he was not joking. He meant to express the essence of mass production: the manufacture of identical products in large quantity. Of course, he knew that it would be easy enough to give his customer a choice of colour; all that was needed was to give the painter at the end of the assembly line three or four spray guns instead of one. But Ford also realized, rightly, that the uniformity of the product would soon be gone altogether once he allowed this first 'option'. To him the uniformity of the product was the key to mass production.

Contrast this with the farm-equipment manufacturer in Southern California who, in the 1930s and the 1940s, designed and made specialized cultivating machines for large-scale farming on irrigated land. Each of his designs was unique. He made, for instance, a machine that performs, with various attachments, all operations needed in large-scale cucumber growing – from preparing the hills in the spring, to harvesting cucumbers at the right stage of their growth, to pickling them. He rarely made more than one of each machine at a time. Yet every one of his more than seven hundred different machines was made up entirely of mass-produced, uniform, standardized parts, which someone in the American economy turned out by the thousands. His biggest job was not to design a machine that identified cucumbers of the right ripeness for pickling, but to find the mass producer of a part that, though originally designed for an entirely different purpose, would, when put on the cucumber cultivator, do what was needed. His machines were mass-produced, but the principle was 'flexible mass production', similar to the productive process used in building the Gothic cathedrals.

The technique for applying the principle of flexible mass production is the systematic analysis of products to find the common pattern that underlies their apparent diversity. Then this pattern can be organized so that the minimum number of standardized parts will make possible the assembly of the maximum number of products. The burden of diversity, in other words, is taken out of manufacturing and shifted to assembly.

General Motors often points out that there are so many options on its cars – colours, body styles, seat fabrics, accessories, and so on – that the customer can actually choose from millions of different final-product combinations. More important – though not often advertised by General Motors – is the fact that all makes of General Motors (Chevrolet, Pontiac, Oldsmobile, Buick, Cadillac) are built from the same parts. They have the same bodies mounted on the same frames with much the same engine, braking, and lighting system. Yet the cars look different, have different characteristics, and represent a great variety of combinations of basic standardized elements. All these cars except Cadillac are put together on the same assembly line. All of them are, in effect, products of rigid mass production and are turned out in a process that has remained almost unchanged since Henry Ford's early days.

To obtain the appearance of diversity from rigid mass production requires, however, a large volume of production for every one of the parts to be assembled. Few industries, other than the automobile industry, can count on such volume. Unless the demand for every version of the end product is very large, rigid mass production can, as Ford saw, turn out only a standardized product.

American Motors, for instance, is at a very real disadvantage because it has to turn out a fair diversity of the end products – at least in looks and styling – without the General Motors volume. And yet it produces 300,000 to 400,000 cars a year – a very large volume by any measure other than that of the American automobile industry.

For most mass-production processes the preferred principle should be flexible mass production. Until recently, however, mechanization and flexible mass production were hard to combine. The tools appropriate to mass production were inherently inflexible.

The computer is rapidly changing this. The computer, and especially the small process computer, which is in effect a part of the machine or machine tool, eliminates the inflexibility of the tool that is the main obstacle to flexible mass production. In traditional mass production any change in product or process requires stopping the process. Change requires altering the machine setup, cleaning tools, changing the position of work and of materials, changing speeds, and so on. As long as this had to be done by hand, it required far too much time. Worse still, changing one tool meant stopping the entire process. Computer control eliminates the time losses. The computer can make the change instantly on the basis of a preset command. Instead of taking hours, changes take seconds or minutes.

This is not automation. (On mechanization and automation, see Chapter 16.) This is a radical improvement in mechanization.

Two examples are the shipbuilders of Japan and Sweden. That these two countries were able in the sixties to gain a dominant position in world shipbuilding and all but crowd out such old and experienced producers as the Scots and the Germans is not the result of lower wages. Swedish wages are, if anything, higher than wages in Germany and Scotland. It is the result of the application of computer control to convert shipbuilding, traditionally a unique-product process, to flexible mass production. As a result, Swedish and Japanese shipyards can build ships from standardized parts and yet turn out final products of great diversity, not only in appearance but also in size, structure, speed, and so on. The job is still, as in the traditional unique-product process, organized by stages. But within each stage the process is a mass-production process in which the parts are standardized but in which the possible combinations of parts have almost unlimited flexibility. The process results both in much lower cost and in much greater speed – and above all, in almost complete predictability of the building cycle and in such tight control of scheduling that – almost for the first time in the history of shipbuilding – a reliable delivery date for the finished product can be set far in advance.

Computerized control requires redesign of the process. It is difficult, expensive, and requires hard, time-consuming analysis of product and process. But wherever it has been used to convert a rigid process to flexible mass production, there has been major cost reduction – sometimes reaching fifty to sixty per cent. Production speeds have been substantially increased. Scheduling has become as reliable as in rigid mass production. At the same time, true marketing has become possible.

Flexible mass production can turn out a very large variety of truly different products and yet have a totally standardized process of production. For this reason it is flexible mass production that will increasingly become the mass-production system of tomorrow, with rigid mass production increasingly confined to the very small number of end products where basic uniformity is in itself a fundamental customer need and customer specification.

## Process production

The fourth system is process production. Here process and product become one.

The classic example of a process industry is the oil refinery. The end products that a refinery will distil from crude oil are determined by the process it uses. It can produce only the oil distillates for which it was built and these only in definite proportions. If new distillates have to be added or if the proportion of the various distillates is to be changed significantly, the refinery has to be rebuilt. Process production is the rule in the chemical industries. It is, with minor variations, the basic system of a milk-processing or a plate-glass plant.

Process production is an integrated system. There are no stages in it; there are no parts. There is only one process. Typically, process production starts with one basic material. But by the nature of that material, crude oil, for example, it ends up with many very different end products. The process itself has high rigidity – more rigidity even than rigid mass production. The end product typically has far more diversity than even unique-product production. Process production requires continuing high volume. The typical process plant in the chemical industry or in the plate-glass industry can operate only at or near peak capacity. Otherwise it has to be shut down.

Because process production is a system, it has tremendous economies and tremendous productivity where it is appropriate. But where it is misapplied, or where it is not truly developed into process production – as in the example of basic steelmaking given above – its rigidity and capital cost tend to outweigh its benefits.

Process production is, or should be, the model for a great many production processes which historically have been organized as unique-product production or as rigid mass production. The basic difference in performance between a well-run telephone system and most post offices is that telephone service is organized as process production and as a true system. Post offices everywhere are organized at best on mass-production principles – and, in effect, by and large, still on unique-product principles with 'stages' of the process and with totally different processes for different 'products', that is, different kinds of mail, or letters versus parcels. To be sure, it is easier to move electronic impulses than it is to move paper, let alone heavy parcels. But wherever a mail service has been able to improve its performance significantly, it has done so by converting its system to process production.

All transportation, whether of mail, freight, or people, should be considered process production. The means of transportation always have to be a system, have to have great rigidity, have to be scheduled and have to be integrated with one another. But each letter, each parcel, let alone each passenger, has a separate destination. There is, therefore, almost infinite diversity of 'end products'. And this can be organized and delivered only by a system that is essentially process production.

## What each principle demands

Each of the four principles has different characteristics and makes different demands. Each has its own costs. Each has its own weaknesses. Each has its own strengths.

*Unique-product* production is labour-intensive. Even when highly mechanized – and it does not lend itself to automation – capital investment will be comparatively low compared to the cost of labour. But it has great flexibility. Costs for the individual product are high, but break-even points are low. Unique-product production can operate at a low volume of output or with considerable fluctuation in output. It makes high demands on skill, but little or no demands on judgement.

*Rigid mass production* is also labour-intensive rather than capital-intensive. But it requires high volume – indeed, very high volume. Even minor variations in output decrease the economy of the system. It needs high skill in the design and maintenance of the process, and little or no skill in actual operations. It requires a high degree of judgement in design, but practically no judgement in operations.

*Flexible mass production* tends to become increasingly capital-intensive, requiring a large initial investment. It still, however, requires a good deal of labour. It requires high volume of total output but has great flexibility with respect to the composition of the output, the product mix. It requires great skill in designing the system and maintaining it. Operating it, as a rule, requires little skill, but a good deal of judgement.

*Process production* requires very high capital investment. The only principle of production appropriate to industries with very high capital investment is process production. They should, therefore, not also be labour-intensive.

Any industry that is both highly capital-intensive and highly labour-intensive is likely to use the wrong principle of production. It has not learned how to apply process-production principles.

Steelmaking is the obvious example. The basic steel industry has in the batch process primarily a unique-product system. There is probably no industry that has worked harder or more successfully on perfecting a unique-product system. Yet the problems the managements of basic-steel companies face are process-production. Basic steelmaking requires high fixed capital and continuous production. Together these requirements mean high break-even points, a need for a high and constant volume of business, and a need to make basic investment decisions for a long time ahead. As a result the cost structure of the steel industry is that of capital-intensive process production. At the same time the basic-steel industry enjoys few of the economic benefits of process production. The steel industry is thus caught in a perpetual squeeze between the cost characteristics of process production and the revenue characteristics of unique-product production. In periods of very rapid growth and high demand, that is, in the early stage of industrialization by and large, it can be very profitable for a few decades. But over any extended period of time, steel industry profitability will always be small and inadequate to the industry's own needs – until such time as the basic steelmaking process shifts from mechanical unique-product production to what would in effect be a chemical flow-process.

The airlines are another example, and so is the hospital. These are inherently highly vulnerable industries or services which combine the worst of two worlds, such as high break-even points and inflexibility of product mix. We usually do not know how to put such industries on true process production, but the more closely such industries or services can attain genuine process production in part of their activities, the better will they perform, both in quality and in economic terms.

Process production has great diversity of product mix, but little or no flexibility. It can produce only the products for which the system has been designed. It requires extreme skill in design. It may require very high skill in operation – on the part of schedulers, pilots, and maintenance people of an airline, for example – or very little skill, as in the typical oil refinery. But it requires a very high degree of judgement by practically every employee.

Since product and process have, so to speak, become one in process production, new products will be created by changes in the process, even if there is no demand for them in the existing market. This is a common occurrence in the chemical industry. There changing the temperature conditions of some reaction may produce a completely new end product. It is also typical of the airlines industry. When a new, bigger plane comes in, a new market has to be created. It is characteristic of process production that the volume of production cannot be increased gradually. The minimum unit of production – whether a new chemical plant or a new jumbo jet – is so large that it requires a quantum jump in production, and with it new markets.

In *unique-product production*, management's first job is to get an order. In both kinds of *mass production*, the job is to build an effective means of distribution and to educate the customer to adapt his wants to the available range of product variety. In *process production*, the first task is to create, maintain, and expand a market and to create new markets. To distribute kerosene lamps free to the Chinese peasants to create a market for kerosene – as Standard Oil did eighty years ago – is a good example of what this means.

In the *unique-product* system the time span of decisions is short. Under both types of *mass production* it becomes longer: a distributive organization, for instance, may take ten years to build. But under a *process system*, decisions are made for an even longer future. Once built, the productive facilities are relatively inflexible and can be changed only at major expense; the total investment is likely to be large; and the development of a market is long range. The marketing systems of the big oil companies are good examples.

## What each system requires of management

Each system requires different management skills and organization. *Unique-product production* requires people good at technical functions. *Mass production*, rigid or flexible, requires management trained in analytical thinking, in scheduling, and in planning. *Flexible mass production* and *process production* require management trained in seeing a business as a whole, in conceptual synthesis, and in decision-making.

There are significant differences with respect to the work force and its management. Unique-product production can usually adjust its work force to economic fluctuations, keeping in bad times only foremen and a nucleus of the most highly skilled. It can, as a rule, find what other skills it needs on the labour market. Because they have limited skills, the workers in mass production must increasingly demand employment stability from the enterprise. At the other extreme the work force in process production represents such an investment in judgement that the business must try to maintain employment stability. It is neither accident nor philanthropy that the oil companies – typical process businesses – have worked so hard to keep employment steady even in bad depression years.

These four principles of production are 'pure' types. There are many businesses – and equally many nonbusinesses (hospitals, for example) – where different parts of the work are best organized on different principles. How then can these principles be combined?

The hospital needs unique-product production. Patient care can be given only on that basis, even though the great majority of patients in any hospital fall into a small number of highly predictable and repetitive categories, such as childbirth, minor orthopaedic surgery, cardiac cases, and so on. At the same time, the medical services, from X-ray to medical laboratory to physical therapy, have to be organized in what is essentially flexible mass production. The same applies to the 'hotel' services – the feeding of patients, the housekeeping, and so on. Other parts of the hospital require real process production. Yet all this has to be integrated into one hospital, one management, and one process and has to be delivered to the same patient at his or her bedside.

The rule for the use of different principles in one organization is simple – though by no means easy to apply. Different principles of production can work well in the same organization, but they must not be mixed in the same stage of a process.

Managers, therefore, need to understand what principles of production are truly appropriate to the different stages of the production process they have to manage. They have to analyse the logic of each stage. And if they find that they require different principles to organize production, they have then to try to separate these stages so that they do not interfere with each other. This organization, however, cannot be done by imitating what others are doing. It requires that management analyse its own work and its own production processes. It also requires that management understand the basic principles of production, their characteristics, their limitations and their requirements.

## Summary

A worker may be unskilled, skilled, or knowledgeable. But all work is essentially of the same kind, follows the same stages and steps, and needs the same treatment to be made productive. It needs analysis, synthesis, controls, and tools. All work has to be organized into a process of production. Production is not the application of tools to materials but of logic to work. There are four such 'logics', four principles of production: unique-product production; rigid mass production; flexible mass production; and process (or flow) production. Each principle has different applications, different requirements, different costs, different limitations, and makes its own demands on management.

# 16 Making Work Productive: Controls and Tools

Work is a process, and any process needs to be controlled. To make work productive, therefore, requires building the appropriate controls into the process of work.

Specifically the process of production needs built-in controls in respect to:

—its direction;
—its quality;
—the quantity it turns out in a given unit of time and with a given input of working;
—its standards, such as machine maintenance or safety;
—its economy, that is, the efficiency with which it uses resources.

Each work process needs its own controls. There is no 'standard' control, but all control systems have to satisfy the same basic demands and have to live up to the same overall specifications.

The first thing to know is that controlling the work process means control of the work, and not control of the worker. Control is a tool of the workers and must never be their master. It must also never become an impediment to working.

The most extreme cases of controls that impede work are to be found not in manufacturing but in retailing and in the hospital. There controls, in the form of almost endless paperwork, have been permitted to become an end in themselves to the point where they encroach upon the work and seriously slow it.

In the hospital, controls are needed in tremendous number,

from medical records to billing to the handling of insurance claims for reimbursement, for the patient's personal physician, and so on. Yet to have the nurse handle this paper flood – as is the practice in the typical hospital – is gross miscontrol. It makes the nurse deskbound so that she has little time for the patient. The remedy is simple: a floor clerk, usually a young management trainee in hospital administration, who takes on the information load including providing the nurses with the information they need to do their own jobs. This is not only economical, since management trainees are paid much less than nurses; it is, above all, the proper use of scarce skills.

It should always be remembered that control is a principle of economy and not of morality. The purpose of control is to make the process go smoothly, properly, and according to high standards. The first question to ask of the control system is whether it maintains the process within a permissible range of deviation with the *minimum effort*. To spend a dollar to protect 99 cents is not control. It is waste. 'What is the minimum of control that will maintain the process ?' is the right question to ask.

Seventy years ago this was clearly understood by the men who built Sears, Roebuck. In the early days of the mail-order business when currency was still metallic, the money in incoming orders was not counted. The orders were weighed, unopened. Sears, Roebuck had run enough tests to know what average weights corresponded to overall amounts of money – and this was sufficient control.

The second thing to know about controls is their basic characteristics. Controls have to be pre-set. There has to be a decision as to the desired performance and as to the permissible deviation from the standard. Control has to be essentially by 'exception': only significant deviation triggers the control. As long as the process operates within the pre-set standards, it is under control and does not require any action.

Third, control has to be by feedback from the work done. The work itself has to provide the information. If it has to be checked all the time, there is no control.

One implication of this – and a very important one – is that inspection is not control. Inspection, especially final inspection, is, of course, needed for both goods and services. But if used as control, it fast becomes too cumbersome, too expensive, and a drag on the process itself. Above all, it does not really control, even if every product is tested and analysed. The end result would still be poor quality, excessive defects, and malfunction.

The control has to be exercised where the malfunction is likely to occur. The control action may then be performed by the machinery itself, as it is in the case of the thermostat that runs the central heating unit of a modern home.

Or the worker may be alerted to take the proper remedial action – and this is also feedback control. What is important is not who takes the action but what action to take. Equally important is that the action be taken as a result of the working of the process itself and at the place where the action is appropriate, that is, the place where correction of the process, or a change in its direction (such as shutting off or turning on the heating unit), is to be performed.

This implies that a control system has to designate the *key point* at which control is to be built in. This is not primarily a technical decision but a managerial one. At what point in the system is there enough information to know whether control action is needed ? At what point in the system is there scope for effective action ? Control at any other point is undesirable. But so is control when it is too late to prevent damage. What part of the process requires continuous control ? What part requires control only at specific stages ? Where is preventive control needed, or at least control at a very early stage ? And, where is control essentially remedial ? These are questions that are rarely asked in designing a control system. Yet unless they are asked – and answered – a control system that truly satisfies the needs of the work process cannot be designed.

## Routines and exceptions

A control system can control only the regular process. It must identify genuine exceptions, but it cannot handle them. It can only make sure that they do not clog the process itself.

Exceptions can never be prevented, but they can be eliminated from the work process. They then can be handled separately and as exceptions. To make a control system take care of exceptions misdirects and undermines both the work process and the control system. A control system that tries to handle the exceptions as well as identifying them will defeat the process. It will sacrifice the 97 per cent we understand to the 3 per cent we do not understand.

The examples that best illustrate this are found in the processing of information in the life insurance business. Every life insurance company handles an avalanche of death claims every day. Every life insurance company has learned that death claims have to be handled fast or else the company rapidly loses its standing in the market. Hence, every life insurance company long ago adopted the rule that routine death claims are to be paid within twenty-four hours.

The great majority – well over 90 per cent – of all the claims are routine and need only to be checked off. Are all the needed forms provided ? Is all the required information in hand ? If the answer is yes – and it should not take more than a few seconds to find this out – payment is authorized.

In a small number of cases, the information is not complete. Perhaps the death certificate is missing, or it has not been signed by a physician, or it does not state a cause of death. Perhaps the name on the death certificate is different from the name on the policy, or the age is significantly different, and other such clerical shortcomings.

Death claims are sorted alphabetically (or sometimes by area) when they are received and then handed to a claims clerk. In the typical American company, until very recently, the claims clerk was expected to handle all the claims in his or her area as they came in. This usually meant that the claims clerk worked up a dozen claims and then came to one where routine checking was not adequate control. The claims clerk then began to work on it. Sometimes the clerk could settle the problem in a few seconds, perhaps by sending it back to the agent in the field with the appropriate form letter asking for whatever information was lacking. But sometimes he or she had to spend half an hour or even an hour on handling one claim. As a result, routine claims backed up. And by twelve o'clock, the clerk was usually way behind, and routine claims that should have been authorized for payment had not been processed.

The typical British insurance company handles this differently. There the claims clerk inspects each claim to see whether it is routine or not. Any claim that is not so simple that it can be cleared for payment immediately is handed over to a special small group of 'experts', usually older and highly experienced claims clerks, who then begin to work on it. In the meantime, the flow of routine claims continues without interruption.

Yet another way of handling this is seen in some European and Japanese life insurance companies. The claims clerk puts aside, on a separate table, every claim which cannot be immediately cleared for payment. So do three or four other claims clerks working within the same claims unit. When the pile of routine claims has dwindled and the pile of non-routine claims has grown, say, around 10:30 or 11 in the morning, the claims clerks then divide the unusual claims among them according to their workload at the moment.

The traditional American system is misapplication of control. It subordinates the routine to the exceptions. The traditional British system is effective control. It eliminates the exceptions from the process, which keeps flowing. But it stultifies the worker; it is a good control system for a machine process rather than for human work. The European or Japanese system satisfies both the demands of work and those of working.

## The patterns of routines

There are three patterns of routines. First is the pattern in which both input and output are highly standardized. This is the case in rigid mass production – and in flexible mass production as well.

Life insurance claims belong in this pattern. The input is totally standardized – a claim for payment because of one event, death of the policy-holder. The output is equally standardized. It is a cheque in payment of the claim. Only the amount of the cheque varies. And the amount, of course, is determined in advance by the policy itself. The handling of life insurance death claims is a perfect example of rigid mass production – perhaps a better one than the automobile assembly line. In this pattern, control consists of organizing the routine flow and screening, with the exceptions handled separately.

In the second pattern, the apparent diversity of events actually represents a set of subpatterns, each of which is highly routinized. One example is casualty insurance, such as insurance against fire, burglary, losses at sea, and so on. Here there seems to be bewildering variety of both risks and of claims. Actually, there are no more than half a dozen patterns.

Wherever a process seems unpredictable the most probable assumption is that it actually consists of a number of rather standard subpatterns. They appear unpredictable only because they interfere with each other. This is, for instance, the case in the hospital. Every patient-admission looks like a unique and patternless event. Yet all but a very small number of cases fall into a dozen or so standard categories. The key to designing a control system is to identify these subpatterns. Each can then be routinized, standards can be set, and a control system established that makes sure that the process operates within a preset range of acceptability.

Finally, there are processes where unique events prevail. They are rare in manufacturing; even unique-product production usually consists of a fairly small number of highly predictable, repetitive subpatterns. But unique-event processes are found, fairly frequently, in some service work.

Workmen's compensation insurance provides for the payment of lost income and damages to people injured while working and as a result of their work. It also pays for the medical costs and rehabilitation of men suffering accidents or contracting occupation-related diseases. Workmen's compensation is largely a process of unique events. No two claims are really alike. Each has to be treated as a separate claim, with respect not only to the payment due, but to the medical, surgical, or rehabilitation action required. Each frequently also calls for changes in work methods or in the tools used in order to eliminate or lessen the hazard for the future. Yet the claims adjuster of workmen's compensation insurers has to have almost complete authority to settle claims. The great majority of claims is settled speedily, to the satisfaction of both the employer and the injured worker, and with a high success in cure or rehabilitation. Workmen's compensation plans have a better record of medical performance than most medical practice has.

The way to handle this pattern of unique events is to think through and define the standards. What are the minimum standards which every single piece of work, a settled workmen's compensation claim, for example, has to satisfy in respect to the investigation of the claim, to the management of the medical or surgical work needed, to the time it takes for settlement, and so on ? What, in other words, are the standards by which a claims adjuster can measure and direct himself ? To be sure, even in such a situation of unique events, there are patterns. But there are too many, and each of them includes too small a proportion of the total phenomena, to devise a control system for each pattern. The only control – but a very effective one – is standards which enable individual workers to develop their own routine and control.

This last pattern is of particular importance because it is the typical pattern for such knowledge work as teaching, medical practice, and any other professional work. The professional, by definition, works alone. By definition he or she also deals with unique events – unique at least within the small universe to which an individual professional is exposed. And then control has to be by standards. The dissatisfaction with the professional that is so widespread today – whether teacher, lawyer, or doctor – is largely based on the lack of such standards, that is, on the lack of a control system appropriate to a unique-events process.

## Work and tools

The final step in making work productive is to fit the right tools to the work, whether the tools be physical, such as a hammer, or conceptual, such as an accounting report.

Different kinds of work require different tools. There are far too many tools, from very simple to very complex, and from very small to giant, to be analysed and presented even in the biggest book. And tool design, tool organization, and tool application are technical subjects rather than managerial ones.

Yet managers, whether they manage industrial production, the processing of information, or knowledge work, need to understand the basic *managerial* requirements of tool usage.

A tool is not necessarily better because it is bigger. A tool is best if it does the job required with a minimum of effort, with a minimum of complexity, and with a minimum of power.

Contrary to popular belief, most assembly-line work, while fully mechanized, is done with small hand tools. They are modified to serve the particular job to be done. But they are still hammers, screwdrivers, mallets, pliers, and so on. Good assembly-line tooling provides the workers with the simplest tool they need for a given job, when they need it, and wherever they need it.

The right question for the manger is not 'Isn't there a bigger tool for the job?' It is always 'What is the simplest, the smallest, the lightest, the easiest tool that will do the job?'

The second simple rule is that the tool has to serve the work. The work does not exist for the sake of the tool; the tool exists for the sake of production. This rule is constantly violated by today's computer users. They become fascinated by the capacity, the speed, the memory, the computational ability of a new generation of computers. As a result, when the new computer arrives, a frantic search begins to find things for it to do. In the end, it is being used to turn out endless reams of information which nobody wants, nobody needs, and nobody can use. Keeping the tool going becomes an end.

The argument for making the work serve the tool rather than the tool serve the work is usually 'The capital investment is so high that the tool can be justified only if it is being used all the time.' It is true that it is wasteful to keep idle a substantial capital investment. Capital costs keep on running whether the tool works or not. Yet it is still infinitely more economical to absorb these costs than to have the expensive tool produce garbage. To use the computer to produce expensive garbage is far more wasteful than not to produce at all.

## Mechanization and automation

The most important thing for a manager to know about tools and work is, however, that tools are the *bridge* between work and working. Tools serve the work. They also serve the worker. They must, therefore, be engineered for making both work productive and the worker achieve. This requires that the manager understand what mechanization is and what constitutes proper mechanization.

Mechanization is a fairly recent word. Most people believe that it pertains only to modern tools, that is, to the tools of an advanced technology. But all tools are 'mechanization'. Over thousands of years, we have changed the energy source for tools from human and animal muscle to wind and water and then to fossil fuels and nuclear power. But tools have changed very little. All tools are an extension of human beings. They either extend the body, as does the hammer, or they extend the mind, as do multiplication table and computer. Or they provide capacities for which the human body is not engineered – such as the wheel or the axe. But all tools are tools of humankind and must, therefore, serve us in the double need of making work productive and worker achieving.

While the fear of technology becoming the master and enslaving man is unfounded – and professed mostly by people who know nothing about technology and understand even less – there is real danger that mechanization will be misapplied. Mechanization to be properly applied must always extend the sphere of human capacity, must always add to human capacity to achieve. If it does not do this, it is poor engineering. It will not even make work more productive. It will, in effect, cut down output.

Specifically, there are two dangers to watch for. The first is the danger of making a person a part of a machine. Human beings are very poor machine parts. If the human effort is misengineered into the system so that it does machine work, the system works poorly. The second danger is to misuse the tool as a divisive element in the work group, thus frustrating the basic need to establish a community bond through working.

The modern assembly line, as Henry Ford set it up, does both. Workers on the traditional automobile assembly line are, in effect, part of the machinery. They do very poorly, very slowly, and very sloppily what a machine should be doing. This is the essence of doing one repetitive motion at the same unvarying speed and rhythm over and over and over again. Worse still, the automobile assembly line makes each worker a threat rather than a resource to his other fellow worker. If one man on the line works a little faster, he threatens his neighbour. When working at his most productive, that is, with varying speeds and rhythms, he becomes a threat to everybody else. And he cannot, by working better, help his neighbour. He is confined to his operation.

What is to be done when mechanization opposes working, that is, when the organization of the tool that is most conducive to making work productive threatens to do harm to working and worker ? One answer – the one that is available in most cases – is to re-engineer mechanization. The other answer is to transcend mechanization and move to automation.

The term automation is a fairly new one. It was coined in the late 1940s by a Ford Motor Company executive. The concept, however, is much older.

The best illustration of what automation means precedes the term – let alone public concern with the phenomenon – by many decades. It is the telephone system. The telephone system does not work 'untouched by human hands', nor does it operate without human work. The user, in dialling the number he wants to reach, programs the system. And this is 'work'. But given these instructions, the system runs itself, switches to the appropriate channels, returns a signal that tells the dialler whether the call is going through or not, and disconnects at the end of the conversation. It does other bookkeeping work, such as recording the calls for billing purposes. If need be, it could easily perform additional chores such as signalling a repair centre that a line is out of order.

The telephone exchange exhibits the *four principles of automation*. First, the entire process is seen as a system. There is, so to speak, no beginning and no end. Everything is integrated. Second, the system is based on the assumption that phenomena of the natural universe are reliable and predictable. Third, the system controls itself through feedback.

Finally, the human workers do not work. They program. They make decisions based on judgement within the range of patterns the system is designed to handle. They may be almost totally unskilled – as is the user of the telephone. Or they may be exceedingly highly skilled, like the people who design microcircuits on automated equipment such as computers, to be produced by totally automated equipment. But whether skilled or unskilled, the workers are discriminating. Their tool is judgement rather than manual or even conceptual skill.

Whenever mechanization reaches the point where the worker is engineered to be a machine part, we can automate. We can design a machine to do machine's work. This may not, in a given case, be desirable or economical. We may not even have the technology as yet to do it, but it is always possible. It is not necessarily the best alternative to re-engineering mechanization to make it serve working as well as work, but it is always an alternative that should be taken seriously.

Automation is not an arrangement of machines. It is not the ultimate in mechanization. It is a basically different concept. It can work perfectly without any machines. The abacus, the manual computer that Japanese and Chinese ten-year-olds use with high speed and accuracy, is, in effect, automation and data processing fully as advanced and as sophisticated as anything the electronic computer does. It does not require machinery and advanced technology, but it embodies the basic concept of automation.

Any work needs its tools. Any work, therefore, needs to be mechanized. 'The workman is only as good as his tools'; but it is also true that the tools work only as well as the workman. In designing tools for work, therefore, the manager has to be conscious of both dimensions, that is, of work and working.

## Beyond manual work

Work analysis, principles of production, controls, and tools have primarily been worked out, for manual work. The question arises whether the same approaches, the same concepts, and the same principles apply to other than manual work.

There is no question of the applicability of the same approaches and the same principles to manual work that is not technically production, that is, to manual work that is not agriculture, mining, or manufacturing, but 'services'. It is also clear that the same approaches, principles, and methods apply, almost without change, to the processing of information, that is, to most clerical work.

Turning out insurance policies, handling orders, billing, key punch operations, and most accounting work are essentially production work. Indeed, most clerical work is mass production – some rigid, some flexible. It requires the same industrial engineering, that is, the same analysis of work, as manual work, the same process of production, the same kinds of control.

Most true service work is not fundamentally different from producing things insofar as the principles of work are concerned. Selling in a retail store is basically flexible mass production. The individual sale varies greatly, but the process varies hardly at all. And it can be organized in standardized parts. It is best organized so as to give the retail clerk a predesigned routine with the appropriate tools but with wide latitude of judgement. Unless, however, the routine has been properly designed and the right tools supplied, even the best judgement on the part of an experienced retail clerk will not produce sales.

What may surprise most people, however, is that we know that the same approaches, principles, and methods also apply to the work of applying and learning known knowledge.

For thousands of years people have been talking about improving teaching – to no avail. It was not until the early years of this century, however, that an educator asked, 'What is the end product ?' Then the answer was obvious. The end product is not teaching. It is, of course, learning. And then the same educator, the Italian physician and teacher Maria Montessori (1870–1952), began to apply systematic analysis of the work and systematic integration of the parts into a process – without, of course, any awareness that this was what she was doing. Montessori's own system is surely not the 'final answer'. But her approaches have provided the foundation for all subsequent work such as that of the Swiss psychologist Jean Piaget, who has studied how children learn, and of the American behaviourists who have studied learning as a dynamic process of continuous work with its own logic and its own controls. In the English 'open classroom' the work of these people has been embodied in a real learning environment. This may be the first major change in education and the first systematic learning work. Its method is specifically the analysis of the work, the integration of the work into a process – a cross between flexible mass production and true process production – the design of the appropriate control system, and the provision of the appropriate tools.

These examples show that the application and learning of knowledge are fundamentally no different from any other work. To be sure, the product is entirely different and so are the materials and the tools. But the process is basically the same. In its application lies one of the greatest managerial opportunities for making work productive.

The most conspicuous area in business in which we need to organize the application and acquisition of already existing knowledge as systematic work is perhaps the development work in industry – that is, the work of converting new knowledge into marketable products or marketable services. The knowledge is already there as a result of research or invention. What is needed now is the application of what we already know. This, by and large, is not yet done systematically. Where development work has been organized according to the methods of work (and again, primarily as flexible mass production), as in some pharmaceutical companies, the results have been impressive. The work goes quickly, is productive, and the developed product or service is likely to be an economic success.

The one area in which it is not yet proven that the systematic methodology of work applies is the generation of new knowledge, invention or research. There is, however, considerable reason to believe that the same methodology should apply at least to substantial parts of the activity.

Edison, perhaps the most productive inventor of the nineteenth century, applied a systematic method to make inventing work productive. He always started out with a clear definition of the product desired. He then broke down the process into consistituent parts and worked out their relationship and sequence. He set specific controls for key points. He laid down the standards, and so on. To be sure, Edison did not take out the 'creative spark'. But he tried, and successfully, to give creativity a solid foundation in system and method. One indication that he may have been on the right path is the large number of his assistants who became successful inventors in their own right, though clearly devoid of outstanding creativity. One of them, Frank J. Sprague (1857–1934), was by all accounts a mere plodder, but his inventions were largely responsible for the electric tramcar.

So far, we have only a few isolated examples – enough to indicate potential but not enough for proof. Clearly, there are limits to methodology – the artist's vision lies well outside its scope (though the artist's work does not). But research, that is, the organized search for new scientific or industrial knowledge, probably falls well within these limitations.

## Summary

Work needs to be controlled in respect to its direction; its quality, the quantities turned out; its standard, and its economy. Control is a tool of the workers and must not be their master or an impediment to working. Control is a principle of economy, and not of morality. Control cannot handle the exception; it can only make sure that the exception does not clog the routine process. Control has to fit the pattern of routine – and there are only three such patterns. Work also needs its appropriate tools, from the plier to the computer print-out. Tools are the bridge between work and working and have to fit both. Tools can be used for mechanization or for automation, each with its own application and requirements. And the systematic management of work – analysis, synthesis into production processes, control and tools – although first developed in respect to manual work, applies to all work: to clerical and services work, to the processing of information, and to the application and learning of known knowledge.

# 17 Worker and Working: Theories and Reality

Since the writings of the human-relations school first came to the notice of managers around World War II, there has been a flood of books, papers, and studies on motivation and achievement, on industrial psychology and industrial sociology, on interpersonal relations at work and on worker satisfaction. Indeed, the literature on managing worker and working, in quantity at least, exceeds the literature in any other management field.

## McGregor's Theory X and Theory Y

The most widely read and most often quoted of these books is probably Douglas McGregor's *The Human Side of Enterprise,* with its two fundamental choices for managing workers, Theory X and Theory Y. McGregor's Theory X – the traditional approach to worker and working – assumes that people are lazy, dislike and shun work, have to be driven, and need both carrot and stick, both reward and threat. It assumes that most people are incapable of taking responsibility for themselves and have to be looked after. By contrast, Theory Y assumes that people have a psychological need to work and want achievement and responsibility. Theory X assumes immaturity. Theory Y assumes that people want to be adults.

McGregor presented these two theories as alternatives and pretended impartiality. Yet no reader ever doubted – or was meant to doubt – that McGregor himself believed wholeheartedly in Theory Y.

There is impressive evidence for Theory Y. On most jobs the workers, even those hostile to boss and organization, want to like their work and look for achievement. In most jobs even the most alienated workers manage to find something that gives them satisfaction.

This was first brought out in the late 1940s, when General Motors conducted a large-scale contest on 'My Job and Why I Like It.' Almost 190,000 workers wrote in and discussed their jobs – by far the largest sample of worker attitudes we have ever obtained. Very few were uncritical. But even fewer found nothing that made them like the job, did not mention some challenge in it, some achievement and satisfaction, some true motivation.

Yet things are far less simple than McGregor's followers would have us believe. In the first place, we have learned that Theory Y is not by itself adequate. Management by Theory Y is not 'permissive'. On the contrary, managing worker and working by putting responsibility on the worker and by aiming at achievement makes exceedingly high demands on both worker and manager, a fact that McGregor noted only somewhat later.

## Maslow's criticism

An ardent enthusiast for Theory Y, the late Abraham H. Maslow, pointed out that the demands are actually very high indeed. Maslow spent one year working closely with a small company in Southern California which at the time tried to practice Theory Y. In the book he wrote on his experience (*Eupsychian Management*), Maslow pointed out that the demand for responsibility and achievement may well exceed what any but the strong and healthy can take. He sharply criticized Theory Y for 'inhumanity' to the weak, the vulnerable, the damaged, who are unable to take on the responsibility and self-discipline which Theory Y demands. Even the strong and healthy, Maslow concluded, need the security of order and direction; and the weak need protection against the burden of responsibility. The world is not, Maslow concluded, peopled by adults. It has its full share of the permanently immature.

Maslow, however, did not conclude that paternalistic oppression is the only way to manage and the only kindness to workers. His conclusion was far more important and far more valid. Maslow – who, until his death a few years later, remained a strong advocate of Theory Y – concluded that it is not enough to remove restraints. One has to *replace* the security of Theory X and the certainty it gives by another but different structure of security and certainty. What commands and penalties do under Theory X must be supplied by other means under Theory Y. Theory Y, in other words, has to go far beyond Theory X. It cannot simply be substituted for it.

This is an important insight. And it is clearly proven by all our experience with Theory Y.

One conclusion from Maslow's work is that Theory Y is not permissive, as so many of its advocates believe. It is not freedom from restraint. It is not indulging the worker, let alone coddling him. It is a stern taskmaster, sterner in many ways than the Theory X which it replaces. It has to achieve what Theory X achieved, and then do a good deal more – or else it will prove too great a burden and will make demands human beings cannot meet.

It has now become clear that Theory X and Theory Y are not, as McGregor maintained, *theories about human nature*. Everybody knows that there are undoubtedly lazy people and there are undoubtedly energetic ones. Far more important, however, is that ordinary, everyday experience teaches us that the same people react quite differently to different circumstances. They may be lazy and resist work to the point of sabotaging it in one situation. They may be motivated to achieve in another one. It is clearly not just human na.ure nor personality structure that is at issue. Or at the very least, there are different human natures which behave differently under different conditions.

Modern American slang talks of being 'turned on' or 'turned

off' by an assignment, a teacher, a job, or a boss. These terms have been criticized as dehumanizing. They refer to people, it is being said, as if they were electrical appliances. But everyday experience shows that this is exactly how a great many people behave. They react rather than act. The motivation, the drive, the impulse lie outside of them.

But this is not compatible with either Theory X or Theory Y. It implies that it is not human nature but the structure of job and work that determines how people will act and what management they will require.

We also now know that individuals can acquire the habit of achievement but can also acquire the habit of defeat. This again is not compatible with either the Theory X or the Theory Y of human nature.

## What is the manager's reality?

The debate over the scientific validity of Theory X versus Theory Y is, therefore, largely a sham battle. The question the manager needs to ask is not 'Which theory of human nature is right?' The question is 'What is the reality of *my* situation and how can I discharge *my* task of managing worker and working in today's situation?'

The basic fact – unpleasant but inescapable – is that the traditional Theory X approach to managing, that is, the carrot-and-stick way, no longer works. In developed countries, it does not work even for manual workers, and nowhere can it work for knowledge workers. The stick is no longer available to the manager, and the carrot is today becoming less and less of an incentive.

The stick of the traditional approach to managing worker and working was hunger and fear. Traditionally, all but a very few in every society barely subsisted. Most lived at the edge of starvation. One bad harvest was enough to force an Indian or Chinese peasant to sell his daughters into prostitution. One bad harvest was enough for him to lose the tiny plot of land that was all that stood between him and beggary. Now, even in only moderately affluent countries, there is an economic floor well above subsistence level, even for the very poor. A worker knows today, in every developed country, that he and his family will not starve if he loses his job. He may have to do without a lot of things he would like to have, but he can survive.

Even where fear exists, it has largely ceased to motivate. Instead of motivation, fear is becoming a demotivator. One reason for this is the spread of education; the other reason is the emergence of the society of organizations. Better education makes people employable. It gives them a wider horizon. Even poorly educated people in today's society now know of opportunities. In a society of organizations it is possible to gain access to a new and different job. Losing one's job is still unpleasant. But it is no longer catastrophic.

Modern behavioural psychology has demonstrated that great fear drives, while remnants of fear, such as exist for most American workers today, cause only resentment and resistance. Fear in all developed countries has lost its coercive power. The lesser fears that still remain do not motivate. They destroy motivation – precisely because they lack full power and full credibility.

### 'Big fear' and 'little fears'

The 'big fear' still motivates where it is truly believable. This is shown by the quite unexpected success which a new approach to 'curing' alcoholism has had. Everybody has 'known' that the true alcoholic cannot stop drinking until he or she is completely down and out, if then. But a good many employers are now finding that a very large percentage of alcoholic workers do indeed stop drinking – permanently – if told flatly that they will otherwise be fired and that potential new employers will be told of their problem, so that they are unlikely to find another job.

But, save in such exceptional cases, the big stick, the horrible fear that drove workers yesterday, is no longer available to today's manager in the developed countries. It is extremely foolish to try to depend on 'little sticks,' that is, on whatever remnants of fear are still available. To be sure, any organization needs disciplinary devices, but their role and purpose are to take care of minor friction. They cannot provide the drive. If misused to drive, disciplinary devices can cause only resentment and resistance. They can only demotivate.

## The overly potent carrot

The carrot of material rewards has not, like the stick of fear, lost its effect. On the contrary, it has become so potent that it must be used with great caution. It has become too potent to be a dependable tool.

The Sunday issue of every newspaper these days contains an article by a learned sociologist or philosopher reporting that people are turning away from material satisfactions. On the front page of the same paper, Sundays *and* weekdays, there is always a story that this or that group of workers – teachers or electricians, newspaper reporters or firemen, salesclerks or stevedores – have presented the biggest wage demand ever or have obtained the biggest wage raise ever.

There is not one shred of evidence for the alleged turning away from material rewards. On the contrary, affluence means that everybody believes that material rewards are and should be within easy reach. Samuel Gompers, (1850–1929), the main founder of the American Federation of Labor and its head until his death, used to define the aims of a union in one word: 'more'. He would surely have to change this today to 'much more'. Antimaterialism is a myth, no matter how much it is extolled. So far, at least, the reality is tremendous and there are steadily rising expectations for more goods and services.

The demands for much more is eventually going to run up against the limitations of the earth's resources and the need to preserve the environment. At least for the foreseeable future, this will mean an even faster shift from goods to services as carriers of satisfaction, and with it, from material-intensive to labour-intensive (and especially knowledge-labour-intensive) wants and purchases. And rising raw-material prices and ecological costs will add fuel to the fire of demands for more, much more, monetary rewards.

It is precisely the rising level of material expectations that makes the carrot of material rewards less and less effective as a motivating force and as a managerial tool.

The size of the raise that is capable of motivating people to work has to become larger. As people get more they do not become satisfied with a little more, let alone with less. They expect much more. This is, of course, one of the major causes of the relentless inflationary pressures that besiege every major economy today. Whereas a 5 per cent wage boost was a major satisfaction a few years ago, the teamsters – or the teachers or the physicians – now demand 40 per cent and expect 20 per cent.

This may be a manifestation of Maslow's rule that the closer a need comes to being satisfied, the larger the increase required to produce the same satisfaction. But the demand for more and much more of material satisfactions has also been accompanied by a change in values that does not fit Maslow's scheme at all. Economic incentives are becoming rights rather than rewards. Merit raises are always introduced as rewards for exceptional performance. In no time at all they become a right. To deny a merit raise or to grant only a small one becomes punishment.

Whatever the explanation, the result of the increasing demand for material rewards is rapidly destroying their usefulness as incentives and managerial tools. The manager must try to de-emphasize the role of material rewards rather than use them as a carrot. If only very large – and steadily larger – raises serve as incentives, then using material incentives becomes self-defeating. The expected result in terms of motivation may be obtained, but the cost will be so high that it exceeds the benefits. The cost will eat up the additional productivity. This has already happened in large measure with respect to share options or extra compensation plans for managers as well as with respect to raises and bonuses for other classes of workers.

## The toxic side effects of the carrot

This also means that the social side effects of the carrot are reaching toxic proportions. A potent medicine always has side effects, and the larger the dosage, the greater the side effects.

Material incentives and rewards are very strong medicine indeed. They therefore are bound to have side effects, which become more pronounced and more dangerous as the dosage required for effectiveness increases. In particular (as noted in Chapter 14) the more total income goes up, the more powerful does dissatisfaction over pay differences become. As all our studies show – beginning with the GM contest 'My Job' in the late 1940s – there is no more effective bar to motivation, than dissatisfaction over one's own pay compared to that of one's peers. Once people's incomes rise above the subsistence level, dissatisfaction with relative incomes is a far more powerful sentiment than dissatisfaction with one's absolute income. The 'sense of injustice,' as Edmond Cahn, an American legal philosopher, convincingly argued, is deeply ingrained in human beings. Nothing is as likely to offend the sense of injustice as dissatisfaction with relative economic rewards in an organization. An organization is a redistributive economy (see Chapter 14); relative economic rewards are therefore power and status decisions reflecting the *worth* of a person or a group.

Reliance on the carrot of economic rewards therefore runs the risk of alienating both the recipient and all others. It runs the risk of dividing the group against itself while uniting it against the employing institution and its management.

Clearly no deemphasis of material rewards is likely. Managers face instead the tremendous challenge of finding some means to relate the growing emphasis on 'much more' to economic reality, that is, to productivity and profitability. Material rewards are too potent to be relied on as the main positive motivator. They can only produce growing inflationary pressure – and growing dissatisfaction.

The limitations of the effectiveness of carrot and stick apply with particular force to two groups in the work force: the new breed of manual workers and knowledge workers.

In managing manual workers, the manager in the developed country more and more has to deal with workers who start out as 'losers', feel rejected, feel already defeated. These are people who have been driven all their lives and yet have not achieved. But losers always learn one thing to perfection: resistance against being driven. They may not be able to achieve, but they know how to sabotage.

Driving the new breed of manual workers therefore will not work. Hunger and fear no longer dominate them as they did their grandparents. But their very failure has made them impervious to pressures.

The knowledge worker will not produce if managed under Theory X. The knowledge worker has to be self-directed and has to take responsibility.

Fear is altogether incompatible with the production of knowledge. It may produce efforts and anxieties, but it will not produce results. And fear inhibits learning, a basic finding of modern behavioural psychology. Rewards will produce learning. In anything that has to do with knowledge, fear will produce only resistance.


## Manager or master

Theory X assumes a 'master'. But in a society of organizations there are no masters. The manager is not a master. He is a superior, but he is a fellow employee. For the first time in history there is a society which lacks masters.

The manager, not being a master, lacks both the master's authority and the master's power. The master's power is independent of the support he receives, either from his servants or from society around him. One can kill a master, but one cannot oust him. But, as the 1960s amply showed, in the case of countless university presidents, for example, even the chief executive of an organization can be ousted, precisely because he is a fellow employee. The authority he exercises is not his own.

In terms of the ancient law of master and servant, the chief executive officer of the largest corporation is a fellow servant. Others may be subordinate in rank, but they are equal in law. They are not the chief executive's servants, they are his fellow workers.

This is much more than a play on words. It means that neither stick nor carrot will actually work if used by a manager, no matter how well they used to work for the master of old.

## Can we replace carrot and stick?

Can we replace the carrot of monetary rewards and the stick of fear with a new carrot and a new stick appropriate to the new managerial reality?

Managers are not the only ones asking this question. The unions are perhaps even more eager to keep the Theory X structure. The unions, after all, have a stake in the master-servant relationship of Theory X. If there were no master, what would the union's role be? Labour leaders derive their sense of mission from opposing Theory X. They know how to behave under it, and have its rhetoric down pat.

When the younger workers in some General Motors plants began to talk about humanizing the assembly line, the greatest resistance did not come from General Motors management. It came from the United Automobile Workers' leadership, which insisted on talking instead about money, pensions, hours off, coffee breaks – and so on. The UAW leaders, in other words, insisted, against their own members, on maintaining and even strengthening a Theory X management on the part of the company.

To look for a new set of drives to take the place of the old carrot and stick seems not only rational but tempting. Such replacement drives are indeed being offered managers in the form of a new 'enlightened psychological despotism,' a modern tyranny.

Most of the recent writers on industrial psychology profess allegiance to Theory Y. They use terms like 'self-fulfilment', 'creativity' and 'the whole person.' But what they mean is control through psychological manipulation. They are led to this by their basic assumptions, which are precisely the Theory X assumptions: human beings are weak, sick, and incapable of looking after themselves. They are full of fears, anxieties, neuroses, inhibitions. Essentially they do not want to achieve but want to fail. They therefore want to be controlled. Indeed, for their own good they need to be controlled – not by fear of hunger and in-centive of material rewards but through a fear of psychological alienation and through the incentive of 'psychological security'.

I know that I am oversimplifying. I know that I am lumping under one heading half a dozen different approaches. But they all share the same basic assumptions, those of Theory X, and they all lead to the same conclusions. Psychological control by the superior, the manager, is possible; and psychological control by the superior, the manager, is 'unselfish' and in the worker's own interest. By becoming his or her workers' psychological ser-vant, however, the manager retains control as their 'boss'.

This may be 'enlightened' compared to the old carrot-and-stick, but it is still despotism. Under this new psychological ap-proach, persuasion replaces command. Those unconvinced by the persuasion would presumably be deemed sick, immature, or in need of psychotherapy to become adjusted. Psychological ma-nipulation replaces the carrot of financial rewards; and playing on individual fears, anxieties, and personality needs replaces the old fear of being punished or of losing one's job.

Psychological despotism, whether enlightened or not, is gross misuse of psychology. The main purpose of psychology is to ac-quire insight into, and mastery of, oneself. What we now call the behavioural sciences were originally called the moral sciences, and 'Know thyself' was their main precept. Using psychology to control, dominate, and manipulate others is self-destructive ab-use of knowledge. It is also a particularly repugnant form of ty-ranny. The master of old was content to control the slave's body.

Here we are concerned, however, neither with the proper use of psychology nor with morality. But can the Theory X structure be maintained through psychological despotism? Can psycho-logical control work?

Psychological despotism should have tremendous attraction for managers. It promises them that they can continue to behave as they have always done. All they need is to acquire a new vocab-ulary. It flatters them. And yet managers, while avidly reading the psychology books and attending psychological workshops, are shying away from trying the new psychological Theory X.

In being leery, managers show sound instincts. Psychological despotism cannot work any more than enlightened despotism worked in the political sphere two hundred years ago – and for the same reason. *It requires universal genius on the part of the ruler.* Managers, if one listens to the psychologists, will have to have insight into all kinds of people. They will have to be in command of all kinds of psychological techniques. They will have to understand an infinity of individual personality structures, individual psychological needs, and individual psychological problems. They will, in other words, have to be all-knowing. But most managers find it hard enough to know all they need to know about their own immediate area of expertise, be it heat-treating or cost accounting or scheduling.

Managers should indeed know more about human beings. They should at least know that human beings behave like human beings, and what that implies. Above all, like most of us, managers need to know much more about themselves than they do. And yet, any manager, no matter how many psychology seminars he or she attended, who attempts to put psychological despotism into practice will very rapidly become its first casualty. Immediate blunders will impair performance.

The work relationship has to be based on mutual respect. Psychological despotism is basically contemptuous – far more contemptuous than the traditional Theory X. It does not assume that people are lazy and resist work, but it assumes that the manager is strong while everybody else is weak. It assumes that the manager knows while everybody else is ignorant. It assumes that the manager is right, whereas everybody else is stupid. These are the assumptions of foolish arrogance.

Above all, the manager-psychologist will undermine his or her own authority. There is, to be sure, need for psychological insight, help, counsel. There is need for the healer of souls and the comforter of the afflicted. But the relationship of healer and patient and that of superior to subordinate are different relationships and mutually exclusive. Each has its own integrity. The integrity of the healer is subordination to the patient's welfare. The integrity of the manager is subordination to the requirements of the common task. In both relationships there is need for authority; but each has a different ground of authority. A manager who pretends that the personal needs of the subordinate for affection, for example, rather than the objective needs of the task, determine what should be done, would not only be a poor manager; no one would – or should – believe him. All he does is to destroy the integrity of the relationship and with it the respect for his or her person and function.

But what then *can* work?

It is not simply McGregor's Theory Y. Managers must indeed assume with Theory Y that there are at least some people in the work force who want to achieve. Otherwise there is little hope. Fortunately the evidence strongly supports this assumption. Managers must further accept it as their job to make worker and working achieving. They must be willing, as a result, to accept high demands on themselves, their seriousness, and their competence. But managers cannot assume, as Theory Y does, that people will work to achieve if only they are given the opportunity to do so. More is needed – much more – to make even the strong and healthy accept the burden of responsibility. The structure we need cannot depend on driving the worker; neither carrot nor stick is dependable any more. But the structure must also provide substitutes for Theory X's security of command, of knowing where one stands, and of being looked after.

## Summary

Whether 'Theory X' or 'Theory Y' – the two most widely discussed theories of the behaviour of people at work – is valid, the manager can no longer rely on Theory X, that is on the stick of fear or the carrot of material incentives. In particular, neither will work if applied to the new breed of young manual workers or to knowledge workers. But Theory Y also has severe limitations and drawbacks. How can we then replace the old Theory X management? Psychological manipulation – that is, Theory X masquerading as Theory Y – will not work. But what does?

# 18 From Personnel Management to the Leadership of People

What does the worker – unskilled or skilled, manual, clerical, or knowledge worker – *need* to be able to take on the burden of responsibility? What tools are needed? What incentives? What security? And what do manager and enterprise have to do to be able to ask workers to take responsibility and to expect them to respond to this demand?

The focus has to be on the job. The job has to make achievement possible. The job is not everything; but it comes first. If other aspects of working are unsatisfactory, they can spoil even the most achieving job – just as a poor sauce can spoil the taste even of the best meat. But if the job itself is not achieving, nothing else will provide achievement.

To enable workers to achieve, they must therefore first be able to take responsibility for their jobs. This requires: (1) productive work; (2) feedback information; and (3) continuous learning.

It is foolish to expect a job to provide achievement when the work has not been studied, the process has not been synthesized, the standards and controls have not been thought through, and the physical information tools have not been designed. It is also managerial incompetence.

## The fallacy of creativity

There is a centuries-old – and continually revived – slogan of the individual's creativity: 'Free people from restraint and they will come up with far better, far more advanced, far more productive answers than the experts.' But there is no evidence to support this belief. Everything we know indicates that creativity can become effective only if the basic tools are given. Everything we know also indicates that the proper structure of work – of any work – is not intuitively obvious.

People have shovelled sand for untold centuries. Most of the time, one can assume, nobody told them how to do it. If making work productive depended on the creativity of people, they would undoubtedly have found the best way of doing the job before the dawn of history. Yet when Taylor first looked at the job in 1885, he found that everything was wrong. The size and shape of the shovel were unsuited to the job. The length of the handle was wrong. The amount of sand the shoveller lifted in one operation was the wrong amount, was indeed the amount most calculated to tire him and do him physical harm. The containers were the wrong shape, the wrong size, and in the wrong position, and so on. Human intuition and creativity had produced an operation that was both backbreaking and inefficient. The process was improved by several orders of magnitude by being analysed and then synthesized again into a single productive operation. And exactly the same total misdesign of work and process after two thousand years of 'creativity' was found when physicians around 1840 first systematically analysed the process of medical diagnosis.

## Feedback information for self-control

The second prerequisite for worker responsibility is feedback information on his own performance. Responsibility requires self-control. That in turn requires continuous information on performance against standards.

There has been a great deal of interest lately in the application of 'behaviour modification' to work. In particular there has been great interest in the approach worked out by a major air freight forwarder, Emery Air Freight, which found out that workers on all levels will manage their own performance if only they are being informed immediately what their performance actually is. Actually we have known this for many years.

The information the worker needs must satisfy the requirements of effective feedback information. It must be timely. It must be relevant. It must be operational. It must focus on his job. Above all, it must be *his* tool. Its purpose must be self-control rather than control of others, let alone manipulation.

The real strength of feedback information – and the major re-inforcer – is clearly that the information is the tool of the worker for measuring and directing himself. The worker does not need praise or reproach to *know* how he is doing. He knows.

## Continuous learning

The third requirement for achievement in work and for a responsible worker is continuous learning.

Continuous learning does not replace training for new skills. It has different aims and satisfies different needs. Above all, it satisfies the need of the employee to contribute what she herself has learned to the improvement of her own performance, to the improvement of her fellow worker's performance, and to a better, more effective, but also more rational way of working.

It is also the one way to come to grips with two basic problems: the resistance of workers to innovation, and the danger that workers will become 'obsolete'.

Continuous learning need not be organized as a formal session, but it always needs to be organized. There is need for the continuing challenge to the worker: 'What have you learned that can make your job and the job of all of us more productive, more performing, and more achieving? What do you need by way of knowledge, by way of tools, by way of information? And how do we best prepare ourselves for new needs, new methods, new performance capacities?'

## Planning and doing

These three prerequisites, (1) productive work, (2) feedback information, and (3) continuous learning, are, so to speak, the planning for worker responsibility for job, work group, and output. They are therefore management responsibilities and management tasks. But they are not 'management prerogatives,' that is, things management does alone, by itself, and unilaterally. Management does indeed have to do the analytical work and make the decisions. But in all these areas the workers themselves, from the beginning, need to be integrated as responsible partners into the planning process. From the beginning they should share in thinking through work and process, tools and information. Their knowledge, their experience, their needs are resources to the planning process. The workers need to be participants in it. Every attempt should be made to make accessible to the workers the necessary knowledge. They need not become industrial engineers or process designers, but the fundamentals of industrial engineering and their application to one's own job and work can be grasped by almost anyone without great difficulty.

Worker *responsibility* for job, work groups, and output cannot be expected, let alone demanded, until the foundations of productive work, feedback information, and continuous learning have been established. Worker *participation* in designing these foundations should be brought into play from the very beginning.

Creativity, if we mean by that undirected, unstructured, untutored, and uncontrolled guessing, is not likely to produce results. But a system that does not tap and put to use the knowledge, experience, resources, and imagination of the people who have to live with the system and make it work is just as unlikely to be effective.

Planning and doing are separate activities, like reading and writing, and require different methods and different approaches. But planner and doer, like reader and writer, need to be united in the same person. They cannot be entirely separate – or the planning will cease to be effective and will indeed become a threat to performance.

The planner is needed to supply the doer with direction and measurement, with the tools of analysis and synthesis, with methodology, and with standards. He is needed also to make sure that the planning of one group is compatible with the planning of the others. But in turn, the planner needs the doer as resource and as feedback control. And unless the planner knows what the doer does and needs, the plan, while theoretically perfect, may never be put into effect. Conversely, unless the doer understands what the planner tries to accomplish, the doer will not perform or will try to resist performance specifications that seem unreasonable, arbitrary, or just plain silly.

But still, the foundations for worker responsibility are planning and are therefore managerial responsibilities.

## The need for clear authority

One more thing is needed to make responsibility acceptable to the workers on all levels: they need to have the security of a clear authority structure. They have to know what areas and decisions are beyond their power and therefore reserved for a different or a higher authority. They have to know where to go for a decision. They have to know whose decision to listen to, and whose order, no matter how peremptory, to disregard as coming from an 'unauthorized' source, that is from someone who has no right to give orders to this or that worker in this or that area.

Also, every organization stands under the threat of the 'common peril'. There is always the chance of an emergency situation which has not been anticipated and for which there are no rules. The common peril may be physical – in business it will more often be economic. Whatever its nature, *one* person has to make the decision in such a situation, and fast, or everybody is endangered. Who this individual is has to be known in advance, or there is chaos. And this leader has to be able to say, 'This needs to be done; *you* do it; *this* way.' The survival of the group depends on his or her unquestioned authority. Without it no one in the group can feel secure.

## Responsibility for job and work groups

The layout of individual jobs to do the work and to meet its standards are the responsibility of workers and work group. So are the design, structure, and relationship of the work group in which these jobs are integrated into a community. The workers may need professional help in this. They may need knowledge, experience, and teaching from their supervisor. They may need advice and service from the industrial engineer and from many other technicians and professionals. Management must retain a veto power and will often exercise it. But the responsibility for job design and work-group design belongs to those who are responsible for output and performance. And that is the worker and the work group.

Worker responsibility for job and group will vary greatly with the kind of work to be done, with the educational skill and knowledge level of the work force, and with cultures and traditions. It will certainly look very different when the workers are research scientists rather than hard-core unemployables from the inner-city ghetto.

But the principles are the same: the worker and the work group are responsible for their own jobs and for the relationships between individual jobs. They are responsible for thinking through *how* the work is to be done. They are responsible for meeting performance goals and for quality as well as for quantity. And they are responsible for improving work, job, tools and processes, and their own skills.

The 'right' structure for the work group is impossible to prescribe from the outside. Work-group structure is complex even if the group is composed of a fairly small number of fairly simple elements – the workers and their individual jobs. It resembles a kaleidoscope. Fairly small shifts drastically change the pattern.

In such a situation the only way to arrive at the right, the best, solution is trial. Outsiders, the industrial engineers, for example, can help. But they cannot analytically arrive at the answer. The group itself, however, usually arrives at a right answer fairly fast and without much trouble. It works things out.

## Assembly line and job enrichment

Pressure for changes in the traditional ways of managing worker and working has been building up these last decades as the 'new breed' has come into the work force and as the old motivating drives of hunger and fear have rapidly lost their power. The pressure has been greatest on the traditional assembly line of manufacturing industry. The conventional view has always been that the assembly line is, by its very nature, incapable of being run any other way than from the top and by command.

Our World War II experience in defence production disproved this long ago. Nothing that is now being proposed goes quite as far in demanding responsibility from the worker as some of the US defence plants of World War II. In one such plant teams of workers assembled highly complex aircraft engines. Each team divided the work differently, but each team outperformed the standards expected of them. There the worker had to take responsibility because of the shortage of industrial engineers, supervisors, and managers.

The lessons of this example are being rediscovered today by one of the most rigid and highly engineered of production processes, the automobile assembly line.

In the United States, Chrysler is experimenting with responsibility on the part of the workers for assembly line operations. In a Chrysler plant in Detroit, employees were actually asked to re-evaluate the entire manufacturing operation. As a result of their comments, the whole plant was reorganized, resulting in higher output with fewer workers.

The most systematic approaches to worker responsibility to automobile assembly line jobs are those taken by the two Swedish automobile makers, Saab and Volvo, both acting under the pressure of severe labour shortages.

In one Swedish plant, one work group takes responsibility for the assembly of the total car. The output standard, that is, the number of cars per hour, and the quality standard are set by the plant. The process has been worked out, but the structure of jobs, their scope, their relationship, and the organization of the work group are worked out by the workers themselves with their supervisors and the industrial engineer.

Outside of the assembly line there is also growing demand for 'job enrichment'. In job enrichment the expert, often an industrial engineer, defines the 'modules' of the work, the individual operations that have to be performed. He or she establishes the standards and analyses the information the worker needs. But then the worker designs his or her own job, that is, the number of modules that constitute 'my' job, their sequence, speed, rhythm. The result is higher output, better quality, and a sharp drop in employee turnover.

IBM and a good many Japanese companies have been practicing job enrichment for decades. And the way claims settlement has been done for decades in some European and Japanese insurance companies (see Chapter 16) is job enrichment pure and simple. We have *known* what to do for a very long time. That it is now being heralded as a discovery is somewhat ironic – but harmless as long as the changes are being made.

What is not so harmless is the belief that job enrichment is *the* answer. It is only a first step. IBM and the Japanese mobilized the energies of the work *group*. Job enrichment confines the workers' responsibility to their own individual jobs. But they also should be expected to assume responsibility for the work group, its relationship in and through the work process, its structure and its cohesion.

## Worker responsibility and the 'new breeds'

Worker responsibility for job and work group is important for all kinds of workers in today's organizations. It is fundamental to a civilization in which three out of every four people at work are employees in organizations.

But worker responsibility is particularly important for three groups of workers – though for different reasons.

The first of these groups is the new breed of young manual workers. These are men and women who arrive at work already rejected, already losers. Yet, though they are the rejects of the educational system, they have had long years of schooling and have, by any historical standard, a high degree of education. They are not the wretched illiterates of the industrial slums of 1850. Their formal knowledge may be limited, but their horizon is wide – if only because of TV. And they are, by and large, not motivated by carrot and stick. They are resentful – in many cases with good reason – because the lack of scholastic success that has condemned them to inferior status does not appear to them a genuine, a true, a valid criterion. At the same time, they have doubts about their own ability to perform and to achieve, about their own dignity. These men and women need achievement to overcome their habit of defeat. Otherwise, they will forever be in a state of smouldering resentment and rebellion. They need responsibility to overcome their feelings of inferiority. They need a challenge in which they can succeed. They are suspicious – every earlier contact with authority has conditioned them to be suspicious. Yet they need self-assurance and security, more than any other group in the work force.

This is, above all, the lesson of the widely publicized revolt of General Motors workers in the 1960s, at the then new Lordstown assembly plant in Ohio. That these young men resented the imposition of the rigid General Motors assembly line discipline is not surprising and is nothing new. At every major assembly plant General Motors had built during the last thirty years, the workers at first reacted the same way. The newspaper account of Lordstown read exactly like the interviews with, and reports on, workers of the big assembly plant in New England which General Motors built in the late 1940s.*

The real difference – and it is an important one – is that the young white and black workers at Lordstown felt almost to a man that they could have done a better job designing their own work and the assembly line than the General Motors industrial engineers did. The Lordstown experience contrasts sharply with the experience in another nearby assembly plant. There workers and foremen participated in the planning and design of work and eventually took responsibility for making the new plant productive even beyond the Lordstown standard.

## The 'pre-industrials'

The second group, an entirely different one whatever its outward similarity, is the large number of recent immigrants from pre-industrial civilizations into modern city and modern organiza-

* See Charles R. Walker and Robert H. Guest, *The Man on the Assembly Line* (Harvard University Press, 1952).

tion: the Turks and other guest workers in Germany, the Sicilians in Torino, Italy, the blacks in the United States, the sharecroppers from the drought-ridden sugar plantations of Brazil's Northeast in Sao Paulo, and Indians from the *pueblo* in Mexico City.

In many ways these workers need paternalism. They need to be looked after. They are not at home in modern society; they are frightened by it, lost in it. But at the same time, they need to be integrated into modern society for their own sake as well as for that of the society to which they move. Otherwise they will become a disturbing and unsettled influence. Again, what is needed is to cultivate in these workers the habit of responsibility and the taste of achievement.

While Fiat in Turin has been largely unable to integrate Sicilian immigrants and has at times been all but paralysed by their despair, anger, and resistance, Olivetti, in nearby Ivrea, has apparently had little trouble with the same Sicilian immigrants. Why this difference? Olivetti went through pretty rough times in the 1960s, after the death of its founder, when the very survival of the company was in jeopardy. At the same time Fiat was enjoying a boom with steadily rising wages and high employment security. Both companies are highly paternalistic. The difference in the two companies' ability to assimilate the Sicilians apparently lies in one factor: at Olivetti there is a long tradition of worker responsibility for job and work group.

## The knowledge worker

Finally there are the knowledge workers, and especially, the advanced knowledge workers. They have to be 'knowledge professionals'. This means that no one can motivate them. They must motivate themselves. No one can direct them. They have to direct themselves. Above all, no one can supervise them. They are the guardians of their own standards, performance, and objectives. They can be productive only if they are responsible for their own job.

## Saving the supervisor

To make the worker responsible for his job and for that of the work group is also the best – and may be the only – way to restore the supervisor to health and function.

For a half century or more first-line supervisors, especially those in manufacturing and clerical work, have seen their roles shrinking in status, in importance, and in esteem. Where a supervisor was 'management' to the employee only half a century ago, he or she has now, by and large, become a buffer between management, union, and workers. And like all buffers, the supervisor's main function is to take the blows.

Indeed, in the modern industrial plant the supervisors are increasingly becoming the 'enemy'. They are separated from those they supervise by an ever-higher wall of resentment, suspicion, and hostility. At the same time, they are separated from management by a lack of technical and managerial knowledge. The position of the supervisors of knowledge workers is just as isolated. Subordinates consider them their spokesman and expect them to protect them and their knowledge area against managerial demands and managerial ignorance. Management, on the other hand, expects the supervisor to integrate the knowledge and expertise of the people in their area with the mission, purpose, and objectives of the institution. Increasingly they find themselves disavowed by both, by subordinates because they are no longer truly scientists or experts but have 'sold out' to management; and by management because they are parochial, departmentalized, and one-sided.

No organization can function well if its supervisory force does not function. Supervisors are, so to speak, connective tissues of an organization. Without them, the parts will not work together as a unit. It is the supervisor's job to be in the middle. Hence he or she must have responsibility, function, and respect in both relationships, upwards to management and downwards to the work group.

The proper role of the supervisor is not to be a cop. It is to be an 'assistant' to the work group and to management – which is

what IBM calls the supervisor – and to provide to both knowledge, information, placing, training, teaching, standard-setting
and guiding. It is not an easy role but it is a workable one. This
role no longer imposes a conflict of loyalties for the supervisor between the work group and management. As the resource to the
achieving worker and work group, the supervisor can again become whole. He or she can serve both the needs of the enterprise
for performance and the personal needs of workers for achievement.

## Plant and office as communities

Plant and office are more than just geographic locations. They
are communities. We speak of the prevailing atmosphere of an
office or of a mill. We study their 'culture'. We speak of 'patterns'
of 'formal' or 'informal' organization, of prevailing 'values', of
'career ladders'. And though there are great differences in degree between the most paternalistic and the most impersonal
plant and office, all are expected to discharge community functions. There is, in other words, a work community.

For workers to be achieving, they must take substantial responsibility for governing the work community. Many decisions
related to the work community have no bearing on the purpose
or performance of the whole organization. They are not business
decisions. They are social decisions, decisions regarding the
affairs of the work community. These decisions should be decentralized. They need to be made in the work community – just
as many business decisions should be decentralized, made by the
operating management to which they apply.

It is a law of governance that it restrict itself to the *necessary*
decisions. Any governing body will be the more effective and
more powerful, the more it refuses to make decisions it does not
have to make. If management makes work-community decisions,
it loads itself down with matters that appear petty to management, though they are of great importance to the work community itself. There are decisions on the cafeteria, on vacation
schedules, on running recreational activities, on safety, on bene-

fit plans, and so on. In the typical enterprise, management people deal with these things – often poorly and always at too great a cost.

## The need for leadership opportunities

At the same time, these areas offer major opportunities for leadership, for responsibility, for recognition, and for learning. The workers who head these activities are important people in the work community. The people making the decisions in these areas are also forced to learn what managing is and what managerial responsibility means. They learn that choices have to be made, priorities have to be set, and that the infinite number of things it would be nice to have must be fitted to the available resources.

Without opportunities for leadership in the work community, the abilities, energies, and ambitions within the work force may be directed against management and the work community. They will be negative, destructive, demagogic. The leader will be the one who can make the most trouble for the bosses rather than the one who can perform the best for the plant community. Responsibility is not by itself a guarantee of performance. But lack of responsibility breeds the demagogue.

## Job security and income stability

Living in fear of loss of job and income is incompatible with taking responsibility for job and work group, for output and performance. That the fear is becoming less pervasive – to the point where it no longer acts as a spur – makes it all the more destructive where it is a factor. It contrasts so sharply with the standard of living and the standard of security to which most workers in a developed society have become accustomed.

To accept the burden of responsibility, workers – the unskilled as well as the skilled worker, and the manual as well as the knowledge worker – need a fair measure of security of job and income. At the same time, however, they need mobility.

The resistance of workers on all levels against higher productivity and against innovation like that at Lordstown is not based solely on the fear of working oneself out of one's own job. Equally important is the fear that the achieving worker will work other workers out of their jobs. As a result, group pressure is exerted against the worker who, by wanting to achieve, becomes a threat to the security of his fellow workers.

Resistance to change and resistance to innovation are not inherent in human nature. Wherever a business has provided real job and income security, resistance to change or to innovation has disappeared.

In the West a *formal* guarantee of jobs and incomes is the exception rather than the rule – though the exceptions are far more numerous than most people (and practically all union leaders) believe. But job security and income assurance have increasingly been built piecemeal into the system.

The first step was unemployment compensation. On top of this, individual companies and individual industries, with or without union contracts, have developed other provisions: supplemental unemployment compensation; severance pay; and seniority rules in layoffs which give older employees effective job security. As a result, labour costs have become more and more inflexible.

## Mobility

There is a belief that American workers, and especially knowledge people, change jobs all the time. But even with respect to managers and professionals – the most mobile groups – this is largely myth.

In the large – and in most small – American companies actual turnover is quite low among managers and professionals. There is considerable turnover in the entrance jobs, that is, in the first three to five years of workers' employment, and in top management jobs. In between, though – among older workers in lower and middle management, and among professional and technical knowledge workers – job change is the exception rather than the rule. In every large American company the great majority of the middle rank positions are filled with people who have changed jobs at most once, and that within a few years after their graduation from college. Their first job change, made when they were still quite young, is usually their last one. After that they may move geographically from one location of the company to another, but they very rarely change employers.

Job stability is also the rule rather than the exception for blue-collar workers in the US. A good indication of this is the experience of the private pension plans in American industry which cover virtually all large and medium-sized enterprises (and probably a majority of small businesses as well). These plans were under sharp attack a few years ago because 'only seventy per cent of the employees actually receive a pension.' The problem arises because in most US pension plans eligibility before 1974 was conditional upon working for the same employer 25 to 30 years. (This is still largely true for the pensions plans of state and city governments. But since 1974, the plans of private businesses have to provide a guaranteed pension after ten years of employment or less.) What this means then is that seventy per cent of the work force have what is in effect lifetime employment; they have spent 25 to 30 years with the same employer.

## Needed: organized placement

Every business – and the economy as a whole – needs a fair degree of labour-cost flexibility. Making job security and employment stability consistent with some flexibility in labour cost requires organized placement activity. The cost of placement is almost insignificant. But without it, labour costs may be 'frozen'. A business may not be able to reduce employment. Or if it does, the cost in severance and other benefits may almost eat up any saving in labour costs. There will still be fear and insecurity unless the employer takes active responsibility, one way or another, for placing employees who have to be let go. Wherever an employer has accepted the commitment to find a job for displaced workers, the result has been psychological security.

In a major depression, placing such workers might be difficult or almost impossible. But the basic problem in job and income security is not general catastrophe. It is the impact on the individual of minor changes, technological advances that obsolete one company, one industry, or one craft; improvements in productivity which lead to a cutting back of the labour force required; minor shifts in economic demands; in transportation economics, in product line, or in process. Statistically these are marginal events. For the individual they are as rare, yet as devastating, as being struck by lightning.

Giving workers a feeling of job security is not a problem of money. The money is already being spent to provide job security and income stability. The need now is, first to make clear the security that exists. And second the mobility that economy, enterprise, and worker all require needs to be organized. What is needed, in other words, is a little intelligence and some hard work.

## Profits, productivity, and benefits

The job as a living is the worker's first concern with respect to the economic dimension of working. But there is also the apparent conflict between wage fund and capital fund, that is, between the worker's economic interest in wage and salary and the need of economy and enterprise (and ultimately of workers) for profits and productivity.

In the United States, at least, this conflict should by now be a thing of the past, for increasingly the American worker is the beneficiary of both the wage fund and the capital fund.

Increasingly American industry – at least the large and middle-sized corporations – is being 'owned' for the employee's benefit by the pension funds as trustees of the employees. By 1990 – or at the latest by the year 2000 – the pension funds and the mutual funds (and most shareholders in mutual funds are low and middle-income employees) will own more than two-thirds of the large and medium-sized businesses of America. Already by now, that is in the late 1970s, these trustees of the workers have become the largest single group of shareholders and owners in the

American economy. They are the only true 'capitalists' around.

Yet the fact that worker and shareowner are becoming one and the same seems to have very little impact, if any, on the workers' hostility towards profit. Even total worker ownership and the elimination of all outside owners does not have much impact, it seems. ·

The worker-owner who resists profits and rejects the needs of the capital fund is, however, not altogether irrational. The fact is that profit is simply too small in relation to wage and salary to tilt the balance for the worker-owner (see Chapter 15).

A second – but not secondary – explanation is that plans which pay out profit shares or productivity shares as *income*, are fairweather plans. They work well as long as profits and productivity go up. They create resentment and frustration the moment profit shares and productivity bonuses no longer go up but go down.

It is a basic fallacy to treat profit as income. Profit is capital fund, that is, savings. Only if profit is used to build a capital fund for the worker can it have meaning. Only then can the function of profit even be understood.

Profitability and the workers' interests may coincide where benefits are linked to profitability. One such benefit might be a retirement provision. If spread over enough years and over a large enough group, an adequate retirement income can be financed by a fairly low annual payment per individual covered. Another area is health care. The individual economic risk goes beyond anything even the rich can carry. But because statistically few require large medical payments in any one year, collective coverage is reasonably cheap. Finally, there is job and income security, again a risk of catastrophe for the individual, but on a probability basis, a fairly low group risk.

These are benefits which can be provided for out of fluctuating profits. In any one year the contribution to a retirement fund, a health plan, or a job and income maintenance fund can fluctuate. What matters is that the contribution averages out to an adequate level over a three to five-year period. That is, low contributions in one year must be compensated for by higher contributions in another, more profitable year.

## What benefits should be

Almost no benefit plan anywhere in the world was planned, designed, thought through. Practically all of them just grew. Indeed, Americans still call them 'fringes' – yet benefits are more than a third of the *total* labour cost of American business, and are rapidly going up (largely because of pension plans) towards forty per cent of total labour costs – which is somewhat wide for a 'fringe'. In Europe and Japan, this fringe is even wider.

In most businesses benefits are the third largest cost next to wages and materials. Yet while individual benefit programmes, such as the retirement plan or the health-care plan, are managed, the benefit system is essentially unmanaged. To leave so large a cost centre unmanaged is poor management. And far more is at stake in benefits than cost. It is high time that management assumes true managerial responsibility for benefits.

We can specify what benefits should be and should do.

1 Benefits need to be structured to give the beneficiary, the worker, the most for the money.

A good example of what not to do is America's most widely used health insurance plan, the nonprofit Blue Cross plan which is particularly popular with unions. Blue Cross health coverage has become increasingly expensive. Yet until recently it did not provide for payment of medical and hospital bills when the worker needs it the most, that is, when he is out of work. Blue Cross pays full expenses for the minor illnesses of the family while the breadwinner is employed – which is a major reason for the high premium. Yet an employed worker in the United States earns more than enough to pay for minor illnesses of his nonworking family members. A $100 'deductible' for medical costs of nonworking dependents would pay for substantial medical cost coverage for up to two years of unemployment. This would be of far greater benefit to the insured than reimbursement for sums which he can easily pay when employed and working.

2 The floor of benefits needs to be fixed, but benefits should be financed on a fluctuating basis with a clear relationship to profitability and perhaps to productivity. Higher benefits (especially

retirement benefits) should be triggered by extraordinary profit-ability and productivity gains.

There must be a *minimum* contribution on the part of the employer, and any deficiency in the benefit fund must be made up periodically. But the more flexibility the employer has, the greater the company's contribution can be. At the same time, the closer and more visible the relationship between benefits and a company's profits, the more benefits will help to reduce the conflict between wage fund and capital fund.

3 Instead of individual benefits and programmes, each with its own contribution, it might be well to decide first the total size of the benefit package and then work out options to give to each group the combination of benefits that best serves its needs.

In some benefit options, employees may cut their cash wage to improve their benefit package – for example, by voluntary extra contributions to a pension fund. Wherever plans of this kind have been offered, they have met with tremendous response, both on the part of the younger workers in general and especially on the part of knowledge workers of all ages. Examples are some stock purchase plans and savings plans of American companies. The Internal Revenue Service has encouraged such a plan for some employees of nonprofit institutions, such as college professors, who can withhold a substantial part of their salary to be invested in their retirement pension, with the income taxable only when received, that is, after retirement and presumably at a much lower rate. This plan has been chosen by a very large proportion of the workers eligible under it – proving that it makes sense to a great many workers to manage cash incomes and benefits as one income stream.

4 The administration of benefits should as much as possible be the responsibility of the work community.

Investing pension-fund money requires professional skill. So does running a mortgage bank for employee housing. But the work community needs to participate, if only to learn. The community should be primarily responsible for the design of benefit programmes and benefit options for various groups in the work force. No one else knows what the true needs are. No one else can convince the work force that choices have to be made and that the available options represent the best balance of choices.

Benefits are likely to continue to be a major worker demand and need. They are, therefore, likely to become a larger rather than a smaller part of the labour costs of an economy. At the same time, they become increasingly the channel through which the capital fund is being fed. It is management's duty to assume responsibility for employee benefits. It is no longer adequate to consider them fringes, as managements do in the West, or benevolence, as managements do in Japan.

## The leadership of people

Fostering responsibility and achievement in the working community requires much more than lessening the roadblocks to productivity. Though reasonable job security and benefits are necessary to a responsible worker, they alone are not sufficient. Managing people for highest productivity requires positive changes in attitude and practice.

There are three traditional approaches to managing people. There is the welfare approach, which sees people as problems needing help. There is the personnel management approach, which sees activities and chores to be performed whenever large numbers of people have to work together. Third is the approach which sees labour as a cost and as a threat and sees the job in controlling cost and in fighting 'crises'.

People are indeed 'problems'. And people do need help. The welfare approach can be highly effective, especially in managing people who truly are helpless.

The best example, at least in the West, is the House of Krupp. Alfried Krupp, who built the German steel firm in the middle of the nineteenth century, was not a brilliant engineer. Nor did Krupp's rise rest on major innovations in product or process. It rested squarely on the tremendous support Alfried Krupp built into his work force. Having grown up in extreme poverty, he, perhaps alone of the major business builders of the mid-nineteenth-century Europe, had compassion for the large masses of unskilled, unlettered, helpless peasants who were being driven out of their wretched tenant hovels by the new 'scientific agriculture.' These peasants fled helter-skelter into the newly industrializing Ruhr Valley. Long before his firm became profitable and prosperous, Krupp provided his workers with housing, schooling, health care, training, small loans at low interest, and so on. Indeed, the Krupp firm at Essen might be called the first welfare state. The workers, who called themselves 'Kruppianers', never forgot the compassion of the original founder. They gave their loyalty to firm and family for an entire century.

But the Krupp example also shows the danger of welfare paternalism. It eventually destroys itself, for it creates expectations which, in the long run, no business enterprise – and no institution – can live up to.

Krupp's paternalism was a major reason, and perhaps *the* reason for the ultimate collapse of the Krupp family. Krupp's over-expansion after World War II was largely motivated by the need to live up to the Krupp promise that every Kruppianer would forever have a job. This in turn meant that the very parts of the Krupp concern that had the least potential for growth in the post-World War II economy had to be expanded the most. This ultimately brought the company to the verge of collapse. The family was ousted from management by the German government and the banks as their price of rescuing the business. Large numbers of old, loyal Kruppianers had to be laid off in the middle of a serious recession in the German coal and steel industry when no other jobs were available.

Even at its most successful, the welfare approach is not an approach for *managing* people. It is an approach for *helping* them. It assumes that people are defined by their weakness. It does not try to find and make productive their strengths. It is a complement to the managing of people rather than its substance.

The welfare approach is a temporary expedient. It is a crutch. As such it may be very effective, may indeed be crucial to survival. But if taken for permanent and seen as the final answer, it will eventually cripple management and workers, company, economy and society.

## Personnel management

The second approach to the management of people is personnel management. It arose during and after World War I as an organized and systematic management function.

Personnel management is methodical and systematic discharge of all the activities that have to be done where people are employed, especially in large numbers: their selection and employment; training; medical services, the cafeteria and safety; the administration of wages, salaries and benefits; and many others.

Personnel management has to be done. Otherwise there is serious malfunction. But personnel management activities bear the same relationship to managing people as vacuuming the living room and washing the dishes bear to a happy marriage and the bringing up of children. If too many dirty dishes pile up in the sink, the marriage may come apart. But spotless dishes do not by themselves contribute a great deal to wedded bliss or to close and happy relationships with one's children. These are hygiene factors. If neglected, they cause trouble. They should be taken for granted.

Personnel management departments have grown at an astronomical rate since World War II in all countries and in all industries. Yet personnel managers everywhere complain that they are 'not listened to', 'not supported', 'have not been truly accepted' by their management colleagues. There is substance to these complaints. But in the main they reflect a feeling on the part of the personnel people that there is something wrong with what they are doing and that they are not addressing themselves to what they profess to deal with, namely the management of people.

There is need in any organization for a 'conscience' with regard to people (see Chapter 34); and conscience functions are top-management work. But personnel management cannot discharge the conscience job; it is too busy with activities. Its usual work is 'support' (again see Chapter 34). But it is primarily support to the work community – and this is where these functions should be lodged.

Last among traditional approaches to managing people is to see them as a cost and a threat.

There is need for the control of labour costs. There is need for the control of labour productivity. There is need for 'fire fighting'. There is need for the organized guerrilla warfare of union relations – or at least we have let this need develop. To take care of these things is necessary and may be crucial. But it is not managing people. It is dealing with problems that result from the failure to manage people. In anything as complex as a modern organization, there will be such failures. But preventing them, or even curing them, does not make the system work and produce.

Managing means making the strengths of people effective. Neither the welfare approach, nor the personnel management approach, nor the control and fire-fighting approach addresses itself to strength, however.

People are weak; and most of us are pitifully weak. People cause problems, require procedures, create chores. And people are a cost and a potential 'threat'. But these are not the reason why people are employed. The reason is their strength and their capacity to perform. And, to say what will be said many times in this book, the purpose of an organization is to make the strengths of people productive and their weaknesses irrelevant.

## 'People are our greatest asset'

Managers are fond of saying, 'Our greatest asset is people.' They are fond of repeating the truism that the only real difference between one organization and another is the performance of people. And most managers know perfectly well that of all the resources, people are the least utilized, and that little of the human potential of any organization is tapped and put to work.

It is perfectly true that the accounting treatment of people shows them as 'costs'. And this characterization does shape the way that management thinks of its people, even though they recognize it as a bookkeeping simplification. (On this see Chapter 31, 'Controls, Control, and Management.') An accounting system that showed people as 'capital investments' might therefore make a difference.

Above all, however, we need *practices*. And practices are easier to obtain than changes in vision or attitude.

First, of course, is the practice of building responsibility and achievement into job and work force that we have already discussed. There is need to have objectives for every job, set by the worker who is to attain the objectives, together with his or her manager. The work itself has to be made productive so that the workers can work at making themselves achieving. And the workers need the demand, the discipline, and the incentive of responsibility.

Second, the manager must treat the people with whom he or she works as a personal *resource*. The manager has to look to them for guidance regarding his or her own job. He or she has to demand of them that they accept it as their responsibility to enable their manager to do a better and more effective job. The manager needs to build upward responsibility and upward contribution into the job of subordinates.

One way to do this is to ask each subordinate to think through and answer a few simple questions: 'What do I do as your manager, and what does your company do that helps you the most in *your* job?'; 'What do I do as *your* manager, and what does the company do, that hinders you the most in *your* job?'; and 'What can you do that will help me, as *your* manager, do the best job for the company?' These may seem obvious questions. But they are rarely asked. Whenever they are asked, the answers turn out to be far from obvious.

Such questions force both manager and subordinate to focus on common performance. They both focus on the purpose of their relationship. And they are likely to induce in managers a new view of the people who work for them. They will make themselves look to subordinates as resources.

## Placement

The final but perhaps the most important element in managing people is to place them where their strengths can become productive.

Personnel management stresses selection for employment. It is debatable whether the results justify the tremendous effort and the elaborate tests, interviews, and selection procedures that have been developed – especially for knowledge workers.

We know how to identify specific physical traits that make an individual less likely to perform a specific manual activity, such as spot-welding in confined small spaces. We know nothing, however, about aspects of character, personality, and talent such as come into play in knowledge work and especially in work as a manager. Most large American companies have large staffs of college recruiters who try to find 'potential' among college and professional school graduates. Insofar as it is the job of these people to attract graduates to their employer, their activity makes sense. But with respect to their ability to 'spot' the 'comers', their record is dismal. Otherwise, three out of every five of their recruits would not quit their first employer within the first two or three years. Random selection of every third applicant would be likely to produce better results. The reason is that we do not know what to look for in management potential, and we have no way of testing it except in performance.

Placement, on the other hand, is left largely to chance. Yet no two people have the same set of strengths and weaknesses. And no one has only strengths; there are no 'universal geniuses'. It is the manager's job to optimize resources. And placement is the way to optimize the most expensive and most valuable resource of them all: the human being.

Such practices will not satisfy the many critics of traditional people management who call for new convictions and for a fundamental change in attitudes. To be sure, treating people as a resource to the manager and emphasis on placement where their strengths can be effective are only 'practices'. But they are a good deal more than empty words. They are hard, demanding work. But they will point organizations towards performance rather than conformance. These practices will not make dull jobs and dull people interesting. But they will go a long way towards preventing interesting jobs and interesting people from being dulled. They will not eliminate the basic functions and tensions of organization and make its problems of economies and power go away. But they might release countervailing forces of trust and achievement. These practices will not make unnecessary the traditional approaches to people as problems, as chores, as cost, and as threat. But, though only the first steps, they move manager and management beyond personnel management and towards leadership of people.

## Summary

What does the worker need to be able and willing to take the burden of responsibility ? The focus has to be on the job; it comes first. To enable workers – unskilled, skilled, or knowledge workers, and managers and professionals as well as rank-and-file workers – to take responsibility requires managerial planning and action. Work must be made productive; feedback must be provided, and continuous learning must be set up. But the worker has to be responsible for the job and for the work group. This is particularly important for three groups: the new breed of young manual workers; the pre-industrials, and knowledge workers. Worker responsibility is also the one way to save the supervisor and restore his or her function. Worker responsibility needs to extend to the affairs of the plant community. To enable workers to take responsibility they need job and income security but also purposeful placement. Worker responsibility is the one way available to lessen the conflict between wage fund and capital fund. What role do employee benefits play ? Worker responsibility finally demands a shift in managerial practices from personnel management to the leadership of people.

# Part Four
# Social Impacts and
# Social Responsibilities

The quality of life is the third major task area for management.
Managements of all institutions are responsible for their
by-products, that is, the impacts of their legitimate activities on
people and on the physical and social environment. They are
increasingly expected to anticipate and to resolve social
problems. They need to think through and develop new policies
for the relationship of business and government, which is
rapidly outgrowing traditional theories and habits. What are the
tasks ? What are the opportunities ? What are the limitations ?
And what are the ethics of leadership for the manager who is a
leader but not a master ?

# 19 Social Impacts and Social Problems

Since the early 1960s, the meaning of the words 'social responsibility of business' has changed radically. Formerly, discussions of social responsibilities of business centred in three areas. One was the question of the relationship between private ethics and public ethics. Is a manager in charge of an organization expected to be guided by the ethics of the individual ? Or does his responsibility to the organization permit him – or perhaps even compel him – to resort to privately unethical behaviour for the good of his organization ? The text for this discussion, consciously or not, is an old saying of politicians: 'What scoundrels we would be if we did in our private lives what we do in our public capacity for our countries.'

The second major topic was the social responsibility which the employer bears towards his employees by virtue of his power and wealth. The classic discussion is to be found in a book by the English Quaker industrialist and philanthropist B. Seebohm Rowntree, *The Human Needs of Labour* (1918).

Finally, social responsibility was the term used to assert – or assign – leadership responsibility to the businessman with respect to the 'culture' of the community: support of the arts, the museums, the opera, and the symphony orchestra; service as a trustee on the boards of educational and religious institutions; and also financial support of philanthropic and other community causes. And in the United States in particular, willingness to serve in governmental or other public positions has become in this century an important social responsibility of the executive.

The traditional approach was not really concerned with the social responsibility of business but with the social responsibility of businesspeople. The greatest emphasis was put on what businesspeople should or might contribute *outside* of business hours.

When social responsibilities are being discussed these days, however, the emphasis is quite different. It is on what business should or might do to tackle and solve problems of society. The emphasis is on the contribution business can make to such social problems as racial discrimination and racial integration in the United States, or on the protection and restoration of the physical environment. One of the best examples of the new attitude comes from Sweden.

Several large Swedish companies, especially a major electrical-apparatus company, were harshly attacked in the late 1960s by the Swedish press for participating in a major electric-power project in Africa. The project was sponsored by the UN and financed by the World Bank; it also had been endorsed by the socialist government of Sweden. Its purpose was to raise the living standards of a desperately poor region of black Africa. But it was located in what was then a Portuguese colony. Hence, it was vehemently argued, the participating Swedish companies 'supported colonialism' by helping to raise the standards of living of the native population. It was their duty, so the argument ran, to work for the 'downfall of colonialism', which would best be achieved by keeping the natives desperately poor rather than have them prosper under an 'imperialist exploiter'.

This new concept of social responsibility no longer asks what the limitations on business are, or what business should be doing for those under its immediate authority. It demands that business take responsibility for social problems, social issues, social and political goals, and that it become the keeper of society's conscience and the solver of society's problems.

But increasingly such social responsibility is also being demanded of nonbusiness institutions in society. Universities, hospitals, and government agencies, but also learned societies – whether of physicists, historians, or linguists – are all increasingly being confronted with similar demands and attacked for not assuming responsibility for society's ills and problems.

## What explains it?

The most popular and most obvious explanation is the wrong one. It is not hostility to business that explains the demands for social responsibility. On the contrary, it is the success of the business system that leads to new and, in many cases, exaggerated expectations. The demand for social responsibility is the price of success.

In developed countries we now take economic performance for granted. This has led to the belief that there is or should be universal capacity for economic performance. It has led us to believe that the same efforts which, within a century, lifted two-fifths of humanity from poverty into affluence can in much less time bring the remaining three-fifths of mankind into rapid economic development.

Nothing in earlier social and economic history equals the recent economic and social development of the American Negro. Within twenty years, from 1950 to 1970, two-thirds of one of the most disadvantaged groups of pre-industrial immigrants have risen from extreme poverty into middle-class status. They have acquired competence and jobs. A larger proportion of their children acquire higher education than of the children of older urban immigrant groups, such as Italians or Poles, who encounter no 'racial' barrier. Yet what most Americans see when they look at the 'problem' of the American blacks is not the success story of the majority. Instead, they see how much is still to be done – and judge the results to be failure. They see that 'the glass is half empty'.

Admittedly the American Negro is a very special case. But still, the difference between what would have been considered near-Utopia only a quarter century ago and what is now considered grim failure illustrates the extent to which success has changed expectations. Even rather well-to-do 'middle-class' people yesterday had few of the good things of life we now expect routinely.

That we can worry about the quality of life is thus very great success. And it is only right and natural that the same leadership groups which were responsible for the success in providing the quantities of life are now expected to assume responsibility for providing the quality of life.

## The disenchantment with government

People look to business for leadership because of a growing disenchantment with government, and a growing disbelief in government's ability to solve major social problems.

Only a generation ago the people who now demand social responsibility from business (or the university) expected government to be able to take care of every problem of society, if not of every problem of the individual as well. There is still, in all countries, pressure for more and more government programmes – though there is also growing resistance to more and more expenditures and taxes. But even the most fervent advocate of an activist government no longer truly expects results, even in countries where respect for and belief in government are still high, such as Japan, Sweden, and Germany. Even the most fervent advocate of a strong government no longer believes that a problem has been solved the moment it has been turned over to government. As a result, the people most concerned with these problems – the liberals and progressives who a generation ago rallied under the banner of 'more government' – now increasingly look to business, to take on the problems that government is not able to solve.

## The new leadership groups

The succession of management to the leadership position in society underlies the demands for social responsibility. In this century the managers of our major institutions have become the leaders in every developed country, and in most developing countries as well. The old leadership groups, whether the aristocracy or the priesthood, have either disappeared entirely or have become insignificant. Even the scientists, the priesthood of the post-World War II period, have lost much of their prestige. The only new leadership groups to emerge are managers – managers of business enterprise and of universities, of government agencies and of hospitals. They command the resources of society. But they also command the competence. It is, therefore, only logical that they are expected to take leadership responsibility for major social problems and major social issues.

The emergence of managers as the major leadership group; the growing disenchantment with government; the shift in focus from the quantities of life to the quality of life – from these shifts the demand has arisen that managers make concern for society central to the conduct of business itself. It is a demand that the quality of life become the business of business. The traditional approach asks, 'How can we arrange the making of cars (or of shoes) so as not to impinge on social values and beliefs, on individuals and their freedom, and on the good society ?' The new demand is for business to make social values and beliefs create freedom for the individual, and produce the good society.

This demand requires new thinking and new action on the part of the managers. It cannot be handled in the traditional manner. It cannot be handled by public relations.

## What is business responsible for?

Social responsibilities – whether of a business, a hospital, or a university – may arise in two areas. They may emerge out of the social impacts of the institution. Or they may arise as problems of the society itself. Both areas are of concern to management because the institution which managers manage lives in society and community. But otherwise the two areas are different. The first deals with what an institution does to society. The second is concerned with what an institution can or should do for society.

The modern organization exists to provide a specific service to society. It therefore has to be in society. It has to be in a community, has to be a neighbour, has to do its work within a social setting. But also it has to employ people to do its work. Its social impacts inevitably go beyond the specific contribution it exists to make.

The purpose of the hospital is not to employ nurses and cooks but to care for patients. But to accomplish this purpose, nurses and cooks are needed. And in no time at all, they form a work community with its own tasks and problems.

These impacts are incidental to the purpose of the organization. But in large measure they are inescapable by-products.

Social problems, by contrast, are malfunctions of society rather than impacts of the organization and its activities.

A healthy business, a healthy university, a healthy hospital cannot exist in a sick society. Management has a self-interest in a healthy society, even though the cause of society's sickness is none of management's making.

## Responsibility for impacts

One is responsible for one's impacts, whether they are intended or not. The social impacts of the organization are management's business.

Because one is responsible for one's impacts, one minimizes them. The fewer impacts an institution has outside of its own specific purpose and mission, the better does it conduct itself, the more responsibly does it act, and the more acceptable a citizen, neighbour and contributor it is. Nonessential impacts, especially those which are not part of the discharge of one's own specific purpose and mission, should be kept to the absolute minimum. Even if they appear to be beneficial, they are outside the proper boundaries of one's function and will sooner or later be resented and resisted.

Impacts are at best a nuisance, at worst a harm. Never beneficial, they always carry within themselves a cost and a threat. Impacts use up resources, burn up or waste raw materials, or tie up management efforts. Yet they add nothing to the value of the product or to the customer's satisfaction. They are 'friction', that is, nonproductive cost.

It is not enough to say, 'But the public doesn't object'. It is, above all, not enough to say that any action that comes to grips with such a problem is going to be 'unpopular', is going to be 'resented' by one's colleagues and one's associates, and is not required. Sooner or later, society will come to regard any such impact as an attack. Then it will exact a high price from those who have not responsibly worked to eliminate the impact or to find a solution to the problem.

Here are some examples.

In the late 1940s and early 1950s, Ford tried to make the American public safety-conscious by introducing cars with seat belts. But sales dropped catastrophically. The company had to withdraw the cars with seat belts and abandon the whole idea. Fifteen years later, the American driving public became safety-conscious, and the car manufacturers were sharply attacked for their 'total lack of concern with safety' and for being 'merchants of death'. And the resulting regulations were written as much to punish the companies as to protect the public.

Several large electric-power companies had tried for years to get the various state utility commissions to approve low-sulphur fuels and cleaning devices in smokestacks. The commissions discouraged them again and again, with the argument that the public was entitled to power at the lowest possible cost. They pointed out that neither a more expensive fuel nor capital investment to clean the smoke could be permitted as a legitimate cost under the state laws governing rates. Yet eventually air pollution became a matter of public concern, and the same power companies were roundly berated for 'befouling the environment'.

Public-service institutions similarly pay the price when they neglect impacts or dismiss them as trivial. Columbia University in New York City was almost destroyed because it had comforted itself with the notion that an impact was trivial. The explosion which rocked Columbia to its foundations in 1968 came over a perfectly harmless and minor matter: a plan to build a new university gymnasium which would be available equally to university students and to the residents of the black ghetto next to Columbia. But the cause for the explosion lay much deeper. It was the conviction of Columbia's management and faculty that a liberal educational institution does not have to concern itself with its impacts on its black ghetto neighbourhood.

## Identifying impacts

The first job of management is, therefore, to identify and to anticipate impacts – coldly and realistically. The question is not 'Is what we do right?' It is 'Is what we do what society and the customer pay us for ?'; and if an activity is not integral to the institution's purpose and mission, it should be considered a social impact, and undesirable.

There is, these days, great interest in technology assessment, which means anticipating impact and side effects of new technology before going ahead with it. The US Congress has actually set up an Office of Technology Assessment. This new agency is expected to be able to predict the new technologies that are likely to become important, and the long-range effects they are likely to have. It is then expected to advise government to encourage some new technologies and discourage others.

This attempt can end only in fiasco. Technology assessment of this kind is likely to lead to the encouragement of the wrong technologies and the discouragement of the technologies we need. For future impacts of new technology are almost always beyond anybody's imagination.

DDT is an example. It was synthesized during World War II to protect American soldiers against disease-carrying insects, especially in the tropics. Some scientists then envisaged the use of the new chemical to protect civilian populations as well. But not one of the many people who worked on DDT thought of applying the new pesticide to control insect pests infesting crops, forests, or livestock. If DDT had been restricted to the use for which it was developed (the protection of humans), it would never have become an environmental hazard; use for this purpose accounted for no more than 5 to 10 per cent of the total at DDT's peak, in the 1960s. Farmers and foresters, without much help from scientists, saw that what killed lice on men would also kill lice on plants and made DDT into a massive assault on the environment.

At the same time, the technology impacts which the experts predict almost never occur. We were told by everybody that automation would have tremendous economic and social impacts – it has had practically none. The computer offers an even odder story. In the late 1940s, nobody predicted that the computer would be used by business and governments. While the computer was a 'major scientific revolution', everybody 'knew' that its main use would be in science and warfare. As a result, the most extensive market research study undertaken at that time reached the conclusion that the world computer market would, at most, be able to absorb 1,000 computers by the year 2000. Now only thirty years later, in the late seventies, there are some 170,000 computers installed in the world, most of them doing mundane bookkeeping work. When it became apparent that business was buying computers for payroll and billing, the experts then predicted that the computer would displace middle management, so that there would be nobody left between the chief executive officer and the foreman. 'Is middle management obsolete?' asked a widely quoted *Harvard Business Review* article in the early 1950s; and it answered this question with a resounding 'Yes'. At exactly that moment, the tremendous expansion of middle-management jobs began. In every developed country, middle-management jobs, in business as well as in government, have grown about three times as fast as total employment in the last twenty years; and their growth has paralleled the growth of computer usage. Anyone depending on technology assessment in the early 1950s would have abolished the graduate business schools as likely to produce graduates who could not possibly find jobs. Fortunately, the young people did not listen and flocked in record numbers to the graduate business schools so as to get the good jobs which the computer helped create.

It is impossible to predict the impacts of technology. The most successful prophet of technology, the French novelist Jules Verne (1828–1905), predicted a great deal of twentieth-century technology a hundred years ago (though few scientists or technologists of that time took him seriously). But he anticipated absolutely no social or economic impacts, only an unchanged mid-Victorian society and economy. Economic and social prophets, in turn, have the most dismal record as predictors of technology. The one and only effect an Office of Technology Assessment is therefore likely to have would be to guarantee full employment to a lot of fifth-rate science-fiction writers. *What we need is impact monitoring rather than impact prediction.*

## How to deal with impacts

Identifying incidental impacts of an institution is management's first responsibility. But how then to deal with them? The objective is clear: impacts on society and economy, community, and individual that are not in themselves the purpose and mission of the institution should be kept to the minimum, or better yet, eliminated altogether.

Wherever an impact can be eliminated by dropping the activity that causes it, this is therefore the best – indeed the only truly good – solution. In most cases the activity cannot, however, be eliminated. Hence there is need for systematic work at eliminating the impact – or at least at minimizing it – while maintaining the underlying activity itself.

The ideal approach is to make the elimination of impacts into a profitable business opportunity. One example is the way Dow Chemical has since the nineteen-fifties tackled air and water pollution. Dow decided, shortly after World War II, that air and water pollution was an undesirable impact that had to be eliminated. Long before the public outcry about the environment, Dow adopted a zero-pollution policy for its plants. It then set about systematically to convert the polluting substances it removes from smokestack gases and watery effluents into saleable products and to create uses and markets for them.

## When regulation is needed

To make elimination of an impact into a business opportunity should always be attempted. But it cannot be done in many cases. More often eliminating an impact means increasing the costs. What was an 'externality' for which the general public paid becomes business cost. It therefore becomes a competitive disadvantage unless everybody in the industry accepts the same rule. In most cases this can be done only by regulation.

Whenever an impact cannot be eliminated without an increase in cost, management must think ahead and work out the regulation which is most likely to solve the problem at the minimum

cost and with the greatest benefit to public and business alike.
And it is then management's job to work at getting right regulation enacted.

The fact that the public sees no issue is not relevant. Indeed it
is not even relevant that the public – as it did in every single one
of the examples above – currently resists actively any attempts on
the part of farsighted business leaders to prevent a crisis. In the
end, there is the scandal. One example is the failure of the international petroleum companies to think ahead and develop the
successor to the 'petroleum concession', the impacts of which
could clearly be anticipated at the end of World War II. Another
example is the failure of US industry to think through the regulation of foreign investment which Canada might have adopted
to preserve both political identity and access to capital.

## The trade-offs

Any solution to an impact problem requires trade-offs. Beyond a
certain level, elimination of an impact costs more in money or
energy, in resources or lives, than the attainable benefit. A decision has to be made on the optimal balance between costs and
benefits. This is something people in an industry understand, as
a rule. But no one outside does – and so the outsider's solution
tends to ignore the trade-off problem altogether.

Where is the right trade-off between the overdue concern for a
natural environment threatened by the strip-mining of coal and
the lives saved in switching from undergound mining to strip-
mining? Underground mining can never be truly safe. It will
also always remain a health hazard because of the coal dust and
the contaminated air in which underground work has to be performed. Strip-mining, on the other hand, is a fairly safe occupa-
tion and has few health hazards. But where is the trade-off
between lives on the one hand, and natural beauty, and clean
unpolluted streams on the other?

But there is, in the strip-mining issue, also a trade-off between the costs of environmental damage and the cost in jobs,
living standards, and in the health hazard of cold homes and the

safety hazards of dark streets implicit in expensive and scarce energy.

What happens if management fails to face up to an impact and to think through the trade-off is illustrated by the American experience with the control of automobile exhausts. That such controls would be needed has been known since the end of World War II, when smog first became a household word in Los Angeles. The automobile industry, however, relied on public relations, which told it that the public was not concerned about smog. Then, suddenly, in the 1960s, the public panicked and forced through drastic emission-control legislation. Whether the new controls will actually cut pollution is quite doubtful. They control exhausts in new cars, but are unlikely to control exhausts in the great majority of cars on the road, which are more than two to three years old. One thing is, however, certain. These exhaust controls will themselves cause substantial new pollution. They increase the energy needed to drive the car and will therefore have to use more petrol. This will require more petroleum refining – one of the most polluting of industrial activities. At the same time, they add substantially to the cost of the car and of automotive service. What the right trade-offs would have been we do not know – for industry did not do its work. But both industry and public will pay and suffer.

Responsibility for social impacts is a management responsibility – not because it is a social responsibility, but because it is a business responsibility. The ideal is to make elimination of such an impact into a business opportunity. But wherever that cannot be done, the design of the appropriate regulation with the optimal trade-off balance – and public discussion of the problem and promotion of the best regulatory solution – is management's job.

## Social problems as business opportunities

Social problems are malfunctions of society. But for the management of institutions, and, above all, for business management, they represent challenges. They are major sources of opportunity. For it is the function of business – and to a lesser degree of the other main institutions – to satisfy a social need and at the same time serve their institution, by making resolution of a social problem into a business opportunity.

The most significant opportunities for converting social problems into business opportunities may therefore not lie in new technologies, new products, and new services. They may lie in solving social problems, that is, in social innovation which then directly and indirectly benefits and strengthens the company or the industry.

The success of some of the most successful businesses is largely the result of such social innovation. Here are some American examples:

Julius Rosenwald, the 'city slicker' who built Sears, Roebuck, invented and for many years financed the County Farm Agent. The social problem he identified was the poverty, ignorance, and isolation of the American farmer who, in the early years of this century, still constituted half the US population. Knowledge that enabled the former to produce more, to produce the right things, and to get more for his efforts was available. But it was inaccessible to the farmer. The County Farm Agent – rather than new technology, new machines or new seeds – became a main force behind the 'productivity explosion' on the American farm. Rosenwald saw a genuine social problem that was also a genuine business opportunity. For as the farmer's position and income grew, so did the Sears market. And Sears came to be identified by the farmers as the 'farmer's friend'.

IBM also owes its rise largely to a frontal attack on a social problem. During the years of the Great Depression IBM was a very small company of little visibility. Hence its action had none of the impact of Ford's $5-a-day wage twenty years earlier (in 1913), which almost overnight tripled the incomes of manual workers and had to be matched rapidly by all major manufacturing companies. Yet in giving workers employment security and then putting them on a salary instead of an hourly wage, IBM was as bold and innovative as Ford had been. IBM's action too was aimed at a major social problem of the time – the fear, insecurity, and loss of dignity that the Depression inflicted on workers in America. It too turned a social disease into a business opportunity. It was this action, above all, which created the human potential for IBM's rapid growth and, then, a decade later, for its aggressive move into the totally new computer technology.

In present-day society one area where a serious social problem might be solved by making it into an opportunity could well be the fatigue, frustration, and 'burning-out' of middle-aged knowledge workers and their need for a second career. The hidden cost of the middle-aged knowledge workers – managers and knowledge professionals – who have 'retired on the job', have lost interest, and just go through the motions, may well be larger than that of Ford's labour turnover in 1913, which had motivated the company to triple prevailing daily wages. At the same time, the frustration and silent despair of these men and women may pose as great a danger to society as the misery, bitterness, and despair of the suffering manual worker of yesterday. Nothing is as corrosive as success turned into frustration. The first company which tackles this problem as an opportunity might well reap benefits fully as great as those reaped by Ford sixty years ago and by IBM forty years ago.

To cure social ills by making them into opportunities for contribution and performance is by no means a challenge to business enterprise alone. It is the responsibility as well of all the other institutions of our society of organizations.

There is a great deal of talk today about the crisis of the university; and the crisis is real. In some places, however, it has been seized as an opportunity. In Great Britain there is the Open University, which uses television to make university education available to anyone who is willing to do the work. In California the medium-sized and little-known University of the Pacific, in Stockton, is building a new kind of university. It utilizes the desire of young people to learn but also to be responsible participants in their learning.

Any business, and indeed any institution, needs to organize innovative efforts to convert social problems into opportunities for performance and contribution. In the last quarter century, organized technological research has become commonplace. Social innovation is still largely left to chance and to the individual entrepreneur who stumbles upon an opportunity. This is no longer adequate. In our society of organizations, every institution needs to organize its research and development for society and community fully as much as it had been organizing it for technology. Management has to organize to identify the issues, the crises, the problems in society and community, and to work at the innovations that will turn their solution into a profitable opportunity.

## The 'degenerative diseases' of society

Not every social problem can be resolved by making it into an opportunity for contribution and performance. Indeed, the most serious of such problems tend to defy this approach.

No business could, for instance, have done much about America's most serious degenerative disease throughout our history – the racial problem. It could not even be tackled until the whole society had changed awareness and convictions – by which time it was almost too late. And even if one management solves such a problem, the rest may not follow. There may be a solution; but while known and visible, it is not being used. The problem stays acute and unresolved.

What then is the social responsibility of management for these social problems that become chronic or degenerative diseases ?

They are management's problems. The health of the enterprise is management's responsibility. A healthy business and a sick society are not compatible. The health of the community is a prerequisite for successful and growing business. It is foolish to hope that these problems will disappear if only one looks the other way. Problems go away because someone does something about them.

To what extent should business – or any other of the special-purpose institutions of our society – be expected to tackle such a problem ? To what extent should these institutions, business, university, or hospital, even be permitted to take responsibility?

Today's rhetoric tends to ignore that question. 'Here is,' former Mayor Lindsay of New York once said, 'the black ghetto. No one knows what to do with it. Whatever government, social workers, or community action try, things seem only to get worse. Therefore big business better take responsibility.'

That Mayor Lindsay frantically looked for someone to take over is understandable; and the problem is indeed desperate and a major threat. But is it correct to make the problem of the black ghetto the social responsibility of management? Or are there limits to social responsibility? And what are they?

## Summary

However much discussed, questions of ethical or moral behaviour of individuals are not central to the issue of the social responsibilities of business and of the other key institutions of modern society, such as school and university, government agency and hospital. Central are first the social impacts that are by-products of the legitimate and necessary conduct of business (or of the institution), and consequences of the fact that the institution exists in a community and has authority over people. Such impacts should always be eliminated or at least minimized. If their elimination cannot be made into an opportunity, there is need for regulation; and it is the responsibility of business to think through and work for the appropriate regulation before there is a scandal. Then there is the issue of the responsibility of business for the ills of society. And finally there is the leadership function of managers in a society in which executives of institutions have become the leadership group.

# 20 The Limits of Social Responsibility

Managers are servants. Their master is the institution they manage, and their first responsibility must therefore be to it. Their first task is to make the institution, whether business, hospital, school or university, perform the function and make the contribution for the sake of which it exists. The person who uses a position at the head of a major institution to become a public figure and to take leadership with respect to social problems, while the company or university erodes through neglect, is not a statesman. He or she is irresponsible and false to a trust.

The institution's performance of its specific mission is also society's first need and interest. Society does not stand to gain but to lose if the capacity of the institution to perform its own specific task is diminished or impaired. Performance of its function is the institution's first social responsibility. Unless it discharges its performance responsibly, it cannot discharge anything else. A bankrupt business is not a desirable employer and is unlikely to be a good neighbour in a community. Nor will it create the capital for tomorrow's jobs and the opportunities for tomorrow's workers. A university which fails to prepare tomorrow's leaders and professionals is not socially responsible, no matter how many 'good works' it engages in.

The first 'limitation' on social responsibility is, therefore, the higher responsibility for the specific performance of the institution which is the manager's master. This needs particular stress with respect to the business enterprise, the economic institution of society. Any solution of a social impact or of a social problem (except to make it into an opportunity for performance and results) creates social overhead costs. These costs can be paid for either out of current costs – that is, by consumer or taxpayer – or out of capital – that is, by fewer and poorer jobs tomorrow and impaired standards of living. The only way to cover costs and to accumulate capital is through economic performance. All other satisfactions of society are being paid for, one way or another, out of the surplus of the economy.

This again underscores the responsibility of managers to anticipate problems and to think through the trade-offs involved in their solutions. At what point does a solution become too expensive for society because it impairs the performance capacity of existing and needed institutions? What is the optimal balance between the need to take care of a social problem and the need to preserve the performance capacity of the existing social institutions? And at what point does one risk losing social performance – and thereby creating new and bigger problems – by overloading the existing institutions? At what point do we achieve the best balance between the old costs and the new benefits?

Managers need to be able to think through the limits on social responsibility set by their duty to the performance capacity of the enterprises in their charge. In the case of the business enterprise this requires knowing the objectives in key areas. For these objectives set the minimum performance goals for the attainment of the enterprise's mission. As long as they can be attained, the enterprise can perform. If the objective in any one area is seriously jeopardized, the performance capacity of the entire business is endangered.

Above all, management needs to know the minimum profitability required by the risks of the business and by its commitments to the future. It needs this knowledge for its own decisions. But it needs it just as much to explain its decisions to others – the politicians, the press, the public. As long as managements remain the prisoners of their own ignorance of the objective need for, and function of, profit – i.e., as long as they think and argue in terms of the 'profit motive' – they will be able neither to make rational decisions with respect to social responsibilities, nor to explain these decisions to others.

## The limits of competence

To take on tasks for which one lacks competence is irresponsible behaviour. It is also cruel. It raises expectations which will then be disappointed.

An institution, and especially a business enterprise, has to acquire whatever competence is needed to take responsibility for its impacts. But in areas of social responsibility other than impacts, right and duty to act are limited by competence.

An institution should refrain from tackling tasks which do not fit into its value system. Skills and knowledge are fairly easily acquired. But one cannot easily change personality. People are not likely to do well in areas they do not respect. If a business or any other institution tackles such an area because there is a social need, it is unlikely to put its good people on the task and to support them adequately. It is unlikely to understand what the task involves. It is almost certain to do the wrong things. As a result, it will do harm rather than good.

What not to do was demonstrated when the American universities in the 1960s rushed into taking social responsibility for the problems of the big city. These problems are real enough. And within the university were to be found able scholars in a variety of areas pertinent to the problems. Yet the tasks were primarily political tasks. The values involved were those of the politician rather than the scholar. The skills needed were those of compromise, of mobilizing energies, and above all, of setting priorities. And these are not skills which the academician admires and respects. They are almost the opposite of the objectivity and the 'finding of truth' which constitute excellence in academia. These tasks exceeded the competence of the university and were incompatible with its value system.

The result of the universities' eager acceptance of these tasks was therefore, inevitably, lack of performance and results. It was also damage to the prestige and standing of the university, and to its credibility. The universities did not help the problems of the city; but they seriously impaired their own performance capacity in their own area.

Management therefore needs to know what it and its institution are truly incompetent for. Business, as a rule, will be in this position of absolute incompetence in an 'intangible' area. The strength of business is accountability and measurability – the discipline of market test, productivity measurements, and profitability requirement. Where these are lacking, businesses are essentially out of their depth. They are also out of fundamental sympathy, that is, outside their own value systems. Where the criteria of performance are intangible, such as 'political' opinions and emotions, community approval or disapproval, mobilization of community energies and structuring of power relations, business is unlikely to feel comfortable. It is unlikely to have respect for the values that matter. It is, therefore, most unlikely to have competence.

In such areas, it is, however, often possible to define goals clearly and measurably for specific partial tasks. It is often possible to convert parts of a problem that by itself lies outside the competence of business enterprise. No one in America has done very well in training hard-core unemployable black teenagers for work and jobs. But business has done far less badly than any other institution. This task can be identified. It can be defined. Goals can be set. And performance can be measured. In such a situation, a business can perform.

Before acceding to the demand that it take on this or that social responsibility, and go to work on this or that problem, management had better think through what, if any, part of the task can be made to fit the competence of its institution. Is there any area which can be defined in terms of tangible goals and measurable performance? If the answer is yes, one is justified in thinking seriously about one's social responsibility. But when the answer is no – and this will be the answer in a good many areas – business enterprise should resist, no matter how important the problems and how urgent the demand for business to take it over. It can only do harm to society and to itself. It cannot perform and therefore cannot be responsible.

## The limits of authority

The most important limitation on social responsibility is the limitation of authority. The constitutional lawyer knows that there is no such word as 'responsibility' in the political dictionary. The term is 'responsibility and authority'. Whoever claims authority thereby assumes responsibility. But whoever assumes responsibility thereby claims authority. The two are different sides of the same coin. To assume social responsibility therefore always means to claim authority.

Every time the demand is made that business take responsibility for this or that, one should ask, 'Does business have the authority and should it have it?' If business does not and should not have authority – and in a great many areas it should not have it – then responsibility on the part of business should be treated with grave suspicion. It is not responsibility; it is lust for power.

Ralph Nader, the American consumerist, sincerely considers himself a foe of big business. Insofar as Nader demands that business take responsibility for product quality and product safety, he is surely concerned with legitimate business responsibility, for performance and contribution. The only question – apart from the accuracy of his facts and the style of his campaign – is whether Nader's demand for perfection is not going to cost the consumer far more than the shortcomings and deficiencies which Nader assails. The only questions are the trade-offs.

But Ralph Nader demands, above all, that big business assume responsibility in a multitude of areas beyond products and services. This can lead only to the emergence of the managements of the big corporations as the ultimate power in a vast number of areas that are properly some other institution's field.

And this is, indeed, the position to which Nader – and other advocates of unlimited social responsibility – are moving rapidly. One of the Nader task forces published in 1972 a critique of the Du Pont Company and its role in the small state of Delaware, where Du Pont has its headquarters and is a major employer. The report did not even discuss economic performance. It dismissed as irrelevant the fact that Du Pont, in a period of general inflation, consistently lowered the prices for its products, which are, in many cases, basic materials for the American economy. Instead the report sharply criticized Du Pont for not using its economic power to force the citizens of the state to attack a number of social problems, from racial discrimination to health care to state schools. Du Pont, for not taking responsibility for Delaware society, Delaware politics, and Delaware law, was called grossly remiss in its responsibility.

One of the ironies of this story is that the traditional liberal or left-wing criticism of the Du Pont Company for many years has been the exact opposite. The complaint used to be that Du Pont, by its very prominence in a small state, 'interferes in and dominates' Delaware and exercises 'illegitimate authority'.

The Nader line is only the best-publicized of the positions which, under the cover of antibusiness slogans, actually plead for a society in which big business is the most powerful, the dominant, the ultimate institution. Of course such an outcome is the opposite of what Nader intends. But it would not be the first time that a demand for social responsibility has had results opposite from those intended.

Yet the 'pure' position of Milton Friedman, the Chicago economist and Nobel Prize winner – to avoid all social responsibility – is not practical either. There are big, urgent, desperate problems. Above all, there is the 'sickness of government' that is creating a vacuum of responsibility and performance – a vacuum that becomes stronger the bigger government becomes. Business and the other institutions of our society of organizations cannot be pure, however desirable that may be. Their own self-interest alone forces them to be concerned with society and community and to be prepared to shoulder responsibility beyond their own main areas of task and responsibility.

But in doing this they have to be conscious of the danger – to themselves and to society. They have to be conscious of the risk. No pluralist society has ever worked unless its key institutions take responsibility for the common good. But at the same time, the perennial threat to a pluralist society is the all-too-easy confusion between the common good and one's own lust for power.

In a few areas, guidelines can be developed. It is not the task of business (or of the university) to substitute its authority for that of the government in areas that are clearly national policy. In a free society a business is, of course, entitled *not* to engage in activities, even though they are sanctioned and even encouraged by governmental policy. It can stay out. But it is surely not entitled to put itself in the place of government. And it is not entitled to use its economic power to impose its values on the community.

## When to say no

Demands for social responsibility which in effect ask of business – or any other institution – that it seize new authority are to be resisted. They are to be resisted in business's own self-interest. They are to be resisted on grounds of true social responsibility. For they are, in effect, demands for irresponsibility; whether they are made sincerely and out of honest anguish, or whether they are rhetoric to cloak the lust for power, is irrelevant. Whenever business, or any other of our institutions, is being asked to take social responsibility beyond its own area of performance and its own impact, it should ask itself, 'Do we possess authority in the area and should we have it ?' And if the answer is no, then the socially responsible course of action is not to yield to the demand.

## Summary

What are the limits of social responsibility for a business or for a hospital ? Such an organization must not damage or destroy its ability to discharge its first and main task in the name of social responsibilities. Whatever the primary function of an organization, whether health care or economic services, that is the reason for its existence and its first responsibility. In addition, it is irresponsible to take on tasks for which elementary competence is lacking. And it is irresponsible – and lust for power – to assume responsibility in areas in which authority is lacking. For responsibility always goes together with authority.

# 21 Business and Government

A crucial social responsibility for the manager, and especially for the business manager, is the relationship of business and government. Yet it is rarely even mentioned when the social responsibilities of management are being discussed.

Few relationships are as critical to the business enterprise as the relationship to the government. Managers have responsibility for this relationship as part of their responsibility to the enterprise itself. It is an area of social impact of the business. To a large extent the relationship to government results from what businesses do or fail to do.

The business-government relationship is also a social problem, for the relationship between business and government in every major country is in disrepair. It urgently needs rethinking, reappraisal, and restructuring. In every developed country – and in most developing ones – there are no clear rules, little common understanding, and at best a confused patchwork of laws and prejudices, regulations, traditions and improvisation. At the same time, there are new major problems which cannot be fitted into the existing relationships. Examples are the environment and the multinational corporation.

Ultimately we will need new political theories appropriate to the realities and needs of a society of organizations. In the meantime, business and government will have to go on with their respective jobs. They will have to know which of these jobs have to be tackled together and which have to be kept apart. It may be too early to think of solutions. But approaches and specifications will have to be designed, if only on a case-by-case basis. And great care will have to be taken lest these temporary solutions commit us to the wrong long-term pattern.

To work out these interim solutions and to watch over them will be primarily the job of the manager. He or she cannot wait for the political philosopher. Too much is at stake, for the enterprise, for the economy, and for society.

To discharge this responsibility the manager needs, above all, to understand the historical background to the government-business relationship. Traditions with respect to this relationship differ greatly in different countries. They largely determine what is considered 'right' and 'appropriate' in individual countries – by politicians, civil servants and political scientists; by the public; and by the business community. These traditions also explain in large part why the government-business relationship is in crisis these days. Yet few books – whether on government or on business – have paid much attention to the historical setting and to the administrative and political theories that underlie the government-business administration.

## The historical models

The two political models that set the pattern for the business-government relationship were very different ones. They might be called, respectively, mercantilism (or in France, *dirigisme*) and constitutionalism. The mercantilist model is the older of the two.

In the mercantilist model the economy is seen as the foundation of political sovereignty and especially of the military strength of the nation. National economy and national sovereignty are both essentially organized *against* an outside world. It is the main function of the economy to provide the means of survival to the nation-state against the threats from the outside. Within the nation-state there may be friction, conflict, competition, dispute. But, as in a beleaguered fortress, all disputes and disagreements stop at the wall.

In the original crude concept of mercantilism (developed in the late seventeenth century) business was seen as the provider of gold and silver with which to pay the soldiers, who in turn protected national independence and survival. Although Adam Smith demolished this line of reasoning, the mercantilist model still sees the economic foundation of political sovereignty in competitive performance abroad. Exports are the objective – and the test.

In the mercantilist model, the businessman is considered socially inferior to the civil servant. This was as true in the France of Louis XIV as in Japan before World War II. Still, the task of the government administrator is to support, strengthen and encourage business – especially exports. With the rise of technology and of the prefessional manager, business became, so to speak, a part of the national establishment. But it is still a junior partner to government.

An example of this is the position which business associations and organizations have in a mercantilist system. In France – and to a considerable extent, in Germany – membership in the trade or industry association is compulsory. In Japan these associations are almost government bodies. The trade association official is often a former civil servant of high rank. He enjoys more status and power than any but the very biggest and strongest members of the industry themselves. Union agreements are typically negotiated by the industry association and are then binding on member companies. The government handles its relations with industry and business through the associations.

The constitutionalist model, developed in the nineteenth century – above all, in the United States – sees government as standing in an adversary relationship to business. The relationship is governed by laws. It is conducted at arm's length.

Constitutionalism accepts that government cannot stay out of economy and business. 'Business,' both concepts say, 'is too important to be left to the business community.' But where the mercantilist guides and directs and pays subsidies, the constitutionalist says 'thou shalt not' and uses antitrust laws, regulatory agencies and criminal indictments. The mercantilist tries to encourage business, provided it moves in the direction he deems right for national political and military strength. The constitutionalist is determined to keep business out of government; it taints. And he sets limits of political morality to business activity.

Jefferson may be said to have been the first constitutionalist – deeply suspicious of business and convinced that the business interest had to be kept out of government. But it was not until the 1820s, when Andrew Jackson was president (twenty-five years later), that constitutionalism became the prevailing intellectual model for business-government relationship in the US.

It was also during the Jackson Administration that constitutionalism fixed the social position of the businessman in American life. Since then, businessmen have been socially equal to any group in American society.

Indeed, in the late nineteenth and early twentieth centuries in the United States, the businessman was perhaps the socially dominant figure. His competitors for social rank were not, as in mercantilist countries, the civil servants, but the clergy and, later on, the university professor. In the constitutionalist model, since Jackson's days, the businessman is also supposed to be a patriot and available, especially in times of crisis, to serve the nation and to assume political leadership positions. And yet, when Franklin D. Roosevelt, a hundred years after Jackson, called businessmen 'malefactors of great wealth', he spoke in the purest constitutionalist vein.

In the constitutionalist tradition, trade and industry associations are looked upon with great suspicion and are rarely involved in the relations between government and the business community. They are not compulsory and have no coercive powers or official standing, no matter how influential they might be behind the scenes as lobbying groups in Congress.

## Models and reality

Both *dirigisme* and constitutionalism are intellectual models of political – or administrative – theory. Reality always falls far short of such an ideal.

Indeed, many critics have called the official US constitutionalist policy position mere hypocrisy and a complete sham. But this misses the powerful impact constitutionalism had and still has. It motivates America's traditional opposition to the 'system'. It explains why the American radical traditionally has opposed business, whereas the European Leftist has traditionally been 'for' business and wants only to replace the 'wicked capitalist' with is own 'good guys' – that is, government administrators.

Constitutionalism also explains the peculiar forms of US economic and business legislation and regulation. But there is considerable substance to the old remark that the US has been Jeffersonian (i.e., constitutionalist) in theory and Hamiltonian (i.e., mercantilist) in practice.

Mercantilism undoubtedly has been far more widely practised. And when the one country that had actually done what economic theory advocated and had kept government out of the economy – Great Britain – shifted, around 1900, to a political approach to business and economy, it shifted towards *dirigisme* rather than towards constitutionalism.

But even the mercantilist model was never fully realized in practice. From the beginning there were tensions in it. Business again and again slipped out of administrative control. Even in Japan, government and the business community see themselves as adversaries as much as partners.

These two models have, for well over a century, been the guides and set the norms. They told governments and politicians what should be. They established the criteria for right and wrong in the public mind. They did not determine the business-government relationship, but they set the limits within which specific relationship problems could be worked out on a case-by-case, issue-by-issue, 'scandal-by-scandal' basis.

## The new problems

By now, however, both models are outdated. Neither model offers much guidance any more, either to government or to business. Neither model can cope with the new relationship problems that demand solutions. The most important – or at least the most visible – of these new problems have been caused by:

—the 'mixed economy';
—the multinational corporation;
—government's loss of its position as *the* institution; and
—the emergence of the professional manager.

1 The first of these realities is today's 'mixed economy'.

Both of these models were developed for a capitalist economy. Both could also function in a socialist economy (for the adaptation of constitutionalism to socialist competition, see Chapter 12). But neither model can handle a mixed economy in which government activities intertwine and compete at the same time.

Every developed economy is a complex mixture of regulations, governmental controls, subsidies and penalties, business autonomy in areas formerly considered government (e.g., autonomous postal services) and direct government operations of business. There are institutions that, although incorporated as private companies, are publicly owned and discharge public functions. There are also government-owned institutions that operate in fairly competitive markets and discharge 'private-sector' functions. And there is a welter of the most complex partnerships. Defence procurement is but one example. In every non-communist country today, defence materials are procured through a contractual relationship – half partnership, half duel – between government and privately owned contractors.

Defence procurement may be considered a special case. In the US, for instance, the mixed economy in defence is still being explained away as a 'temporary emergency' thirty-five years after the end of World War II. Everyone concerned knows that there is nothing temporary about it and that the fiction of 'temporary emergency' is a major cause of the serious problems in defence procurement. Yet everyone concerned also knows that any attempt to think through and restructure the relationship would immediately run into philosophical contradictions and irreconcilable differences between 'what ought to be' and what is needed. As one high Defense Department official once put it, 'We know it's chaos; but that's still better than paralysis.'

There are going to be more and more *joint tasks* in which government and business will have to work as a team, with leadership taken by one or the other as the situation demands. There are the tasks of the environment. There is the enormous task of conserving the resources of the world. There are the problems of the big city. There is research – technological as well as social. Quality-of-life tasks are perhaps by definition joint tasks that non-governmental institutions have to take social responsibility for doing while governments provide direction and money.

This is difficult enough to fit in with *dirigisme*. The civil servant no longer guides and shapes a separate business community. In some relationships he will have to be a partner, and not necessarily the senior partner. In some relationships (banking and insurance, for example) he has to become the spokesman for business against public policy. In others, especially in relations with 'multinationals', private businesses represent the 'public policy' of their own government, for instance in European unification or in developing underdeveloped economies. The civil servant then defends 'private interests' of domestic industry.

*Dirigisme* can still accept this – though the strain is great. But the mixed economy is quite incompatible with the constitutionalist model, which explains the extreme difficulty American political parties, American political rhetoric, and American political commentators have in explaining the way government and economy actually work.

2 The second factor which cannot be made to fit in the traditional models is the multinational corporation. The multinational corporation is a response to the divorce of economy and sovereignty after three hundred years of marriage. The economy can no longer be defined as a national economy even in the biggest and most powerful countries. Yet sovereignty is still exclusively national. There is no sign of anything to take the place of the nation-state as the political sovereign. Yet there is a genuine world economy that carries the economic dynamics and actually determines economic developments worldwide. It has direct impact on economic behaviour, activity, and results within the national economies, but it is largely impervious to political sovereignty.

The mercantilist model is most directly challenged by the development of which the multinational corporation is both carrier and effect. To mercantilism this divorce is unthinkable; yet it is happening. This was clearly understood by General De Gaulle, when he was President of France in the 1950s and 1960s. His decision not to permit French businesses to go multinational was completely rational. It was also completely futile.

The constitutionalist model has a hard time coping with the multinational corporation. It is no accident that US populism is now attacking the multinational corporation. For the mercantilist tradition, the crime of the multinational corporation is that it is not an instrument of political sovereignty and cannot be one. For the populist of the American constitutionalist tradition, the crime of the multinational corporation is that it is not an instrument of American morality and cannot be one. On the contrary, it must fit itself in every country to the prevailing legal and moral beliefs of the political sovereignty in the country where it operates.

3 In the society of organizations, government becomes one special-purpose institution rather than *the* institution. Such a society creates social responsibility for the nongovernment leadership groups, and especially for the business manager. It thereby undermines the uniqueness of government's position and role.

What made De Gaulle so impressive a figure was his refusal to accept this. De Gaulle instead insisted on the unchallenged primacy of the state – not only over the economy but equally over arts and education. This made De Gaulle consistent and clear. But it also made his policy appear old-fashioned and in the end almost absurd, even to fervent admirers of a great man.

But the constitutionalist too has difficulty with a society in which business is expected to assume social responsibility. His position all along, and the basis for his insistence on an adversary relationship to business, has been that business has to be restrained, policed, regulated, limited – and if need be, punished – lest it behave irresponsibly and antisocially. Hence the ambivalence, approaching schizophrenia, of the traditional American liberal who demands in the same breath that GM or IBM be split up and that they mobilize their resources to solve major social problems.

4 Finally, there is the emergence of the professional manager as against the owner-entrepreneur. The traditional models speak of the businessman. But the reality of today is the manager. This means that the managers of business have emerged as a group which in origin, education, background and values closely re-

sembles the civil servant. At the same time the civil servants (as well as the leadership groups in other institutions) are in the process of becoming managers.

The emergence of managers as a powerful group of leaders is particularly incompatible with the mercantilist model. But equally incompatible for the constitutionalist tradition is the growing trend towards considering business management as the model for public administration.

It may be argued that these are problems for goverment rather than for business. But too much is at stake for business and management to disregard the fact that the traditional, inherited relationship models cannot adequately organize and structure relationship realities any more.

## Guidelines

Specific problems have to be dealt with, even though there are no known solutions, no new political theory, no new and more adequate model. What is needed are 'specifications'. What is needed are criteria by which specific answers to specific problems – pragmatic and temporary – can be tested and judged.

1 The first such specification is that the economic organizations of society – business and their managers – require autonomy and accountability:

—in the interest of the economy;
—for the sake of strong and effective government;
—in the interest of society.

'Accountable Enterprise' might be a better slogan than the by now overused 'Free Enterprise'.

To be accountable for performance, economic institutions and their managers have to have autonomy. One cannot be accountable for what one has no authority over and cannot control. Business enterprises and managements have to be under the performance test or they cease to perform. They have to be able to allocate society's and economy's resources in a rational manner against objective criteria, or resources will be misallocated.

This is not a matter of ownership. It requires market test and market decision, in the three economic dimensions – the market for goods and services, the market for capital and investment and the market for jobs and careers.

Of the three, the capital market may be most crucial. It is in the capital market that resources for the future are allocated on the basis of performance expectation. And it is the capital market which, therefore, needs self-determination as well as regulation.

But there is need also for an open-ended economy, an economy in which businesses can be born and also die. It is a basic weakness of a state-owned or state-controlled economic system that businesses are not allowed to go bankrupt and can only rarely be liquidated. Yet clearly the welfare of society and economy demands a healthy business metabolism.

The performance capacity of government also rests on autonomy for business and management. A political process at best makes allocation decisions poorly and painfully. They clog government and overload it to the point where it cannot move at all, cannot make decisions, cannot devote itself to the governmental tasks properly.

Society too requires management autonomy. Managers of the major organizations are collectively the leadership groups of the society of organizations. But a healthy society requires a pluralism of leadership groups with different values, different priorities, different 'styles'. It requires alternatives – in careers and career ladders, in points of view, in life-styles. Otherwise it degenerates into conformity and loses its capacity for change. When the need for change arises, no one can even imagine a behaviour different from what everyone in the leadership group is accustomed to and considers 'right', if not a fixed 'law of nature'. At the same time, those among the able and ambitious who do not fit easily into the one pattern of the one leadership group are alienated.

2 Society also needs a healthy and functioning government, especially the complex and interdependent society ours has become.

Government is needed as the political decision-maker perhaps more than ever before. At the same time, the capacity of government to be the political decision-maker is increasingly jeopardized by its weight, size, and bureaucracy. It is increasingly jeopardized by government tendency to take on too many things, to promise too much and to 'do' too much. The fatter government becomes, the flabbier and weaker it actually is.

Business and business management cannot restore government to health. This is a political job. But they can at least be conscious of the need and avoid, in working out the business-government relationship, whatever might weaken the performance capacity of government as the central political decision-maker. In this area their responsibility is *Primum non nocere* – 'not knowingly to do damage'.

## The multinational corporation

3 The twin needs for economic autonomy and effective government come together in one major problem of the business-government relationship.

The multinational corporation is a central economic achievement of the period since World War II and perhaps the most fruitful social innovation of the century. It is also a hard problem. What is needed is to work out a relationship that safeguards both a true world economy and the political sovereignty of national governments in peaceful coexistence. Otherwise we will impair or destroy that most promising development, the multinational business, and undermine the capacity for political vision and action and for political community.

4 The need to think through the business-government relationship is not really the result of a crisis of business. It is the result of a serious crisis of government. Yet business managers will have to look upon the relationship to government and society as their task. They cannot wait for the political scientist or the theoretical economist. A purely negative attitude that fights every 'encroachment of government' is not going to be effective. All it can do is delay. Positive, affirmative action is needed.

We do not need more laws. No country suffers from a shortage of laws these days. We need a new model. Yet all we can expect are temporary answers to specific problems. These answers should, however, be compatible with minimum specifications: they should preserve the autonomy and accountability of business enterprise and business management; they should safeguard a free and flexible society capable of change; they should harmonize the world economy of the multinational and the sovereignty of the nation-states; and they should encourage strong and performing government.

## Summary

One of the most important dimensions of social responsibility is the government-business relationship. It is crucial to the functioning of business and to the functioning of government as well. Yet both traditional theories for organizing the relationship – the mercantilist one and the constitutionalist one – are increasingly becoming inappropriate and ineffectual. No new theory is yet available; but business has a responsibility – and an opportunity – for thinking through and shaping the relationship to enable both government and business to function.

# 22 The Ethics of Responsibility

Countless sermons have been preached and printed on the ethics of business and the businessperson. Most have nothing to do with business and little to do with ethics.

One main topic is plain, everyday honesty. Businesspeople, we are told solemnly, should not cheat, steal, lie, bribe or take bribes. But nor should anyone else. Men and women do not acquire exemption from ordinary rules of personal behaviour because of their work or job. Nor, however, do they cease to be human beings when appointed vice-president, city manager or college dean. And there have always been a number of people who cheat, steal, lie, bribe or take bribes. The problem is one of moral values and moral education. There is not a separate ethics of business, nor is one needed.

The other common theme in the discussion of ethics in business has nothing to do with ethics. Such things as the employment of call girls to entertain customers are not matters of ethics but matters of aesthetics. 'Do I want to see a pimp when I look at myself in the mirror while shaving ?' is the real question.

It would indeed be nice to have fastidious leaders. Alas, fastidiousness has never been prevalent among leadership groups, whether kings and counts, priests or generals, or even 'intellectuals' such as the painters and humanists of the Renaissance or the Chinese tradition. All a fastidious man can do is withdraw personally from activities that violate his self-respect and his sense of taste.

Lately these old sermon topics have been joined, especially in the US, by a third one. Managers, we are told, have an 'ethical responsibility' to take an active and constructive role in their community, to serve community causes, give their time to community activities and so on.

There are many countries where such community activity does not fit the traditional mores; Japan and France would be examples. But where the community has a tradition of 'voluntarism', as in the US, managers should indeed be encouraged to participate and to take responsible leadership in community affairs and community organizations. Such activities should, however, never be forced on them. Nor should managers be appraised, rewarded or promoted according to their participation in voluntary activities. Ordering-or pressuring them into such work is abuse of organizational power – and illegitimate.

## Leadership groups but not leaders

A problem of ethics that is peculiar to the manager arises from the fact that the managers of institutions are *collectively* the leadership groups of the society of organizations. But *individually* a manager is just another employee.

This is clearly recognized by the public. Even the most powerful head of the largest corporation is unknown to the public. Even most of the company's employees barely know his name and would not recognize his face. He may owe his position entirely to personal merit and proven performance. But he owes his authority and standing entirely to his institution. Everybody knows GE, the Telephone Company, Mitsubishi and Unilever. But who heads these great corporations – or for that matter, the University of California, the Ecole Polytechnique in Paris or St Mary's Hospital in London ? The question is of direct interest and concern primarily to the management group within these institutions.

It is therefore inappropriate to speak of managers as leaders. They are 'members of the leadership group'. The group, however, does occupy a position of visibility, prominence, and authority. It therefore has responsibility – and it is with this responsibility that the preceding chapters of this section are concerned.

But what are the responsibilities, what are the ethics of the individual manager, as a member of the leadership group ?

Essentially being a member of a leadership group is what traditionally has been meant by the term 'professional'. Membership in such a group confers duties. To expect every manager to be a leader is futile. There are, in a developed society, thousands, if not millions, of managers – and leadership is always the rare exception and confined to a very few individuals. But as a member of a leadership group a manager stands under the demands of a professional ethic of responsibility.

## Primum non nocere

The first responsibility of a profession was spelled out clearly, in Greece, 2,500 years ago, in the Hippocratic Oath which every young physician still swears : *primum non nocere* – 'Above all, not knowingly to do harm.'

No professional, whether doctor, lawyer, or manager, can promise that he or she will indeed do good for the client. All they can do is try. But they can promise that they will not knowingly do harm. Professionals have to have autonomy. They cannot be controlled, supervised or directed by the client. Decisions have to be entrusted to their knowledge and judgement. But it is the foundation of their autonomy, and indeed its rationale, that they see themselves as 'affected with the client's interest'. Professionals, in other words, are private in the sense that they are autonomous and not subject to political or ideological control. But they are in public in the sense that the welfare of their client sets limits to their deeds and words. And *primum non nocere*, 'not knowingly to do harm', is the basic rule of professional ethics.

There are important areas where managers, and especially business managers, still do not realize that in order to be permitted to remain autonomous and private, they have to impose on themselves the responsibility of the professional ethic. They still have to learn that it is their job to scrutinize their deeds, words, and behaviour to make sure that they do not knowingly do harm.

One, perhaps the most important one, of these areas has already been discussed. The manager who fails to think through and work for the appropriate solution to an impact of the business because it makes him unpopular in the club knowingly does harm. He or she knowingly abets a cancerous growth. That this is stupid has been said. That this always in the end hurts the business or the industry more than a little temporary 'unpleasantness' would have hurt has been said too. But it is also gross violation of professional ethics.

But there are other areas as well. American managers, in particular, tend to violate the rule not knowingly to do harm with respect to:

—executive compensation;
—the use of benefit plans to impose 'golden fetters' on people in the company's employ; and
—in their profit rhetoric.

Their actions and words in these areas tend to cause social disruption. They tend to conceal healthy reality and to create disease, or at least social hypochondria. They tend to misdirect and to prevent undetstanding. And this is grievous social harm.

## Executive compensation and economic inequality

Contrary to widespread belief, incomes today have become far more equal (in developed countries) than in any society of which we have a record. And they have tended to become steadily more equal as national and personal incomes increase. Equally contrary to popular rhetoric, income equality is greatest in the United States.

Specifically, in the typical American business the inequality of income between the lowest-paid people and the people in charge – that is, between the machine operator and the manager of a large plant – is at most one to four, if taxes are taken into account. The take-home pay of the machine operator after taxes in 1970 was around $7,500 a year; the after-tax income of very few plant managers was larger than $25,000, all bonuses included. If fringes are taken into account, the ratio is even lower, i.e., one to three (or $12,000 to $35,000 maximum). And similar ratios prevail in other developed countries.

Whether the degree of inequality of incomes that actually prevailed in the US economy is 'too high' or 'too low' is a matter of opinion. But clearly it is much lower than the great majority of the American public accepts or even considers desirable. Every survey shows that an 'income ratio of 1 to 10 or 12' between the blue-collar in the factory and the 'big boss' would be considered 'about right'. That would make the 'after-tax take-home pay' of the 'big boss' somewhere around $75,000 to $100,000 a year, which would be equal to a pre-tax salary of at least $200,000. Only a mere handful of executives earn that much, bonuses included. If the comparison is made – as it should be – between total incomes including fringes, deferred compensation, share options and all other forms of extra compensation, a 1 to 12 ratio would work out to an after-tax top figure of $150,000. And no more than a dozen or so top people in the very largest companies have a pre-tax 'total compensation package' of $300,000 and up (needed to produce an after-tax value of $150,000). The 'extremely rich' are not employed executives; they are either heirs of the millionaires of pre-tax days or owners of small businesses.

The facts of increasing income equality in US society are quite clear. Yet the popular impression is one of rapidly increasing inequality. This is dangerous illusion. It corrodes. It destroys mutual trust between groups that have to live together and work together. It can only lead to political measures that can seriously harm society, economy and the manager as well.

The belief in growing income inequality in the US partly reflects America's racial problem. The emergence in big cities of a nonworking population of blacks has created a marginal but highly visible group suffering from extreme inequality of incomes. That the income of the employed Negro has been going up rapidly and is likely, within a decade or so, to be equal to that of the employed white doing the same kind of work – and that four-fifths of the American Negroes are employed and working – tends to be obscured by the dire poverty of the much smaller but highly concentrated groups of unemployed or unemployables in the black ghettos of the core cities.

Another reason for the widespread belief in growing inequality is inflation. Inflation is a corrosive social poison precisely because it makes people look for a villain. The economists' explanation that no one benefits by inflation, that is, that no one gets the purchasing power that inflation takes away from the income recipients, simply makes no sense to ordinary experience. Somebody must have benefited, somebody 'must have stolen what is rightfully mine'. Every inflation in history has therefore created class hatred, mutual distrust and beliefs that, somehow, 'the other fellow' gains illicitly at 'my' expense. The middle class becomes paranoid in an inflationary period and turns against the 'system'. The inflations of the 1960s and 1970s in the developed countries were no exceptions.

But the main cause of the dangerous delusion of increasing inequality of income is the widely publicized enormous *pre-tax* incomes of a few men at the top of a few giant corporations, and the – equally widely publicized – 'extras' of executive compensation, e.g., share options.

The $500,000 a year which the chief executive of one of the giant corporations is paid is largely 'make-believe money'. Its function is status rather than income. Most of it, whatever tax loopholes the lawyers might find, is immediately taxed away. And the 'extras' are simply attempts to put a part of the executive's income into a somewhat lower tax bracket. Economically, neither serves much purpose. But socially and psychologically they 'knowingly do harm'. They cannot be defended.

One way to eliminate the offence is for companies to commit themselves to a maximum range of *after-tax* compensation. The 1 to 10 ratio that the great majority of Americans would consider perfectly acceptable, would, in fact, be wider than the actual range of most companies. (There should, I would argue, be room, however, for an occasional exception: the rare, 'once-in-a-life-time', very big, special bonus to someone – a research scientist, manager or salesman – who has made an extraordinary contribution.)

Equally important is acceptance of social responsibility on the part of the managers to work for a rational system of taxation,* which eliminates the temptation of 'tax gimmicks' and the need for them.

There is a strong case for adequate incentives for performing executives. And compensation in money is far preferable to hidden compensation such as perquisites. The recipient can choose what to spend the money on, rather than, as in the case of 'perks', taking whatever the company provides, be it a chauffeur-driven car, a big house or (as in the case of some Swedish companies) a governess for the children. Indeed it may well be that real incomes in American business are not sufficiently unequal.

What is dangerous, however, is the delusion of inequality. The basic cause is the tax laws. But the managers' willingness to accept, and indeed to play along with, an antisocial tax structure is a major contributory cause. And unless managers realize that this violates the rule 'not knowingly to do damage', they will, in the end, be the main sufferers.

* We know the specifications of such a system – and they are simple: *no* preferential tax rates for *any* personal income, whether from salaries or from capital gains, and a limit on the maximum tax – say 50 per cent of total income received.

## The danger of 'golden fetters'

A second area in which the manager of today does not live up to the commitment of *primum non nocere* is closely connected with compensation.

Since World War II compensation and benefits have been increasingly misused to create 'golden fetters'.

Retirement benefits, extra compensation, bonuses, and share options are all forms of compensation. From the point of view of the enterprise – but also from the point of view of the economy – these are 'labour costs' no matter how they are labelled. They are treated as such by managements when they sit down to negotiate with the union. But increasingly, if only because of the bias of the tax laws, these benefits are being used to tie employee to employer. They are being made dependent on staying with the same employer, often for many years. And they are structured in such a way that leaving a company's employ entails drastic penalties and actual loss of benefits that have already been earned.

Golden fetters do not strengthen the company. They lead to 'negative selection'. People who know that they are not performing in their present employment – that is, people who are clearly in the wrong place – will often not move but stay where they know they do not properly belong. But if they stay because the penalty for leaving is too great, they resist and resent it. They know that they have been bribed and were too weak to say no. They are likely to be sullen, resentful and bitter the rest of their working lives.

It is incumbent, therefore, on the managers to think through which of these benefits should properly – by their own rationale – be tied to continued employment. Share options might, for instance, belong here. But pension rights, performance bonuses, participation in profits and so on, have been 'earned' and should be available to the employee without restricting rights as a citizen, an individual and a person. And, again, managers will have to work to get the tax law changes that are needed.

## The rhetoric of the profit motive

Through their rhetoric, managers make it impossible for the public to understand economic reality. This violates the requirement that they not knowingly do harm. This is particularly true of the United States but also of Western Europe. For in the West, managers still talk constantly of the profit motive. And they still define the goal of their business as profit maximization. They do not stress the need for capital. They almost never even mention the cost of capital, let alone that a business has to produce enough profit to obtain the capital it needs at minimum cost.

Managers constantly complain about the hostility to profit. They rarely realize that their own rhetoric is one of the main reasons for this hostility. For indeed in the terms management uses when it talks to the public, there is no possible justification for profit, no explanation for its existence, no function it performs. There is only the profit motive, a desire of some anonymous capitalists – and why that desire should be indulged in by society any more than bigamy, for instance, is never explained. But profitability is a crucial *need* of economy and society.

In any pluralist society responsibility for the public good has been the central problem and issue. The pluralist society of organizations is no exception. Its leaders represent 'special interests', that is, institutions designed to fulfil a specific need of society. The leaders of this society are the servants of such institutions. At the same time, they are the major leadership group of the society. They have to serve both their own institution and the common good. If the society is to function, let alone if it is to remain a free society, the people we call managers will remain 'private' in their institutions. No matter who owns them and how, they will remain autonomous. But they will also have to be 'public' in their ethics.

In this tension between the private functioning of the manager, the necessary autonomy of the institution and its accountability to its own mission and purpose, and the public character of the manager, lies the specific ethical problem of the society of organizations. *Primum non nocere* may seem tame compared to the rousing calls for 'statesmanship' that abound in today's manifestos on social responsibility. But, as the physicians found out long ago, it is not an easy rule to live up to. Its very modesty and self-constraint make it the right rule for the ethics managers need, the ethics of responsibility.

## Summary

The individual manager, even the chief executive of a giant corporation, has in this century become anonymous, unassuming – just another employee. But together the managers of our institutions – business, universities, schools, hospitals and government agencies – are the leadership groups in the modern society of organizations. As such they need an ethics, a commitment and a code. The right one is the code developed more than two thousand years ago for the first professional leadership group, the physician: 'Above all not knowingly to do harm.'

# Part Five
# The Manager's
# Work and Jobs

It is responsibility for contributing to the results of the enterprise, not 'responsibility for the work of others' that makes a manager. It is responsibility for his own work. There is a distinct 'work of the manager'; there are distinct 'managerial jobs'. There is a distinct way to manage managers: by objectives and self-control. As we move from 'middle management' to the 'knowledge organization' there are new and different requirements. Most important, managers have to be managed in a way that engenders a spirit of performance in them.

# 23 Why Managers?

Managers are the basic resource of the business enterprise. In a fully automatic factory there may be almost no rank-and-file employees. But there will be managers – in fact, there will be many more than there were in the factory of yesterday.

Managers are the most expensive resource in most businesses – and the one that depreciates the fastest and needs the most constant replenishment. It takes years to build a management team, but it can be depleted in a short period of misrule. The number of managers and the investment that each manager represents are increasing steadily. Parallel with this goes an increase in the demands of the enterprise on its managers. These demands have doubled in every generation, and there is no reason to expect the trend to slow during the next decades.

During the last quarter century managers everywhere have subjected themselves to a steady barrage of speeches, and programmes in which they tell each other that their job is to manage the people under them, urge each other to give top priority to this responsibility, and furnish each other with copious advice and expensive gadgets for 'downward communications'. But I have yet to sit down with a manager, whatever his or her level or job, who was not primarily concerned with upward relations and upward communications. (See also Chapter 30, 'Managerial Communications.') Every vice-president feels that relations with the president are the real problem. And so on down to the first-line supervisor, the production foreman, and chief clerk, who are quite certain that they could get along with their people if only the 'boss' and the personnel department left them alone.

This is not, as personnel people seem inclined to think, a sign of the perversity of human nature. Upward relations are properly a manager's first concern. To be a manager means sharing in the responsibility for the performance of the enterprise. Anyone who is not expected to take this responsibility is not a manager.

These problems of upward relations that worry the manager – the relationship to the boss; doubts as to what is expected in terms of performance; difficulty in getting the department's point across, or programme accepted; concern that one's activity be given full weight; the relations with other departments and with staff people, and so forth – are all problems of managing managers.

## The rise, decline and rebirth of Ford

The story of Henry Ford, his rise and decline, and of the revival of his company under his grandson, Henry Ford II, has been told so many times that it has passed into folklore:

Henry Ford, starting with nothing in 1905, had fifteen years later built the world's largest and most profitable manufacturing enterprise. The Ford Motor Company, in the early twenties, dominated and almost monopolized the American automobile market and held a leadership position in most of the other important automobile markets of the world. In addition, it had amassed, out of profits, cash reserves of a billion dollars or so.

Yet only a few years later, by 1927, this seemingly impregnable business empire was in shambles. Having lost its leadership position and barely a poor third in the market, it lost money almost every year for twenty years or so, and remained unable to compete vigorously right through World War II. In 1944 the founder's grandson, Henry Ford II, then only twenty-six years old and without training or experience, took over, ousted two years later his grandfather's cronies in a palace coup, brought in a totally new management team and saved the company.

It is not commonly realized that this dramatic story is far more than a story of personal success and failure. It is, above all, what one might call a controlled experiment in mismanagement.

The first Ford failed because of his firm belief that a business did not need managers and management. All it needed, he believed, was the owner-entrepreneur with his 'helpers'. The only difference between Ford and most of his contemporaries in business was that, as in everything he did, Henry Ford stuck uncomprisingly to his convictions. He applied them strictly, firing or sidelining any one of his 'helpers', no matter how able, who dared act as a 'manager', make a decision or take action without orders from Ford. The way he applied his theory can only be described as a test, one that ended up by fully disproving Ford's theory.

In fact, what makes the Ford story unique and important is that Ford *could* test the hypothesis. This was possible in part because he lived so long, and in part because he had a billion dollars to back his convictions. Ford's failure was not the result of personality or temperament. It was first and foremost the result of his refusal to accept managers and management as necessary, as a necessity based on task and function rather than in 'delegation' from the 'boss'.

## GM – the countertest

In the early twenties, while Ford was trying to prove that managers are not needed, Alfred P. Sloan, Jr, the newly appointed president of General Motors, put the opposite thesis to the test. GM at that time was almost crushed by the towering giant of the Ford Motor Company. It was barely able to survive as a weak number two. Little more than a haphazard financial speculation, GM had been stitched together out of small failing automobile companies sold because they could not stand up to Ford's competition. GM had not one winning car in its line, no dealer organization and no financial strength. Each of the former owners had stayed on and had been allowed to mismanage his former business his own way as if it had been his own personal property. When Sloan became president of GM, he thought through what the business and structure of GM should be and converted his undisciplined barons into a management team. Within five years GM had become the leader in the American automobile industry and has remained the leader ever since.

When Henry Ford's grandson put Sloan's hypothesis to the test again twenty years later, the Ford Motor Company was nearly bankrupt. The entire billion dollars of cash assets it had held in the early twenties had been poured into paying for the deficits since. As soon as young Henry Ford II took over in 1946, he set out to do for his company what Sloan had done for GM two decades earlier. He created a management structure and a management team. Within five years the Ford Motor Company regained its potential for growth and profit, both at home and abroad. It became the main competitor to General Motors and even outstripped GM in the fast-growing European automobile market.

## The lesson of the Ford story

The lesson of the Ford story is that managers and management are the specific need of the business enterprise, its specific organ and its basic structure. Enterprise clearly cannot do without managers. One cannot argue that management does the owner's job by delegation. Management is needed not because the job is too big for any one individual, but because managing in enterprise is something essentially different from managing one's own property.

Henry Ford failed to see the need to change to managers and management because he believed (as the textbooks still tell us) that a large and complex business enterprise 'evolves' organically from the small one-man shop. Of course, Ford started small. But growth brought more than a change in size. At some point quantity turned into quality. At some point Ford became a *business enterprise*, that is, an organization requiring different structure and different principles – an organization requiring managers and management.

Management did not evolve out of the small owner-managed firm as a result of its growth. It is a new concept, designed for enterprises that were large and complex to begin with.

The large American railroad of the nineteenth century – which wrestled with the engineering task of building a railbed, the financial task of raising very large sums of capital, and the political-relations tasks of obtaining charters, land grants, and subsidies – was the first enterprise that can be said to have been 'man-

310 The Manager's Work and Jobs

aged'. Indeed, the management structure designed shortly after the Civil War for the first long-distance American railroads has remained essentially unchanged to this day.

It was not until thirty or forty years later that the concept of management was transferred from the enterprise that started out large to the enterprise that had grown large. Andrew Carnegie and John D. Rockefeller, Jr, introduced management into the steel and petroleum industries, respectively. A little later still, Pierre S. du Pont restructured the family chemical company (E. I. du Pont de Nemours & Co) and gave it a management, both to make it capable of growth and to preserve family control. The management structure Pierre du Pont built in his family company between 1915 and 1920 became, a few years later, the starting point for the General Motors structure of 'professional management' after the du Ponts had acquired control of the near-bankrupt and floundering automotive conglomerate and had made Sloan president.

## Management as a 'change of phase'

The change from a business which the owner-entrepreneur can run with 'helpers' to a business that requires a management is what the physicists call a 'change of phase' such as the change from water to ice. It is an abrupt change from one state of matter, from one fundamental structure, to another. Sloan's example shows that it can be made within one and the same organization. But Sloan's restructuring of GM also shows that the job can be done only if basic concepts, basic principles, and individual vision are changed radically.

Henry Ford wanted no managers. The result was that he misdirected managers, set up their jobs improperly, created a spirit of suspicion and frustration, misorganized his company, and stunted or broke management people. The only choice managers have in these areas is therefore whether management jobs will be done well or badly. But the jobs themselves will exist, because there is an enterprise to be managed. And whether the jobs are done right or not will determine largely whether the enterprise will survive and prosper or decline and ultimately fall.

**Summary**

Managers are not helpers and their jobs are not delegated. Their jobs are autonomous and grounded in the needs of the enterprise. The only choice is between doing the managerial jobs well or badly – but the jobs exist because there is an enterprise that has to be managed.

# 24 Design and Content of Managerial Jobs

A manager's job should always be based on a task necessary to attain the company's objectives. It should always be a real job – one that makes a visible and, if possible, measurable contribution to the success of the enterprise. It should have the broadest rather than the narrowest scope and authority. Managers should be directed and controlled by the objectives of performance rather than by their bosses.

The activities that have to be performed and the contributions that have to be made to attain the company's objectives should always determine what managerial jobs are needed. A manager's job exists because the task facing the enterprise requires it – and for no other reason. The job has to have its own authority and its own responsibility. *For managers must manage.*

The job should always have managerial scope and proportions. Since a manager is someone who takes responsibility for, and contributes to, the final results of the enterprise, the job should always embody the maximum challenge, carry the maximum responsibility, and make the maximum contribution.

## Common mistakes in designing managerial jobs

There is no formula that will guarantee the right job design for a managerial job. Yet six common mistakes that impair the effectiveness of manager and managerial organization can be avoided.

1 *The too-small Job*. The most common mistake is to design the job so small that a good manager cannot grow. Any managerial job is, in all likelihood, a terminal job – that is, a job on which the incumbent will stay until he or she retires. Even in rapidly growing organizations this is the rule rather than the exception.

The number of jobs at the top is inevitably far smaller than the number of jobs at the bottom. Out of every ten people on a given organizational level, no more than two or three can normally expect even one promotion. The rest are likely to stay where they are. They may get bigger titles and, as a rule, more money. But what they do is unlikely to change a great deal.

If a job is designed so small that the incumbent can learn everything about it in a few years, most managers will be frustrated, bored, and will stop really working. They will 'retire on the job'. They will risist any change, any innovation, any new idea, for change can only be a change for the worse for them and threaten their security. Knowing very well that they are not actually contributing any more, they are fundamentally insecure.

Managerial jobs should, therefore, be designed to allow a person to grow, to learn, and to develop for many years to come. There is little harm, as a rule, in a job that is designed too big. This mistake shows up soon and can easily be corrected. A job that is too small, however, is an insidious, slow poison which paralyses both the manager and the organization.

All managerial jobs should be designed to provide satisfaction through performance. The job itself should challenge and reward. If the main satisfaction of the job is promotion, the job itself has lost significance and meaning. And since the majority in managerial positions are bound to be disappointed in their hopes for promotion – by arithmetic rather than by organization politics – it is unwise to focus on promotion. The emphasis should always be on the job itself rather than on the next job.

In fact, there are few things quite as dangerous as an organization in which promotions are so rapid as to become the accepted reward for doing a decent job.

An extreme example is the situation of some of the large New

York commercial banks. Very few young people were hired in the banking industry in the thirties and forties when commercial banks in New York were shrinking rather than expanding. When the banking business expanded again after World War II, a series of mergers (such as the one between the Chase Bank and the bank of the Manhattan Company, which created the Chase Manhattan) actually created a surplus of managers. By the early fifties, however, large numbers of the men who had started before 1929 reached retirement age, and the banks began to hire large numbers of young people, fresh out of college or graduate business school. Within seven or eight years many of them rose to positions of substantial pay and exalted title such as vice-president and senior vice-president. Before they were thirty, large numbers of these 'young comers' reached, in other words, what must be their terminal position. Yet – in large part because these young people did not have much experience – these jobs, whatever the big title and the good salary, were quite limited in scope and authority. And by the time they were forty, many of these people had become bored, cynical, frustrated, and no longer excited about the job and its challenge.

A company that is expanding rapidly is well-advised to bring into important positions a few seasoned and older outsiders who have made a career elsewhere. Otherwise it is bound to create expectations among its own young managers, which, a few years later, it must frustrate.

Another important reason why jobs and a job structure focused on rapid promotion are to be avoided is that they result in an unbalanced age structure. Both an age structure that is overbalanced on the side of youth and one overbalanced on the side of age create serious organizational turbulence.

The management structure needs continuity and self-renewal. There must be continuity so that the organization does not have suddenly to replace a large number of experienced but old managers with new and untried ones. And there has to be enough 'managerial metabolism' that new ideas and new faces can assert themselves. A management group that is all of the same age is a management group headed for crisis. Yet the management group that is uniformly old may be preferable to the one that is uniformly too young. At least then the crisis is over sooner.

2 *The nonjob.* Worse even than the job that is too small is the job that is not really a job, the job of the typical 'assistant to'.

The managerial job must have specific objectives and a specific purpose and function. A manager must be able to make a contribution that can be identified. The manager must be accountable.

But the typical assistant does not have a job that can make a contribution. He cannot be held accountable and his function, purpose, and objectives cannot be identified. He is a 'helper' who does whatever the boss thinks needs to be done or whatever the assistant can 'sell' to the boss. Such a job corrupts. The holder becomes either a wire-puller who abuses his influence with an important executive or a toady who tries to make his career by licking his boss's boots. The assistant position also corrupts the organization. No one ever knows what the role, authority, and actual power of the assistant are. As a rule, other managers will flatter him, use him, and exploit his insecurity of tenure.

3 *Balancing Managing and Working.* Managing is work. But it is not, by itself, full-time work. The way to design a managerial job is to combine 'managing' with 'working', that is, responsibility for a specific function or job of one's own. As a rule, the manager should be both a manager and an individual career professional.

A manager should have enough to do – otherwise he or she is likely to try to do the subordinates' work for them. The common complaint that managers do not 'delegate' usually means that managers do not have enough to do and therefore take on the job the subordinate should be doing. But also, it is rather frustrating not to have work of one's own – especially for people who have grown up in the habit of work. And it is not particularly desirable for a manager not to have a job of his own. He or she soon loses the sense of workmanship and the respect for hard work without which, however, a manager is likely to do more harm than good. A manager should be a 'working boss' rather than a 'co-ordinator'.

4 *The One-Person Job.* As far as possible, a manager's job should

be designed so that it can be done by one person working alone and with the people in the unit which he or she manages. It is a mistake to design a job so that it requires continuous meetings, continuous 'cooperation' and 'coordination'. There is no need, especially nqt in managerial jobs, to inflict extra 'human relations'. The job by its very nature requires more human relations than most people are capable of. And one can either work or meet. One cannot do both at the same time.

Another mistake that is fairly common – and usually unnecessary – is to design a job in which the incumbent has to spend a great deal of time travelling. Just as one cannot meet and work at the same time, one cannot travel and work at the same time. Person-to-person and face-to-face meetings with colleagues, associates, subordinates, customers and superiors are absolutely essential. There is no substitute. But it is far better to spend a substantial amount of time once every two years with the managers and the main customers of a subsidiary company than to 'commute' – that is, leave New York on Tuesday, spend Wednesday in Paris and be back on the job in New York on Thursday. This means only that no work gets done for four days: one needs, after all, at least one day to recover from this futile attempt to be in two places at once.

5 *Titles as Rewards*. Titles should never be used as rewards, let alone to cover up lack of function. Titles 'in lieu of a raise' are not nearly as bad, nor as common, as titles 'in lieu of a job'.

An example is the large commercial bank, both in the United States and in Germany. In the United States everybody has to be a vice-president or at least an officer. In Germany everybody has to be a Herr Direktor. There are reasons for this. The customer of a bank, say the head of a small business, will not discuss his financial problems with anybody but an officer. But this also deforms. It makes dissatisfied those who do not get the title, perhaps because their job does not entail close customer contact. It adds greatly to the dissatisfaction of people who reach the exalted title of vice-president at an early age and then find that they are locked into the same humdrum routine for the rest of their working lives.

The rule should be: for first-rate work we pay – and pay well.

But we change title only when function, position and responsibility change. Titles do create expectations. They do imply rank and responsibility. To use them as empty gestures – that is, as substitutes for rank and responsibility – is asking for trouble.

6 *The Widow-Maker job.* Finally, jobs that are 'widow-makers' should be rethought and restructured. In the heyday of the great sailing ships, around 1850, just before the coming of steam, every shipping company had a 'widow-maker' on its hands once in a while. This was a ship which, for reasons nobody could figure out, tended to get out of control and kill people. After it had done this a few times a prudent ship-owner pulled the ship out of service and broke it up, no matter how much money he had invested in it. Otherwise, he soon found himself without captains or mates.

In many companies there are jobs which manage to defeat one good manager after the other – without any clear reason why. These jobs seem to be logical, seem to be well constructed, seem to be do-able – yet nobody seems to be able to do them. If a job has defeated, in a row, two individuals who in their previous assignments had done well, it should be restructured. It then usually becomes clear, though only by hindsight, what was wrong with the job in the first place.

One typical 'widow-maker' has been the job of international vice-president in the large American company. Nobody seems to know why the job should not work, but in most cases one good executive after the other fails in it. The reason is usually that the company has outgrown the volume of business which justifies treating 'international' as a stepchild. But this becomes clear only in retrospect, after one has restructured the job and has found the manager who can do the work.

The 'widow-maker' job is sometimes the result of accident. One man who somehow combined in himself temperamental characteristics which are not usually found in one person, created the job and acquitted himself well. In other words, what looked like a logical job was an accident of personality rather than the result of a genuine function. But one cannot replace personality.

## Job structure and personality

The abuse of titles and the 'widow-maker' job relate closely to one of the most hotly debated issues with respect to managerial jobs and managerial structure: Should the organization be structured so that jobs fit people? Or should the organization be 'functional', with people fitted to jobs?

As commonly propounded, this is not a real problem. Quite obviously, people have to fill the jobs, and therefore jobs have to fit people. We will indeed have to design jobs that really fit people, answer their needs, and fulfil their expectations. We will, increasingly, see 'organization planning' in large companies, that is, attempts to make jobs fit people and serve them.

Yet organization structure has to be impersonal and task-focused. Otherwise it is impossible to have continuity and to have people succeed each other. If the job is designed for an individual rather than for a task, it has to be restructured every time there is a change in the incumbent. And, as experienced managers know, one cannot restructure *one* job. There is a true 'domino effect', a true chain reaction. Restructuring a job usually means restructuring a score of jobs, moving people around and upsetting everybody. And for this reason, jobs have to be designed to fit a task, rather than a particular person.

There is one exception: the exceedingly rare, truly exceptional man for whose sake the rule should be broken.

Alfred P. Sloan, Jr, the architect of General Motors, was adamant that jobs had to be impersonal and task-focused. But he made one exception to accommodate one of the great inventors of our century, Charles F. Kettering. Kettering was an exceedingly difficult man, and he was a man who disregarded every single organizational rule. Yet his inventions, from the selfstarter to the redesign of the diesel engine, were of major importance. Sloan offered to set up Kettering as an independent researcher. But Kettering wanted to be vice-president and a 'big businessman'. Sloan gave in, but the moment Kettering retired, the job was redesigned – from 'resident genius' to manager of a large research laboratory.

The design of a job has to start out with the task, but it also has to be a design that can accommodate people with different temperaments, habits and behaviour patterns. This is a major reason why managerial jobs ought to be designed big rather than small. A job has to be big enough to provide satisfaction and achievement to a good manager, working in his or her own way.

'A job should be small enough so that a good manager can get his arms around it' is a common saying. It is the wrong rule. 'A job should be specific enough so that a good manager can go to work on it, but so big that he can't get his arms around it' is the right rule.

'Style' should never be a consideration, either in designing a managerial job or in filling it. The only requirement of a managerial job, and the only test of the incumbent, is performance. Every organization needs a clear understanding of the kind of behaviour that is unacceptable. There must be a clear definition of the nonpermissible action, especially towards people, whether inside the business – employees – or outside – suppliers and customers. But within these limits a manager should have the fullest freedom to do the job the way it best suits individual temperament and personality.

'Style' is packaging. The only substance is performance.


## The span of managerial relationships

In discussing how big a manager's job should be, the textbooks often start out with the observation that one person can supervise only a very small number of people – the so-called span of control. This in turn leads to that managerial atrocity: levels upon levels, which impede cooperation and communication, stifle the development of tomorrow's managers and erode the meaning of the management job.

In the first place, the principle of the span of control is rarely cited properly. It is not how many people report to a manager that matters. It is how many people *who have to work with each other* report to a manager. What counts are the number of relationships, not the number of individuals.

The president of a company who has reporting to him a number of senior executives, each concerned with a major function, should indeed keep the number of direct subordinates to a fairly low number – between eight and twelve is probably the limit. These subordinates – the chief financial officer, the head of manufacturing, the head of marketing and so on – have to work every day with each other and with the company's president. If they do not work together, they do not work at all. Therefore, the president is engaged in a great many relationships even though the number of direct subordinates may be quite small.

By contrast, a regional vice-president of Sears, Roebuck can – and does – have several hundred store managers report to him. Each store is separate. There is no need whatever for interaction between two different stores. All the stores do the same kind of work and have the same job. They can all be appraised and measured by the same yardsticks. Theoretically, there is no limit to the number of store managers a regional vice-president of Sears can manage and supervise. The limit is set by geography rather than by the span of control.

The second shortcoming of the span-of-control argument is that it assumes that a manager's main relationship is downward. But this is only one dimension. The manager, in the traditional definition as someone responsible for the work of other people, has a downward relationship, to be sure. But every manager and every career professional also has a superior. Indeed many managers, no matter what the organization chart says, have more than one boss. And the upward relationship to the superior is at least equal in importance to the downward relationship to the subordinates. Most important, however, managers and career professionals always have sideways relations, relationships with people who are neither their subordinates nor their superiors and, indeed, stand in no relationship of authority and responsibility to them. Yet these relationships are crucial both for the manager's own ability to do the work, and for the effectiveness of that work.

What is needed, therefore, is to replace the concept of the span of control with another and more relevant concept: the span of managerial relationships.

We do not know how wide this span can be. Certainly, there

are limits. We do know, however, that the span of managerial relationships is crucial in the design of a managerial job.

In the first place, these relationships define the place of the manager in the managerial structure. Second, they largely define what his or her job is – for these relationships are a crucial and essential part of the job content. Finally, they do set limits – since a job that is all 'relationships' and no 'work' is not a job at all. In designing managerial jobs it is just as important to think through the managerial relationships and to make sure that they do not exceed an individual's grasp as it is to think through the specific function.

Again it is better to make the span of managerial responsibilities too wide rather than too narrow. This goes for the number of subordinates with whom a manager works and who constitute the unit and the team. It goes also for upward relationships. The only area in which I would strongly counsel to keep rather tight limits on the span of managerial relationships are the sideways relationships. A managerial job, ideally, should have few sideways relationships – every one of them of prime importance, both for the functioning of the entire organization and for the achievement of the manager's own function and objectives. It is not only that these are time-consuming relationships. If there are too many, they will be treated superficially, will not be thought through, and will not be worked at. And the common weakness of many organizations is, by and large, the lack of adequate concern for, and adequate work on, sideways relationships.

## Defining a manager's job

A manager's job is defined in several ways.

1 There is first the specific function, the job itself. This should always be a permanent, continuing job, one expected to be needed for a good long time to come. An example would be manager of market research or manufacturing manager. Both obviously are jobs which will have to be done for the foreseeable future.

2 But the functional definition of the job, which is what is expressed in the typical job description or position guide, does not

define the specific contribution which a specific manager is expected to make. While the function is, at least in intent, permanent, there are assignments 'here and now' which are what the enterprise and the manager's boss should hold the manager accountable for. They contribute the second definition of a managerial position and job.

Managers should ask themselves the question at least once a year, and always when taking on a new job: 'What specific contribution can my unit and I make which, if done really well, would make a substantial difference to the performance and results of my company?'

The position guide and job description are, so to speak, the mission statement of a managerial job. They correspond to the definition of 'what is our business and what should it be' for the enterprise as a whole. The assignments are the objectives and goals. They need, therefore, specific targets, a deadline, a clear statement of who is accountable and a built-in measurement by feedback from results.

It is the mark of a performing manager that these assignments always exceed the scope of the job as outlined in the job description. A job description usually represents what has already been done; what needs to be done to make the future always exceeds and goes beyond what has been done in the past.

3 A managerial job is defined by relationships – upwards, downwards, and sideways.

4 It is finally defined by the information needed for the job and by a manager's place in the information flow.

All managers should ask themselves, 'What information do I need to do my job and where do I get it?' They should make sure that whoever has to provide that information understands the manager's needs – not only in terms of what is needed but also how it is needed.

Managers need to think through the question 'And who depends on information from me, and in what form, upwards, downwards, and sideways?'

These four definitions which together describe a manager's job are the manager's own responsibility. He or she should be ex-

322 The Manager's Work and Jobs

pected to write his own job description; to work out his own proposal for the results and contributions for which he and the unit should be accountable; to work out and think through his relationships; and finally to define both his information needs and the information contribution. Indeed, responsibility for thinking through the four dimensions of the job is a manager's first responsibility, of which he should never be relieved. A superior has both the duty and the responsibility to approve or disapprove what the individual manager proposes. But the responsibility for thinking and proposing is the manager's. There is no difference in this respect between a 'managing' job, that is, one with direct responsibility for the work of other people, and a job as a career professional.

## The manager's authority

Saying that each manager's job must be given the broadest possible scope and authority is just rephrasing the rule that decisions be pushed down the line as far as possible and be made as close as possible to the action to which they apply. In its effects, however, this requirement leads to sharp deviations from the traditional concept of delegation from above.

Top management decides what activities and tasks the enterprise requires. The analysis begins with the desired end product: the objectives of business performance and business results. From these the analysis determines step by step what work has to be performed.

But in organizing the manager's job we have to work from the bottom up. We have to begin with the activities on the 'firing line' – the jobs responsible for the actual output of goods and services, for the final sale to the customer, for the production of blueprints and engineering drawings.

The managers on the firing line have the basic management jobs – the ones on whose performance everything else ultimately rests. Seen this way, the jobs of higher management are aimed at helping the firing-line managers do their job. Viewed structurally and organically, it is the firing-line managers in whom all authority and responsibility centre; only what they cannot do themselves passes up to higher management.

Obviously there are real limits to the decisions the firing-line managers can or should make, and to the authority and responsibility they should have. A firing-line manager is limited as to the extent of his authority. A production foreman has no business changing a salesman's compensation, and a regional sales manager has no authority in somebody else's region. A manager is also limited with respect to the kind of decision he can make. Clearly, he should not make decisions that affect other managers. He should not alone make decisions that affect the whole business and its spirit. It is only elementary, for instance, not to allow any manager to make alone and without review a decision on the career and future of one of his subordinates.

Firing-line managers should not be expected to make decisions which they cannot make. A person responsible for immediate performance does not have the time, for instance, to make long-range decisions. A production man lacks the knowledge and competence to work out a pension plan or a medical programme. These decisions certainly affect him and his operations. He should know them, understand them, indeed participate as much as is humanly possible in their preparation and formulation. But he cannot make them. Hence he cannot have the authority and responsibility for them; for authority and responsibility should always be task-focused. This applies all through the management hierarchy up to the chief executive.

There is one simple rule for setting limitations on the decisions a manager is authorized to make. The management charter of General Electric's Lamp Division, in paraphrasing the US Constitution, expresses it by saying: 'All authority not expressly and in writing reserved to higher management is granted to lower management.' This is the opposite of the old Prussian idea of a citizen's rights: 'Everything that is not expressly commanded is forbidden.' In other words, the decisions that a manager is not entitled to make within the extent of the task should always be spelled out; for all others he or she should be supposed to have authority and responsibility.

# 25 Developing Management and Managers

The years since 1950 have seen a boom in management development within the wider boom in management as a whole. In the mid-1940s, when I first became interested in this subject, I could find only two companies that had given serious thought to the development of managers: Sears, Roebuck in America and Marks & Spencer in England. At that time there were only three university programmes in America for the continuing advanced education of managers: the Sloan Program at MIT, the programmes at New York University for the continuing education of managers and young professionals in banking and finance; the Advanced Management Program at Harvard.

Ten years later, in the mid-fifties, the number of companies with specific management development programmes ran to some three thousand. And a great many universities in the United States offered all kinds of advanced management programmes.

Today, it is impossible to count the number of companies that, one way or another, work on the development of management and managers. The large company that does not make specific provision for such work and does not have a management development staff of its own is the exception. And so is the university-level business school without some form of management development programme. In addition, many outside organizations – trade associations, consulting firms and so on – have gone into management development work.

## Why management development?

Basic business decisions require an increasingly long lead time. Since no one can foresee the future, management cannot make rational and responsible decisions unless it selects, develops and tests the men and women who will have to take care of these decisions – the managers of tomorrow.

for a good manager to grow in. They need satisfaction through performance rather than through promotion or title. Their jobs need to be designed around job and position; assignments; relationships; and information needs. They need authority to do their tasks. And they have to derive their own objectives from those of the institution they serve.

Indeed, as has been said before (in Chapters 9 through 12), the manager in a public-service institution needs proper job design, proper job content and proper job structure even more than the manager in a business. Yet, few public-service institutions seem to pay much attention to managerial *jobs*; their emphasis tends to be on title rather than on function, on procedure rather than on performance. The design of truly managerial jobs is the first – but may also be the biggest – step towards improving both performance and morale in public-service institutions.

## Summary

A manager's job should always be based on a necessary task. It should be a real job which makes a visible (if not a measurable) contribution towards the objectives of the entire enterprise. It should have the broadest scope and authority possible. Managers should be directed and controlled by the objectives of performance rather than by their superior. In designing managerial jobs, six specific mistakes are to be avoided. Should managerial jobs fit people, or should managers fit managerial jobs? There is a need to design the span of managerial responsibility – and there are four ways of defining a managerial job. Managers are mutually dependent on superiors and subordinates. Their final duty is towards the enterprise.

## Managers, their superiors, their subordinates, and the enterprise

The manager's relationship to superiors and subordinates are two-way relationships. Both are formal and informal relationships of authority as well as of information. *Both are relationships of mutual dependence.*

The manager has responsibilities downwards, to subordinates. He or she has first to make sure that they know and understand what is demanded of them. He has to help them set their own objectives. Then he has to help them to reach these objectives. He is responsible for their getting the tools, the staff, the information they need. He has to help them with advice and counsel, and, if need be, to teach them how to do better. A one-word definition of this downwards relationship might be 'assistance'.

The objectives of a managerial unit should always consist of the performance that it has to contribute to the success of the enterprise. Objectives should always focus upwards.

But the objectives of the manager who heads the units include what he himself has to do to help subordinates attain their objectives. The vision of a manager should always be upwards – towards the enterprise as a whole. But his responsibility runs downwards as well – to the people on his team. Seeing his relationship towards them as duty towards them and as responsibility for making them perform and achieve rather than as 'supervision' is a central requirement for organizing the manager's unit effectively.

The final duty of the manager is towards the enterprise. A manager's job and function are grounded in the real needs of the enterprise rather than in title or delegation of power.

Each manager, therefore, has to derive from the objectives of the enterprise the definition of his or her own objectives and those of the unit he or she heads.

The discussion in this chapter has focused on the manager in business enterprise. But everything said here applies just as much to managers in the public-service institution, and especially to managers in the government agency. They need jobs big enough

The demand for executives is steadily growing. A developed society increasingly replaces manual skill with theoretical knowledge and the ability to organize and to lead – in short with managerial ability. In fact, ours is the first society in which the basic question is not 'How many educated people can society spare from the task of providing subsistence?' It is 'How many uneducated people can we afford to support?'

But management development is also necessary to discharge an elementary responsibility that a business enterprise owes to society. Continuity, especially of the big business enterprise, is vital. Our society cannot afford to see such wealth-producing resources jeopardized through lack of competent successors to today's management.

The members of a modern society look to their work for more than a livelihood. They look to it also for satisfactions that go beyond the economic, that is, for pride, self-respect and achievement. Management development is just another name for making work and industry more than a way of making a living. By offering challenges and opportunities for the individual development of each manager to his or her fullest ability, the enterprise discharges, in part, the obligation to make a job in organizations a 'good life'.

And if we know one thing today, it is that managers are made and not born. There has to be systematic work on the supply, the development, and the skills of tomorrow's management. It cannot be left to luck or chance.

## Why manager development?

Individual managers need development just as much as company and society do. A manager should, first, keep alert and mentally alive. He or she needs to stay challenged. The manager must acquire today the skills that will be effective tomorrow. He also needs an opportunity to reflect on the meaning of his own experience and – above all – he needs an opportunity to reflect on himself and to learn to make his strengths count. And then he needs development as a person even more than he needs development as a manager.

One of the strengths, but also one of the weaknesses, of a knowledge worker is to expect satisfaction and stimulation from work. In that respect, the knowledge workers are badly spoiled during their early formative years. Manual workers whether skilled or unskilled, do not expect the work to challenge, stimulate or develop them. The manual worker expects only a living from the work. The knowledge worker expects a life out of it.

Thus, knowledge workers, and especially highly accomplished knowledge workers, are likely to find themselves in a spiritual crisis in their early or mid-forties. By that time the majority will have reached, inevitably, their terminal positions. Perhaps they will also have reached what, within their business, is their terminal function – whether this be market research, personnel training, or metallurgy. Suddenly their work will not satisfy them any more. After fifteen or twenty years in market research in their industry, they know all there is to know about it. What was tremendously exciting when the job was new is boring and humdrum fifteen years later.

Managers have to be able, in other words, to develop lives of their own, outside the organization, before they are in their mid-forties.

They need this for themselves, but they need it also for the organization. For the manager who, at age forty-five, 'retires on the job' because he has no more interest in life, is not likely to make any further contribution to the business. He owes it to himself – and to the business – to develop himself as a person, so that he can build his own life and not depend entirely upon the organization, or further promotion or on new and different work. He needs to focus on his own personality, on his own strengths and on his own interests.

We will have to learn to develop *second careers* for accomplished professional and managerial people when they reach their late forties or so. We will have to make it possible for people who have worked for twenty years or so in a business and in a function – that is, for most managers – to find new challenge, new opportunity and new contributions in doing something different, or at least in being effective in different surroundings and in a different institution.

But what do we really mean by the terms 'management development' and 'manager development' ? Any boom such as we have experienced these last two decades is suspect. Undoubtedly there have been as many fads as there have been sound ventures. There must be – and there are – quite a few quacks, and many more who preach management development only because it is the fashionable thing to do.

## What management development is not

For these reasons, it is best to start by spelling out what management and manager development are not.

1 It is not taking courses. Courses are a tool of management development. But they are not management development.

Any course – whether it is a three-day seminar in a special skill or a two-year 'advanced' programme three evenings a week – has to fit the development needs of a management group or the development needs of an individual manager. But the job, the superior and the development planning of both company and individual are far more important developmental tools than any course or courses.

Indeed, some of the most popular courses are of questionable value. I have come to doubt, for example, the wisdom of courses which take a manager away from the job for long periods of time. The most effective courses, in my experience, are those that are done on the manager's own time and after hours – the evening programmes offered by a good many metropolitan universities, for instance. And the most effective full-time courses alternate periods at school with periods at work; a manager spends a week or two off the job in an intensive learning experience, after which he or she is immediately reinforced by going back to work and applying the things that were learned.

Managers are action-focused; they are not philosophers and

should not be. Unless they can put into action right away the things they have learned, the course will not 'take'. It will remain 'information' and never become 'knowledge'. Pedagogically it is unsound not to have action to strengthen learning, that is, not to be able to put into practice on Monday what one has learned the preceding Friday. Finally, managers who have been away 13 weeks on an advanced course may well find themselves 'displaced persons' and homeless when they get back to work after such a long absence.

2 Manager development and management development are not promotion planning, replacement planning or finding potential. These are useless exercises. They may even do harm.

The worst thing a company can do is to try to develop the 'comers' and leave out the others. Ten years hence, 80 per cent of the work will have to be done by those left out. If they have not developed themselves to the point where they can understand, accept, and put into action the vision of the few 'comers', nothing will happen. The eight out of every ten who were not included in the programme will, understandably, feel slighted. They may end up by becoming less effective, less productive, less willing to do new things than they were before.

The attempt to find 'potential' is altogether futile. It is less likely to succeed than simply choosing every fifth person. Performance is what counts, and the correlation between promise and performance is not a particularly high one. Five out of every ten 'high potential' young workers turn out to be nothing but good talkers by the time they reach forty. Conversely, five out of every ten young employees who do not look 'brilliant' and do not talk a good game will have proven their capacity to perform by the time they are in their early forties.

Also, the idea that the purpose of management development is to find 'replacements' negates the entire reason for the activity. We need management development precisely because tomorrow's jobs and tomorrow's organizations are going to be different from today's jobs and today's organization. If all we had to do were to replace yesterday's and today's jobs, we would be training people as apprentices under their present bosses.

The worst kind of replacement planning is the search for a 'crown prince'. A crown prince either has a legal right to succeed, or else being chosen is likely to destroy him. No matter how carefully concealed, picking a crown prince is an act that the whole organization very rapidly recognizes. And then all the other possible contenders unite against the crown prince and work to bring him down – and they usually succeed.

3 Finally, management development and manager development are not means to 'make people over' by changing their personalities. Their aim is to make them effective. Their aim is to enable people to use their strengths fully, and to make them perform the way they are, rather than the way somebody thinks they ought to be.

An employer has no business with a subordinate's personality. Employment is a specific contract calling for specific performance, and for nothing else. Any attempt of an employer to go beyond this is immoral as well as illegal intrusion of privacy. It is abuse of power. An employee owes no 'loyalty', no 'love', and no 'attitudes' – he owes performance and nothing else.

Management and manager development deal with the skills people need. They deal with the structure of jobs and of management relations. They deal with what an employee needs to learn to make skills effective. They should concern themselves with changes in behaviour likely to make a person more effective. They do not deal with who the person is – that is, with personality or emotional dynamics.

Attempts to change a mature individual's personality are bound to fail in any event. By the time he or she comes to work, personality is set. The task is not to change personality, but to enable a person to achieve and to perform.

## The two dimensions of development

Development is not one, but two related tasks that affect each other. One task is that of *developing management*. Its purpose is the health, survival and growth of the enterprise. The other task is *manager* development. Its purpose is the health, growth and achievement of the individual, both as a member of the organization and as a person. *Management* development is a function and activity of the organization – no matter how it is being discharged. *Manager* development is the responsibility of the individual, though company and superior have important parts to play.

Management development starts out with the question 'What kind of managers and career professionals will this business need tomorrow in order to achieve its objectives and to perform in a different market, a different economy, a different technology, a different society ?'

Management development concerns itself with questions such as the age structure of the management group or the skills that managers should acquire today to qualify for tomorrow. It also focuses on the organizational structure and the design of managerial jobs to satisfy the needs and aspirations of tomorrow's 'career customer', that is, tomorrow's young manager or young career professional. The market for jobs and careers has become a genuine mass market. Every organization, therefore, needs to design a 'career product' that will attract and satisfy the career customer of tomorrow.

Whether management development requires a separate staff depends on the size and complexity of the business. It is certainly not an activity that should require a great many people and run a great many programmes. But it does need power and prestige, for its object is to change the basic planning of the company, the structure of its organization and the design of managerial jobs. At the core of the task are planning the market, designing the product, and obsoleting existing jobs and existing organizational structures. Management development, seen this way, is an innovator, a disorganizer, a critic. Its function is to ask with respect to the company's human organization, 'What is our business and what should it be ?'

The *development of a manager* focuses on the person. Its aim is to enable an individual to develop his or her abilities and strengths to the fullest extent and to find individual achievement. The aim is excellence.

No one can motivate a person towards self-development. Motivation must come from within. But a person's superior and the company can do a good deal to discourage even the most highly motivated, and to misdirect his or her development efforts. The active participation, the encouragement, the guidance from both superior and company are needed for manager-development efforts to be fully productive.

The starting point for any manager-development effort is a performance appraisal focused on what the manager does well, what he can do well, and what limitations to his performance capacity he needs to overcome to get the most out of his strengths. Such an appraisal, however, should always be a joint effort. It requires work on the part of the employee himself; it has to be self-appraisal. But it also requires active leadership by the manager.

In appraising themselves people tend either to be too critical or not critical enough. They are likely to see their strengths in the wrong places and to pride themselves on nonabilities rather than on abilities.

There is, typically, the first-class engineer who judges himself to be a good manager because he is 'analytical' and 'objective'. Yet, to be a manager requires, equally, empathy, ability to understand how others do their work and a keen sense of such 'nonrational' factors as personality. There is the sales manager who considers her strengths to lie in 'strategy' – in reality she is a shrewd negotiator; and what she means by strategy is 'next week's bargain sale'. Only too frequently there is the good analyst and adviser who does not realize that he lacks the emotional courage to make hard and lonely decisions.

An appraisal should be based on the performance objectives which the managers set for themselves in cooperation with their superiors. It should start with their performance against these objectives. It should never start out with 'potential'. It should ask 'What has this manager done well – not once, but consistently ?' This should lead to a recognition of the manager's strengths and of the factors which prevent him or her from making these strengths fully effective. But a self-development appraisal should also ask, 'What do I want from life ? What are my values, my aspirations, my directions ? And what do I have to do, to learn, to change, to make myself capable of living up to my demands on myself and my expectations of life ?' This question, too, is much better asked by an outsider, by someone who knows and respects the person but at the same time can have the insight which most of us do not possess about ourselves.

Self-development may require gaining new skills, new knowledge, and new manners. But above all, it requires new experience. The most important factors in self-development, apart from insight into one's own strengths, are experience on the job and the example of the superior. Self-appraisal, therefore, should always lead to conclusions regarding the needs and opportunities of the manager, both with respect to what he or she has to contribute and with respect to the experience he or she needs. The question should always be asked, 'What are the right job experiences for this person to help strengths develop the fastest and the furthest ?'

Development is always self-development. For the enterprise to assume responsibility for the development of a person is idle boast. The responsibility rests with the individual, his abilities, his efforts. No business enterprise is competent, let alone obligated, to substitute its efforts for the self-development efforts of the individual. To do this would be foolish pretension.

But all managers in a business have the opportunity to encourage individual self-development or to stifle it, to direct it or to misdirect it. They should be specifically assigned the responsibility for helping all those working with them to focus, direct and apply self-development efforts. And every company can make available to its managers development challenges and development experiences.

It is a necessity for the spirit, the vision and the performance of today's managers that they be expected to develop those who will manage tomorrow. Just as no one learns as much about a subject as the one who is forced to teach it, no one develops as much as the individual who is trying to help others to develop themselves. Indeed, no one can develop himself unless he works on the development of others. It is in and through efforts to develop others that managers raise their demands on themselves.

The best performers in any profession always look upon those they have trained and developed as the proudest monument they can leave behind.

And again, developing both management and managers is as needed – and requires the same approaches – in the public-service institution as in business enterprise.

But above all, today's managers and career professionals have a responsibility to develop themselves. It is a responsibility they have towards their institution, as well as towards themselves.

We hear a great deal today about the organization man and about alienation of people in organizations. I doubt whether there is more conformity in today's organization than there was in yesterday's small village with its tremendous pressures of class and kin, of caste and custom. I doubt seriously whether there is more alienation today than in earlier societies. But whether conformity and spiritual despair today are greater or less than they used to be, the one effective counterforce to both is the individual's commitment to self-development, the individual's commitment to excellence.

## Summary

Since 1950 there has been a boom in management development – and it is based on genuine needs of organizations and managers alike. But it is as yet rarely understood that there is *management* development tied to the needs of the organization, and *manager* development tied to the needs of the individual – and that the two are different. Manager development is self-development, although the superior and the organization can encourage or stifle it. And the aim of manager development is excellence.

# 26 Management by Objectives and Self-Control

Each member of the enterprise contributes something different, but all must contribute towards a common goal. Their efforts must all pull in the same direction, and their contributions must fit together to produce a whole – without gaps, without friction, without unnecessary duplication of effort.

Every job in the company must be directed towards the objectives of the whole organization if the overall goals are to be achieved. In particular, each manager's job must be focused on the success of the whole. The performance that is expected of managers must be directed towards the performance goals of the business. Results are measured by the contribution they make to the success of the enterprise. Managers must know and understand what the business goals demand of them in terms of performance, and their superiors must know what contribution to demand and expect. If these requirements are not met, managers are misdirected and their efforts are wasted.

Management by objectives requires major effort and special techniques. In a business enterprise managers are not automatically directed towards a common goal. On the contrary, organization, by its very nature, contains four factors that tend to misdirect: the specialized work of most managers; the hierarchical structure of management; the differences in vision and work and the resultant isolation of various levels of management; the compensation structure of the management group.

To overcome these obstacles requires more than good intentions. It requires policy and structure. It requires that management by objectives be purposefully organized and be made the living law of the entire management group.

## The specialized work of managers

An old story tells of three stonecutters who were asked what they were doing. The first replied, 'I am making a living.' The second kept on hammering while he said, 'I am doing the best job of stonecutting in the entire country.' The third one looked up with a visionary gleam in his eyes and said, 'I am building a cathedral.'

The third man is, of course, the true manager. The first man knows what he wants to get out of the work and manages to do so. He is likely to give a 'fair day's work for a fair day's pay.' But he is not a manager and will never be one. It is the second man who is the problem. Workmanship is essential – an organization demoralizes if it does not demand of its members the highest workmanship they are capable of. But there is always a danger that the true workman, the true professional, will believe that he is accomplishing something when in effect he is just polishing stones or collecting footnotes. Workmanship must be encouraged in the business enterprise. But it must always be related to the needs of the whole.

Most managers and career professionals in any business enterprise are, like the second man, concerned with specialized work. A person's habits as a manager, his vision and values, are usually formed while he does functional and specialized work. It is essential that the functional specialist develop high standards of workmanship, that he strive to be 'the best stonecutter in the country'. For work without high standards is dishonest; it corrupts the worker and those around him. Emphasis on, and drive for, workmanship produces innovations and advances in every area of management.

That managers strive to do the best job possible – to do 'professional personnel management,' to run 'the most up-to-date plant,' to do 'truly scientific market research' – must be encouraged. But this striving for professional workmanship in functional and specialized work is also a danger. It tends to divert the manager's vision and efforts from the goals of the business. The functional work becomes an end in itself. In far too many instances the functional managers no longer measure their performance by its contribution to the enterprise but only by professional criteria of workmanship. They tend to appraise subordinates by their craftsmanship and to reward and to promote them accordingly. They resent demands made for the sake of business performance as interference with 'good engineering,' 'smooth production,' or 'hard-hitting selling.' The functional manager's legitimate desire for workmanship can become a force that tears the enterprise apart and converts it into a loose association of working groups. Each group is concerned only with its own craft. Each jealously guards its own 'secrets'. Each is bent on enlarging its own domain rather than on building the business. The remedy is to counterbalance the concern for craftsmanship with concern for the common goal of the enterprise.

## Misdirection by the boss

The hierarchical structure of management makes the danger even greater. Because of his rank, whatever the boss does and says, his most casual remarks, his habits, even his mannerisms, tend to appear to his subordinates as calculated, planned and meaningful. 'All you ever hear around the place is human-relations talk; but when the boss calls you on the carpet it is always because overtime is too high; and when it comes to promoting a guy, the plums always go to those who do the best job filling out accounting-department forms.' This is one of the most common tunes, sung with infinite variations on every level of management. It leads to poor performance – even in cutting overtime. It also expresses loss of confidence in, and absence of respect for, the company and its management.

Yet the manager who misdirects subordinates in this way does not intend to do so. He genuinely considers human relations to be the most important task of his plant managers. But he talks about overtime because he feels that he has to establish himself with his men as a 'practical man', or because he thinks that he shows familiarity with their problems by talking 'shop' with them. He stresses the accounting-department forms only because they annoy him as much as they do his men – or he may just not want to have any more trouble with the comptroller than he can help. But to his subordinates these reasons are hidden; all they see and hear is the question about overtime, the emphasis on forms.

The solution to this problem requires a structure of management that focuses the eyes of managers and their bosses on what the job – rather than the boss – demands. To stress style and manner – as does a good deal of current management literature – is likely instead to worsen the problem. Indeed, everyone familiar with business today has seen situations in which a manager's attempt to avoid misdirection through changing his style has converted a fairly satisfactory relationship into a nightmare of embarrassment and misunderstanding. The manager himself becomes so self-conscious as to lose all easy relationship with his men. And the men in turn react with: 'So help us, the old man has read a book; we used to know what he wanted of us, now we have to guess.'

## Differences in levels of management

Misdirection can result from a difference in concern between various levels of management. This problem, too, cannot be solved by attitudes and good intentions; for it is rooted in the structure of any enterprise. Nor can it be solved by 'better communications', for communications presuppose common language, and it is precisely that which is usually lacking.

It is no accident that the old story of the blind men meeting up with an elephant on the road is so popular among management people. Each level of management sees the same 'elephant' – the business – from a different angle of vision. The production foreman, like the blind man who felt the elephant's leg and decided that a tree was in his way, tends to see only the immediate production problems. Top management – the blind man touching the trunk and deciding a snake bars his way – tends to see only the enterprise as a whole. It sees shareholders, financial problems, altogether a host of highly abstract relations and figures. Operating management – the blind man feeling the elephant's belly and thinking himself up against a landslide – tends to see things functionally. Each level needs its particular vision; it could not do its job without it. Yet, these visions are so different that people on different levels talking about the same thing often do not realize it – or, as frequently happens, believe that they are talking about the same thing when in reality they are poles apart.

## Misdirection by compensation

The most serious force for misdirection within the management group may be the pay structure. At the same time, it is the hardest one to remove. Somehow management people have to be paid, but every compensation system is liable to misdirect.

Compensation is cost to the enterprise and income to the recipient. It also always expresses status, both within the enterprise and in society. It entails judgements on the managers' worth as much as on their performance. It is emotionally tied to all our ideas of fairness, justice and equity. Money is, of course, quantitative. But the money in any compensation system expresses the most intangible, but also the most sensitive, values and qualities. For this reason, there can be no truly simple or truly rational compensation system.

Any compensation system determines a person's place within the group. How one's pay relates to the pay of others, and especially to the pay of one's peers, is always more important than the absolute amount of the salary. (On this see Chapter 14.) Compensation must always try to balance recognition of the individual with stability and maintenance of the group. No attempt at a 'scientific formula' for compensation can therefore be completely successful. The best possible compensation plan is of necessity a compromise among the various functions and meanings of compensation, for the individual as well as for the groups. Even the best plan will still misdirect as well as direct and encourage the wrong as well as the right behaviour.

Yet there is hardly a more powerful signal for managers than compensation and compensation structure. Its importance to them goes far beyond the economic meaning of money. It conveys to them the values of their top management and their own worth within the management group. It expresses in clear and tangible form a manager's position, rank and recognition within the group. At today's high tax rates a little more money means, as a rule, very little to senior managers. It is, in effect, only so much more income tax to pay. But the status symbol of a little more money and its emotional impacts, are incalculable.

The most damaging misdirection may result from those apparently eminently 'fair' compensation systems that relate a manager's pay directly to performance. Performance is usually measured by return on investment during the current year. If we want to *measure* performance, there is no other way. Yet, if return on investment or current profits are overemphasized, the managers of decentralized business will be misdirected towards slighting the future in favour of the present.

An able management team heading one of the major divisions of a chemical company failed for years to develop a badly needed new product. Year after year they reported to their top management that the new product was not yet quite ready. Finally, when the division manager was asked bluntly why he stalled on a project that was clearly vital to the success of his business, he answered: 'Have you looked at our compensation plan? I myself have a guaranteed salary. But my entire management group gets its main income from a bonus geared to return on investment. The new product is the future of this business. But for five or eight years there will be only investment and no return. I know we are three years late. But do you really expect me to take the bread out of the mouths of my closest associates?' This story had a happy ending. The compensation plan was changed – somewhat in line with the plan Du Pont has had for years with respect to new developments. Du Pont does not put the cost of a development into the investment base of a division or a subsidiary until the new product has been introduced on the market.

And within a year or two the new product was out and selling.

The preference should be for simple compensation systems rather than for complex ones. It should be for compensation systems that allow judgement to be used and that enable pay to be fitted to the job of the individual rather than imposing one formula on everybody. But I would be the last person to claim that a 'fair', let alone a 'scientific', system can be devised. All one can do, to repeat, is to watch lest the compensation system reward the wrong behaviour, emphasize the wrong results, and direct people away from performance for the common good.

## What should the objectives of a manager be?

Just as 'eternal vigilance is the price of freedom,' constant effort is needed to prevent misdirection. The superior needs to understand what to expect of subordinate managers. The subordinates, in turn, need to be able to know what results they should hold themselves accountable for. Without special effort, superior or subordinate will not know and understand this, and their ideas will not be compatible, let alone identical.

Each manager, from the 'big boss' down to the production foreman or the chief clerk, needs clearly spelled-out objectives. Otherwise confusion can be guaranteed. These objectives should lay out what performance each managerial unit is supposed to achieve. They should lay out what contribution a manager and his or her unit are expected to make to help other units obtain their objectives. Finally, they should spell out what contribution the manager can expect from other units towards the attainment of these objectives. Right from the start, in other words, emphasis should be on teamwork and team results.

These objectives should always derive from the goals of the business enterprise. A statement of his own objectives based on those of the company and of the manufacturing department should be demanded even of the foreman on the assembly line. The company may be so large as to make the distance between the individual foreman's production and the company's total output enormous. Yet the foreman must focus on the objectives of the company and needs to define his results in terms of his unit's contribution to the whole of which it is a part.

The objectives of every manager should spell out his or her contribution to attainment of company goals in all areas of the business. Obviously, not every manager has a direct contribution to make in every area. The contribution that marketing makes to productivity, for example, may be indirect and hard to define. But if a manager's unit is not expected to contribute towards one of the areas that significantly affect prosperity and survival of the business, this fact should be clearly brought out. For managers must understand that business results depend on a balance of efforts and results in a number of areas. This is necessary both to give full scope to the craftsmanship of each function and specialty, and to prevent the empire-building and jealousy of the various functions and specialties. It is necessary also to avoid overemphasis on any one key area.

This is particularly important for service staffs and for such highly specialized groups as the computer people. They may not always be able to relate their work directly to business objectives and business results. But unless they try to, they are likely to direct their work away from business objectives and business results.

To obtain balanced efforts, the objectives of all managers on all levels and in all areas should also be keyed to both short-range and long-range considerations. And, of course, all objectives should always contain both the tangible business objectives and such 'intangible' objectives as manager development, worker performance and attitude and social responsibility. Anything else is shortsighted and impractical.

## Management by drives

Proper management requires balanced emphasis on objectives, especially by top management. It avoids the all-too-common business malpractice – management by crisis and drives.

That things always revert to their original state three weeks after a drive is over, everybody knows and apparently expects. The only result of an economy drive is likely to be that messengers and typists get fired, and that $35,000 executives are forced to do $175-a-week work typing their own letters – and doing it badly. And yet many managements fail to draw the obvious conclusion that drives are, after all, not the way to get things done.

Over and above its ineffectiveness, management by drive misdirects. It puts all emphasis on one phase of the job to the detriment of all other aspects. 'For four weeks we cut inventories,' a case-hardened veteran of management by crisis once summed it up. 'Then we have four weeks of cost-cutting, followed by four weeks of human relations. We just have time to push customer service and courtesy for a month. And then the inventory is back where it was when we started. We don't even try to do our job. All top management talks about, thinks about, preaches about, is last week's inventory figure or this week's customer complaints. How we do the rest of the job they don't even want to know.'

In an organization that manages by drives, people either neglect their job to get on with the current drive or silently organize to sabotage the drive in order to get the work done. In either event they become deaf to the cry of 'wolf'. And when the real crisis comes, when all hands really should drop everything and pitch in, they treat it as just another case of management-created hysteria. Management by drive is a sure sign of confusion. It is an admission of incompetence. It is a sign that management does not think. Above all, it is a sign that the company does not know what to expect of its managers and that, not knowing how to direct them, it misdirects them.

## How should managers' objectives be set and by whom?

The goals for the jobs of all managers must be defined by the contribution they have to make to the success of the larger unit of which they are a part. The objectives of the direct sales manager's job should be defined by the contribution she and her district sales force have to make to the sales department; the objectives of the project engineer's job by the contribution he, his engineers and draftsmen make to the engineering department. The objectives of the general manager of a decentralized division should be defined by the contribution the division has to make to the objectives of the parent company.

Higher management must reserve the powers to approve or disapprove these objectives. But their development is part of a manager's responsibility; indeed, it is the manager's first responsibility. It means, too, that every manager should responsibly participate in the development of the objectives of the higher unit of which he is a part. To 'give a *sense* of participation' (to use a pet phrase of human relations jargon) is not only not enough. It is the wrong thing. Being a manager means *having* responsibility. Precisely because his aims should reflect the objective needs of the business, rather than merely what the boss – or the manager himself – wants, he must be committed to the objectives with a positive act of assent. Managers must know and understand the ultimate business goals, what is expected of them and why, what they will be measured against and how. There must be a meeting of minds within the entire management of each unit. This can be achieved only when all the contributing managers are required to think through what the unit objectives are and are led to participate actively and responsibly in the work of defining them. And only if lower managers participate in this way can the higher managers know what to expect of them and make exacting demands.

This is so important that some of the most effective managers I know go one step further. They have each of their subordinates write a 'manager's letter' twice a year. In this letter to the superior, managers first define the objectives of the superior's job and of their own job as they see them. They then set down the performance standards that they believe are being applied to them. Next, they list the things they must do to attain these goals – and the things within their own units they consider the major obstacles. They list the things the superiors and the company do that help them and the things that hamper them. Finally, they outline what they propose to do during the next year to reach their goals. If their superiors accept this statement, the 'manager's letter' becomes the charter under which the manager operates.

This device, like no other I have seen, brings out how easily the unconsidered and casual remarks of even the best boss can confuse and misdirect. One large company has used the manager's letter for ten years. Yet almost every letter still lists as objectives and standards things that baffle the superior to whom the letter is addressed. And whenever he asks, 'What is this ?' he gets the answer, 'Don't you remember what you said last spring going down in the elevator with me ?'

The manager's letter also brings out whatever inconsistencies

346 The Manager's Work and Jobs

there are in the demands made on a person by his or her superior
and by the company. Does the superior demand both speed and
high quality when he can get only one or the other? And what
compromise is needed in the interest of the company? Does the
boss demand initiative and judgement of his people but also that
they check back with him before they do anything? Does the
superior ask for ideas and suggestions but never uses them or dis-
cusses them? Does the company expect of a small engineering
force that it be available immediately whenever something goes
wrong in the plant and yet bend all its efforts to the completion of
new designs? Does it expect managers to maintain high standards of performance but forbid them to remove poor performers?
Does it create the conditions under which people say, 'I can get
the work done as long as I can keep the boss from knowing what I
am doing?'

As the manager's letter illustrates, managing managers requires special efforts not only to establish common direction, but
to eliminate misdirection. Mutual understanding can never be
attained by 'communications down,' can never be created by
talking. It results only from 'communications up.' It requires
both the superior's willingness to listen and a tool especially designed to make lower managers heard.


## Self-control through measurements

The greatest advantage of management by objectives is perhaps
that it makes it possible for managers to control their own performance. Self-control means stronger motivation: a desire to do
the best rather than do just enough to get by. It means higher performance goals and broader vision. Even if management by objectives were not necessary to give the enterprise the unity of
direction and effort of a management team, it would be necessary
to make possible management by self-control.

So far in this book I have rarely talked of control; I have talked
of measurement. This was intentional. Control is an ambiguous
word. It means the ability to direct oneself and one's work. It can
also mean domination of one person by another. Objectives are

the basis of control in the first sense. Using them as the basis of control in the second sense would defeat their purpose. Indeed, one of the major values of management by objectives is that it enables us to substitute management by self-control for management by domination.

To control their own performance, managers need to know more than what their goals are. They must be able to measure their performances and results against the goal. Managers must have clear and common measurements in all key areas of a business. These measurements need not be rigidly quantitative nor need they be exact. But they have to be clear, simple and rational. They have to be reliable – at least to the point where their margin of error is acknowledged and understood. And they have to be self-explanatory, understandable without complicated interpretation or philosophical discussion.

All managers should have the information they need to measure their own performance and they should receive it soon enough to make any changes necessary for the desired results. This information should go to the managers themselves, and to their superiors. It should be the means of self-control, not a tool of control from above.

This needs particular stress today, when the ability to obtain such information is growing rapidly as a result of technological progress in information gathering, analysis and synthesis. In the past, information on important facts was either not obtainable at all or could be assembled only so late as to be of little use. This was not an unmixed curse. It made effective self-control difficult; but it also made difficult domination of a manager from above. In the absence of information with which to control him, the manager had to be allowed to work as he saw fit.

The new ability to assemble measuring information will make possible effective self-control. If used properly, it will lead to a tremendous advance in the effectiveness and performance of management. But if this new ability is abused to impose control on managers from above, the new technology will inflict incalculable harm by demoralizing management and by seriously lowering the effectiveness of managers.

## lf-control and performance standards

nagement by objectives and self-control asks for self-discipline. It forces the managers to make high demands on themselves. It is anything but permissive. It may well lead to demanding too much rather than too little. This has indeed been the main
criticism levelled against the concept. (See Chapter 17, especially the discussion of Maslow's criticism of Theory Y.)

Management by objectives and self-control assumes that people want to be responsible, want to contribute, want to achieve.
That is a bold assumption. Yet we know that people tend to act
as they are expected to act.

A manager who starts out by assuming that people are weak,
irresponsible and lazy will get weakness, irresponsibility and
laziness. A manager who assumes strength, responsibility and desire to contribute may experience a few disappointments. But the
first task of managers is to make effective the strengths of people.
And this they can do only if they start out with the assumption
that people – and especially managers and professional contributors – want to achieve.

Above all, they must make this assumption with regard to the
young educated people of today who will be tomorrow's managers. These young people may not know what they mean when
they demand to be allowed to 'make a contribution'. But their demand is the right one. They are right also that management, as it
has been practised so far, does not act on the assumption that the
young educated people want to make a contribution. They need
to be subjected – and to subject themselves – to the discipline and
the demands of management by objectives and self-control.

## A philosophy of management

What the business enterprise needs is a principle of management
that will give full scope to individual strength and responsibility,
as well as common direction to vision and effort, one that will
establish team work and harmonize the goals of the individual
with the common good. Management by objectives and self-

control makes the interest of the enterprise the aim of every manager. It substitutes for control from outside the stricter, more exacting and more effective control from inside. It motivates managers to action, not because somebody tells them to do something or talks them into doing it, but because the objective task demands it. They act not because somebody wants them to but because they themselves decide that they have to – they act, in other words, as free men and women.

I do not use the word 'philosophy' lightly. Indeed, I prefer not to use it at all; it's much too big a word. But management by objectives and self-control may properly be called a philosophy of management. It rests on a concept of the job of management. It rests on an analysis of the specific needs of the management group and of the obstacles it faces. It rests on a concept of human action, behaviour, and motivation. Finally, it applies to every manager, whatever his or her level and function, and to any organization whether large or small. It insures performance by converting objective needs into personal goals. And this is genuine freedom.

## Summary

Each member of the enterprise contributes something different; but all must contribute towards a common goal, a common performance. Each should strive towards workmanship in his or her work. Yet professional excellence is a means towards a common objective. By its very nature, the organization tends to misdirect away from the common objective. Organizations therefore require management by objectives so as to integrate individual efforts into common performance. Managers' objectives need to be set by themselves. And they should be used for self-control. Management by objectives and self-control can truly be called a 'philosophy of management for free men and women.'

# 27 From Middle Management to Knowledge Organization

In the early 1950s when computer and automation were the headline makers, the disappearance of middle management was widely predicted. By 1980, we were told, middle management would have disappeared. All decisions would be made by the computer or by top management on the basis of a 'total information system'.

Few predictions have been disproven so fast and so completely. Just when the predictions were being widely publicized, the middle-management boom began. And it has continued ever since. Indeed, the fifties, sixties and seventies might be called the era of middle management. No other group in the work force has been growing so fast.

There was, indeed, during this period a powerful force at work reducing the number of middle-management jobs. It was not, however, the computer, automation or any other new technology. It was the press of mergers, takeovers and acquisitions, especially in the US and in Great Britain. It consolidated or closed countless sales and accounting offices – and abolished middle-management positions by the score. Yet despite this force, the demand for middle-rank managerial people grew steadily except in periods of economic recession, as in Great Britain in the late sixties and in the US in 1970 and 1971. In companies not directly affected by mergers or acquisitions and in public-service institutions, the demand grew spectacularly.

Here are some examples from manufacturing, the economic sector where automation has been most widely applied and where computers have become as commonplace as smokestacks were a few generations ago. A large American automobile company recently built a major manufacturing plant to turn out the entire production of a new model. It was the company's first major automotive plant since 1949, when a similar plant, designed for a similar production volume, was opened. The number of rank-and-file employees, both blue-collar and clerical, is almost one-third less than that of the earlier plant. This is the result, however, of normal increases in productivity rather than of a shift of the process to automation. The top-management group in the new plant is about the same size. But the middle-management group, that is, the group that is paid more than a general foreman and less than the plant's general manager, is almost five times the size of the middle-management group in the 1949 plant.

In England one of the large materials companies –a worldwide leader in its industry – grew by 45 per cent between 1950 and 1970. The top-management group at the end of the period was actually somewhat smaller as the result of two reorganizations in which older members of the founding families were replaced by professional managers. The rank and file, both in the factories and in the office, grew by about a fifth. But the middle group tripled.

These examples actually understate the growth rate of middle management. During this same period, industries that have a high proportion of middle managers in their employ grew faster than most other industries. The symbol of economic dynamism in the United States economy of 1970 was no longer General Motors. It was IBM. And at IBM, or at any other computer manufacturer, the middle group is far bigger than it is in traditional manufacturing industries such as automobile or steel. The same is true of the pharmaceutical companies which grew so rapidly in the twenty years between 1950 and 1970.

Top management in the hospital – however one defines it – has not grown. There is still a hospital administrator, perhaps with an assistant in larger hospitals, there are the trustees and a medical director. Rank-and-file employment in terms of number of employees per patient day has gone down rather than up. It is in the kitchen, in maintenance, and in the other rank-and-file areas that hospitals have become a good deal less labour-intensive. But the middle ranks – technicians, engineers, accountants, psychologists and social workers – have exploded. Their number has grown at least fourfold – in some big teaching hospitals even faster.

## The needed correction

Growth at such rates always overshoots the target. It is bound to be wasteful. There is overstaffing because it is the fashion to go in for this or that activity whether it is needed or not. There is overstaffing because times are good and it is easier to yield to a demand for more people than to fight it. And in such a period of explosive growth no one pays much attention to the organization of the work. Yet expansion of such magnitude always changes the nature of the work rather than merely adding quantity. If the work and its organization are not studied and changed, waste, duplication of effort and organizational obesity follow.

Examples of wasteful overstaffing in the middle ranks abound. The worst are some American defence projects. To design the Mirage fighter, the best military plane of the 1950–1970 period, the French employed some seventy engineers and designers who did the job in record time. A comparable American development might have been staffed with three thousand engineers and designers and have taken four times as long. In the end the project might have come out with an inferior design at infinitely greater cost.

The middle-management boom therefore had to lead to a 'middle-management depression'. At the first significant economic setback, there had to be a sharp correction. This came first in Great Britain, where the fairly sharp recession of the late 1960s coincided with a peak in mergers and takeovers, resulting in lay-offs of middle-rank executives and professionals. In the United States, in the 1970 and 1971 recession, the reaction was far milder. Here there was a sharp two-year curtailment of college recruiting for management and professional positions, with very few layoffs of middle-management people already on the payroll (except in the particularly distressed aerospace and defence industries).

Such a reaction, however painful, is fundamentally healthy. It always goes too far, of course. But at least it forces management to think through what the work is and what it needs. Such thinking is particularly important for middle-management work.

There are few areas where overstaffing does as much damage. It costs a great deal more than money. It costs performance and motivation.

Such a reaction is always short-lived. It was over in the United States by 1973; then middle-management growth resumed. Even in Great Britain, despite severe economic problems, middle-management growth picked up again after 1972.

## The danger of overstaffing

Knowledge work – the specific work of middle managers – should always be demanding. It should be lean and should err, if at all, on the side of understaffing. An overstaffed middle-management organization destroys motivation. It destroys accomplishment, achievement and satisfaction. In the end, it destroys performance.

The middle-management boom and the resulting overstaffing, especially in larger companies, did indeed undermine morale and motivation. Overstaffing is a main reason for the dissatisfaction and disenchantment of so many of the young middle-rank people whom business, governments, school systems and hospitals recruited in large numbers during the fifties and sixties. They are well paid and well treated, but there is not enough for them to do. There is not enough challenge, not enough contribution, not enough accomplishment. There is too much sheer busyness. When able young educated people are asked to explain their growing preference for a job in a small company or in the medium-sized city administration, they always say, 'At least I'll have something to do.'

The first lesson is to keep the middle ranks lean. 'What really needs to be done?' is the first question. And the second and equally important one is 'What no longer needs to be done and should be cut back or cut out?' The first lesson is the *need for weight control*.

What needs even more thought and attention is, however, the *work* of middle management and its organization. Expansion of the middle ranks not only produced a qualitative change – it was itself produced by a change in the nature of the middle-management function.

Middle management will probably continue to expand. But future growth will have to be directed, controlled, managed. It will have to be based on an understanding of the changing nature of middle management and of the resulting need for change in function, relationship and structure.

## Where the growth occurred

The real growth of middle-rank people in management jobs has been in functions which, a generation ago, were hardly known. The new middle managers are the knowledge professionals: manufacturing engineers and process specialists; computer programmers, tax accountants and market analysts; product and market managers; advertising and promotion specialists.

Traditional middle managers were essentially commanders of people. The new middle managers are essentially suppliers of knowledge. Traditional middle managers had authority downwards, over the people who report to them. The new middle manager essentially has responsibility sideways and upwards, that is, to people over whom he or she exercises no command authority.

Above all, the traditional middle managers had largely routine jobs. They did not make decisions; they carried them out. At the most, they implemented them and adapted them to local conditions. Their job was to keep running a system that they had neither designed nor were expected to alter.

This role was, of course, the traditional definition of a manager as someone who is responsible for the work of others rather than responsible for his or her own work. It also underlay the traditional social structure of management outside the US and Japan, especially in Europe.

In the United States and Japan top management has traditionally been recruited from middle management, that is, from people who worked their way up in the business. In European countries this was not so. In England there was – and to some extent still is

– a tremendous gulf between managers and 'the board', that is, top management. Even in large companies the board was until recently recruited from people who had never discharged operating management functions, if not from people who had never worked in a business, such as distinguished former public servants. In Holland, for instance, top management, even in the large and professionally managed companies, rarely comes out of operations. Throughout Europe most top-management people often make their careers in government and then move directly into senior management jobs in business. Operating managers who come up in the business are normally considered unfit for top jobs, even if they are university graduates.

That this social structure could work – and work very well in many cases – shows that the European view of the traditional middle manager as being concerned with routines rather than with decisions, and with maintenance of ongoing operations rather than with direction, had a good deal of validity. But this view is not valid with respect to the new middle manager.

## The decision impact of the new middle manager

Because the new middle managers are knowledge professionals, their actions and decisions have direct and major impact on the business, its ability to perform, and its direction.

Here are some fairly typical examples.

Product managers in a company like Procter & Gamble's soap and detergent business are definitely middle management by rank and compensation. They have no command authority. The work is being carried out by people who report to their respective functional bosses, the manufacturing manager, the sales manager, the head of the chemical and development laboratories and so on. But product managers are held responsible for the development, the introduction and the performance of a product in the marketplace. Product managers decide what the product's specifications should be. They determine its price. They decide where and how to test-market it. They set the sales goals. They do not have direct command authority and cannot issue an order,

356 The Manager's Work and Jobs

but they do control the advertising and promotion budget, which largely determines the success of any new consumer product.

Quality control engineers in a machine tool company also have no command authority and have no one, except junior quality engineers, reporting to them. But they oversee the design and structure of the manufacturing process. Their quality control standards largely decide the costs of the manufacturing process and the performance of the manufacturing plant. The manufacturing manager or the plant manager actually makes the decisions. But the quality control manager can veto them.

The tax accountant also has no command, can give no orders, and often has no one reporting to him except his secretary. Yet, in effect, he has veto power over even top-management decisions. His opinion on the tax consequences of a course of action often determines both what a company can do and how it must do it.

The product manager at Procter & Gamble, the quality engineer, and the tax accountant are not 'line' managers. But neither are they 'staff'. Their function is not advice and teaching. They do 'operating' work. And they have top-management impacts even though they are not top management in rank, compensation or function.

To be sure, they cannot make some of the key decisions – what our business is and what it should be; where to allocate key resources of capital and people. But even with respect to these decisions they contribute the essential knowledge without which the key decision cannot be effectively made. And the key decisions cannot be carried out unless these new middle managers build them into their own knowledge and work, on their own responsibility and on their own authority. In Chapter 1 we argued that the knowledge professionals are managers even though no one reports to them. Now we see that in their impacts and responsibilities they are top management even though they may be five or six organizational levels down.

## The knowledge organization

Middle management has not disappeared. Indeed, not even the traditional middle manager has disappeared. But yesterday's middle management is being transformed into tomorrow's *know-ledge organization*.

This requires restructuring both individual jobs and the organization. In the knowledge organization the job, all the way down to the lowest professional or managerial level, has to focus on the company's objectives. It has to focus on contribution and have its own objectives. It has to be organized according to assignment. It has to be thought through and structured according to the flow of information both to and from the individual position. And it has to have a place in the decision structure. It can no longer be designed in terms of downwards authority alone. It has to be recognized instead as multidimensional.

Traditionally, middle-management jobs have been designed narrowly. The first concern has been with the limits on a middle manager's authority. In the knowledge organization we will instead have to ask, 'What is the greatest possible contribution this job can make?' The focus will have to shift from concern with authority to stress on responsibility.

## The need for clear decision authority

The knowledge organization demands clear decision authority. It demands thinking through what decision belongs where. The knowledge organization is far more complex than the simple 'line' organization it is replacing. Unless decision authority is clearly spelled out, it will tend to become confused.

The knowledge organization is also designed to take greater risks. Operating no longer is a 'routine' in which the norms are clear. It is a decision-making organization rather than one that just keeps the machinery running at a preset speed and for already known results. Things will go wrong in unexpected ways. And unless authority to change the decision is built into the decision itself, malfunction is bound to result.

A major pharmaceutical company decided to introduce eight new products in one year – twice as many as the company had ever introduced before in a single year. An elaborate multinational strategy was worked out in yearlong sessions of task forces assembled from all functions, all levels and all major territories.

Some products were to be introduced first into European markets, some into the American market, some first with general practitioners of medicine, others with specialists or in hospitals. When the products were brought out, the two that had been considered the weakest unexpectedly developed into best sellers while the two supposedly strongest products ran into unforeseen troubles that sharply slowed their growth. In planning the strategy, no one had asked, 'If things do not work out as planned, who is going to be responsible for changing the plan?' As a result, there were endless reports, endless studies, endless meetings – and no action. In the end, the company lost much of the benefit of its accomplishments. The two products that had shown unexpected success did not receive the support needed to exploit their acceptance by the medical profession. Competitors quickly moved in with imitations and reaped much of the harvest. Clinical testing and marketing efforts on the two products that had run into unexpected difficulties either should have been cut back sharply or should have been raised sharply. Everyone saw that, but no one had the authority to make the decision.

In the knowledge organization of the new middle management any programme, any project, and any plan will have to ask and answer the question 'Who has the authority to change the plan?' And this will lead to far greater authority in middle management than even the American middle management tradition ever envisaged. Even line managers will need more rather than less authority in the knowledge organization.

## Top management's role in the knowledge organization

In the knowledge organization, top management can no longer assume that the 'operating people' do as they are being told. It has to accept that the middle ranks make genuine decisions. But the operating organization can also no longer assume that it can do its job in isolation from top management as it used to do in the European tradition. It must understand top-management decisions. Indeed, middle management in the knowledge organization must take responsibility for 'educating' top management.

Top management must understand what the knowledge organization tries to do, what it is capable of doing, and where it sees the major opportunities, the major needs, the major challenges to the enterprise. Finally, middle management must insist that top management make decisions on what the business is and what it should be, on objectives, strategies and priorities. Otherwise the middle ranks cannot do their own job.

Top management needs to understand the knowledge organization. It needs to establish communication with it. The traditional American assumption that the people in top management know the middle manager's job because they have been through it is no longer valid. Even executives who have risen into top management through the middle-management organization can no longer expect to have been exposed directly to more than a small sample of the functional work of the knowledge organization. And some of the most important areas of middle management will no longer prepare and test a person for top-management positions.

Indeed some of the most capable people in such areas will not even want to get into top-management work but will prefer to stay in their specialty. The computer specialist wants, as a rule, to stay within that area of specialization and work on information and information technology. Equally, most researchers want to stay in research, whether in physical and technical fields, in research on people or in economic research.

The most important 'public' in the knowledge organization for top management – and the one that most needs a relationship to top management – are the younger and highly specialized knowledge workers. They are least likely to understand what top management is trying to do, least likely to see the business whole, least likely to focus on company objectives and performance. Yet they are likely, because of their knowledge, to have impact early in their careers. In business of any size or complexity the top-management group needs to organize its relationship to these younger knowledge professionals.

Each member of the top-management team might sit down a few times a year with a group of younger knowledge people and say to them, 'I have no agenda. I have nothing I want to tell you. I am here to listen. It is your job to tell me what you think we in top management need to know about your work and how you think we can make it most productive. It is your job to tell me where you see the problems and opportunities for this company and to tell me what top management does to help you in your job and what we do that hampers you. I shall insist on only one thing: that *you* have done *your* homework and that you take seriously your responsibility to inform me and to educate me.'

Overall in the knowledge organization it is top-management's job to mobilize, to organize, to place and to direct knowledge. Knowledge people – and that means managers and career professionals in today's organization – cannot be seen and treated as inferiors. They are middle in rank, pay, authority. But they are juniors and colleagues rather than subordinates.

'Management' means, in the last analysis, the substitution of thought for brawn and muscle, of knowledge for folkways and superstition, and of cooperation for force. It means substituting responsibility for obedience to rank, and authority of performance for authority of power. The knowledge organization, therefore, is what management theory, management thinking, management aspirations have been about all along. But now the knowledge organization is becoming accomplished fact. The tremendous expansion of managerial employment since World War II converted the middle ranks into knowledge professionals – people paid for putting knowledge to work and for making decisions that have impact on performance capacity, results and future directions of the whole enterprise. The task of making these new knowledge people in the middle ranks truly effective and achieving has barely begun. It is a central task in managing managers.

## Summary

Middle management, in 1950 predicted to disappear, has instead expanded spectacularly. But it has changed. Yesterday's middle manager is becoming today's knowledge professional – a well educated, well-paid professional who is employed to supply knowledge rather than to supervise people. This requires restructuring both individual jobs and the organization. It requires stress on responsibility rather than stress on authority – but also a rethinking of authority and decision structures. It also requires a change in the role of top management.

# 28 The Spirit of Performance

The purpose of an organization is to enable ordinary human beings to do extraordinary things.

No organization can depend on genius; the supply is always scarce and unreliable. It is the test of an organization to make ordinary people perform better than they seem capable of, to bring out whatever strength there is in its members, and to use each person's strength to help all the other members perform. It is the task of organization at the same time to neutralize the individual weaknesses of its members. The test of an organization is the spirit of performance.

The spirit of performance requires that there be full scope for individual excellence. The focus must be on the strengths – on what people can do rather than on what they cannot do.

'Morale' in an organization does not mean that 'people get along together.' The test is performance. Human relations that are not grounded in the satisfaction of good performance in work are actually poor human relations. There is no greater indictment of an organization than that the strength and ability of the outstanding individual threatens the group and that his or her performance becomes a source of difficulty, frustration and discouragement for the others.

Spirit of performance in a human organization means that its energy output is larger than the sum of the efforts put in. It means the creation of energy. This cannot be accomplished by mechanical means. A machine cannot deliver more energy than is put into it. To get out more than is being put in is possible only in the moral sphere.

By morality I do not mean preachments. Morality, to have any meaning at all, must be a principle of action. It must not be speeches, sermons or good intentions. *It must be practices.* Specifically:

1 The focus of the organization must be on *performance.* The first requirement of the spirit of performance is high performance standards, for the group as well as for each individual. The organization must cultivate in itself the habit of achievement.
2 The focus of the organization must be on *opportunities* rather than on problems.
3 The *decisions that affect people* – their placement and their pay, promotion, demotion and severance – must express the values and beliefs of the organization. They are the true controls of an organization.
4 Finally, in its people decisions, management must demonstrate that it realizes that *integrity* is one absolute requirement of managers, the one quality that they must bring with them and cannot be expected to acquire later on. And management must demonstrate that it requires the same integrity of itself.

## The danger of safe mediocrity

The constant temptation of every organization is safe mediocrity. The first requirement of organizational health is a high demand on performance. Indeed, one of the major reasons for demanding that management be by objectives and that it focus on the objective requirements of the task is the need to have managers set high standards of performance for themselves.

This requires that performance be understood properly. Performance is not hitting the bull's-eye with every shot – that is a circus act that can be maintained only over a few minutes. Performance is rather the consistent ability to produce results over prolonged periods of time and in a variety of assignments. A performance record must include mistakes. It must include failures. It must reveal a person's limitations as well as strengths. And there are as many different kinds of performance as there are different human beings. One person will consistently do well, rarely falling far below a respectable standard, but also rarely excel through brilliance or virtuosity. Another will perform only adequately under normal circumstances but will rise to the demands of a crisis or a major challenge and then perform like a true 'star'. Both are 'performers'. Both need to be recognized. But their performances will look quite different.

The one to distrust, however, is the person who never makes a mistake, never commits a blunder, never fails in what he tries to do. Either he is a phony, or he stays with the safe, the tried and the trivial.

A management which does not define performance as a balance of success and failure over a period of time is a management that mistakes conformity for achievement, and absence of weaknesses for strengths. It is a management that discourages its organization. The better a person is, the more mistakes he will make – for the more new things he will try.

The person who consistently renders poor or mediocre performance should be removed from the job for his or her own good. People who find themselves in a job that exceeds their capacities are frustrated, harassed, anxiety-ridden people. One does not do people a service by leaving them in a job they are not equal to. Not to face up to failure in a job is cowardice rather than compassion.

One also owes it to the manager's subordinates not to tolerate poor performance in their boss. They have a right to be managed with competence, dedication and achievement. Subordinates have a right to a boss who performs, for otherwise they themselves cannot perform.

One owes it finally to all the people in the organization not to put up with a manager who fails to perform. The entire organization is diminished by the manager or career professional who performs poorly or not at all. It is enriched by the one who performs superbly.

At first sight the Japanese seem to violate this rule. For few, if any, people are ever fired for nonperformance in the Japanese organization. Actually the Japanese organization may be as demanding and even as competitive as any in the West. The poor or mediocre performer is not fired. He is quickly side-tracked and assigned to activities that are in effect 'made work'. And both he and the organization know it. Moreover, while everyone advances in pay and title according to seniority, there is a day of reckoning at or around age forty-five when the very few who will become top management are chosen for the many others who will, ten years later, retire as section managers or department directors.

The only thing that is proven by a person's not performing in a given assignment is that management has made a mistake in giving him or her that assignment. It is a mistake that managers cannot avoid, no matter how carefully they work on the placement of people. 'Failure' in such a case may mean only that a first-rate career professional has been miscast as a manager. It may mean that someone excellent at running an existing operation has been miscast as an innovator and entrepreneur. Or it may mean the opposite: that a person whose strength lies in doing new and different things has been miscast to head a continuing, well-established and highly routinized operation.

Failure to perform on the part of an individual who has a record of proven performance is a signal to think hard about the person and the job. And sometimes, of course (see the discussion of the 'widow-maker' job in Chapter 24), it is the job rather than the person that is at fault.

George C. Marshall, Chief of Staff of the US Army in World War II, was an uncompromising and exacting boss who refused to tolerate mediocrity, let alone failure. 'I have a duty to the soldiers, their parents, and the country, to remove immediately any commander who does not satisfy the highest performance demands,' Marshall said again and again. But he always asserted, 'It was my mistake to have put this or that man in a command that was not the right command for him. It is therefore *my* job to think through where he belongs.' Many of the men who emerged in World War II as highly successful commanders in the US Army were once in the course of their careers removed by Marshall from an early assignment. But then Marshall thought through the mistake *he* had made – and tried to figure out where that man belonged. And this explains, in large measure, why the American Army, which had gone into World War II without a single one of its future general officers yet in a command position, produced an outstanding group of leaders in a few short years.

### 'Conscience' decisions

The toughest cases, but also the most important ones, are those of people who have given long and loyal service to the company but who have outlived their capacity to contribute.

There is, for instance, the bookkeeper who started when the company was in its infancy and grew with it until, at age fifty or so, she finds herself controller of a large company and totally out of her depth. The woman has not changed – the demands of the job have. She has given faithful service. And where loyalty has been received, loyalty is due. But still, she must not be allowed to remain as controller. Not only does her inability to perform endanger the company, her inadequacy demoralizes the entire management group and discredits management altogether.

Such cases – fortunately not too numerous – challenge the conscience of an organization. To keep the controller in her job would be betrayal of the enterprise and of all its people. But to fire a person who has given thirty years of faithful service is also betraying a trust. And to say, 'We should have taken care of this twenty-five years ago,' while true, is not much help.

The decision in such cases must be objective, that is, focused on the good of the company: the person must be removed from the job. Yet the decision is also a human decision which requires utmost consideration, true compassion, and an acceptance of obligations. That Henry Ford II could revive the moribund Ford

Motor Company after World War II was in large measure the result of his understanding the crucial importance of these 'conscience cases'.

At that time, none of the nine management people in one key division was found to be competent to take on the new jobs created in the course of reorganization. Not one was appointed to these new jobs. Yet, for these nine men, jobs as technicians and experts were found within the organization. It would have been easy to fire them. Their incompetence as managers was undisputed. But they had also served loyally through very trying years. Henry Ford II took the line that no one should be allowed to hold a job without giving superior performance, but he also held that no one should be penalized for the mistakes of the previous management. The company owes its rapid revival largely to the strict observance of this rule.

The frequent excuse in a conscience case, 'We can't move him; he has been here too long to be fired,' is bad logic and rarely more than a weak-kneed alibi. It harms the performance of management people, their spirit and their respect for the company.

But to fire such a manager is equally bad. It violates the organization's sense of justice and decency. It shakes its faith in the integrity of management. 'There, but for the grace of God, go I,' is what everybody will say – even though he or she would be the first to criticize if management left an incompetent in a position of importance.

A management that is concerned with the spirit of the organization therefore takes these cases exceedingly seriously. They are not too common, as a rule – or at least, they should not be. But they have impact on the spirit of the organization way beyond their numbers. How they are handled tells the organization both whether management takes itself and its job seriously, and whether it takes the human being seriously.

## Focus on opportunity

An organization will have a high spirit of performance if it is consistently directed towards opportunity rather than towards problems. It will have the thrill of excitement, the sense of challenge, and the satisfaction of achievement if its energies are put where the results are, and that means on the opportunities.

Of course, problems cannot be neglected. But the problem-focused organization is an organization on the defensive. It is an organization that feels that it has performed well if things do not get worse.

A management that wants to create and maintain the spirit of achievement therefore stresses opportunity. But it will also demand that opportunities be converted into results.

A management that wants to makes its organization focus on opportunity demands that opportunity be given pride of place in the objectives and goals of each manager and career professional. 'What are the opportunities which, if realized, will have the greatest impact on performance and results of the company and of my unit?' should be the first topic to which managers and career professionals should address themselves in their performance and work plan.

## 'People' decisions – the control of an organization

An organization that wants to build a high spirit of performance recognizes that 'people' decisions – on placement and on pay, on promotion, demotion and firing – are the true 'control' of an organization. They, far more than the accountant's figures and reports, model and mould behaviour. For the people decisions signal to every member of the organization what it is that management really wants, really values, really rewards.

The company that preaches 'our first-line supervisors are expected to practise human relations' but that always promotes the supervisor who gets paperwork in on time, neatly done, will not get 'human relations'. Even the dumbest foreman will learn very soon that what the company really wants is neat paperwork.

Indeed an organization tends to overreact to the people decisions of management. What to top management may look like an innocuous compromise to remove an obstacle or to solve a political impasse may well be a clear signal to the organization that management wants one kind of behaviour while preaching another.

Placement and promotion are the most crucial people decisions. They, above all, require careful thinking and clear policy and procedures with high standards of fairness and equity. They should never be made on the basis of opinions and on a person's 'potential'. They should always be based on a factual record of performance against explicit goals and objectives.

But the best placement and promotion procedures do not by themselves insure that these crucial decisions strengthen the spirit of the organization rather than impair it. For this, top management must build itself into the promotion process. Above all, it must make sure that it participates in the key decisions on promotion, the decisions that spell out to the organization what management's values and beliefs really are and at the same time determine – often irrevocably – the top management of tomorrow.

All top managements take an active role in the decisions on promotion to the jobs directly below or in the top-management group: the promotion into position of general manager of major divisions or into position as the head of major functional areas, such as manufacturing or marketing. But few top managements, especially in larger businesses, take much interest in the promotion decisions just below the top group, that is, into such jobs as head of market research, plant manager, or even marketing manager of a division. They leave these decisions to the top people in the respective functions or divisions. Yet these upper-middle-management jobs are truly *the* management to the organization. People further down, and especially the younger managers and career professionals, know very well that their own careers depend on these upper-middle people rather than on the big boss. And it is the decision on filling these upper-middle spots that in effect determines who, a few years hence, will be eligible for a top-management assignment.

Above all, these promotional decisions have great symbolic value. They are highly visible and signal to the entire organization, 'This is what this company wants, rewards, and recognizes.' For this reason, old and experienced organizations, such as the

Army and the Catholic Church, put their main concern in promotions on upper-middle management – in the Army on promotion to the rank of colonel, and in the Catholic Church on selecting an auxiliary bishop.

## Integrity, the touchstone

The final proof of the sincerity and seriousness of a management is uncompromising emphasis on integrity of character. This, above all, has to be symbolized in management's 'people' decisions. For it is character through which leadership is exercised; it is character that sets the example and is imitated. Character is not something managers can acquire; if they do not bring it to the job they will never have it. It is not something one can fool people about. A person's co-workers, especially the subordinates, know in a few weeks whether he or she has integrity or not. They may forgive a great deal; incompetence, ignorance, insecurity or bad manners. But they will not forgive a lack of integrity. Nor will they forgive higher management for choosing such a person.

Integrity may be difficult to define, but what constitutes lack of integrity of such seriousness as to disqualify a person for a managerial position is not. Someone whose vision focuses on people's weaknesses rather than on their strengths should never be appointed to a managerial position. The manager who always knows exactly what people cannot do, but never sees anything they can do, will undermine the spirit of the organization. Of course, a manager should have a clear grasp of the limitations of subordinates, but should see these as limitations on what they can do, and as challenges to them to do better. A manager should be a realist; and no one is less realistic than the cynic.

A person should not be appointed if he or she is more interested in the question 'Who is right?' than in the question 'What is right?' To put personality above the requirements of the work is corruption and corrupts. To ask 'Who is right?' encourages one's subordinates to play safe, if not to play politics.

Management should not appoint anyone who considers intelligence more important than integrity. This is immaturity – and usually incurable. It should never promote a person who has shown that he or she is afraid of strong subordinates. This is weakness. It should never put into a management job a person who does not set high standards for his own work. For that breeds contempt for the work and for management's competence.

A man might himself know too little, perform poorly, lack judgement and ability, and yet not do too much damage as a manager. But if he lacks in character and integrity – no matter how knowledgeable, how brilliant, how successful – he destroys. He destroys people, the most valuable resource of the enterprise. He destroys spirit. And he destroys performance.

This is particularly true of the people at the head of an enterprise. For the spirit of an organization is created from the top. If an organization is great in spirit, it is because the spirit of its top people is great. If it decays, it does so because the top rots; as the proverb has it, 'Trees die from the top.' No one should ever be appointed to a senior position unless top management is willing to have his character serve as the model for his subordinates.

This chapter has talked of 'practices'. It has not talked of 'leadership'. This was intentional. There is no substitute for leadership. But management cannot create leaders. It can only create the conditions under which potential leadership qualities become effective; or it can stifle potential leadership. The supply of leadership is much too uncertain to be depended upon for creating the spirit that the enterprise needs to be productive and to hold together.

Practices, though seemingly humdrum, can always be practised whatever a person's aptitudes, personality or attitudes. Practices require no genius – only application. They are things to do rather than to talk about.

And the right practices should go a long way towards bringing out whatever potential for leadership there is in the management group. They should also lay the foundation for the right kind of leadership. For leadership is not magnetic personality – that can just as well be a glib tongue. It is not 'making friends and influencing people' – that is flattery. Leadership is lifting a person's vision to higher sights, the raising of a person's performance to a higher standard, the building of a personality beyond its normal limitations. Nothing better prepares the ground for such leadership than a spirit of management that confirms in the day-to-day practices of the organization strict principles of conduct and responsibility, high standards of performance, and respect for individuals and their work.

## Summary

The purpose of organization is to enable ordinary human beings to do extraordinary things. The test of an organization is therefore the spirit of performance. This requires specific practices rather than preachment. It requires above all realization that integrity is the one absolute requirement of managers.

# Part Six
# Managerial Skills

Managing is specific work. As such it requires specific skills.
Among them are:

—making effective decisions;
—communication within and without the organization;
—the proper use of controls and measurements;
—skill in budgeting and in planning work;
—skill in using analytical tools, that is, the management sciences.

No manager is likely to master all these skills. But every manager
needs to understand what they are, what they can do for him,
and what, in turn, they require of him.

## 29 The Effective Decision

Executives do many things in addition to making decisions. But only executives make decisions. The first managerial skill is, therefore, the making of effective decisions.

There are countless books on the techniques of decision-making. Complex logical and mathematical methods have been developed for the decision-making process. But there is little concern with the essential process itself. What is a 'decision'? What are the important elements in it?

The only people who have developed a systematic and standardized approach to decision-making are the Japanese. Their approach violates every rule in the books on decision-making. According to the books, the Japanese should never be able to arrive at any decision, let alone an effective one. Yet, their decisions are highly effective. It might, therefore, be fruitful to take a look at the Japanese way of decision-making in order to find out the elements of the process.

### How the Japanese make decisions

If there is one point on which all authorities on the subject of Japan are in agreement, it is that Japanese institutions, whether business or government agencies, make decisions by consensus. The Japanese, we are told, debate a proposed decision throughout the organization until there is complete agreement on it. And only then do they make the decision.

This, every experienced Western manager will say with a shudder, is not for us, however well it might work for the Japanese. This approach can lead only to indecision or politicking, or at best to a compromise that offends no one but also solves nothing.

But what stands out in Japanese history, as well as in today's

Japanese management behaviour, is the capacity for reaching radical and highly controversial decisions. Let me illustrate.

No country was more receptive to Christianity than sixteenth-century Japan. The hope of the Portuguese missionaries that Japan would become the first Christian country outside of Europe seemed justified. Yet the same Japan made a 180-degree turn in the early seventeenth century. Within a few years it completely suppressed Christianity and shut itself off from all foreign influences – indeed, from all contact with the outside world – and stayed that way for 250 years. Then, in the Meiji Restoration of 1867, Japan executed another 180-degree turn and opened itself to the West – something no other non-European country managed to do.

The key to this apparent contradiction is that the Westerner and the Japanese mean something different when they talk of 'making a decision'. In the West, all the emphasis is on the *answer* to the question. Our books on decision-making try to develop systematic approaches to giving an answer. To the Japanese, however, the important element in decision-making is *defining the question*. The important and crucial steps are to decide whether there is a need for a decision and what the decision is about. And it is in this step that the Japanese aim at attaining consensus. Indeed, it is this step that, to the Japanese, is the essence of the decision. The answer to the question (what the West considers *the* decision) follows from its definition.

During the process that precedes the decision, no mention is made of what the answer might be. This is done so that people will not be forced to take sides; once they have taken sides, a decision would be a victory for one side and a defeat for the other. Thus the whole process is focused on finding out what the decision is really about, not what the decision should be. Its result is an agreement that there is (or is not) a need for a change in behaviour.

All of this takes a long time. Westerners dealing with the Japanese are thoroughly frustrated during the process. They do not understand what is going on. They have the feeling that they are being given the runaround.

To take a specific example, it is very hard for a US executive to understand why the Japanese with whom he or she is negotiating a licence agreement keep sending new groups of people every few months who start what the Westerner thinks are 'negotiations' as if they had never heard of the subject. One delegation takes copious notes and goes back home, only to be succeeded six weeks later by another team of people from different areas of the company who again act as if they have never heard of the matter under discussion, take copious notes and go home.

Actually – though few of my Western friends believe it – this is a sign that the Japanese take the matter seriously. They are trying to involve the people who will eventually have to carry out the agreement in the process of obtaining consensus that a licence is indeed needed. Only when all of these people have come together on the need to make a decision will the decision be made to go ahead. Only then do negotiations really start – and then the Japanese usually move with great speed.

When the Japanese reach the point we call a decision, they say they are in the *action stage*. Now top management refers the decision to what the Japanese call the 'appropriate people.' Selection of these people is a top-management decision; on it depends the specific answer to the problem that is to be worked out. For, during the course of the discussions leading up to the consensus, it has become quite clear what basic approaches certain people or groups would take to the problem. Top management, by referring the question to one group or the other, in effect picks the answer – but an answer which by now will surprise no one.

What are the advantages of this process? And what can we learn from it?

In the first place, it makes for very effective decisions. While it takes much longer in Japan to reach a decision than it takes in the West, from that point on they do better than we do. After making a decision, we in the West spend much time 'selling' it and getting people to act on it. Only too often the decision is sabotaged by the organization; or, what may be worse, it takes so long to make the decision truly effective that it becomes obsolete, if not wrong, by the time the people in the organization actually make it operational.

The Japanese, by contrast, need to spend absolutely no time on selling a decision. Everybody has been presold. Also, their process makes it clear where in the organization a certain answer to a question will be welcomed and where it will be resisted. So there is plenty of time to work on persuading the dissenters, or on making small concessions to them which will win them over without destroying the integrity of the decision.

Every Westerner who has done business with the Japanese has learned that the apparent snail's pace of the negotiating stage, with its endless delays and endless discussion of the same points, is followed by a speed of action that is truly breathtaking. It may take three years before a licensing agreement can be reached, during which time there is no discussion of terms, no discussion of what products the Japanese plan to make, no discussion of what knowledge and help they might need. And then, within four weeks, the Japanese are ready to go into production. They make demands on their partners for information and people which the Westerners are totally unprepared to meet. Now it is the Japanese who complain, and bitterly, about the 'endless delay and procrastination' of the Westerner. For they understand our way of making a decision and acting on it no better than we understand their way.

The Japanese process is focused on understanding the problem. The desired end result is action and behaviour on the part of people. This almost guarantees that all the alternatives will be considered. It focuses management attention to essentials. It does not permit commitment until management has decided what the decision is all about. Japanese managers may come up with the wrong answer to the problem, but they rarely come up with the right answer to the wrong problem. And that, as all decision-makers learn, is the most dangerous course, the irretrievably wrong decision.

Above all, their system forces the Japanese to make big decisions. It is much too cumbersome to be put to work on minor matters. It takes far too many people far too long to be wasted on anything but truly important matters that will lead to real changes in policies and behaviour. Small decisions, even when obviously needed, are for that reason very often not made at all in Japan.

With us it is the small decisions which are easy to make – decisions about things that do not greatly matter. Anyone who knows Western businesses, government agencies, or educational institutions knows that their managers make far too many small decisions as a rule. And nothing causes as much trouble in an organization as a lot of small decisions. Whether the decision concerns moving the water cooler from one end of the hall to the other or the phasing out of one's oldest business makes little emotional difference. One decision takes as much time and generates as much heat as the other.

In the West we are moving in the Japanese direction. At least, this is what the many task forces, long-range plans, strategies and other approaches are trying to accomplish. But we do not build into the development of these projects the selling which the Japanese process achieves before the decision. Its absence explains in large measure why so many brilliant reports of task forces and planners never get beyond the planning stage.

What are the essentials of the Japanese method of decision-making? First the focus is on deciding what the decision is all about. The Japanese do not focus on giving an answer; they focus on defining the question.

Second, the Japanese bring out dissenting opinions. Because there is no discussion of the answer till there is consensus about the question, a wide variety of opinions and approaches is being explored.

Third, the focus is on alternatives rather than on the 'right solution'. The process also suggests the level at which a decision should be made, and the person who should make it. And it eliminates selling a decision. It builds effective execution into the decision-making process.

The specific Japanese system is unique. It could not be used without the special social organization of Japan and of Japanese institutions. But the principles which the Japanese put to work in their decision-making process are generally applicable. They are the essentials of effective decision-making.

## Facts or opinions?

A decision is a judgement. It is a choice between alternatives. It is rarely a choice between right and wrong. It is at best a choice between 'almost right' and 'probably wrong' – but much more often a choice between two courses of action, neither of which is provably more nearly right than the other.

Most books on decision-making tell the reader: 'First find the facts.' But managers who make effective decisions know that one does not start with facts. One starts with opinions. These are, of course, nothing but untested hypotheses and, as such, worthless unless tested against reality. To determine what is a fact requires first a decision on the criteria of relevance, especially on the appropriate measurement. This is the hinge of the effective decision, and usually its most controversial aspect.

But also, the effective decision does not, as so many texts on decision-making proclaim, flow from a 'consensus on the facts'. The understanding that underlies the right decision grows out of the clash and conflict of opinions and out of the serious consideration of competing alternatives.

Only by starting out with opinions can the decision-maker find out what the decision is all about. People do, of course, differ in the answers they give. But most differences of opinion reflect an underlying – and usually hidden – difference as to what the decision is actually about. They reflect a difference regarding the question that has to be answered. Identifying the alternative questions is thus the first step in making effective decisions.

People inevitably start out with an opinion; to ask them to search for the facts is impossible and undesirable. They will simply do what everyone is far too prone to do anyhow: look for the facts that fit the conclusion they have already reached. And no one has ever failed to find the facts he is looking for. Good statisticians know this and distrust all figures – they either know the fellow who found them or they do not know him; in either case they are suspicious.

The only rigorous method, the only one that enables us to test an opinion against reality, is based on the clear recognition that opinions come first. Then no one can fail to see that we start out with untested hypotheses – in decision-making, as in science, the only starting point. One does not argue them; one tests them to find out which are worthy of serious consideration, and which are invalidated by the first test against observable experience.

Effective decision-makers therefore encourage opinions. But they insist that the people who voice them also think through what it is that the 'experiment' – that is, the testing of the opinion against reality – would have to show. The effective executive, therefore, asks, 'What do we have to know to test the validity of this hypothesis?' 'What would the facts have to be to make this opinion tenable?' And it becomes a habit for everyone to think through and spell out what needs to be looked at, studied, and tested. People who voice an opinion also *need* to take responsibility for defining the factual findings that can be expected and should be looked for.

Perhaps the crucial question here is 'What is the measurement appropriate to the matter under discussion and to the decision to be reached?' Whenever one analyses the way a truly effective decision has been reached, one finds that a great deal of work and thought went into finding the appropriate measurement.

## The need for dissent and alternatives

Unless one has considered alternatives, one has a closed mind. This, above all, explains why the Japanese deliberately disregard the second major command of the textbooks on decision-making and create discussion and dissent as a means to consensus.

Executive decisions are not made well by acclamation. They are made well only if they are based on the clash of conflicting views, the dialogue between different points of view, the choice between different judgements. The first rule in decision-making is that one does not make a decision unless there is disagreement.

Alfred P. Sloan, Jr, is reported to have said at a meeting of one of the GM top committees, 'Gentlemen, I take it we are all in complete agreement on the decision here.' Everyone around the table nodded assent. 'Then,' continued Mr Sloan, 'I propose we postpone further discussion of this matter until our next meeting, to give ourselves time to develop disagreement and perhaps gain some understanding of what the decision is all about.'

Sloan was anything but an 'intuitive' decision-maker. He always emphasized the need to test opinions against facts and the need to make absolutely sure that one did not start out with the conclusion and then look for the facts that support it. But he knew that the right decision demands adequate disagreement.

There are three reasons that dissent is needed. First, it safeguards the decision-maker against becoming the prisoner of the organization. Everybody always wants something from the decision-maker. Everybody is a special pleader, trying – often in perfectly good faith – to obtain a favourable decision. This is true whether the decision-maker is the president of the United States or a junior engineer working on a design modification. The only way to break out of the prison of special pleading and preconceived notions is to make sure of argued, documented, thought-through disagreements.

Second, disagreement alone can provide alternatives to a decision. And a decision without an alternative is a desperate gambler's throw, no matter how carefully made it might be. There is always a high possibility that the decision will prove wrong – either because it was wrong to begin with or because a change in circumstances makes it wrong. If one has thought out alternatives during the decision-making process, one has something to fall back on, something that has already been studied and understood. Without such an alternative, one is likely to flounder dismally when reality proves a decision to be inoperative.

Above all, disagreement is needed to stimulate the imagination. In all matters of true uncertainty such as the executive deals with – whether the sphere be political, economic, social or military – one needs creative solutions which create a new situation. And this means that one needs imagination – a new and different way of perceiving and understanding.

Great imagination is, I admit, not in abundant supply. But

neither is it as scarce as is commonly believed. Imagination needs to be challenged and stimulated, however, or else it remains unused. Disagreement is the most effective stimulus to the imagination that we know.

The effective decision-maker, therefore, organizes dissent. This protects the organization against being taken in by plausible but false or incomplete solutions. It provides alternatives to choose from, and also ensures that there will be a back-up plan. And it forces the imagination. Dissent converts the plausible into the right and the right into the good decision.

## The trap of 'being right'

Effective decision-makers do not start out with the assumption that one proposed course of action is right and that all others must be wrong. Nor do they start out with the assumption 'I am right and the other person is wrong'. They start out with the commitment to find out why people disagree.

Effective executives know, of course, that there are fools around and that there are mischief-makers. But they do not assume that the person who disagrees with what they themselves see as clear and obvious is, therefore, either a fool or a knave. They know that unless proven otherwise, the dissenter has to be assumed to be reasonably intelligent and reasonably fair-minded. Therefore, it has to be assumed that he or she has reached the so obviously wrong conclusion because of seeing a different reality and a different problem. The effective executive, therefore, always asks, 'What does this person see that would make so different a position seem to him rational?' The effective executive is concerned first with *understanding*. Only then can one even think who is right and who is wrong.

Needless to say, this is not done by a great many people, whether executives or not. Most people start out with the certainty that how they see things is the only way to see at all. As a result, they never understand what the decision – and indeed the whole argument – is really all about.

The American steel executives have never asked the question

'Why do these union people get so terribly upset every time we mention the word "featherbedding"?' The union people, in turn, have never asked themselves why steel managements make such a fuss over featherbedding when every single instance thereof they have ever produced has proved to be petty and irrelevant to boot. Instead, both sides have worked mightily to prove each other wrong. If either side had tried to understand what the other one sees and why, both would be a great deal stronger, and labour relations in the steel industry might be a good deal healthier.

No matter how high emotions run, no matter how certain it seems that the other side is completely wrong and has no case at all, the executive who wants to make the right decision works hard to see opposition as a means to think through the alternatives. He or she uses conflict of opinion as a tool to make sure all aspects of an important matter are looked at carefully.

## Is a decision necessary?

There is one question the effective decision-maker asks: 'Is a decision really necessary?' *One* alternative is always the alternative of doing nothing.

One has to make a decision when a condition is likely to degenerate if nothing is done. This also applies with respect to opportunity. If the opportunity is important and is likely to vanish unless one acts with dispatch, one acts – and one makes a radical change.

Theodore Vail's contemporaries around 1900 agreed with him as to the degenerative danger of government ownership. But they wanted to fight it by fighting symptoms – fighting this or that bill in the legislature, opposing this or that candidate and supporting another, and so on. When president of the Bell Telephone System, Vail alone understood that this is the ineffectual way to fight a degenerative condition. Even if one wins every battle, one can never win the war. Vail saw that drastic action was needed to create a new situation. He alone saw that private business had to make public regulation into an effective alternative to nationalization.

At the opposite end are those conditions that one can, without being unduly optimistic, expect to take care of themselves even if nothing is done. If the answer to the question 'What will happen if we do nothing?' is 'It will take care of itself', one does not interfere. Nor does one interfere if the condition, while annoying, is of no importance and unlikely to make much difference.

The great majority of decisions will lie between these extremes. The problem is not going to take care of itself; but it is unlikely to turn into degenerative malignancy either. The opportunity is only for improvement rather than for real change and innovation; but it is still quite considerable. If we do not act, in other words, we will in all probability survive. But if we do act, we may be better off.

In this situation the effective decision-maker compares effort and risk of action to risk of inaction. There is no formula for the right decision here. But the guidelines are so clear that decision in the concrete case is rarely difficult. They are:

—act if on balance the benefits greatly outweigh cost and risk; and

—act or do not act; do not 'hedge' or compromise.

The surgeon who takes out only half the tonsils or half the appendix risks as much infection and shock as if the whole job were done. And the condition has not been cured, has indeed been made worse. The surgeon either operates or doesn't. Similarly, the effective decision-maker either acts or he doesn't act. He does not take half-action. This is the one thing that is always wrong.

## Who has to do the work?

When they reach this point, most decision-makers in the West think they can make an effective decision. But, as the Japanese example shows, one essential element is still missing. An effective decision is a commitment to action and results. If it has to be 'sold' *after* it has been made, there will be no action and no results – and, in effect, no decision. At the least, there may be so much delay as to make the decision obsolete before it has become truly effective.

The first rule is to make sure that everyone who will have to do something to make the decision effective – or who could sabotage it – has been forced to participate responsibly in the discussion. This is not 'democracy'. It is salesmanship.

But it is equally important to build the action commitments into the decision from the start. In fact, no decision has been made unless carrying it out in specific steps has become someone's work assignment and responsibility. Until then, there are only good intentions.

Converting a decision into action requires answering several distinct questions: 'Who has to know of this decision?' 'What action has to be taken?' 'Who is to take it?' 'And what does the action have to be so that the people who have to do it *can* do it?' The first and the last of these are too often overlooked – with dire results.

A story that has become a legend among management scientists illustrates the importance of the question 'Who has to know?' A major manufacturer of industrial equipment decided to discontinue one model. For years it had been standard equipment on a line of machine tools, many of which were still in use. It was decided, therefore, to sell the model to present owners of the old equipment for another three years as a replacement, and then to stop making and selling it. Orders for this particular model had being going down for a good many years, but they shot up temporarily as former customers reordered against the day when the model would no longer be available. No one had asked, 'Who needs to know of this decision?' Therefore nobody informed the clerk in the purchasing department who was in charge of buying the parts from which the model itself was being assembled. His instructions were to buy parts in a given ratio to current sales – and the instructions remained unchanged. When the time came to discontinue further production of the model, the company had in its warehouse enough parts for another eight to ten years of production, parts that had to be written off at a considerable loss.

Above all, the action must be appropriate to the capacities of the people who have to carry it out.

A chemical company found itself, in the early 1960s, with

fairly large amounts of blocked currency in two West African countries. To protect this money, it decided to invest in local businesses which would contribute to the local economy, would not require imports from abroad, and would, if successful, be the kind that could be sold to local investors when currency remittances became possible again. To establish these businesses, the company developed a simple chemical process to preserve a tropical fruit which is a staple crop in both countries and which, up until then, had suffered serious spoilage in transit to its markets.

The business was a success in both countries. But in one country the local manager set the business up in such a manner that it required highly skilled and technically trained management, not easily available in West Africa. In the other country, the local manager thought through the capacities of the people who would eventually have to run the business and worked hard at making both process and business simple. He staffed from the start with nationals of the country, even at the highest levels.

A few years later it became possible again to transfer currency from these two countries. But though the business flourished, no buyer could be found for it in the first country. No one available locally had the necessary managerial and technical skills. The business had to be liquidated at a loss. In the other country so many local entrepreneurs were eager to buy the business that the company got back its original investment with a substantial profit.

The process and the business built on it were essentially the same in both places. But in the first country no one had asked, 'What kind of people do we have available to make this decision effective ? And what can they do ?' As a result, the decision itself became frustrated.

All this becomes doubly important when people have to change behaviour, habits or attitudes to make a decision effective. One has to make sure that responsibility for the action is clearly assigned and that the people responsible are capable of carrying it out. One also has to make sure that their measurements, standards for accomplishment and incentives are changed simultaneously. Otherwise, the people will get caught in a paralysing internal emotional conflict.

If the greatest rewards are given for behaviour contrary to that which the new course of action requires, then everyone will conclude that this contrary behaviour is what the people at the top really want and are going to reward.

## The right and the wrong compromise

The decision is now ready to be made. The specifications have been thought through, the alternatives explored, the risks and gains weighed. Who will have to do what is understood. It is reasonably clear what course of action should be taken. At this point the decision does indeed almost 'make itself'.

And it is at this point that most decisions are lost. It becomes suddenly quite obvious that the decision is not going to be pleasant, is not going to be popular, is not going to be easy. It becomes clear that a decision requires courage as much as it requires judgement. There is no inherent reason why medicines should taste horrible – but effective ones usually do. Similarly, there is no inherent reason why decisions should be distasteful – but most effective ones are.

The reason is always the same: there is no 'perfect' decision. One always has to pay a price. One always has to balance conflicting objectives, conflicting opinions and conflicting priorities. The best decision is only an approximation – and a risk. And there is always the pressure to compromise to gain acceptance, to placate strong opponents of the proposed course of action, or to hedge risks.

To make effective decisions under such circumstances requires starting with a commitment to what is right rather than with the question 'Who is right?' One has to compromise in the end. But unless one starts out with the closest one can come to the decision that will truly satisfy objective requirements, one ends up with the wrong compromise – that abandons essentials.

For there are two different kinds of compromise. One kind is expressed in the old proverb 'Half a loaf is better than no bread.'

The other kind is expressed in the story of the Judgement of Solomon, which was clearly based on the realization that 'half a baby is worse than no baby at all.' In the first instance, objective requirements are still being satisfied. The purpose of bread is to provide food, and half a loaf is still food. Half a baby, however, is not half of a living and growing child. It is a corpse in two pieces.

It is fruitless and a waste of time to worry about what is acceptable. The things one worries about seldom happen. And objections and difficulties no one thought about suddenly turn out to be almost insurmountable obstacles. One gains nothing, in other words, by starting out with the question 'What is acceptable?' And in the process of answering it, one loses any chance to come up with an effective – let alone with the right – answer.

## The feedback

Feedback has to be built into the decision to provide continuous testing, against actual events, of the expectations that underlie the decision. Few decisions work out the way they are intended to. Even the best decision may run into snags, unexpected obstacles, and all kinds of surprises. Even the most effective decision eventually becomes obsolete. Unless there is feedback from the results of a decision, it is unlikely to produce the desired results.

This requires that the expectations be spelled out clearly – and in writing. It requires an organized effort to follow up. And this feedback is part of the decision and has to be worked out in the decision process.

When General Eisenhower was elected president, his predecessor, Harry Truman, said: 'Poor Ike; when he was a general, he gave an order and it was carried out. Now he is going to sit in that big office and he'll give an order and not a damn thing is going to happen.'

The reason why 'not a damn thing is going to happen' is not that generals have more authority than presidents. It is that military organizations learned long ago that futility is the lot of most orders and organized the feedback to check on the execution of the order. They learned long ago that to go oneself and look is the only reliable feedback. Reports – all an American president is normally able to mobilize – are not much help. All military services have long ago learned that the officer who has given an order goes out and sees for himself whether it has been carried out. At the least he sends one of his own aides; he never relies on what he is told by the subordinate to whom the order was given. Not that he distrusts the subordinate, but he has learned from experience to distrust communications.

## Summary

Decision-making is not a mechanical job. It is risk-taking and a challenge to judgement. The 'right answer' (which usually cannot be found anyway) is not central. Central is understanding of the problem. Decision-making is not an intellectual exercise. It mobilizes the vision, energies and resources of the organization for effective action.

# 30 Managerial Communications

We have more attempts at communications today, more attempts to talk to others. There is a surfeit of communications media, unimaginable to the men who, around the time of World War I, started to work on the problems of communicating in organizations. Communications in management has become a central concern to students and practitioners in all institutions – business, the military, public administration, hospital, university and research. In no other area have intelligent men and women worked harder or with greater dedication than psychologists, human relations experts, managers and management scholars have worked on improving communications in our major institutions.

Yet communications has proven as elusive as the Unicorn. The noise level has gone up so fast that no one can really listen any more to all that babble about communications. But there is clearly less and less communicating. The communications gap within institutions and between groups in society has been widening steadily – to the point where it threatens to become an unbridgeable gulf of total misunderstanding.

In the meantime, there is an information explosion. Every professional and every executive suddenly has access to data in inexhaustible abundance. All of us feel – and overeat – very much like the child who has been left alone in the candy store. But what has to be done to make this data yield information, let alone knowledge? We get a great many answers. But the one thing clear so far is that no one really has an answer. Despite information theory and data processing, no one yet has actually seen, let alone used, an 'information system', or a 'data base'. The one thing we do know is that the abundance of information changes the communications problem and makes it both more urgent and more difficult.

There is a tendency today to give up on communications. In psychology, for instance, the fashion today is the T-group with its sensitivity training. The avowed aim is not communications, but self-awareness. T-groups focus on the 'I' and not on the 'Thou'. Ten or twenty years ago it was fashionable to stress 'empathy'; now it's 'doing one's thing'. However needed self-knowledge may be, communication is needed at least as much.

Despite the sorry state of communications in theory and practice, we have learned a good deal about information and communications. Most of it, though, has not come out of the work on communications to which we have devoted so much time and energy. It has been the by-product of work in a large number of seemingly unrelated fields, from learning theory to genetics and electronic engineering. We also have experience – though often of failure– in many practical situations in all kinds of institutions. We may indeed never understand 'communication'. But 'communications in organizations' – call it *managerial communications* – we do know something about by now.

## What we have learned

We have learned, mostly through doing the wrong things, four fundamentals of communications.

1 Communication is perception.
2 Communication is expectation.
3 Communication makes demands.
4 Communication and information are different and indeed largely opposite – yet interdependent.

1 *Communication is perception.* An old riddle posed by the mystics of many religions – the Zen Buddhists, the Sufis of Islam, and the Rabbis of the Talmud – asks : 'Is there a sound in the forest if a tree crashes down and no one is around to hear it ?' The right answer to this is no. There are sound waves. But there is no sound unless someone perceives it. Sound is created by perception. Sound is communication.

It is the *recipient* who communicates. The so-called communicator, the person who emits the communication, does not communicate. He or she utters. Unless there is someone who hears, there is no communication. There is only noise. The communicator speaks or writes or sings – but he does not communicate. Indeed, he cannot communicate. He can only make it possible (or impossible) for a recipient – or rather, 'percipient' – to perceive.

Perception, we know, is not logic. It is experience. This means, in the first place, that one always perceives a configuration, a pattern. One cannot perceive single specifics. They are always part of a total picture. The 'silent language',* – gestures, tone of voice, the environment, not to mention the cultural and social context – cannot be dissociated from the spoken language. In fact, without them the spoken word has no meaning and cannot communicate.

*As Edward T. Hall called it in the title of his pioneering work (Doubleday, 1959).

The same words, for example, 'I enjoyed meeting you', will be heard as having a wide variety of meanings. Whether they are heard as warm or as icy-cold, as endearment or as rejection, depends on their setting in the 'silent language'. Without its place in the total configuration of occasion, value, 'silent language', and so on, the phrase has no meaning at all. By itself it cannot make communication possible. It cannot be understood. Indeed it cannot be heard. To paraphrase an old proverb of the human-relations school: 'One cannot communicate a word; the whole man always comes with it.'

But we know about perception also that one can perceive only what one is capable of perceiving. Just as the ear does not hear sounds above a certain pitch, so the mind does not perceive what is beyond its range of perception. It may, of course, hear physically, or see visually, but these sensations cannot become communication unless they are meaningful.

In Plato's *Phaedo*, Socrates points out that one has to talk to people in terms of their own experience. One has to use carpenters' metaphors when talking to carpenters, the language of sailors when talking to sailors and so on. One can communicate only in the recipient's language or terms. And the terms have to be experience-based. It does very little good to try to explain terms to people. They will not be able to receive the terms if they are not related to their own experience.

In communicating, the first question has to be 'Is this communication within the recipient's range of perception? Can he receive it?'

The 'range of perception' is, of course, physiological and largely (though not entirely) set by physical limitations of man's animal body. When we speak of communication, however, the most important limitations on perception are usually cultural and emotional rather than physical.

That fanatics are not being convinced by rational arguments, we have known for thousands of years. Now we are beginning to understand that it is not 'argument' that is lacking. Fanatics do not have the ability to perceive a communication that goes beyond their range of emotions. First their emotions would have to be altered. No one is really 'in touch with reality', if by that we mean complete openness to evidence. The distinction between 'sanity' and 'paranoia' does not lie in the ability to perceive, but in the ability to learn, to change one's emotions on the basis of experience.

One rarely realizes that something that is obvious to us and is clearly validated by our own emotional experience, has other dimensions, a 'back' and 'sides', which are entirely different and which, therefore, lead to entirely different perceptions. The story about the blind men and the elephant in which each one, encountering this strange beast, feels one of the elephant's parts and reports an entirely different conclusion, is simply a metaphor of the human condition. There is no possibility of communication until this is understood.

2 *Communication is expectation.* As a rule we perceive what we expect to perceive. We see largely what we expect to see, and we hear largely what we expect to hear. That the unexpected may be resented is not the important thing – though most of the work on communications in business and government suggests it is. What is truly important is that the unexpected is usually not received at all. It is not seen or heard, but ignored. Or it is misunderstood.

On this we now have a century or more of experimentation. The results are clear. The human mind attempts to fit impressions and stimuli into a frame of expectations. It resists vigorously any attempts to make it 'change its mind', that is, to perceive what it does not expect to perceive. It is, of course, possible to alert the human mind to the fact that what it perceives is contrary to its expectations. But this first requires that we understand what it expects to perceive. It then requires that there be an unmistakable signal – 'this is different'. A gradual change in which the mind is supposedly led by small steps to realize that what is perceived is not what it expects to perceive will not work. It will rather reinforce expectations. This makes it even more certain that what will be perceived is what the recipient expects to perceive.

Before we can communicate, we must know what the recipient expects to see and hear. Only then can we know whether communication fits into expectations – and what they are – or whether there is need for an 'awakening' that breaks through the recipient's expectations and forces a realization that the unexpected is happening.

3 *Communication makes demands*. Many years ago psychologists stumbled on a strange phenomenon in their studies of memory. In order to test memory, the psychologists compiled a list of words that were shown to their experimental subjects. As control, a list of nonsense words, mere jumbles of letters, was devised. Much to the surprise of these early experimenters almost a century ago, their subjects showed totally uneven memory retention of individual words. More surprisingly, they showed amazingly high retention of the nonsense words. The explanation of the first phenomenon is fairly obvious. Words are not mere information. They do carry emotional charges. And, therefore, words with unpleasant or threatening associations tend to be suppressed, words with pleasant associations retained. In fact, this selective retention by emotional association has since been used to construct tests for emotional disorders and for personality profiles.

The relatively high retention rate of nonsense words was a greater puzzle. It was expected that no one would really remember words that had no meaning at all. But it has become clear over the years that the memory for these words, though limited, exists precisely because these words have no meaning. With respect to them, memory could be said to be truly 'mechanical', showing neither emotional preference nor emotional rejection.

Communication is always 'propaganda'. The sender always wants 'to get something across'. Propaganda, we now know, is both a great deal more powerful than the rationalists, with their belief in 'open discussion', admit, and a great deal less powerful than the myth-makers of propaganda wanted us to believe. The danger of total propaganda is not that the propaganda will be believed. The danger is that nothing will be believed and that every communication becomes suspect. In the end, no communication is received. Everything anyone says is considered a demand and is resisted, resented and in effect not heard at all. The end results of total propaganda are not fanatics, but cynics.

Communication, in other words, always makes demands. It always demands that the recipient become somebody, do something, believe something. It always appeals to motivation. If communication fits in with the aspirations, values and purposes of the recipient, it is powerful. If it goes against them, it is likely not to be received at all. At its most powerful, communication brings about 'conversion', that is, a change of personality, values, beliefs and aspirations. But this is the rare event, and one against which the basic psychological forces of every human being are strongly organized. Even the Lord, the Bible reports, first had to strike Saul blind before he could raise him up as Paul. Communications aiming at conversion demand surrender. By and large, therefore, there is no communication unless the message can key in to the recipient's own values.

4 *Communication and information are different and indeed largely opposite – yet interdependent.* Communication is perception; information is logic. As such, information is purely formal and has no meaning. It is impersonal rather than interpersonal. The more it can be freed of the human component, of emotions and values, expectations and perceptions, the more valid and reliable and informative it becomes.

All through history, the problem has been how to get a little information out of communications. The problem has been to isolate the information content from an abundance of perception. Now, all of a sudden, we have the capacity to provide information – both because of the conceptual work of the logicians and because of the technical work on data processing and data storage by computer. We have the opposite problem from the one mankind has always struggled with. We have the problem of handling information that is devoid of any communication content.

The requirements for effective information are the opposite of those for effective communication. Information is, for instance, always specific. We perceive a pattern in communications; but we convey specific individual data in the information process. Indeed, information is, above all, a principle of economy. The fewer data needed, the better the information. And an overload of information leads to information blackout. It does not enrich, but impoverishes.

The prototype information system may well have been the peculiar language known as *Armee Deutsch* (Army German) which served as the language of command in the Imperial Austrian Army prior to 1918. Designed for an army in which officers and men often had no language in common, it functioned remarkably well with fewer than two hundred specific words – 'fire', for instance, or 'at ease' – each of which had only one possible meaning. The meaning was always an action. And the words were learned in and through actions. The tensions in the Austrian Army after many decades of nationalist turmoil were very great indeed. Social interaction between members of different nationalities serving in the same unit became increasingly difficult. But to the very end, the information system functioned. It was completely formal; completely rigid; completely logical in that each word had only one possible meaning. It rested on pre-established communication regarding the specific response to a certain set of sound waves. This example shows also that the effectiveness of an information system depends on the willingness and ability to think through carefully what information is needed by whom for what purposes, and then on the systematic creation of communication among the various parties to the system as to the meaning of each specific input and output. The effectiveness, in other words, depends on the pre-establishment of Communication.

## Why downward communications cannot work

For centuries we have attempted communication 'downwards'. This, however, cannot work, no matter how hard and how intelligently we try. It cannot work, first, because it focuses on what *we* want to say. It assumes, in other words, that the utterer communicates. But we know that all he or she does is utter. Communication is the act of the recipient. What we have been trying to do is to work on the sender (specifically on the manager) to make him capable of being a better communicator. But all one can communicate downwards are commands. One cannot communicate downwards anything connected with understanding, let alone with motivation. This requires communication upwards, from those who perceive to those who want to reach their perception.

This does not mean that managers should stop working on clarity in what they say or write. Far from it. But it does mean that how we say something comes only after we have learned what to say. And this cannot be found out by 'talking to'. 'Letters to the Employees,' no matter how well done, will be a waste unless the writer knows what employees expect to perceive and want to do. They are a waste unless they are based on the recipient's rather than the senders' perception.

When the Human Relations School of Elton Mayo, fifty years ago, recognized the failure of the traditional approach to communications, its suggestion was to listen. Instead of starting out with what 'we', the management, want to 'get across', the executive should start out by finding out what subordinates want to know. To this day, the human relations prescription remains the classic formula.

But 'listening' does not work either. Of course, listening is a starting point for communication. But it is not adequate, by itself. Listening assumes that the superior will understand what he is being told. It assumes, in other words, that the subordinates can communicate. But it is hard to see why the subordinate should be able to do what the superior cannot do. There is no reason, in other words, to believe that listening results any less in misunderstanding and miscommunications than does talking. In addition, the theory of listening does not take into account that communication is demand. It does not bring out the subordinate's preferences and desires, values and aspirations. It may explain the reasons for misunderstanding. But it does not lay down a basis for understanding.

Nor does more and better information solve the communications problem. On the contrary, the more information, the greater is the need for functioning and effective communication. The more effective the information process, the more impersonal and formal will it become; the more will it separate human beings and thereby require separate, but also much greater, efforts, to re-establish the human relationship of communication. The effectiveness of the information process will depend increasingly on our ability to communicate. In the absence of effective communication (the present situation) the information revolution cannot really produce information. All it can produce is data.

The information explosion is the most compelling reason to go to work on communications. Indeed, the frightening communications gap all around us – between management and workers; between business and government; between faculty and students, and between both of them and university administration; between producers and consumers – reflects the problem.

## What can managers do?

Can we say anything constructive about communication? Can we do anything? We can say that communication has to start from the intended recipient of communications rather than from the sender. In terms of traditional organization, we have to start upwards. Downward communications cannot work and do not work. They come *after* upward communications have successfully been established.

But we can also say that it is not enough to listen. The upward communication must be focused on something that is common to recipient and sender. It must be focused on what already motivates the intended recipient. It must, from the beginning, be informed by the recipient's values, beliefs and aspirations.

Management by objectives is thus a prerequisite for functioning communication. It requires the subordinate to think through and present to the superior his own conclusions as to what major contribution to the organization he should be expected to perform and should be held accountable for.

What the subordinate comes up with is rarely what the superior expects. Indeed, the first aim of the exercise is precisely to bring out the divergence in perception between superior and subordinate. But the perception is focused, and focused on something that is real to both parties. To realize that they see the same reality differently is in itself already communication.

Management by objectives gives the intended recipient of communication – in this case the subordinate – access to experience that enables him or her to understand. He is given access to the reality of decision-making, the problems of priorities, the choice between what one likes to do and what the situation demands, and above all, the responsibility for a decision. He may not see the situation the same way the superior does – in fact, he rarely will or even should. But he may gain an understanding of the complexity of the superior's situation and of the fact that the complexity is not of the superior's making, but inherent in the situation itself.

And these communications, even if they end in a 'no' to the subordinate's conclusions, are firmly focused on the aspirations, values and motivation of the intended recipient. In fact, they start out with the question 'What would you *want* to do ?' They may then end up with the command 'This is what I tell you to do.' But at least this forces the superior to realize that he or she is overriding the desires of the subordinate. It forces him to explain, if not to try to persuade. At least he knows that he has a problem – and so does the subordinate.

A performance appraisal based on what a person can do and has done well, is a foundation for communications. He starts out with the subordinate's concerns, expresses his perception and focuses his expectations. He makes communications his tool rather than a demand on him. And he recognizes that communication requires shared experience.

There can be no communication if it is conceived as going from the 'I' to the 'Thou'. Communication works only from one member of 'us' to another. Communication in organization is not a *means* of organization. It is the *mode* of organization.

## Summary

We know that communication in organizations:
—is perception;
—is expectations;

—makes demands;
and that communications and information are different, yet interdependent.

We know that downward communications do not work – only upward communications do. And we know that effective communication in organizations requires management by objectives. Communication is not between 'me' and 'you'. It is always from one member of 'us' to another.

# 31 Controls, Control, and Management

In the dictionary of social institutions, the word 'controls' is not the plural of the word 'control'. Not only do more controls not necessarily give more control, but the two words have different meanings altogether. The synonyms for controls are measurements and information. The synonym for control is direction. Controls pertain to means, control to an end. Controls deal with facts, that is, with events of the past. Control deals with expectations, that is, with the future. Controls are analytical, concerned with what was and is. Control is normative and concerned with what ought to be.

We are rapidly acquiring great capacity to design controls due to a great improvement in techniques, especially in the application of logical and mathematical tools and in the ability to process and analyse large masses of data very fast. What does this mean for control? Specifically, what are the requirements for these greatly improved controls to give better control to management? For, in the task of a manager, controls are purely a means to an end. The end is control.

The person in a business who is charged with producing the

controls is the controller. But most executives – including most controllers themselves – would consider it gross misuse and abuse of controllership were this controller to use controls to exercise control in the business. This, they would argue, would actually make the business be 'out of control' altogether.

The reasons for this apparent paradox lie in the complexity both of human beings and of the social task.

If we deal with a human being in a social institution, controls must become personal motivation that leads to control. Instead of a mechanical system, the control system in a human-social situation is a system based on will. That we know very little about the will is not the central point. A translation is required before the information yielded by the controls can become grounds for action – the translation of one kind of information into another, which we call *perception*.

In the social institution there is a second complexity, a second 'uncertainty principle'. It is almost impossible to determine ahead of time the responses appropriate to a certain event in a social situation.

We can, and do, build controls into a machine which slow down the turning speed whenever it exceeds a certain figure. We can do this either by mechanical means or by instrumentation which shows a human operator what the turning speed is, and which gives him the specific, unambiguous instruction to turn down the speed when the indicator reaches a certain point. But a control-reading 'profits are falling' does not indicate, with any degree of probability, the response 'raise prices', let alone suggest by how much; the control-reading 'sales are falling' does not indicate the response 'cut prices', and so on. There is a large number of equally probable responses – so large that it is usually not even possible to identify them in advance. There is also no indication in the event itself which of these responses is even possible, let alone appropriate or right. The event itself may not be meaningful. But even if it is, it is by no means certain what it means. And the probability of its being meaningful is a much more important datum than the event itself – and one which is almost never to be discerned by analysing the event.

## The characteristics of controls

There are three major characteristics of controls in business enterprise (or in any other social institution).

1 *Controls can be neither objective nor neutral.* When we measure the rate of fall of a stone, we are totally outside the event itself. By measuring we do not change the event; and measuring the event does not change us, the observers. Measuring physical phenomena is both objective and neutral.

In a perceptual situation of the complexity we deal with in business enterprise, the act of measurement is neither objective nor neutral. It is subjective and of necessity biased. It changes both the event and the observer. Events in the social situation acquire value by the fact that they are being singled out for the attention of being measured. No matter how 'scientific' we are, the fact that this or that set of events is singled out for being 'controlled' signals that it is being considered to be important.

Everybody who ever watched the introduction of a budget system has seen this happen. For a long time – in some companies forever – realizing the budget figures becomes more important than what the budget is supposed to measure, namely economic performance. Managers, upon first being exposed to a budget system, often deliberately hold back sales and cut back profits rather than be guilty of 'not making the budget'. It takes years of experience and a very intelligent budget director to restore the balance. And there are any number of otherwise perfectly sane research directors who act on the conviction that it is a greater crime to get research results for less than the budgeted amount than not getting any research results at all while spending all the 'proper' budget money.

*Controls in a social institution such as a business are goal-setting and value-setting.* They are not 'objective'. They are of necessity moral. The only way to avoid this is to flood the executive with so many controls that the entire system becomes meaningless, becomes mere 'noise'.

Controls create vision. They change both the events measured and the observer. They endow events not only with meaning but with value. And this means that the basic question is not 'How do we control?' but 'What do we measure in our control system?'

2 *Controls need to focus on results.* Business (and every other social institution) exists to contribute to society, economy and individual. In consequence, *results* in business exist only on the outside – in economy, in society and with the customer. It is the customer who creates a 'profit'. Everything inside a business – manufacturing, marketing, research and so on – creates only costs. In other words, the managerial area is concerned with costs alone. But results are entrepreneurial.

We can easily record and therefore quantify efficiency, that is, efforts. We have very few instruments to record and quantify effects. But even the most efficient buggy-whip manufacturer would no longer be in business. It is of little value to have the most efficient engineering department if it designs the wrong product. The Cuban subsidiaries of US companies were by far the best run and, apparently, the most profitable – let alone the least 'troublesome' – of all US operations in Latin America. This was, however, irrelevant to their takeover by the Castro government. And it mattered little, I daresay, during the period of IBM's great expansion in the 1950s and 1960s how 'efficient' its operations were; its basic entrepreneurial idea was the right, the effective one.

The outside, the areas of results, is much less accessible than the inside. The central problem of the executive in the large organization is insulation from the outside. This applies to the President of the United States as well as to the president of United States Steel. What today's organization therefore needs are synthetic sense organs for the outside. If modern controls are to make a contribution, it would be, above all, here.

3 *Controls are needed for measurable and nonmeasurable events.* Business, like any other institution, has important results that are incapable of being measured. Any experienced executive knows companies or industries bound for extinction because they cannot attract or hold able people. Every experienced exec-

utive also knows that this is a more important fact about a company or an industry than last year's profit statement. Any logician who tried to tell an executive that this statement, being incapable of unambiguous definition, is a 'nonstatement' dealing with a 'nonproblem', would be quickly – and correctly – dismissed as an ass. The statement cannot be defined clearly, let alone 'quantified', but it is anything but 'intangible' (as anyone ever having to do with such a business quickly finds out). It is just nonmeasurable. And measurable results will not show up for a decade.

But business also has measurable and quantifiable results of true meaning and significance. There are all those that have to do with past economic performance. For these can be expressed in terms of the very peculiar measurement of the economic sphere, money.

This does not mean that these are 'tangibles'. Indeed most of the things we can measure by money are totally 'intangible' – take depreciation, for instance. But they are measurable.

The measurable results are things that happened; they are in the past. There are no facts about the future. Measurable events are primarily inside events rather than outside events. The important developments on the outside, the things which determine that the buggy-whip industry disappears and that IBM becomes a big business, are not measurable until it is too late to have control.

A balance between the measurable and the nonmeasurable is therefore a central and constant problem of management and a true decision area. Measurements that do not spell out the assumptions with respect to the nonmeasurable statements that are being made – at least as boundaries or as restraints – misdirect and misinform. Yet the more we can quantify the measurable areas, the greater the temptation to put all emphasis on those. And the greater, therefore, the danger that what looks like better controls will actually mean less control, if not a business out of control altogether.

## Specifications for controls

To give the manager control, controls must satisfy seven specifications:

—they must be economical;
—they must be meaningful;
—they must be appropriate;
—they must be congruent;
—they must be timely;
—they must be simple; and
—they must be operational.

1 *Control is a principle of economy.* The less effort needed to gain control, the better the control design. The fewer controls needed, the more effective they will be. Indeed, adding more controls does not give better control. All it does is create confusion.

The first question the manager therefore needs to ask in designing or in using a system of controls is 'What is the minimum information I need to know to have control?'

The answer may vary for different managers. The company's treasurer needs only to know the total amount invested in inventories and whether it is going up or down. The sales manager needs to know the half dozen products that together account for 70 per cent of inventory, but total inventory amount is not of primary importance to him or her. Neither the treasurer nor the sales manager needs complete inventory figures, except once or twice a year; a fairly small sample should give them all the information they need. But the warehouse clerk needs daily figures – and in detail.

The capacity of the computer to spew out huge masses of data does not make for better controls. On the contrary, what gives control is asking the question 'What is the *smallest* number of reports and statistics needed to understand a phenomenon and to be able to anticipate it?' And then one asks, 'And what is the minimum of data regarding this phenomenon that gives a reasonably reliable picture?'

2 *Controls must be meaningful.* That means that the events to be

measured must be significant either in themselves (e.g., market standing) or they must by symptoms of at least potentially significant developments (e.g., a sudden sharp rise in labour turnover or absenteeism).

Controls should always be related to the key objectives and to the priorities within them, to 'key activities' and to 'conscience areas'. Controls should, in other words, be based on a company's definition of what its business is, what it will be, and what it should be.

## Controls follow strategy

Whatever is not essential to the attainment of a company's objectives should be measured infrequently and only to prevent deterioration. It should be strictly controlled by 'exception'. A standard should be set, measurement should be periodical and on a sample basis, and only significant shortfalls below the established standard should be reported.

That we can quantify something is no reason for measuring it. The question is 'Is this what a manager should consider important?' 'Is this what a manager's attention should be focused on?' 'Is this the proper focus for control, that is, for effective direction with maximum economy of effort?'

3 *Controls have to be appropriate to the character and nature of the phenomenon measured.* This may well be the most important specification; yet it is least observed in the actual design of controls.

Because controls have such an impact, it is important that we select not only the right ones but also the appropriate ones, to enable controls to give right vision and to become the ground for effective action. The measurement must present the events measured in structurally true form. Formal validity is not enough.

Formal complaints or grievances coming out of a work force are commonly reported as 'five grievances per thousand employees per month'. This is formally valid. But is it structurally valid? Or is it misdirection? The impression this report conveys is, first, that grievances are distributed throughout the work force in a random manner. And second, the report gives the impression that they are a minor problem, especially if we deal with five grievances per thousand employees per month. This, while formally valid, completely misrepresents and misinforms.

Grievances are a social event. And social events are almost never distributed in the 'normal distribution' we find in the physical world. The great majority of departments in the plant, employing 95 per cent of the work force, normally does not have even a single grievance during one year. But in one department, employing only a handful of people we have a heavy incidence of grievances – so the 'five per thousand' may well mean (and in the actual example from which I took these figures, did mean) a major grievance per person per month. If this department happens to be the final assembly through which all the production has to pass, and if the workers in this department go out on strike when their grievances are being neglected by a management which has been misled by its own controls, the impact can be shattering. In this case, it bankrupted the company.

Most measurements of sales performance, whether of the entire sales force or of the individual salesperson, report sales in total dollars. But in many businesses this is an inappropriate figure. The same dollar volume of sales may mean a substantial profit, no profit at all, or a sizable loss – dependent on the product mix sold. An absolute sales figure not related to product mix, therefore, gives no control whatever – neither to the individual salesperson, nor to the sales manager, nor to top management.

These are elementary things. Yet few managers seem to know them. The traditional information systems (especially traditional accounting) conceal appropriateness rather than highlight it. Without controls that bring out clearly what the real structure of events is, the manager lacks knowledge and therefore will tend to do the wrong things. For all the weight of the daily work pushes him or her towards allocating energies and resources in proportion to the *number* of events. There is a constant drift towards putting energies and resources where they can have the least results, that is, on the vast number of phenomena which, together, account for practically no effects.

4 *Measurements have to be congruent with the events measured.*

Alfred North Whitehead (1861–1947), the distinguished logician and philosopher, used to warn against the 'danger of the false concreteness'. A measurement does not become more 'accurate' by being worked out to the sixth decimal when the phenomenon is only capable of being verified within a range of 50 to 70 per cent. This is 'false concreteness', and misleading.

It is an important piece of information that this or that phenomenon cannot be measured with precision but can be described only within a range or as a magnitude. To say 'we have 26 per cent of the market' sounds reassuringly precise. But it is usually so inaccurate a statement as to be virtually meaningless. What it really means, as a rule, is 'we are not the dominant factor in the market, but we are not marginal either'. And even then the statement is no more reliable than the definition of the market that underlies it.

It is up to the manager to think through what kind of measurement is appropriate to the phenomenon it is meant to measure. He has to know when 'approximate' is more accurate than a firm-looking figure worked out in great detail. He has to know when a range is more accurate than even an approximate single figure. He has to know that 'larger' and 'smaller', 'earlier' and 'later', 'up' and 'down' are quantitative terms and often more accurate, indeed more rigorous, than any specific figures or range of figures.

5 *Controls have to be timely.* Frequent measurements and very rapid 'reporting back' do not necessarily give better control. Indeed, they may frustrate control. The time dimension of controls has to correspond to the time span of the event measured.

It has lately become fashionable to talk of 'real time' controls, that is, of controls that inform instantaneously and continuously. There are events where 'real time' controls are highly desirable. If a batch of antibiotics in the fermentation tank spoils as soon as temperature or pressure deviate from a very narrow range for more than a moment or two, 'real time' monitoring on a continuous basis is obviously needed. But few events need such controls. And most cannot be controlled by them. 'Real time' is the wrong time span for real control.

Children planting a garden are so impatient, it is said, that they tend to pull out the radishes as soon as their leaves show, to see whether the root is forming. This is 'real time' control – misapplied.

Similarly, the attempt to measure research progress all the time is likely to confound research results. The proper time span for research is a fairly long one. Once every two or three years, research progress and results should be rigorously appraised. In between such appraisals, an experienced manager keeps in touch. He or she watches for any indication of major unexpected trouble, and, even more, for any sign of unexpected breakthroughs. But to monitor research in 'real time' – as some research labs have been trying to do – is pulling up the radishes.

There is also the opposite danger, of not measuring often enough. It is particularly great with developments that (a) take a fairly long time to have results, and (b) have to come together at a point in the future to produce the desired end result.

6 *Controls need to be simple.* Every major New York commercial bank worked in the 1960s on developing internal controls, especially of costs and of allocation of efforts. Everyone spent a great deal of time and money on the task and came up with control manuals. In only one of the banks are the manuals being used, to the best of my knowledge. When the executive in that bank was asked how he explained this, he did not (as his interviewer expected him to) credit a massive training programme or talk about his 'philosophy'. He said instead, 'I have two teenage daughters. They know nothing about banking and are not terribly good at figures. But they are bright. Whenever I had worked out an approach to controlling an activity, I took my intended procedure home in draft form and asked my girls to let me explain it to them. And only when I had it so simple that they could explain back to me what the procedure was intended to accomplish and how, did I go ahead. Only then was it simple enough.'

Complicated controls do not work. They confuse. They misdirect attention away from what is to be controlled, and towards the mechanics and methodology of the control. But if the user has to know how the control works before he can apply it, he has no control at all. And if he has to sit down and figure out what a measurement means, he has no control either.

7 *Finally, controls must be operational.* They must be focused on action. Action rather than information is their purpose. The action may be only study and analysis. In other words, a measurement may say, 'What goes on we don't understand; but something goes on that needs to be understood.' But it should never just say, 'Here is something you might find interesting.'

This then means that controls – whether reports, studies or figures – must always reach the person who is capable of taking controlling action. Whether they should reach anyone else – and especially someone higher up – is debatable. But their prime addressee is the manager or professional who can take action by virtue of his or her position in the flow of work and in the decision structure. And this further means that the measurement must be in a form that is suitable for the recipient's needs.

Workers and first-line supervisors should receive measurements and control information that enable them to direct their own immediate efforts towards results they can control. Instead, typically, the first-line supervisor receives each month a statement of the quality control results for the entire plant – and the worker receives nothing. And top management usually receives the information and measurements operating middle managers need and can use, and little or nothing of pertinence to their own top-management job.

The reason for this is largely a confusion between control as domination of others and control as rational behaviour. Unless controls are means towards the latter, and this means towards self-control, they lead to wrong action. They are miscontrol.

## The ultimate control of organization

There is one more important thing to be said. There is a fundamental, incurable, basic limitation to controls in a social institution. This lies in the fact that a social institution is both a true entity and a fiction. As an entity it has purposes of its own, a performance of its own, results of its own – and survival and death of its own. These are the areas of which we have been speaking so far. But a social institution is comprised of persons, each with his or her own purpose, ambitions, ideas and needs. No matter how authoritarian the institution, it has to satisfy the ambitions and needs of its members, and do so in their capacity as individuals, but through *institutional* rewards and punishments, incentives and deterrents. The expression of this may be quantifiable – such as a raise in salary. But the system itself is not quantitative in character and cannot be quantified.

Yet here is the real control of the institution, that is, the ground of behaviour and the cause of action. People tend to act as they are being rewarded or punished. To them, this is the expression of the true values of the institution and of its true purpose and role.

A system of controls which is not in conformity with this true, this only effective, this ultimate control of the organization, which lies in its people decisions, will therefore at best be ineffectual. At worst, it will cause neverending conflict and will push the organization out of control.

## Summary

*Controls* and *Control* are different. Controls are the means, control the needed end. Controls can neither be objective nor neutral in a human organization. They are goal-setting and value-setting. Controls need to focus on results. Controls are needed for measurable and nonmeasurable events. Controls have specifications that must be satisfied for effective control. And people decisions are the ultimate control of an organization.

# 32 The Manager and the Budget

Next to double-entry bookkeeping and the copying machine, budgets are the most commonly used management tools. Practically every business, large or small, has a budget of some sort. And so has every hospital and every university. Above all, no government agency in the world operates without an annual budget. In fact, budgets are the only management tool which originated in governmental, rather than in business, practice.

The original budget, as it was first developed in its modern form in England during the nineteenth century, listed revenues from taxes, custom duties and so on on one side, and expenses on the other. This showed whether the government's finances would be in surplus or in deficit and thereby whether to increase revenues, cut expenditures, or borrow money. It also provided the legal basis for a government department to spend money. Unless authorized in the budget, an expenditure was illegal. It was thus the first effective check on the bureaucracy, the first systematic and orderly way of telling the governmental executive how much to spend for what purpose.

All budgets, no matter how constructed, still serve these original purposes. They enable management – whether of a business, of a hospital, or of a government agency – to pull together its commitments, its plans and projects, and all its costs in one comprehensive document; the budget contrasts total expenditure with the total of expected revenues, thus arriving at a forecast of financial sources and financial requirements for the entire organization. Budgets still establish what is planned and authorized expenditure. And then budgets enable managers on every level to see whether events over the budget period actually follow the course predicted, or whether there is a shortfall of revenues, an excess of cost over the budget, or a significant change in economic performance of an enterprise, department, project or product.

Almost every business today uses the budget to forecast and to control its financial needs and financial position. In particular, a budget is needed to enable the financial manager to anticipate the cash requirements of the business and to make sure that it obtains the necessary cash resources ahead of time. Every budget process, therefore, develops a 'cash flow' budget. In most businesses there is also a capital budget – usually extending over more than one year – which sets expected needs for capital against the various sources of capital and thus provides the basis for allocation of capital resources among various capital expenditures (for example between proposals for expanding capacity and proposals for developing additional markets). At the same time, the capital budget enables management to see whether the plans for obtaining capital are adequate to the capital needs of the business and to take timely action to bring the two into balance.

### The budget is a managerial tool

But the budget has grown to be far more than a financial tool. It is, above all, a managerial tool. It is the tool around which an experienced manager organizes all planning. It is the best tool for making sure that key resources, and especially the resource of performing people, are assigned to priorities and to results. It is equally a tool of integration for the entire work force, and especially a tool of integration for the managers in the organization. And it is a tool that enables the manager to know when to review and revise the plans, either because results are different from what is expected – whether better or worse – or because environment, economic conditions, market conditions, or technologies have changed and no longer correspond to the assumptions of the budget.

The starting point for the budgeting process, especially in a business, should always be *expected results*. What results do we expect to obtain in this business over the course of the next twelve or twenty-four months? What results do we expect in this research department over the course of the next year or the next five years? Only when the expected results have been thought through carefully does one ask: And what *efforts* does this require?

Budgets are expressed in monetary terms. But monetary terms

should be seen as symbolic expression – a kind of shorthand – for the actual efforts needed, and should be based on 'real values'; that is, on raw material needed, on work needed, on manufacturing capacity needed. Budgets, in other words, should always be used as a tool to think through the relationship between desired results and available means. If they are looked at simply as a statement of cost, they soon cease to be the managers' tool for planning and control. Instead they may degenerate into a straight-jacket that controls the manager and inhibits correct action.

In particular, it is important to avoid the worst pitfall of budgeting, the pitfall into which government budgets tend to fall. This is the tendency to regard last year's expenditures as being 'about right' and to project them into the new budget. Typically, in this kind of budgeting, the manager starts out with the budget for last year and then either adds ten per cent across the board or cuts ten per cent across the board. This may give her a 'symmetrical' budget. But it also means that she has not used the budget as a planning tool and is unlikely to use resources where they are needed.

## Zero-based budgeting

Growing in popularity as a remedy against this sort of projected budget is 'zero-based budgeting'. Rather than starting with last year's expenditures, the manager starts with the results he or she wants to achieve in a given area and asks 'Is it the right area ? Is it a priority area ?' And then 'What is really needed to obtain these results ?'

In a large and complex enterprise, it is difficult to subject all expenditure areas to these questions every year. Yet it should always be done for important expenditure areas. For less important areas, the budgeting that adjusts last year's budget to next year's expectations might serve for a few years. In such areas, zero-based budgeting might be done every three years or so, rather than yearly. On such a rotating schedule, zero-based budgeting can, and should, be used in every organization as a tool for the periodic systematic review of all products, markets and activities. Thus it serves as the tool of systematic abandonment of the obsolescent, the unproductive, the unnecessary.

Just as important as zero-based budgeting is the realization that any time period for budgeting is an arbitrary one. A great many of the expenditures for which a manager budgets are, of necessity, geared to much longer periods than one year. This applies particularly to capital expenditures. In the first year of a project – building a new plant, for instance – expenditures might be very low and confined to what is needed to do preliminary engineering and architectural drawings. But this, in effect, commits the business to very large expenditures in subsequent years. And if those are not made because the money is not available, the sums spent the first year are wasted. The same applies to a great many other activities: research work; management and manager development; training, whether of workers in the plant or of salespeople; or sales promotion and advertising. All these activities require continuous efforts over long time periods to have any results. To budget for them on an annual basis is, therefore, self-delusion and likely to lead to waste in subsequent years when it is being discovered that the sums needed to make the activity produce the desired result are not available. These activities require life cycle budgeting that shows the efforts needed over the life of the project or activity.

## Types of costs

Accountants have long distinguished three kinds of costs: One is *variable costs*, that is, costs that should fluctuate with the volume of operations, such as the cost of raw materials needed to produce a certain product, or the cost of direct labour needed in its manufacture. Second is *fixed costs*, that is, costs to which the enterprise is committed by law or by past decisions, such as interest payments on money borrowed to build a new plant, the cost of maintaining the plant, real estate taxes, and insurance premiums. The cost of maintaining an employee pension plan is also a fixed cost. Finally, the account speaks of *administered costs*, that is, the costs of such activities as research, advertising and promotion, manager development, activities of the field sales force. These costs are determined neither by the level of operations nor by commitments made in the past, but represent managerial decisions.

## Life-cycle budgeting

Accountants debate whether these distinctions are still meaningful ones. Increasingly, for instance, 'labour' is becoming a fixed rather than a variable cost. But for budgeting purposes, the system is still useful. Anything that is likely to be a fixed cost and anything that is administered cost has, by definition, a time span well beyond one year. Therefore, it should never be budgeted on an annual basis alone. Rather, the budget should start out with the appropriate time cycle. Then it should ask: What portion of the expenditure needed over this time cycle belongs in this current budgeting period?

The best known example of such 'life-cycle' budgeting is the life-cycle costing which Robert NcNamara introduced into the American defence budget while Secretary of Defense under President Kennedy in the early 1960s. Under the budgeting process of the US government, as it had been practised earlier, the Armed Services submitted their requests for money for the development of a new weapon, such as a new fighter plane, on an annual basis. In other words, they asked for enough money to get a project started, without disclosing how much money it would take to get the project finished. Then, when the first few hundred million dollars had been spent they always argued that to abandon a product because its costs were going up sharply (as the new plane moved from drawing board into production) would lead to a waste of money already spent. When the first prototype of the plane rolled off the production line and when it became apparent that there would be need for an expensive and extensive training programme, and also for very large sums of money to buy replacement parts for the plane, they could argue that not to provide these sums in the future budget would mean a waste of very large sums already spent. Under life-cycle cost-ing, the Armed Services are supposed to present total cost estimates over the life of the proposed weapon, including the training expenses and the expense for maintaining, repairing, and replacing equipment. This, in theory at least, enables the Secretary of Defense, the President and the Congress to know in advance the size of the commitment and its impact on future budgets.

Life-cycle costing, or some variant thereof, is increasingly be-coming standard practice in business as well. In fact, it is poor budgeting to assume that a new project – whether a capital in-vestment or an activity such as an advertising programme or a training programme – will cost less in the future. Only the un-successful programme does not require additional money; it can, and should, be abandoned. The plant that turns out not to be needed should be sold. The training programme that does not produce trained people should be scrapped. If the product does well in the market, if the plant turns out the right product at the right cost, and if the training programme really trains people, it will always require more money in the future – and it should. In budgeting capital expenses, fixed expenses, and administered ex-penses, the manager should always think through how much more money will be required to run with success. Success com-mits the organization to increasing the effective support for the programme.

## Operating budget and opportunities budget

For this reason alone, a great many companies increasingly sep-arate the budget into two parts. One is the operating budget, which deals with all the things that are already being done. The other part is sometimes called the opportunities budget; it deals with the new things that might be done, with the products, mar-kets, activities, programmes that represent either something genuinely new or a new way of doing old work. The operating budget tends to be many, many pages thick. The opportunities budget, by contrast, is usually very short. But the manager who has learned how to budget spends just as much time, as a rule, on the brief opportunities budget as on the lengthy operational budget. In analysing the operational budget, the manager asks: 'What is the *minimum* that needs to be done in this area to prevent damage ? How much effort and how many resources have to be put into this activity to keep it going ? What is the lowest cost to obtain adequate results ?' In the terms of modern economic theory, his approach is one of 'satisficing'. He does not try to 'maximize'. He does not try to 'optimize'. He tries to 'satisfice' the minimum requirements needed to prevent unacceptable performance.

In respect to the opportunities budget, the first question is always: Is this the right opportunity ? And if the answer is 'yes', then the question becomes: What is the optimum, in terms of resources and money, this opportunity can absorb at the present level ? Can we hope to speed up the development process of a badly needed new product by putting more people to work on it ? Will this only create confusion ? It is just as dangerous, in the early stages of an opportunity, to over-supply money and resources as it is to under-supply them.

Failure to ask this questions is, in large measure, responsible for the failure of so many of the programmes of the War on Poverty; they were killed by kindness. They were smothered in money, at a time when they needed only a few first-rate people to experiment, develop, learn and demonstrate. The money brought with it a tremendous bureaucracy that was far too busy with its own internal mechanics to produce results, or even to know when results were being achieved. And the public, being led by the lush budgets of these programmes to expect immediate breakthroughs, became disenchanted when results were slow in coming – as they have to be in educational or health-care programmes which, by definition, have long lead-times.

## Budgeting human resources

In order to budget properly, the manager has to use the budget as a tool for assignment control. Most budgets provide only for money and specify where it should be spent. They do not contain the necessary provisions to make reasonably sure that the expected results can indeed be obtained. They do not provide for the only resource that can produce results: accomplished people.

That last, and most crucial, step in the budget process (and one that is rarely taken) is determining who should be accountable for what activity and for what expected results. Unless the name of a person to do the work is listed against each budget expenditure, this decision has not been made. The only decision that has been made is to spend the money – and this, of course, is the easy part.

In budgeting, a manager starts out with his or her opportunities and priorities. And in respect to each of them, the manager asks: 'And whose job is it? Is that the right person? Is he or she capable of producing results? Is that person available to do the job?'

Budgeting, in other words, is not a substitute for effective decisions. It is a tool of planning and decision-making. And money is not a substitute for thinking, performance, and competence. People think. People perform. People have competence. They need money, to be sure, but without the people money will only be wasted.

In addition to being the manager's planning tool, budgeting is also one of the most effective tools for communication and integration. Budgeting always tries to present a picture of each part of a business. But it also shows how each part relates to the ends and needs of the whole. Budgeting therefore demands that the manager in charge of the whole, and each of the people in charge of the parts, discuss the budget jointly. The manager of each unit needs to take leadership responsibility in the budgeting process. The budget for the entire business is, in essence, the total of the budgets for all its parts. Conversely, the budget for each part is derived from the budget of the whole.

Properly used, therefore, the budget becomes an important communications and integration device for the manager. It should induce effective upward communication, which brings to the manager the point of view, priorities, concerns, and needs of each subordinate unit. It should also provide sideways communication, enabling managers in other areas to understand what their colleagues are trying to accomplish and what they require. And it should be an effective tool of integration that enables the manager to convey to the people who work for him or her an understanding of the needs of the entire business – of the decisions that have to be made, the priorities that have to be set, and especially of the personnel assignments that derive from the budget.

A budget authorizes some expenditures and denies others. It highlights and supports some opportunities, but by doing so plays down or denies support to other opportunities and activities. It is a tool for making decisions that affect everybody in the organization. Therefore, the budget can sometimes be seen as a tool to limit managers, or as their own escape from accountability, thus inhibiting motivation. But when properly used, it can become a tool to stimulate and unify, to make understood and comprehensible the common interest, and to motivate even those whose pet projects have had to be denied.

## Budgeting and control

The budget is a tool of managerial control. It shows the manager how the organization is performing in each major area. Are we 'on budget'? Or are we 'under budget'? One look at the figures can show us every month, every three months, every year. And by the same token, the budget also shows when there is a need to revise the forecast – because things go better, worse, or differently than expected.

Businesses typically look upon the budget as an early warning system for danger and lack of performance, and this is an important function. But performance against budget should also be seen as an early warning system for opportunities, that is, for performance that is *better* than expected.

One illustration of a budget control which does both is a very simple colour code developed by a large multinational investment firm, operating in Latin America, that supplies initial capital for new industries and new businesses. The budget for all the investments of the company in any given Latin American country is shown on one big wall chart in the conference room in the company's headquarters. Each is coded in one of four colours: green – things are going according to budget; yellow – watch out, there might be trouble; red – there is trouble; and blue – things are going better or faster than expected. Management in this company has learned to spend as much (or more) time on blue areas as on the yellow and red ones.

Suppose a new business finds that its new plant is being built faster than was originally expected. It therefore can start marketing its new product a year earlier. What does this mean for hiring people, for building a distributive system, for starting advertising and promotion, for ordering raw materials and for working capital requirements ? If these are not supplied, the opportunity which the unexpected success in building the plant represents will be lost.

Control by the budget enables the manager to disregard all the items which proceed according to budget, while those which significantly deviate from budget, whether on the plus or on the minus side, can easily be identified. In fact, it is sound budget practice to show separately every month or every quarter the items with significant deviation from budget forecast and to have an explanation of the deviation available, so that the manager can decide whether the deviation requires action.

However, different items in the budget obviously differ greatly in their importance, from the most critical to the most trivial. And often, control by exception is not adequate for the most important. Increasingly, therefore, especially in complex operations, a 'critical factors budget' is being used. (It was developed first, in the 1920s, by General Motors.)

The best-publicized version of a critical factors budget is probably the budget developed for the Armed Services of the United States, under the Secretaryship of Robert McNamara in the early 1960s. For every weapons system, for every command, for every major project, the question is asked: What are the few major items which account together for 75 to 80 per cent of the total budget ? And what are the few items which together account for 75 to 80 per cent of the combat readiness of the Armed Services of the United States, or of the Strategic Air Command, or the naval task force ? These items – and altogether they only account for a few hundred items of a defence budget which numbers millions, if not billions, of items – are then reported on specifically and in considerable detail. All the other items are reported on only if and when they deviate significantly from pre-set standards. And the less important the item, either in terms of money or in its impact on US combat readiness and strategy, the greater is the range within which fluctuations in performance as against budget are not reported to higher levels of management.

Another important and widely used refinement is the 'milestone budget', which controls disbursements and makes them dependent on achieving pre-set results. The budget may, for instance, authorize spending on sales promotion and distribution of a new product, subject to the successful completion of market testing by a given time and within a given budget. Until that milestone has been reached, the additional expenditure, while authorized and provided for, cannot be made. Milestone budgeting is particularly important in capital projects, such as a major building, a major research programme, or product development and product introduction.

## The Gantt Chart

The budget cuts across the entire organization – whether a whole company, a division, or a department. It controls all its revenues and contrasts them with all its expenditures. It presents, for each time period, a portrayal – or at least an X-ray – of the entire organization and indicates where control is needed. But it does not give the manager the tools for planning and control of individual projects, and especially of complex projects extending over a long period of time.

To build a big oil tanker, a major chemical plant, a new paper mill, or an office skyscraper is a five-year task. The finished product is an integrated whole. But it is the result of a great many different activities and goes through different stages. Some of them have to be done in sequence. Electric wiring and plumbing in the office building, for instance, cannot be installed until the frame has been completed. But they must be installed before any work on the interior is done. Other work can be done in parallel. The engine for the tanker and the power train that connects the engine to the propeller will be worked on while the hull is being built and may even have to be begun before work on the hull begins. Yet the contracting firm responsible for building the ship or the skyscraper is committed to a definite completion date and often has to pay heavy penalties if the job is not finished on time. It is also, typically, committed to a definite cost.

The tool to control such projects is the *Gantt Chart* (named after the American pioneer of scientific management, Henry L. Gantt, 1861–1919, who first developed this tool for the tasks of World War I). The Gantt Chart and its many recent refinements, such as the Critical Path Chart (developed by the Dupont Chemical Company in the 1950s) and PERT (Program Evaluation and Review Technique, developed by the US Navy in the late 1950s) is the most elegant and effective tool of planning and control at the manager's disposal. It is not used nearly as widely as it should be.

Gantt's basic idea was stunningly simple. Traditionally, planning for a major complex job began with the beginning, the first step. And it then went, step by step, towards the end. Gantt proposed to start with the end product. 'On December 15, 1917,' he argued, 'we have promised to deliver a finished destroyer, complete and ready to be put into service. What is the last step that has to be done to reach this completion date? And when will that step have to be started so that the ship will actually be ready by the promised delivery date? And what then is the step before, and before that, and before that, all the way back to the beginning?' The results of this analysis are usually shown in a series of parallel bar charts, each of which represents a major activity or effort. There are two types of such bars. One represents efforts that can only be made *after* something else has been done, for example installing the turbine in the destroyer, which presupposes finishing the hull of the ship. The other bars represent activities which are not dependent on the completion of some other work, such as training the crew or designing the instrument panel. Yet each of these efforts has to be started at a given point if it is to come together in the completed final product at the desired time.

During the 1960s, the Japanese and Swedish shipyards established themselves as the world's leaders and captured the largest shares of the world's shipbuilding business. Their cost for labour and material were not much lower than those of traditional shipyards in Great Britain or the United States. Yet they could underbid traditional shipyards by a substantial margin. They could also promise far shorter delivery dates – and make good on their promises. A major reason was that the Japanese and the Swedes used Gantt Charts; other builders had resisted the approach and had continued to plan in the traditional way, that is, step by step from the beginning to the end. As a result, traditional shipyards again and again found that needed supplies, sub-assemblies, or training activities had simply not been planned and provided for, with the result of sharply increasing costs and delaying completion of the finished work.

For extremely complex programmes, such as the building of a huge chemical factory complex or of a new weapons system, Gantt Charts of greater complexity are required: Critical Path Charts or PERT Charts (the difference between these two methods are both minor and purely technical). These are simply methods that enable the manager to stay in control of a great many different efforts that must interlock and interact at many points in time. A starting point for these methods is something Gantt himself understood very well. In every major project there is one 'critical path', that is, one sequence of stages that takes the longest and cannot easily be telescoped, speeded up, or cut short.

In building the skyscraper office building, for instance, no interior work can be done until the frame, roof, floors, wiring and plumbing, and shafts for elevators have been finished. Once all this has been accomplished, the rest of the work can be scheduled with considerable freedom. The critical path is that of erecting the main structure. The rest of the work has to be organized around it. But renting office space in the skyscraper is also a critical path. Trying to find tenants may well have to begin *before* the ground is broken. And if the building fills up more slowly than was originally expected, finishing the last twenty-five or thirty floors of the building may not have the same urgency it seemed to have when the plans were drawn. There is thus, in building and designing a big office building, both a critical path to construction and a critical path to renting. And the two have to mesh.

Above all, Critical Path and PERT methods enable the manager to see what action can be taken to offset unfavourable developments, such as delays in time or increases in costs. Where can resources be switched from less to more critical areas? What must be added or sacrificed to make up for lost time or to speed up a project? How much time might be gained or lost by spending more or less money?

The Gantt Chart need not be complicated, except in the case of truly complex systems work. But there should always be a Gantt Chart when a project extends over a considerable time period or when a project requires a substantial number of different activities that must come together in time or space. Without a plan that starts from the intended termination point and works backwards through the needed stages to the starting point, even simple projects are likely to get out of control in respect to time and cost.

## Judging performance by using the budget

Managers also need to be able to plan the performance of the human organization and to control it. They need to do this, both in terms of the groups that comprise the organization (divisions, departments, sections, activities) and in terms of the individuals who make up these groups.

The manager needs to know first: What performance is expected from this group or from this person? And then the manager needs to know: What performance has been achieved? The starting point, in other words, is performance planning rather than performance appraisal. The starting point for performance of the human organization, like the starting point in the Gantt Chart, has to be the intended result. As has been said before many times in this book, this must be focused on objectives and should be considered a major responsibility of the organizational unit and of the individual manager and professional.

## Summary

The budget enables the manager to allocate resources for results, to balance income and expenditures, and to control events in time to take corrective action. The Gantt Chart and its various refinements, such as the Critical Path Chart or PERT Chart, enable a manager to plan a major project, to allocate resources rationally to the various stages and kinds of work needed to complete the project, and to control progress towards completion of the project, both in respect to the time needed and to the cost incurred. Performance planning for units and individuals and performance appraisal, finally, enable the manager to make productive the people, the knowledge, the vision and the motivation of the human organization, to focus human energy on performance and to make organizational performance, in turn, redound to individual development.

# 33 The Manager and the Management Sciences

The first management scientist was that unknown Italian who invented double-entry bookkeeping sometime in the twelfth or thirteenth century. No other management tool can compare with it in simplicity, elegance, and utility. Double-entry bookkeeping, with all its offspring and variations, is still the only truly universal 'management science', the only tool of systematic analysis that every business, and indeed every institution, uses every day.

But no one ever talked of double-entry bookkeeping as management science. That term made its appearance after World War II. 'Management,' it seemed to say, 'was to be made rigorous, scientific, quantitative.' The new tools would substitute certainty for guesswork, knowledge for judgement, 'hard facts' for experience. These were the heady days when it was widely predicted that the computer would replace the manager. And a good many of the management scientists, awed by their new shiny tools, similarly saw themselves 'taking over' decision-making control.

Most managers have long learned that the computer will not replace managers. Most have learned that the computer is a tool – very useful if properly employed, but a tool nonetheless. Most managers also know by now that the management sciences are tools. It would have been more prudent – and more modest – to speak of 'management analysis' rather than of 'management sciences'.

Still, the management sciences are tools with high potential for contribution. There is no more reason for a manager to be a management scientist than there is reason for a physician to be a blood chemist or a bacteriologist. But a manager needs to know what to expect of the management sciences and how to use them as managerial tools, just as the physician needs to know what to expect of blood chemistry and bacteriology and how to use them as diagnostic tools.

For this managers first need to understand what the management sciences try to do – and what they should be doing. They next need to know what contributions to expect of them. Few managers, so far, have acquired the skill of making the management sciences contribute to their managerial work. Few, so far, are putting these new tools to effective work.

## Promise and performance

Most managers know that they need better tools. Most have learned through bitter experience that intuition is unreliable, if not downright treacherous, if used as the only basis for decision. Indeed, most experienced managers have long suspected what a leading management scientist of today, Jay W. Forrester of MIT, brilliantly demonstrated: complex systems actually behave 'counter-intuitively'; the course of action suggested by common sense tends to be wrong. And markets, technologies, and business are very complex systems indeed.

When management science first appeared, it was therefore hailed by managers with glad cries. Since then, a whole new profession has come into being: the management scientists, with their own professional associations, their own learned journals, their own departments in universities, business schools and colleges of technology, and with good jobs in large numbers within industry.

And yet management science has been a disappointment. It has not lived up to its promise. It certainly has not revolutionized the practice of management. Few managers, indeed, pay much attention to it.

The widening gap between the claims and promises of management science and its use by business is recognized – and deplored – by both management scientists and managers. Not unexpectedly, each blames the other. Managers complain that management scientists concern themselves with trivia and 're-invent the wheel'. Management scientists, in turn, tell horror stories of 'resistance by reactionary managers'.

There is a good deal to both complaints. But the truth is more complex – and far more important than who is to blame.

## Why management science fails to perform

There is one fundamental insight underlying all management science. It is that the organization is a system of the highest order. The parts of the system are human beings contributing voluntarily of their knowledge, skill, and dedication to a joint venture. And one thing characterizes all genuine systems, whether mechanical, like the control of a missile, biological like a tree, or social like the business enterprise; it is interdependence. The whole of a system is not necessarily improved if one particular function or part is improved or made more efficient. In fact, it may well damage the system or even destroy it. In some cases the best way to strengthen the system may be to weaken a part – to make it less precise or less efficient. For what matters in any system is the performance of the whole; this is the result of growth and dynamic balance, adjustment and integration rather than of mere technical efficiency.

Primary emphasis on the efficiency of parts in management science is therefore bound to do damage. It is bound to optimize precision of the tool at the expense of the health and performance of the whole. (That the enterprise is a social rather than a mechanical system makes the danger all the greater, for the other parts – the people – do not stand still. They either respond so as to spread the maladjustment throughout the system or organize for sabotage.)

But when we look at the actual work done by management scientists in business, we find little that lives up to the basic insight with which management science starts out.

The bulk of the work done so far concerns itself with the sharpening of already existing tools for specific technical functions – such as quality control or inventory control, warehouse location or freight-car allocation, machine loading, maintenance scheduling, or order handling. A good deal of the work is little more than a refinement of industrial engineering, cost accounting or procedures analysis. Some, though not very much, attention has been given to the analysis and improvement of functional efforts – primarily those of the manufacturing function but also, to some extent, of marketing and money management.

But there has been little work, little organized thought, little emphasis on managing an enterprise – on the risk-making, risk-taking, decision-making job. Throughout management science – in the literature as well as in the work in progress – the emphasis is on techniques rather than on principles, on mechanics rather than on decisions, on tools rather than on results and, above all, on efficiency of the part rather than on performance of the whole.

There are a few significant exceptions. At the General Electric

Company, almost twenty years of effort have led to the development of genuine models of whole businesses showing their basic economic characteristics and principal interrelationships. Similar work has been done at the British Coal Board. The potential is there. But most of the actual work has concerned itself with doing a little better what we already know how to do. We did control inventories, after all, or allocate freight cars, well before the advent of management science. And it is unlikely that any business will survive rather than die, or prosper rather than languish, because we now know how to do these things better – even significantly better.

What explains this underuse – or misuse – of such potentially powerful tools ?

The first clue lies, perhaps, in the origin of the management sciences – and the origin is an unusual one indeed. Every other human discipline began with a crude attempt to define what its subject was. Then people set to work fashioning concepts and tools for its study. But the management sciences began with the application of concepts and tools developed within a host of other disciplines for their own particular purposes. It may have started with the discovery in World War II that certain mathematical techniques, hitherto applied to the study of the physical universe, could also be applied to the study of military operations.

As a result, the focus of much of the work in the management sciences has not been on such questions as 'What is the business enterprise ?' 'What is managing ?' 'What do the two do, and what do the two need ?' Rather, the focus has been 'Where can I apply my beautiful gimmick ?' The emphasis has been on the hammer rather than on driving in the nail, let alone on building the house. In the literature of operations research, for instance, there are several dissertations along the lines of '155 applications of linear programming', but I have not seen any published study on 'typical business opportunities and their characteristics'.

What this indicates is a serious misunderstanding on the part of the management scientist of what 'scientific' means. Scientific is not – as many management scientists naively seem to think – synonymous with quantification. If this were true, astrology would be the queen of the sciences. It is not even the application of the scientific method. After all, astrologers observe phenomena, derive the generalization of a hypothesis therefrom, and then test the hypothesis by further organized observation. Yet astrology is superstition rather than science because of its childish assumption that there is a real zodiac, that the signs in it really exist, and that their fancied resemblance to some such earthly creature as a fish or a lion defines their character and properties (whereas all of them are nothing but the devices navigators of old invented to help them remember the position of the stars they used to steer by).

In other words, 'scientific' presupposes a rational definition of the universe of the science (that is, of the phenomena which it considers to be real and meaningful) as well as the formulation of basic assumptions or postulates which are appropriate, consistent, and comprehensive. This job of defining the universe of a science and of setting its basic postulates has to be done, however crudely, before the scientific method can be applied. If it is not done, the scientific method cannot be applied. If it is done, the scientific method becomes applicable and indeed powerful.

Management science still has to do this job of defining its universe. If it does this, then all the work done so far will become fruitful – at least as preparation and training ground for real achievement. The first task for management science, if it is to be able to contribute rather than distort and mislead, is therefore to define the specific nature of its subject matter.

This might include as a basic definition the insight that the business enterprise is made up of human beings. The assumptions, opinions, objectives and even the errors of people (and especially of managers) are thus primary facts for the management scientist. Any effective work in management science really has to begin with analysis and study of them.

Starting, then, with this recognition of what there is to be studied, management science must next establish its basic assumptions. It might first take note of the vital fact that every business enterprise exists in the economy and in society; that even the mightiest is the servant of its environment, by which it can be dismissed without ceremony; but that even the lowliest affects and moulds economy and society instead of just adapting to them. In other words, the business enterprise exists only in an economic and social ecology of great complexity.

The basic postulates might further include the following ideas:

1 The business enterprise produces neither things nor ideas but humanly determined values. The most beautifully designed machine is still only so much scrap metal until it has utility for a customer.

2 Measurements in the business enterprise are complex symbols, such as money – at the same time both highly abstract and amazingly concrete.

3 Economic activity, of necessity, is the commitment of present resources to an unknowable and uncertain future – a commitment, in other words, to expectations rather than to facts. Risk is of the essence, and risk-making and risk-taking constitute the basic function of enterprise. And risks are taken not only by the general manager, but right through the whole organization by everybody who contributes knowledge – that is, by every manager and professional specialist. This risk is something quite different from risk in the statistician's probability; it is the risk of the unique event, the irreversible breaking of the pattern.

4 Inside and outside the business enterprise there is constant irreversible change; indeed, the business enterprise exists as the agent of change in a modern society, and it must be capable both of purposeful evolution to adapt to new conditions and of purposeful innovation to change the conditions.

Some of this is often said in the prefaces of books on the management sciences. It generally stays in the preface, however. Yet for the management sciences to contribute to business understanding, let alone become 'sciences', postulates like the foregoing ought to be the fabric of its work. Of course we need quantification – though it tends to come fairly late in the development of a discipline (only now, for instance, can scientists really quantify in biology). We need the scientific method. And we need work on specific areas and operations – careful, meticulous detail work. But above all, we need to recognize the particular character of business enterprise and the unique postulates necessary for its study. It is on this vision that we must build.

The first need of a management science is, then, that it respects itself sufficiently as a distinct and genuine discipline.

## The fear of risk-taking

The second clue to what is lacking in the management sciences as applied today is the emphasis throughout its work on 'minimizing risk' or even on 'eliminating risk' as the goal and ultimate purpose of its work.

To try to eliminate risk in business enterprise is futile. Risk is inherent in the commitment of present resources to future expectations. Indeed, economic progress can be defined as the ability to take greater risks. The attempt to eliminate risks, even the attempt to minimize them, can only make them irrational and unbearable. It can only result in that greatest risk of all: rigidity.

The main goal of a management science must be to enable business to take the right risk. Indeed, it must be to enable business to take greater risks – by providing knowledge and understanding of alternative risks and alternative expectations; by identifying the resources and efforts needed for desired results; by mobilizing energies for contribution; and by measuring results against expectations, thereby providing means for early correction of wrong or inadequate decisions.

All this may sound like mere quibbling over terms. Yet the terminology of risk minimization does induce a hostility to risk-taking and risk-making – that is, to business enterprise – in the literature of the management sciences. It wants to subordinate business to technique, and it seems to see economic activity as a sphere of physical determination rather than as an affirmation and exercise of responsible freedom and decision.

This is worse than being wrong. This is lack of respect for one's subject matter – the one thing no science can afford and no scientist can survive. Even the best and most serious work of good and serious people – and there is no lack of them in the management sciences – is bound to be undermined by it.

The second requirement for a management science is, then, that it take its subject matter seriously.

## What managers need to know

But managers too share in the blame for the gap between the potential and the actual contribution of the management sciences. And by and large, the manager's share may be the greater one, and the contribution the manager needs to make – and has not made – the truly crucial need of management science and management scientist.

However, the management scientist's typical complaint about the manager is, bluntly, nonsense. It is the complaint that the manager does not bother to learn management science and remains ignorant. To demand that a tool user understand what goes into the making of the tool is admission of incompetence on the part of the tool maker. The tool user, provided the tool is made well, need not – and indeed should not – know anything about the tool. How many drivers know how the carburettor works – or even that their car has one ?

The basic problem is much more serious than the unwillingness of managers to learn a few mathematical techniques. Managers, by and large, have failed to take managerial responsibility for management scientists and management sciences. They have refused to accept the fact that the management scientist, like any other high-grade specialist, depends on the manager for direction and effectiveness. They have left the management sciences unmanaged – and are therefore largely responsible for their degenerating into a box of tricks, a 'management gadget bag' of answers to nonexisting questions in many cases.

We know, by and large, what managers need: a systematic supply of organized knowledge for the risk-taking decisions of business enterprise in a complex and rapidly changing technology, economy, and society.

Tools are needed to measure expectations and results and as

effective means for common vision and communication among the many functional and professional specialists, each with his or her own knowledge, logic, and language, whose combined efforts are needed, however, to make the right business decisions, to make them effective and to produce results.

Managers need something teachable and learnable if only because our world needs far too many people with managerial vision and competence to depend on the intuition of a few 'natural-born' geniuses; and only the generalizations and concepts of a discipline can really be learned or taught.

This becomes clear when one looks at the few places where management sciences have produced results. In every single case this is not because the management scientists have done anything they are not doing every place. It is because managers have asked the right questions and have managed the management sciences.

One example is a large manufacturer with a broad product line, selling directly to the public through thousands of outlets, such as department stores, discount chains and hardware stores. Its executives came to their management scientists and said, 'Everybody in this industry knows that extending credit to wholesalers and retailers is the way to get sales. And everybody also knows that there is a point where the additional credit risks outbalance the additional sales. Are these the right assumptions on which to base our selling and credit policies?' The management scientists came back six months later and said, 'No, these are the wrong assumptions. What everybody knows is, as so often happens, not true. What is true is that in our industry you can get additional sales by extending credit to the biggest and best customers who are also good credit risks, and to the smallest and worst customers who are also the poorest credit risks. You cannot get additional sales by extending credit to the "average" customer who is also an "average" credit risk'. As a result, the company completely changed its policy. It cut off credit from the small accounts – and while it lost some sales, it greatly improved its selling and credit performance. And it extended credit to its big and best accounts. The total amount of credit it now extends is actually less than what it used to extend when it had a very tight credit policy. But it now has a rational understanding of the relationship between credit, sales, and credit risk.

In other words, what managers need to do to make management science capable of contribution is to think through the areas in which they need to have basic assumptions tested.

Managers expect management scientists to come up with answers when nobody has asked them the right question. They expect the management scientist, that is, a technical specialist, to know better than a manager what the needs, problems and questions of a business are.

Above all, they expect final answers. But the great strength of management science – whether its methods be those of the physical sciences, of economics, or of the social sciences (and a good management scientist needs to be at home in all three areas) – is its capacity for asking questions. The manager will have to give answers. For answers in business are always judgement, always choice between alternatives of different and yet uncertain risks, always a blend of knowledge, experience and hopes.

Managers, as a rule, expect the management sciences to come up with one best solution. But what the management sciences should be able to contribute are the alternatives available to the manager. They should be expected to say, 'Here are four or five different courses of action. Not one of them is perfect. Each has its own risks, its own uncertainties, its own limitations, and its own costs. Each of them, however, satisfies at least some of the major specifications. You, the manager, will have to choose between them. You will have to decide on one of them, at least as the lesser evil. Which one you choose is your decision. It is your judgement regarding the risks the company can take. It is your judgement with respect to the things you can sacrifice and the things you have to insist on. But at least you now know what choices are available to you.'

Finally the manager should expect management scientists to provide understanding rather than formulas. The formulas are the tools of the management scientist and are of little interest to managers. If they cannot assume that the management scientist knows his craft, they had better get another management scientist. But understanding, that is, insight into what a decision is really about, is something they should hold the management scientist accountable for. What the management sciences can contribute – and should be expected to contribute – is understanding that a certain decision, while it looks like a decision on manufacturing, is really a decision on marketing. It is a decision on what customers will want, will be willing to pay for, will buy. What a manager should expect from management scientists is to hear, 'Look, the problem you assigned us is the wrong problem. This is the problem we ought to be working on'.

The greatest contribution a group of management scientists made to the pharmaceutical company which employed them was not solutions. It was to say to management, 'All your efforts, all your energies, all your attention are focused on the new products. But three-quarters of your income today and for the foreseeable future will come from drugs that have been in the inventory at least three years. Nobody manages them, nobody sells them, nobody knows what to do with them. In fact, nobody has the slightest interest in them. The only thing we know is that the way to keep old drugs in the market is completely different from what is needed to introduce new ones. What managing an existing product line of old and established drugs requires we do not know. This, however, is what we should be studying.'

These four demands and expectations:

—that the management scientists test assumptions;
—that they identify the right questions to ask;
—that they formulate alternatives rather than solutions;
—that they focus on understanding rather than on formulas

are the keys to making the management sciences productive. They all are based on the assumption that the management sciences are not methods of computation but tools of analysis. They all assume that the purpose of the management sciences it to help with diagnosis. They are insights and not prescriptions.

But they all require also that the manager take responsibility for the management sciences. They all require that the manager manage these tools. They all require of the manager that he or she decide, in close working relationship with the management scientists, what the management scientists should go to work on. They should not go to work on the things that are interesting to the management scientists and easily amenable to their tools. They should go to work on the areas in which a manager needs understanding. And if these are areas in which the tools are not particularly appropriate, areas, for instance, in which quantification is difficult or perhaps even impossible, this should not deter manager or management scientists. Insight, understanding, ranking of priorities, and a 'feel' for the complexity of an area are as important as precise, beautifully elegant mathematical models – and in fact usually infinitely more useful and indeed even more 'scientific'. They reflect the reality of the manager's universe and of his tasks.

## Summary

It is up to the manager to convert the management sciences from potential to performance. To do this he has to understand what the management sciences are and what they can do. He has to understand the peculiar limitations which are inherent in the management sciences largely as a result of their origin and history. But above all he has to understand that the management sciences are the manager's tools, and not the tools of the management scientist. And it is up to the manager to focus these tools on managerial tasks and direct them towards managerial contributions.

# Part Seven
# Managerial Organization

Organization structure is the oldest and most thoroughly
studied area in management. But we face new needs in
organization that the well-known and well-tested structural
design of 'functional' and 'decentralized' organization cannot
adequately satisfy. New structural designs are emerging: the
task-force team; simulated decentralization; the systems
structure. We have learned that organization does not start with
structure but with building blocks. There is no one right or
universal design; each enterprise needs to design around the key
activities appropriate to its mission and its strategies. Three
different kinds of work – operating, innovative, and top-
management – have to be accommodated under the same
organizational roof. Organization structure needs to be both
task-focused and person-focused and to have both an
authority axis and a responsibility axis.

## 34 Structures and Strategies

Organization studies leading to reorganizing companies, divisions, and functions have been one of the more spectacular 'growth industries' of the last few decades. Everybody, whether business, government department or armed service, research laboratory, Catholic diocese, university administration or hospital seems to be forever engaged in reorganizing.

There are reasons for this interest in organization and for the underlying conviction that inherited organization structures or structures that 'just grew' are unlikely to satisfy the needs of the enterprise. Above all, we have learned the danger of the wrong organization structure. The best structure will not guarantee results and performances, but the wrong structure is a guarantee of nonperformance. All it produces are friction and frustration. The wrong organization spotlights the wrong issues, aggravates irrelevant disputes and makes a mountain out of trivia. It accents weaknesses instead of strengths. The right organization structure is thus a prerequisite of performance.

Until very recently, interest in organization was to be found only in very large businesses. The earlier examples – Alfred P. Sloan's organization structure for General Motors in the early 1920s, for one – all came from large businesses.

Today, we know that organization becomes most critical when a small business grows into a medium-sized one, and a simple business into a complicated one. The small business that wants to grow, even into only a medium-sized business, has to think through and work out the right organization to enable it both to function as a small business and to be able to grow into something bigger. Similarly, the simple one-product, one-market business faces crucial organization problems the moment it adds even a little diversity or complexity.

## Yesterday's final answers

But while we have accepted that organization and management structure are crucial, we are fast outgrowing yesterday's 'final answers'.

Twice in the short history of management we have already had the 'final answer' to organization. The first time was around 1910 when Henri Fayol, the French industrialist, had thought through the functions of a manufacturing company. At that time the manufacturing business was, of course, the truly important organizational problem, and the functions he defined then – such as engineering, manufacturing, and marketing – still apply to manufacturing businesses today.

A generation later one could again say that we 'knew'. Fayol had given 'the answer' for the single-product manufacturing business. Alfred P. Sloan, Jr, in organizing General Motors in the 1920s, made the next step. He found 'the answer' for organizing the complex and large manufacturing company. The Sloan approach used Fayol's functional organization for the subunits, the individual 'divisions', but organized the business itself on the basis of 'federal decentralization'. This structure is based on decentralized authority and coordinated control. After World War II it became the organization model worldwide, especially for larger organizations.

Another generation later, by the early 1950s, it was becoming clear that the General Motors model was no more adequate to new and important challenges in organization than Fayol's model had been adequate to the realities of a very big business which Alfred P. Sloan, Jr faced when he tackled the task of making General Motors manageable and managed.

Where they fit the realities of an organization, Fayol's and Sloan's models are still unsurpassed. Fayol's functional organization is still the best way to structure a small business, especially a small manufacturing business. Sloan's federal decentralization is still the best structure for the big multiproduct company. None of the new design structures comes nearly as close to fulfilling the design specifications of organization structure as do functional organization and federal decentralization *if and when they fit.* But more and more of the institutional reality that has to be structured and organized does not fit. Indeed, the very assumptions that underlay Sloan's and Fayol's work are not applicable to major organization needs and challenges.

## Traditional assumptions and current needs

The best way, perhaps, to show the current needs of organization structure is to contrast the basic characteristics of GM which Sloan so successfully structured with current needs and realities of organization and structure.

1 General Motors is a manufacturing business, producing and selling highly engineered goods. Fayol too was concerned with a business producing physical goods, specifically a fair-sized coal-mining company. Today we face the challenge of organizing the large business that is not primarily a manufacturing business. There are not only the large financial institutions and the large retailers. There are worldwide transportation companies, communications companies, companies that, while they do manufacture, are mainly in customer service (such as most computer businesses). Then there are all the nonbusiness service institutions with which Chapters 9 to 12 dealt. These nonmanufacturing institutions are increasingly the true centre of gravity of any developed economy. They employ the most people. They both contribute and take the largest share of gross national product. They are the fundamental organization problems today.

2 General Motors is essentially a single-product, single-technology, single-market business. More than four-fifths of its sales are automotive. The cars that GM sells differ in details, such as size, horsepower, and price, but they are essentially one and the same product.

By contrast, the typical businesses of today are multiproduct, multitechnology, and multimarket businesses. They may not be 'conglomerates', but they are diversified. And their central problem is a problem General Motors did not have: the organization of complexity and diversity.

3 General Motors is still primarily a US company. It dominates the American automobile industry and looms very large on the international automobile market. But Australia is the only market outside the US dominated by GM. In Europe it is at best number four. Organizationally the world outside the United States is still, for GM, 'separate' and 'outside'.

By contrast, the most rapid growth in the last twenty-five years has been the multinational company, that is, the company for which a great many countries and a great many markets are all of equal importance, or at least are all of major importance.

4 Because GM is a one-product and one-country company, information is not a major organizational problem and need not be a major organizational concern. Everyone in GM speaks the same language, whether by that we mean the language of the automotive industry or American English. Everyone fully understands what the other one is doing or should be doing, if only because, in all likelihood, he has done a similar job himself. GM can therefore be organized according to the logic of the market place, and the logic of authority and decision. It need not, in its organization, concern itself a great deal with the logic and the flow of information.

By contrast, multiproduct, multitechnology, and multinational companies do have to concern themselves in their organizational design and structure with organization according to the flow of information. They have to be sure that their organization structure does not violate the logic of information. And for this GM offers no guidance – GM did not have to tackle the problem.

5 Four out of every five GM employees are production workers, either manual workers or clerks on routine tasks. GM, in other words, employs yesterday's, rather than today's, labour force.

But the basic organization problem today is knowledge work and knowledge workers. They are the fastest-growing element in every business. In the service institutions, they are the core employment.

6 Finally, General Motors has been a 'managerial' rather than an 'entrepreneurial' business – i.e., one that starts and develops new businesses and products. The strength of Sloan's approach lay in its ability to manage superbly what was already there and

known. General Motors has not been innovative – altogether the automobile industry has not been innovative since the days before World War I.

But the challenge is increasingly going to be entrepreneurship and innovation. We need an innovative organization – in addition to a managerial one. And for this, the General Motors model offers no guidance.

But of course we have learned a great deal in the three-quarters of a century since Fayol's generation first tackled organization. We know what the job is. We know the major approaches. We know what comes first. We know what will not work – though not always what will. We know what organization structure aims at and therefore what the test of successful organization design is.

## What we have learned

1 The first thing we have learned is that Fayol and Sloan were right: organization structure will not just 'evolve'. The only things that develop spontaneously in an organization are disorder, friction, and malperformance. Nor is the right structure 'intuitive' any more than Greek temples or Gothic cathedrals were. Traditions may indicate where the problems are, but traditions are no help in solving them. *Organization design and structure require thinking, analysis, and a systematic approach.*
2 We have learned that the first step is not designing an organization structure; that is the last step. The first step is identifying and organizing the *building blocks* of organization, that is, the activities that have to be built into the final structure and that carry the 'structural load' of the final organization.

We now know that building blocks are determined by the kind of *contribution* they make. And we know that the traditional classification of the contributions – the 'staff and line' concept of conventional American organization theory – is more of a hindrance to understanding than a help.
3 '*Structure follows strategy.*' Organization is not mechanical. It is not 'assembly'. It cannot be 'prefabricated'. Organization is

unique to each individual business or institution. For we now know that structure, to be effective, must follow strategy.

Structure is a means for attaining the objectives and goals of an institution. Any work on structure must therefore start with objectives and strategy. This is perhaps the most fruitful new insight we have gained in the field of organization. It may sound obvious, and it is. But some of the worst mistakes in organization building have been made by imposing an 'ideal' or 'theoretical' organization on a living business.

Strategy – that is, the answers to the questions 'What is our business, what should it be, what will it be?' – determines the purpose of structure. In doing that, it determines the key activities in a given business or service institution. Effective structure is the design that makes these key activities capable of functioning and of performance. And in turn the key activities are the 'load-bearing elements' of a functioning structure. Organization design is, or should be, concerned first with the key activities; the rest are secondary.

## The three kinds of work

There are different kinds of work in every organization, however small and simple.

There is first operating work, the work of managing what is already in existence and known, building it, exploiting its potential, taking care of its problems.

There is always top-management work. And (as will be discussed in Chapter 38) it is different work, with its own tasks and requirements.

Finally, there is innovative work. It too is different work, requiring different things with respect to both operations and top management.

As we shall see later in this part, none of the available design principles can be used to organize all three different kinds of work. Yet each needs to be organized. And they all need to be integrated into one overall organization.

## What we need to unlearn

There are also a few things we need to unlearn. Some of the noisiest and most time-consuming battles in organization theory and practice are pure sham. They pose an 'either/or'; yet the right answer is 'both' – in varying proportions.

1 The first of these sham battles which better be forgotten is the one between task-focus and person-focus in job design and organization structure. To repeat what has been said already (Chapter 24), *structure* and *job design* have to be task-focused. But *assignments* have to fit both the person and the needs of the situation. Work, to say it once more, is objective and impersonal; the job itself is done by a person.

2 Somewhat related to this old controversy is the discussion of hierarchical, or scalar, versus free-form organization.

Traditional organization theory knows only one kind of structure applicable alike to building blocks and whole buildings: the so-called *scalar organization*, that is, the pyramid of superior and subordinates. Traditional organization theory considers this structure suitable for all tasks.

Today another organization theory is becoming fashionable. It maintains that shape and structure are what we want them to be. They are, or should be, 'free-form'. Everything – shape, size, and apparently tasks – derive from interpersonal relations. Indeed the purpose of the structure is to make it possible for each person to 'do my own thing'.

The first thing to say about this controversy is that it is simply not true that one of these forms is regimentation and the other freedom. The amount of discipline required in both is the same; they only distribute it differently.

A hierarchy does not, as the critics claim, make the superior more powerful. On the contrary, the first effect of hierarchical organization is to protect the subordinate against arbitrary authority from above. It does this by defining carefully the sphere within which the subordinate has the authority; the sphere within which the superior cannot interfere. It protects the subordinate by making it possible for him to say, 'This is *my* assigned job.' Protection of the subordinate underlies also the scalar principle's insistence that a person have only one superior. Otherwise the subordinate is likely to find himself caught between conflicting demands, conflicting commands, and conflicts of interest as well as of loyalty. 'Better one bad master than two good ones,' says an old peasant proverb.

At the same time, the hierarchical organization gives the most *individual* freedom. As long as the incumbent does the assigned duties of the position, he or she has done the job. He or she has no responsibility beyond it.

The term free-form organization is somewhat misleading. What is meant is organization designed for specific tasks rather than for supposedly 'eternal' purposes. In particular, it means organization of work in small groups and teams.

This (as will be discussed in some detail in later chapters of this part) demands, above all, great self-discipline from each member of the team. Everybody has to do 'the team's thing'. Everybody has to take responsibility for the work of the entire team and for its performance. Indeed, Abraham Maslow's criticism of Theory Y (Chapter 17) for making inhuman demands on that large proportion of people who are weak, vulnerable, timid, impaired, applies with even greater force to free-form organization. The more flexible an organization, the stronger the individual members have to be and the more of the load they have to carry.

Both individual members and the entire organization need some element of hierarchy in any structure. There has to be someone who can make a decision or the organization deteriorates into a never-ending bull session. Knowledge organizations especially need to have decision authority and specific, designated 'channels' defined with great clarity. Every organization will find itself in a situation of common peril once in a while. And then all perish unless there is clear, unambiguous, designated *command* authority vested in one person.

Just as statesmen long ago learned that both good laws and good rulers are needed for government to function well, so organization builders will have to learn that sound organization structure needs *both* a hierarchical structure of authority and the capacity to organize task forces, teams, and individuals for work both on a permanent and a temporary basis.

3 At bottom these sham battles – between task focus and person-focus and between scalar and free-form organization – reflect the belief of traditional organization theory that one best principle alone is 'right' and that it is also always 'right'. There must be *one final answer*.

Instead of the 'one right' principle, *three* new major design principles have emerged in the thirty years since World War II ended, to join Fayol's functions and Sloan's federal decentralization. These three – the *team, simulated decentralization*, and *systems management* – do not replace the older designs. None of them could lay claim to being a 'universal' principle; indeed, all three have serious structural weaknesses and limited applicability. But they are the best answers available for certain kinds of work, the best structures available for certain tasks, and the best approaches to such major organization problems as top management and innovation in many industries.

## The building blocks of organization

In designing the building blocks of organization four questions face the organizer.

1 What should the units of organization be ?
2 What components should join together, and what components should be kept apart ?
3 What are the best size and shape for the different components ?

The traditional approach to identifying the basic units of organization has been to analyse *all* the activities needed for performance in the enterprise. This produces a list of typical functions of a manufacturing business or of a retail business.

This approach to the typical functions sees organization as mechanical, as an assemblage of functions. Organizations will indeed use typical activities – though not necessarily all of them. But how the structure is to be built depends on the results needed. Organizing has to start out with the desired results.

## The key activities

What we need to know is not all the activities that might conceivably have to be housed in the organization structure. What we need to know are the load-bearing parts of the structure, the *key activities*.

Organization design, therefore, starts with these questions:

—In what area is excellence required to obtain the company's objectives?
—In what areas would nonperformance endanger the results, if not the survival, of the enterprise?

Here are some examples of the kind of conclusions these questions lead to.

Sears, Roebuck in the United States and Marks & Spencer in England are in many ways remarkably similar enterprises, if only because the founders and builders of Marks & Spencer consciously modelled their company on Sears, Roebuck. But there is a pronounced difference in the organizational placement and role of the 'laboratory' in these two companies. Sears defines its business as being 'the buyer for the American family' and uses its laboratory to test the merchandise it buys. Accordingly, the laboratory, while large, competent, and respected, is organizationally quite subordinate. Marks & Spencer, on the other hand, defines its business as 'developing upper-class goods for the working-class family'. As a result, the laboratory is central to Marks & Spencer's organization structure. The laboratory, rather than the buyer, decides what new products are desirable, develops the new merchandise, designs it, tests it, and then has it produced. Only then does the buyer take over. As a result, the head of the Marks & Spencer laboratory is a senior member of management and, in many ways, the chief business planner.

Any company that shows understanding success made the key

activities – and especially those in which excellence is needed to attain business objectives – the central elements in its organization structure.

But equally important are the questions 'In what areas could malfunction seriously hurt us ? In what areas do we have major vulnerability ?' These questions, however, are seldom asked.

The New York brokerage community, by and large, did not ask it during the boom years of the 1960s. If it had, it would have realized that malfunction of the 'back office', where customer orders, customer accounts and securities are handled, could seriously endanger the business. Failure to organize the back office as a key activity was the single most important cause of the severe crisis that overtook Wall Street in 1969 and 1970. The one Wall Street firm that had asked those questions, Merrill Lynch, had organized the back office as a load-bearing key activity in its structure. It emerged from the crisis the giant of the brokerage business.

Finally, the question should be asked 'What are the *values* that are truly important to *us* in this company ?' It might be product or process safety. It might be product quality. It might be the ability of the company's dealers to give proper service to the customer and so on. Whatever the values are, they have to be organizationally based. There has to be an organizational component responsible for them – and it has to be a key one.

These three questions identify the key activities. And they in turn will be the structural elements of organization. The rest, no matter how important, no matter how much money they represent, no matter how many people they employ, are secondary. Obviously, they have to be analysed, organized, and placed within the structure. But the first concern must be those activities that are essential to the success of a business strategy and to the attainment of business objectives. They have to be identified, defined, organized, and centrally placed.

This means that business should always analyse its organization structure when its strategy changes. Whatever the reason – a change in market or in technology, diversification, or new objectives – a change in strategy requires reanalysing the key activities and adapting the structure to them. Conversely, reorganization that is undertaken without a change in strategy is either superfluous or indicates poor organization to begin with.

## The contribution analysis

From the earliest days of concern with organization, the most controversial question has been 'What activities belong together and what activities belong apart ?'

There are, by and large, four major groups of activities that contribute in different ways:

There are, first, *result-producing activities*, activities that produce measurable results which can be related, directly or indirectly, to the performance of the entire enterprise. Some of these activities are directly revenue-producing. Others contribute measurable results.

There are, second, *support activities* that, while needed and even essential, do not by themselves produce results but have results only through the use made of their 'output' by other components of the business.

There are, third, activities that have no direct or indirect relationship to the results of the business, activities which are truly ancillary. They are *housekeeping activities*.

Finally, and different in character from any of these, is the *top-management activity*, which will be discussed separately in Chapter 38.

Among the result-producing activities, some directly bring in *revenues*. In service institutions, the comparable activities are those that directly produce 'patient care' or 'learning'. Selling and all the work needed to do a systematic and organized selling job, such as sales forcasting, market research, sales training, and sales management belong in this category. Here also belongs the treasury function, that is, the supply and management of money in the business.

The second group of result-producing activities are those that do not generate revenue but are directly related to the results of the entire business, or of a major revenue-producing segment. I call them *result-contributing* rather than result-producing.

Manufacturing is typical of these activities. Training belongs here too, as do recruitment and employment. These are the activities concerned with supplying qualified and trained people to the enterprise. Purchasing and physical distribution are result-contributing but not revenue-producing activities. 'Engineering', as the term is normally understood in most manufacturing businesses, is a result-contributing but not a revenue-producing activity. In a commercial bank 'operations', the handling of data and papers, belong here. In a life insurance company, claims settlement is result-contributing. Labour negotiations and many other similar 'relations' activities are result-contributing though not revenue-producing.

The third group of result-producing activities are *informational*. They do produce a 'finished product' needed by everyone in the system. Yet information, by itself, does not produce any revenue. It is 'supply' to revenue and cost centres alike.

First among the *support activities*, which do not by themselves produce a product but are input to others, stand the *conscience* activities. These activities set standards, create vision, and demand excellence in *all* the key areas where a business needs to strive for excellence. 'Conscience' may seem an odd term for this function, but it is a good one. The task of the conscience activities is not to help the organization improve on its present activities. Its task is to hold the organization to its own standards, to remind the organization what it should be, but isn't, doing.

Conscience activities tend to be slighted in most organizations. But every company – and every service institution – needs to provide itself and its managers with vision, with values, with standards and with some provision for reviewing performance against these standards.

Another support function is *advice and teaching*. The contribution is not in what the activity itself does or can do, but in the impact it has on the ability of others to perform. The 'product' is increased performance capacity of the rest of the organization.

A good many of the 'relations' activities are also support, the legal staff and the patent department, for example.

The last group of activities defined by their contribution are the *housekeeping activities*, ranging from the medical department to the people who clean the floor, from the plant cafeteria to the management of pension and retirement funds, from finding a plant site to taking care of all the record-keeping requirements imposed on business by government. These functions contribute nothing directly to the results and performance of the business. Their malfunction, however, hurts the enterprise. They serve legal requirements, the morale of the work force, or public responsibilities. Of all activities they are the most diverse. And of all activities they tend to get the shortest shrift in most organizations.

This is a rough classification, and far from scientific. Some activities may belong in one category in one business, in another one in a second business and in a third company will be left fuzzy and without clear classification at all.

Why classify then? The answer is that activities that differ in contribution have to be treated differently. Contribution determines ranking and placement.

Key activities should never be subordinated to activities that are not key.

Revenue-producing activities should never be subordinated to nonrevenue-producing activities.

And support activities should never be mixed with revenue-producing and result-contributing activities. They should be kept apart.

## The 'conscience' activities

Activities that are the conscience of an organization must never be subordinated to anything else. They also should never be placed with any other activity; they should be clearly separate.

The conscience function of giving vision, of setting standards, and of reviewing performance against standards is basically a top-management function. But it has to work with the entire management group. Every business, even a small one, needs this function. In a small business, it need not be set up as a separate function but can be part of the top-management job. In any business of more than medium size, however, the function usually has to be set up and staffed separately.

However, there should be very few people actually doing the conscience job. It is a job for a single individual rather than a staff. It is a job for a person whose performance has earned the respect of the management group. It is not a job for a 'specialist'. It is best discharged by a senior member of the management group with proven performance record who has manifested concern, perception and interest in the area for which she or he is supposed to act as conscience.

Only those few areas that are vital and central to a company's success and survival should become areas of conscience. Objectives and strategy determine what conscience activities are needed. Managing people is always a conscience area, and so is marketing. The impact of a business on its environment, its social responsibilities, and its relations with the outside community are also basic conscience areas. Innovation (whether technological or social innovation) is likely to be a conscience area for any large business.

Beyond these, however, there is no formula.

The tenure of the few conscience executives should be limited as a rule. No matter how greatly a conscience executive may be respected, and no matter how successful, he or she will eventually wear out either integrity or welcome. This is a good place for a senior person to end a distinguished career. A younger person in the job should be moved out after a few years – preferably back into a 'doing' job.

## Making service staffs effective

There are similarly stringent rules with respect to advisory and teaching activities, that is, with respect to service staffs.

There should be very few of them. They should be set up only in key activity areas. The secret of effective services work is concentration rather than busyness.

Advisory and teaching staffs should never try to do a little bit of everything. They should zero in on a very small number of crucial areas. Rather than serve everybody, they should select areas within the organization where the managers are receptive and do not have to be 'sold', and where success will generate the greatest effect throughout the whole company.

The staffs and their activities should be kept lean.

The supply of people of the right temperament for this kind of work is not large. To do a decent job in an advisory and teaching capacity requires someone who genuinely wants others to get the credit. It requires an individual who starts out with the aim of enabling others to do what *they* want to do, provided only that it is neither immoral nor insane. It requires further someone who has the patience to let others learn rather than go and do the work single-handed. And finally, it requires someone who will not abuse a position in headquarters close to the seat of power to politick, to manipulate and to play favourites. People who possess these personality traits are rare. Yet people in services work who lack these qualities can do only mischief.

One basic rule for advisory and teaching staffs is that they abandon an old activity before they take on a new one. Otherwise they will soon start to 'build empires' or to produce 'canned goods', that is, programmes and memoranda, rather than developing the knowledge and performance capacity of those whose job it is to produce. They will also otherwise be forced to use second-raters rather than people of outstanding competence. Only if they are required to abandon an old activity before taking on a new one will they be able to put really first-rate people on every job.

Advisory and teaching activities should never 'operate'. A common weakness of personnel staffs is that they operate. They run the labour negotiations, they do a lot of housekeeping chores such as managing the cafeteria, or they train. As a result the advisory and teaching work does not get done. The 'daily crisis' in operations takes precedence over the work of advice and teaching, which can always be postponed.

Advisory and teaching work should not be a career. It is work to which managers or career professionals should be exposed in the course of their growth. But it is not work which a person should normally do for long. As a career it corrupts. It breeds contempt for 'those dumb operating people', that is, for honest work. It puts a premium on being 'bright', rather than on being right. It is also frustrating work because one does not have results of one's own but results only at secondhand.

But it is excellent training, excellent development, and a severe test of a person's character and ability to be effective without having the authority of command. It is an experience everyone who rises to the top of an organization should have. But it is an exposure no one should suffer for more than a short time.

## The two faces of information

Information activities present a special organizational problem. They have two faces, two dimentions, and two directions. Unlike most other result-producing activities, they are not concerned with one stage of the process but with the entire process itself. This means that they have to be both centralized and decentralized.

The traditional organization chart expresses this in the two different lines that connect an information activity to 'bosses'. A solid line connects the activity to the head of the unit for which it provides information, and a dotted line connects it to the central information group. A monthly operating statement, for example, might go both to the head of the operating unit and to the company controller.

One conclusion from this is that information work should be kept separate from other kinds of work. American business has typically violated this rule by putting accounting (a traditional information activity) into the same component as the treasurer (the result-producing operating work of supplying capital and managing money in the business). The justification has been that both 'deal with money'. But, actually, accounting does not deal with money; it deals with figures. The result of the traditional approach has been to slight financial management.

The tough question with respect to information activities is which of them belong together and which should be kept apart. There is much talk today about 'integrated total information systems'. This implies that all – or at least most – information activities should be in one component. Insofar as this means that new and different information activities, such as operations research or a computer system, should not be subordinated to traditional accounting, the point is well taken. But should they be coordinated ? Or should they be separate ?

## Housekeeping

The last group of activities according to their contribution are housekeeping activities. They should be kept separate from other work, or else they will not get done. The problem is not that these activities are particularly difficult. Some are. Many others are not. The problem is that they are not even indirectly related to results. Therefore, they tend to be looked down upon by the rest of the organization.

One reason for the tremendous increase in health-care costs in the US is managerial neglect of the 'hotel services'. The people who dominate the hospital, the doctors and nurses, all know that the hotel services are essential. Patients do not get well unless they are reasonably comfortable, are fed, have their beds changed and their rooms cleaned. But these are not professional activities for a doctor, nurse or X-ray technician. They are not willing to yield an inch to make it possible for the people in charge of the hotel services to do their jobs. They are not willing to have these activities represented on the upper levels of hospital management. As a result, they are left unmanaged. And this means they are done badly and expensively.

This same sort of neglect extends even to activities in which a great deal of money is at stake. Few companies in the United States for instance have done even an adequate job of managing their employees' pension funds, despite the enormous amount of money involved. It is an activity which does not, it seems, have any relationship to results, and therefore it is an activity which tends to be relegated to somebody else.

One way out is to turn housekeeping activities over to the work community to run (see Chapter 18). They are activities *for* the employees, and they are therefore best managed *by* the employees. Or, such activities may be farmed out to some outsider whose business it is to run a pension fund or to manage a cafeteria.

But insofar as a company's management has to do these things itself – and picking a plant site and building a factory is something a company has to do for itself, or at least has to participate in actively – housekeeping activities ought to be kept separate from all others. They require different people, different values, different measurements – and should require little supervision by business management itself.

There is one overall rule: activities that make the same kind of contribution can be combined in one component under one management, whatever their technical specialization. Activities that do not make the same kind of contribution do not, as a rule, belong together.

It is feasible and often best to put all advising and teaching activities, whether these be in personnel, in manufacturing, in marketing, or in purchasing, in one 'services' group under one manager. Similarly, in any but large companies, one person might well be the company's conscience in all major conscience areas. Contribution rather than skill determines function.

## Decision analysis

Identifying key activities and analysing their contributions defines the building blocks of organization. But placing the structural units that make up the organization requires two additional pieces of work: an analysis of decisions and an analysis of relations.

What decisions are needed to obtain the performance objectives ? What kinds of decisions are they ? On what level of the organization should they be made ? What activities are involved in, or affected by, them ? Which managers must therefore participate in the decisions – at least to the extent of being consulted beforehand ? Which managers must be informed after they have been made ? The answers to these questions determine where work begins.

In one large company, well over 90 per cent of the decisions that managers had to make over a five-year period were found to be 'typical', falling in a small number of categories. In only a few cases would it have been necessary to ask, 'Where does this decision belong ?' had the problem been thought through in advance. Yet, because there had been no decision analysis, almost three-quarters of the decisions had to 'go looking for a home'. Most of them went to a much higher level of management than was needed. The company's components had been organized so that the activities that should have made key decisions were placed so low as to be without authority and also without adequate information to make them.

Four basic characteristics determine the nature of any business decision.

First, is the degree of *futurity* in the decision. For how long into the future does it commit the company ? And how fast can it be reversed ?

Buyers at Sears, Roebuck have practically no limit as to the amount to which they can commit the company. But no buyer or buying supervisor can either abandon an existing product or add a new one without approval of the head of the entire buying operation who, traditionally, is the second or third in command in the entire Sears, Roebuck organization. Similarly, the foreign exchange trader in a major commercial bank traditionally has only the loosest limit on the amounts to which she can commit the bank. But she cannot start trading in a new currency without approval from high authority in the bank.

The second criterion is the *impact* a decision has on other functions, on other areas, or on the business as a whole. If it affects only one function, it is of the lowest order and should be made fairly low in the organization. Otherwise it will either have to be made on a higher level, where the impact on all affected functions can be considered, or it must be made in close consultation with the managers of the other affected functions. To use technical language, 'optimization' of process and performance of one function must not be at the expense of other functions. This is undesirable 'suboptimization'.

One example of a decision that looks like a purely 'technical' one affecting one area only, but that actually has impact on many areas, is a change in the methods of keeping the parts inventory in a mass-production plant. This affects all manufacturing operations. It makes necessary major changes in assembly. It affects delivery to customers – it might even lead to radical changes in marketing and pricing, such as the abandonment of certain designs and models. The technical problems in inventory-keeping – though considerable – pale into insignificance compared to the problems that any change in inventory-keeping will produce in other areas. To 'optimize' inventory-keeping at the expense of these other areas cannot be allowed. Yet suboptimization will be avoided only if the decision is recognized as being of a fairly high order and handled as one affecting the entire process. Either it has to be reserved for management higher than the plant, or it requires close consultation among all functional managers.

The character of a decision is also determined by the number of *qualitative factors* that enter into it; basic principles of conduct, ethical values, social and political beliefs and so on. If such value considerations are involved, the decision moves into a higher order. It requires either determination or review at a higher level. The most important and most common of qualitative factors are human beings. This, of course, underlies the strong recommendation in Chapter 28 for top-management people to play an active part in the decisions on promotion to upper levels of middle management.

Finally, decisions can be classified as periodically *recurrent* or *rare*. The recurrent decision requires establishing a general rule, that is, it requires making a decision in principle. Since suspending an employee deals with a person, the general rule has to be made at a fairly high level in the organization. But the application of the rule to the specific case, while also a decision, can then be placed on a much lower level.

The rare decision, however, has to be treated as a distinct

event. Whenever it occurs, it has to be thought through.

A decision should always be made at the lowest possible level and as close to the scene of action as possible. However, a decision should always be made at a level high enough to insure that all activities and objectives affected are fully considered. The first rule tells us how far down a decision *should* be made. The second how far down it *can* be made. It tells us which managers must share in the decision and which must be informed of it. The two together tell us where certain activities should be placed. Managers charged with responsibility for a given decision should be high enough to have the authority to make typical decisions pertaining to their work, and low enough to have the detailed knowledge and the first-hand experience, 'where the action is'.

## Relations analysis

The final step in designing the building blocks of organization is an analysis of relations. It tells us where a specific component belongs.

The basic rule in placing an activity within the organization structure is to impose on it the *smallest possible number of relationships* and to make the crucial relations, that is, the relationship on which depend its success and the effectiveness of its contribution, easy, accessible, and central to the unit. *The rule is to keep relationships to a minimum and make each count.*

This rule explains why functions are not groups of related skills. If we followed the functional principle, we would, for instance, put production planning into a planning component where all kinds of planners would work together. The skills needed in production planning are closely related to all other operational planning skills. Instead, we put the production planner into manufacturing and as close as possible both to the plant manager and to the first-line supervisors. This is where the planner belongs according to key relationships.

There is often a conflict between placement according to decision analysis and placement according to relations analysis. By and large, one should try to follow the logic of relations as far as possible.

## Symptoms of poor organization

There is no perfect organization. At its best an organization structure doesn't cause trouble. But what are the most common mistakes in designing the building blocks of organization and joining them together? And what are the most common symptoms of serious flaws in organization?

The most common and the most serious symptom of poor organization is an increase in the number of management levels. A basic rule of organization is to build the fewest *possible* management levels and forge the shortest possible chain of command.

Every additional level makes it more difficult to attain mutual understanding by creating more noise and distorting the message. Every additional level distorts objectives and misdirects attention. Every link in the chain sets up additional stresses and creates one more source of inertia, friction, and slack.

The second most common symptom of poor organization is recurring organizational problems. No sooner has a problem supposedly been 'solved' than it comes back again in a new guise.

A typical example in a manufacturing company is product development. The marketing people think it belongs to them; the research and development people are equally convinced that it belongs to them. But placing it in either component simply creates a recurring problem. Actually both placements are wrong. In a business that wants innovation, product development is a key, revenue-producing activity. It should not be subordinated to any other activity. It deserves to be organized as a separate component.

Solving the recurrent organization problem requires making the right analyses – the key activities analysis, the contributions analysis, the decisions analysis and the relations analysis. An organization problem that comes back more than a couple of times should not be treated mechanically by shuffling little boxes on an organization chart. It indicates lack of thinking, lack of clarity and lack of understanding.

Equally common and equally dangerous is an organization structure that puts the attention of key people on the wrong, the irrelevant, the secondary problems. Organization should put the attention of people on major business decisions, on key activities, and on performance and results. If, instead, it puts attention on proper behaviour, on etiquette, on procedure, then organization misdirects. Then organization is a bar to performance.

There are several common symptoms of poor organization which, usually, require no further diagnosis. There is, first, the symptom of *too many meetings* attended by too many people.

Whenever executives, except at the very top level, spend more than a fairly small fraction of their time – maybe a quarter or less – in meetings, this is by itself evidence of poor organization. Too many meetings indicate that jobs have not been defined clearly, have not been structured big enough, have not been made truly responsible. The need for meetings indicates that the decisions and relations analyses either have not been made at all or have not been applied. The rule should be to minimize the need for people to get together to accomplish anything.

An organization in which people are constantly concerned about feelings and about what other people will or will not like is not an organization that has good human relations. On the contrary, it is an organization that has very poor human relations. Good human relations, like good manners, are taken for granted. Constant anxiety over other people's feelings is the worst kind of human relations.

An organization that suffers from this – and a great many do – can be said unequivocally to suffer from overstaffing. It might be overstaffed in terms of activities. Instead of focusing on key activities, it tries to do a little bit of everything – especially in advice and teaching activities. Or the individual activities may be overstaffed. It is in crowded rooms that people get on each other's nerves, poke their elbows into each other's eyes, and step on each other's toes. Where there is enough distance they do not collide. Overstaffed organizations create work rather than performance. They also create friction, sensitivity, irritation and concern with feelings.

It is a symptom of malorganization to rely on 'coordinators', 'assistants', and other such *whose job it is not to have a job*. This indicates that activities and jobs have been designed too narrow, or that activities and jobs, rather than being designed for one defined result, are expected to do a great many parts of different tasks. It usually indicates also that organizational components have been organized according to skill rather than according to their contribution or their place in the process. Skill always contributes only a part rather than a result. If the organization is by skill, one needs a coordinator to put back pieces together that should never have been separated in the first place.

## 'Organizitis' as a chronic affliction

A good many businesses, especially large, complex ones, suffer from the disease of 'organizitis'. Everybody is concerned with organization. Reorganization is going on all the time. At the first sign of any trouble, be it only a spat over a specification between a purchasing agent and the people in engineering, the cry goes up for the 'organization doctors', whether outside consultants or inside staff. And no organizational solution ever lasts long. Indeed few organizational arrangements are given enough time to be tested and worked out in practice before another organization study is begun.

In some cases this does indeed suggest malorganization. 'Organizitis' will set in if organization structure fails to come to grips with fundamentals. It is brought on especially by not rethinking and restructuring the organization after a fundamental change in the size and complexity of a business or in its objectives and strategy.

But just as often 'organizitis' is a form of hypochondria. It therefore should be emphasized that organizational changes should not be undertaken often and should not be undertaken lightly. Reorganization is a form of surgery, and even minor surgery has risks.

The demands for organization studies or for reorganization as a response to minor ailments should be resisted. No organization will ever be perfect. A certain amount of friction, of incongruity, of organizational confusion is inevitable. And the test of good organization is not perfection on paper. It is performance at work.

## Summary

Twice in the short history of management did we believe we had the right answer to organization. Once was during the time of World War I in Henri Fayol's 'functions' and, again, a generation later, in Alfred Sloan's 'federal decentralization'. If and when they fit, these two designs are still our best answers. But increasingly we have to structure organizations where neither of these two designs fit. Increasingly we have had to develop new and additional design principles: we now have five.

We have learned a great deal about organization in the last 75 years. We know the specifications for effective organization. We know that we have to organize, in one and the same structure, three distinct kinds of work: operating work, top-management work, and innovating work. We know that structure follows strategy and that structure is therefore not mechanical but must be developed from the purposes, goals and objectives of an organization, and on the foundation of the key activities needed to attain objectives. We have learned that organizing starts with 'building blocks' of organization. We know what activities belong together and what activities should be kept apart. We know the symptoms of poor organization. And we know that there is no one final answer.

Good organization structure does not guarantee performance. But poor or inappropriate structure impedes performance – and performance is the test of organization structure.

# 35 Work- and Task-Focused Design

The 'organization architect' has available today *five design principles*, five distinct ways of organizing activities and ordering relationships. Two of them are traditional: Henri Fayol's functional structure, and Alfred P. Sloan's federal decentralization.

Three are new: team organization; simulated decentralization; and the system structure.

Each of these five was developed to meet specific needs. The first impression is therefore that they represent expediency rather than design, let alone logic. But in reality, these designs express different *design logics*. Each takes one general dimension of managerial organization and builds a structure around it.

## Formal specifications

Organization structure must satisfy minimum requirements with respect to: clarity; economy; the direction of vision; understanding by the individual of his or her own task and the task of the whole; decision-making; stability and adaptability; and perpetuation and self-renewal.

1 *Clarity*. All managerial components, and all individuals within the organization, especially all managers, need to know where they belong, where they stand, where they have to go for whatever is needed, whether information, cooperation, or decision. Clarity is by no means the same thing as simplicity. Indeed, structures that look simple may lack clarity. And seemingly complex structures may have great clarity.

A structure in which workers do not know without an elaborate organization manual where they belong, where they have to go and where they stand, creates friction, wastes time, causes bickering and frustration, delays decisions and is altogether an impediment, rather than a help.

2 *Economy*. Closely related to clarity is the requirement of economy. One should be able to control, to supervise and to coax people to perform with a minimum effort. Organization structure should make self-control possible and should encourage self-motivation. And the smallest possible number of people, especially of people of high-performance capacity, should have to devote time and attention to keeping the machinery going.

In any organization some of the effort has to be used to keep the organization running and in good repair. Some time will have to be spent on 'internal control', 'internal communications', and 'personal problems'. But the less of the input of the organization has to be used to keep it going, the more of the input can become output. The organization will be more economical, and the more of its 'input' can become performance.

3 *The direction of vision*. Organization structure should direct the vision of individuals and of managerial units towards performance rather than towards efforts. And it should direct vision towards *results*, that is, towards the performance of the entire enterprise.

Performance is the end that all activities serve. Indeed, organization can be likened to a transmission that converts activities into the one 'drive' – performance. Organization is the more efficient the more 'direct' the transmission is, that is, the less it has to change the speed and direction of individual activities to make them yield performance. The largest possible number of managers should perform as business people rather than as 'experts' or 'bureaucrats'. As many as possible should be tested against performance and results rather than primarily by standards of administrative skill or professional competence.

4 *Understanding one's own task and the common task*. An organization should enable all individuals, especially all managers and professionals to *understand their own tasks*.

But at the same time, an organization should enable everyone to *understand the common task, the task of the entire organization*. All members of the organization, in order to relate their efforts to the common good, must understand how their tasks fit in with the task of the whole. And, in turn, they must know what the task of the whole implies for their own tasks, their own contributions, their own directions. Communications therefore need to be helped rather than hampered by organizational structure.

5 *Decision-making*. None of the available design principles is primarily structured around a 'decision model'. Yet decisions have to be made, made on the right issues and at the right level, and have to be converted into work and accomplishment. An organization design, therefore, needs to be tested to find whether it impedes or strengthens the decision-making process.

A structure that forces decisions to go to the highest possible level of organization rather than be settled at the lowest possible level clearly hampers decision-making. So does a decision structure that obscures the need for crucial decisions, or that focuses attention on the wrong issues, such as jurisdictional disputes.

6 *Stability and adaptability*. An organization needs *stability*. It must be able to do its work even though the world around it is in turmoil. It must be able to build on its performance and achievement of yesterday. It needs to be able to plan for its own future and continuity.

The individual needs also a 'home'. Nobody gets much work done in an airport waiting room; no one gets much work done as a transient. The individual needs to belong to a 'community' in which he or she knows people and is known by them, and in which his or her own relationship is anchored.

But stability is not rigidity. On the contrary, organization structure requires *adaptability*. A totally rigid structure is not stable; it is brittle. Only if the structure can adapt to new situations, new demands, new conditions will it be able to survive.

7 *Perpetuation and self-renewal*. Finally, an organization needs to be able to *perpetuate itself*. It needs to be able to *provide for its self-renewal*. These two needs entail a number of demands.

An organization must be capable of producing tomorrow's leaders from within. One minimum requirement for this is that it must not have so many levels of management that an able person, entering a management job early, say at age 25, cannot normally reach the top rungs of the promotion ladder while still young enough to be effective.

One self-renewal requirement is the ability of an organization structure to prepare and test an individual on each level for the next level above. It must especially prepare and test today's junior and middle managers for senior and top-management positions. For perpetuation and self-renewal, an organization structure must also be *accessible to new ideas* and must be willing and able to do new things.

## Meeting the specifications

Some of these specifications clearly conflict. No design principle could fully satisfy all of them. Any organization structure capable of performance and continuity will however have to satisfy all these specifications to some degree. This means compromises, trade-offs, balancing. It also implies that several design principles rather than one are likely to be used even for simple organization. For if any one of these specifications goes totally unsatisfied, the enterprise will not perform. Organization building therefore requires understanding the available design principles, their requirements, their limitations, and their 'fit' against the design specifications.

The first thing to know about the available design principles is their logic. Functional organization and team organization are organized around task and work. Both kinds of decentralization are organized around results. The systems structure is organized around relationships.

## Three ways of organizing work

All work, physical as well as mental, can be organized in three ways.

It can be organized by stages in the process. In building a house we first build the foundation, then the frame and the roof, and finally the interior.

It can be organized so that the work moves where the skill or tool required for each of the steps is located. The traditional metal-working unique-product plant has rows of reamers and lathes in one aisle, stamping machines in another, heat treating equipment in a third, with the pieces of metal moving from one set of tools and their skilled operators to another.

Finally, we can organize the work so that a team of workers with different skills and different tools moves to the work, which itself is stationary. A movie-making crew – the director, the actors, the electricians, the sound engineers – 'goes on location'. Each does highly specialized work, but they work as a team.

Fayol's 'functional organization' is commonly described as organizing work into 'related bundles of skill'. Actually it organizes work both by stages and by skills. Such traditional functions as manufacturing or marketing involve a very wide variety of unrelated skills – the machinist's skill and the production planner's skill in manufacturing, for example, and the salesperson's skill and the market researcher's skill in marketing. But manufacturing and marketing are distinct stages in a process. Other functions, such as accounting and personnel, are, however, organized by skills. But in any functional organization the work is moved to the stage or the skill. The work moves, while the position of the worker is fixed.

In the team structure, however, work and task are, so to speak, 'fixed'. Workers with different skills and different tools are brought together in a team. The team is assigned a piece of work or to a job whether this is a research project or the architectural design of a new office building.

Both functional and team structures are old designs. The Egyptian pyramid builder organized work functionally. And the organized and permanent team of the 'hunting band' goes back even further, to the last Ice Age.

Work and task have to be structured and organized. Any organization has to apply either functional or team or both to design work and task. Many organizations, as will be discussed later in this chapter, should apply both. And all need to understand both.

## The functional structure

Functional design has the great advantage of *clarity*. Everybody has a 'home'. Everybody *understands his or her own task*. It is an organization of high *stability*.

But the price for clarity and stability is that it is difficult for people, up to and including the top functional people, *to understand the task of the whole* and to relate their own work to it. While stable, the structure is *rigid* and resists adaptation. It does not prepare people for tomorrow, does not *train and test* them. On the whole, it tends to make them want to do what they already do a little better, rather than to seek new ideas and new ways of doing things.

The strengths and the limitations of the functional principle give it peculiar characteristics with respect to the *economy* specification. At its best, functional organization works with high economy. Very few people at the top need to spend much time on keeping the organization running, that is, on 'organizing', 'co-ordination', 'conciliation', and so on. The rest can do their work. But at its fairly common worst, functional organization is grossly uneconomical. As soon as it approaches even a modest size or complexity, 'friction' builds up. It rapidly becomes an organization of misunderstanding, feuds, empires and Berlin-Wall building. It soon requires coordinators, committees, meetings, troubleshooters, special dispatchers, which waste everybody's time without, as a rule, solving much. And this tendency towards conflict exists not only between different 'functions'. The large functional unit with its subdivisions and subfunctions is also prone to internal inefficiency and also requires more and more managerial effort to keep it running smoothly.

The basic strength as well as the basic weakness of functional organization is its *effort-focus*. Every functional manager considers his or her function the most important one. This emphasizes craftsmanship and professional standards. But it also makes people in the functional unit tend to subordinate the welfare of the other functions, if not of the entire business, to the interests of their unit. There is no real remedy against this tendency in the functional organization. The wish of every function to improve its own standing in the organization is the price paid for the worthy desire of each manager to do a good job.

*Communications* are fairly good in a small functional organization, but they too break down as the size of the organization increases. Even within an individual functional unit – a marketing department, for example – communications weaken if the unit becomes large or complex. People are then increasingly specialists, interested primarily in their own narrow specialty.

As a decision-making structure functional organization – even if fairly small – works poorly. For decisions in a functional organization cannot, as a rule, be made except at the highest level. No one except the executive at the top sees the entire business. As a result, decisions are easily misunderstood by the organization and are often poorly implemented. And because a functional organization has high stability but low adaptability, the challenge to do something truly new and different is likely to be suppressed rather than brought out in the open and faced up to.

*Functional organization* also does poorly in *developing, preparing, and testing* people. Functional organization puts the major emphasis on a person's acquiring the knowledge and competence that pertain to a particular function. Yet the functional specialist may become narrow in vision, skills, and loyalties. In a functional organization there is a built-in emphasis on not showing too much curiosity about the work of other functions or specialties. That is, narrow departmentalization is encouraged.

These limitations and weaknesses of functional organization were apparent from the very first. A good deal of thought has therefore been given to offsetting them, and to offsetting in particular the greatest weakness: the tendency of functional organization to misdirect the vision of functional people from contribution and results to efforts and busyness.

## Its limited scope

Even where functional organization applies, its scope is limited to operating work. Top management is 'work' (see Chapter 38), but it is not 'functional' work. And functional organization is the wrong organization for it. Wherever applied, it has made for a weak top management.

The functional principle is even less applicable to innovating work (see Chapter 37, 'The Innovative Organization'). In innovation, we try to do something not done before, that is, something we do not yet know. We need the individual skills of the various disciplines in innovation, but we do not know where and when they will be needed, for what time, in what degree, or in what volume. The innovative task therefore cannot be organized on the basis of functional organization. It is incompatible with it.

## Where functionalism works

Functionalism works very well in the kind of business for which it was designed. The model for Henri Fayol's functional design early in this century was the coal-mining company he ran. It was a fairly large business at that time but would be considered rather small today. Except for a few engineers, it employed only manual workers who all did one kind of work. A coal mine has only one product, and it varies only in size. Coal requires no treatment beyond simple washing and sorting. Coal had, at least at that time, only a few markets – steel mills, railroads and steamships, power plants, and homeowners. But in these markets it had practically a monopoly, and while the machinery and tools for mining coal were changing rapidly in Fayol's day, the process itself did not change at all. There was not much scope for innovation.

Fayol's company is the kind of business that the functional design principle organizes well. Anything more complex, more dynamic, or more innovative demands performance capacities that the functional principle does not possess. If used beyond the limits of Fayol's model, functional structure rapidly becomes costly in terms of time and effort. It also runs a high risk of directing the energies of the organization away from performance and towards mere busyness. In businesses that exceed Fayol's model, in size, in complexity, or in innovative scope, functional design should be used only as *one* principle and never as *the* principle. And even in businesses that fit Fayol's model, top-management design and structure require a different design principle.

## The team

A team is a number of people – usually only a few – with different backgrounds, skills, and knowledge, and drawn from various areas of the organization who work together on a specific and defined task. There is usually a team leader or team captain. The leader is often permanently appointed for the duration of the team's assignment. But leadership at any one time places itself according to the logic of the work and the specific stage in its progress. There are no superiors and subordinates, there are only seniors and juniors.

Every business – and every other institution – has been using teams all along for one-time tasks, but we have only recently recognized what the hunting bands of our nomadic Ice Age ancestors knew – the team is also a useful principle for permanent, structural design. The mission of the team is a specific task: hunting expedition or product development. But the team itself can be permanent. Its composition may vary from task to task. Its base remains, however, fairly constant even though individual members may scatter between tasks or belong, at one and the same time, to a number of teams.

The hospital may be the clearest example of the team. The structural component in the hospital is a team mobilized from the 'services' for the needs of the individual patient as defined by the team captain, the physician, with the nurse as the executive officer of the group.

In the hospital everyone directly concerned with patient care, that is, everyone on the team, is supposed to take personal responsibility for the success of the whole team's effort. The doctor's orders are law in a hospital. Yet physical therapists who are told, for instance, to give rehabilitation exercises to a patient are expected to notice when the patient seems to run a fever, to stop the exercises, and to notify the nurse immediately and ask for a temperature reading. They will not hesitate to counter-mand a doctor's orders within their own sphere. The doctor may order an orthopaedic patient to be measured for crutches and taught how to use them. The physical therapist may take one look and say, 'You don't need crutches; you'll be better off using a cane right away or just walking on your walking cast without any support.'

Performance responsibility rests with the whole team. Each nurse as leader draws on the resources of the whole organization as needed. At one stage she brings in X-ray technicians, at another, physical therapists, at another stage, medical laboratory technicians, and so on. The composition of the team may be different for every patient, but the team leader who carries primary responsibility will also tend to work again and again with the same three or four people in each functional area.

## The requirements of team design

Team design requires a continuing mission in which the specific tasks change frequently. If there is no continuing mission, there might be a temporary task force, but not an organization based on the team as a permanent design. If the tasks do not change, there is no need for team organization and no point to it.

A team needs a clear and sharply defined objective. It must be possible all the time to feed back from the objectives to the work and performance of the whole team and of each member.

A task force needs leadership. It can be a permanent leader – physician and nurse on the patient-care team in the hospital, or the recognized head of a top-management team. Or leadership can shift with each major phase. But if it does, one person must be clearly designated to decide, at a given stage, who takes team leadership for a particular phase of the task. This is not leadership responsibility for making the decision and giving the command. It is leadership responsibility for deciding who among the team members has the decision and command authority for a particular phase. A team is therefore not 'democratic'. It emphasizes authority. But the authority is task-derived and task-focused.

The team as a whole is always responsible for the task. The in-

dividual members contribute their particular skills and knowledge. But every individual is always responsible for the output
and performance of the entire team rather than only for his or
her own work. The team is the unit.

Team members need not know each other well to perform as a
team. But they do need to know each other's function and potential contribution. 'Rapport', 'empathy', 'interpersonal relations'
are not needed. Mutual understanding of each other's job and
common understanding of the common task are essential.

It is therefore the team leader's first job to establish clarity:
clarity of objectives and clarity with respect to everybody's role
including the leader's own.

## The strengths and limitations of the team principles

The team has obvious strengths. Everybody always knows the
work of the whole and holds himself or herself responsible for it.
It is highly receptive to new ideas and new ways of doing things.
And it has great adaptability.

It also has great shortcomings. It has clarity only if the team
leader creates it. It has poor stability. Its economy is low; a
team demands continuing attention to its management, to the
relationships of people within the task force, to assigning people
to jobs, to explanation, deliberation, communication, and so on.
Much of the energy of the members goes into keeping things running. Although each person on the team understands the common task, he does not always understand his own specific task.
He may be so interested in what others are doing that he pays inadequate attention to his own assignment.

Teams are adaptable. They are receptive to new ideas and to
new ways of doing things. They are the best means available for
overcoming functional isolation and narrow interest. All career
professionals should serve on a few teams during their working
life.

Still, teams do only a little better than straight functional organization in preparing people for higher management responsibilities or in testing them in performance. A team makes neither

for clear communications nor for clear decision-making. The whole group must work constantly on explaining both to itself and to managers throughout the rest of the organization what it is trying to do, what it is working on and what it has accomplished. The team must constantly make sure that the decisions that need to be made are brought into the open. There is a real danger otherwise that teams will make decisions they should not make – decisions, for instance, that irreversibly commit the whole company.

Teams fail – and the failure rate has been high – primarily because they do not impose on themselves the self-discipline and responsibility required because of their high degree of freedom. No task force can be 'permissive' and function.

But the greatest limitation of the team structure is size. Teams work best when there are few members. The hunting band had seven to fifteen members. So do the teams in team sports such as football, baseball and cricket. If a team gets much larger it becomes unwieldy. Its strengths, such as flexibility and the sense of responsibility of the members diminishes. Its limitations – lack of clarity, communication problems, overconcern with its internal relationships – become crippling weaknesses.

## The scope of team organization

Its size limitation determines the scope of applicability of the team principle of organization.

It is the best available design principle for top-management work. Indeed (as will be discussed in Chapter 38) it is probably the *only* appropriate design principle for top management. The team is also the preferred design principle for innovative work (see Chapter 37).

But for most operating work the team is not appropriate *by itself and alone* as the design principle of organization. It is a complement – though a badly needed one – to functional design. It may well be that it is team organization that will make the functional principle fully effective and will enable it to do what its designers had hoped for.

## Team design and knowledge organization

The area where team design as a complement to functional organization is likely to make the greatest contribution is in knowledge work. The knowledge organization is likely to balance 'function' as a person's 'home' with 'team' as his or her 'place of work' (The technical term for this is 'matrix organization').

Knowledge work by definition is specialized work. The shift from middle management to knowledge organization therefore brings a host of specialists into the management group as operating people. The traditional pattern of functions is being replaced by an enormous number of new functions. Of course many of them can, and should, be grouped together. Still, while the tax specialist will often be put together with other 'financial' people, either in accounting or in the treasurer's department, tax work is different and separate. This also applies to product managers or market managers, who are related alike to the traditional marketing function, the traditional research and development function, and the traditional manufacturing function.

This requires better functional management. The organization must decide what specialties are needed or it will drown in useless learning. It must think through what the key activities are in which specialized knowledge is needed, and it must make sure that knowledge work in the key areas is provided for in depth and with excellence. Knowledge work in other areas must either not be done at all or must be kept in low key.

A specialty must be managed to assure that it makes the management contribution to the enterprise for the sake of which it has been established. Management must anticipate today the new specialties that will be needed tomorrow and the new demands that will be made tomorrow on existing specialties. There is need, in other words, for functional concern with what in Chapter 25 I called *management development*.

There is great need for concern with, and for management of, the specialists themselves. Do they work on the truly important things, or do they fritter away their time? Do they do over again what they already know how to do, or do they work on creating new potential and new performance capacity? Are they being used productively, or are they just being kept busy? Are they developing both as professionals and as persons?

These are crucial questions that cannot be answered by checking how many hours a person works. They require knowledge of the functional area and genuine functional management.

Much knowledge work will undoubtedly be organized on a strictly functional basis. Much will also be done by individuals who, in effect, are an 'organizational component' by themselves.

An increasing number of knowledge workers, however, will have a functional home but do their work in a team with other knowledge workers from other functions and disciplines. The more advanced knowledge is, the more specialized it has to be. And specialized knowledge is a fragment, if not mere 'data'. It becomes effective only as input to other people's decisions, other people's work, other people's understanding. It becomes 'results' only in a team.

Knowledge organization will therefore increasingly have two aspects: a functional one, managing the individual and his or her knowledge; and another one, the team, managing work and task. Seen one way, this undermines the functional principle and destroys it. Seen another way, it saves the functional principle and makes it fully effective. It certainly requires strong, professional, effective, functional managers and functional components.

The team is clearly not a cure-all. It is a difficult structure requiring great self-discipline. It has severe limitations and major weaknesses.

But it is also not, as many managers still believe, only a temporary measure for dealing with nonrecurring 'special problems'. It is a genuine design principle of organization. It is the best principle for such *permanent* organizing tasks as top-management work and innovating work. And it is an important and perhaps essential complement to functional structure – in mass-production work, whether manual or clerical, and above all, in knowledge work. It is probably the key to making functional skill fully effective in the knowledge organization through the matrix organization of which a functional skill-oriented component is one axis and the task-oriented team the other axis.

## Summary

There are available to us now FIVE different design principles. Each satisfies some of the design specifications but none satisfies all of them. Each of the design principles has strengths, limitations, and rigorous requirements for effectiveness. And each expresses a different design logic. The first two design principles, functional organization and team organization, are organized around the logic of work and task. Though often seen as in conflict, they are largely complementary, especially for knowledge work, which is increasingly being organized in matrix organizations using both, functional and team design.

# 36 Result- and Relation-Focused Design

## Federal decentralization

In *federal decentralization* a company is organized in a number of self-governing businesses. Each unit is responsible for its own performance, its own results, and its own contribution to the total company. Each unit has its own management which, in effect, runs its own 'autonomous business'.

Federal decentralization assumes that the activities *within* an autonomous business are organized on the functional principle – though, of course, the use of teams is not excluded. The autonomous businesses of a decentralized structure are designed to be small enough to put the strengths of a functional structure to work while neutralizing its weaknesses.

But the starting point of decentralization is different. Functional and team organization start with work and task. They assume that the results are the sum total of the efforts. 'If only efforts are organized properly, the right results will follow' is the underlying premise. Decentralization, by contrast, starts out with the question 'What results do we aim for ?' It tries to set up the right business first, that is, the unit that will have the best capacity for results and especially for results in the marketplace. Then the question is asked 'What work, what efforts, what key activities have to be set up and organized *within* the autonomous business ?'

It is desirable to set up the same, or at least a similar, functiona structure for all the autonomous businesses within a company All Sears stores, regardless of size or location, have, for instance, a store controller, an operations manager, and department heads for major merchandise areas. All GM manufacturing divisions have the same seven key functions : engineering, manufacturing, master-mechanic, purchasing, marketing, accounting, and personnel, with the head of each reporting directly to the division's general manager.

But care should be taken lest this desirable similarity becomes stifling uniformity.

The General Electric reorganization of 1950–52 provides an example of what not to do. GE decided that the 'typical manufacturing business' has five key functions : engineering, manufacturing, marketing, accounting and personnel. That this did not fit nonmanufacturing businesses such as the General Electric Credit Corporation, everyone saw, of course. But two things were not seen – and the result was considerable damage. First, some manufacturing businesses needed additional and different key functions, or at least they needed a different arrangement of the same functional work. For example, in the computer business, product development and customer service are far too important to be subordinated to engineering and marketing. GE's failure in the computer business had many causes, but imposing the functional structure of a typical manufacturing business was a major factor. Second, some businesses that looked like manufacturing businesses were really innovative businesses. These units were genuine businesses and result centres, but they had no 'product'; they were set up to develop one. They had no 'market', but a research and development contract, usually from the US government. They did not 'manufacture'; at most they had a model shop to build a few prototypes. Yet the functions of a typical manufacturing business were imposed on them. Some of these innovative development businesses managed to survive by quiet sabotage of the official structure. Others were seriously damaged – by having to carry a heavy load of functions they did not need and, above all, by misdirection of vision and efforts.

## The strength of federal decentralization

Of all design principles available so far, federal decentralization comes closest to satisfying all the design specifications listed in Chapter 35. It also has the widest scope. Both operating work and innovative work can be organized as decentralized autonomous businesses. And while top management obviously cannot be set up as an autonomous business, federal decentralization of the business, if done properly, makes for strong and effective top managements. It frees top management for the top-management tasks.

Federal decentralization has great *clarity* and considerable *economy*. It makes it easy for all members of the autonomous business to *understand their own tasks* and to understand *the task of the whole business*. It has high *stability* and is yet *adaptable*.

It focuses the *vision* and efforts of managers directly on business performance and results. The danger of self-deception, of concentrating on the familiar but old and tired rather than on the difficult but new and growing, or of allowing unprofitable lines to be carried on the backs of the profitable ones, is much lessened. Reality is not easily obscured by overhead costs. It is not hidden somewhere in the figures for total sales.

With respect to *communications* and *decisions*, the federal organization is the only satisfactory design principle we have. Since the entire management group, or at least the upper ranks within it, share a common vision and a common perception, they tend to communicate easily. And usually, for that reason, communication between people in different kinds of work is encouraged all the way down the line rather than frowned upon. Decision-making is also likely to be placed at the proper level without great effort. The focus tends to be on the right rather than the wrong issue, and on the important rather than the trivial decision.

The greatest strength of the federal principle lies, however, in *manager development*. Of all known principles of organization, it alone prepares and tests people for top-management responsibility at an early stage. This by itself makes it the principle to be used in preference to any other.

In a federally organized structure, the managers are close enough to business performance and business results to focus on them. They are close enough to results to get immediate feedback from business performance on their own tasks and work. Because *management by objective and self-control* becomes effective, the number of people or units under one manager no longer is limited by the span of control; it is limited only by the much wider span of managerial responsibility.

Above all, the general managers of the decentralized businesses are truly top management, if only in a small business. They face most of the challenges of the top-management job in an independent company – the one exception being, as a rule, the responsibility for financial resources and their supply. They have to make decisions. They have to build a team. They have to think about markets and processes, people and money, today and tomorrow. As a result, they are being tested in an autonomous command. Yet they are being tested fairly early in their career, and at a reasonably low level. A mistake can, therefore, be unmade without too much damage to the company, and, equally important, without too much damage to the person. No other known principle of organization, whether in business or in any other institution, satisfies the need to *prepare* and *test* people for tomorrow's leadership positions nearly as well as the federal principle does.

The search for a system that will prepare and test tomorrow's leaders is the oldest problem of political theory and political practice. No political system has ever solved it adequately. The principle of federal decentralization does not solve it fully. The autonomous manager of a decentralized business is still not faced with the full responsibility, let alone with the full loneliness, of the top position. But the federal principle comes closer to a solution than any other known design.

## The requirements of federal decentralization

Federal decentralization has strict requirements. It also makes very substantial demands for responsibility and self-discipline.

Decentralization must not create a weak centre. On the contrary, one of the main purposes of federal organization is to *strengthen* top management and to make it capable of doing its own work rather than being forced to supervise, coordinate, and prop up operating work. Federal decentralization works only if the top-management job is clearly defined and thought through.

The test of effective federal decentralization is top-management strength. Top management in a decentralized company must first accept its responsibility for thinking through 'what our business is and what it should be'. It must accept the responsibility for setting the objectives for the entire company and for working out the strategies for obtaining these objectives. It must, in other words, accept the responsibility for its own job. A federal structure is a shambles if top management does not live up to the responsibilities of its own tasks.

Top management must think through carefully what decisions it reserves for itself. There are decisions that have to do with the entire company, its integrity, and its future. But there are also decisions that should be made on the basis of what is good for an individual autonomous business. To distinguish between the two, and to make each kind of decision correctly, requires somebody who sees the whole and is responsible for the whole.

At General Electric, for instance, only corporate top management can make the decision to abandon a business or go into a new one. At General Motors, top management at the central office sets the price ranges within which each automobile division's products have to fall. It thus controls the competition between the major units of the company. At Sears, Chicago headquarters decides what kinds of goods – hard goods, appliances, fashion goods and so forth – each store must carry.

Specifically, there must be *three reserved areas* if the business is to remain a whole rather than splinter into fragments. Top management, and top management alone, can decide what technologies, markets and products to go into, what businesses to start and what businesses to abandon, and also what the basic values, beliefs and principles of the company are.

Second, top management must reserve control of the allocation of the key resource of capital. Both the supply of capital and its investment are top-management responsibilities which cannot be turned over to the autonomous units of a federal organization.

The other key resource is people. The people in a federally organized company, and especially managers and key professionals, are a resource of the entire company rather than of any one unit. The company's policies with respect to people and decisions on key appointments in the decentralized autonomous business are thus the third area for top-management decisions – though of course, autonomous businesses managers need to take an active part in them. And a decentralized company must have a strong, respected, and senior executive in top management who is the company's conscience with respect to people.

Federal decentralization requires centralized controls and common measurements. Whenever a federal organization gets in trouble, the reason is always that the measurements at the disposal of the centre are not good enough. As a result personal supervision has to be substituted. Both the managers of the autonomous businesses and top management must know what is expected of each business, what is meant by 'performance', and what developments are important. To give autonomy one must have confidence. And this requires controls that make 'opinions' unnecessary. To manage by objectives one must know whether goals are being reached or not, and this requires clear and reliable measurements.

A federal structure requires common vision. A federal unit of a company is autonomous, but it is not independent and should not be. Its autonomy is a means towards better performance for the entire company. Its managers should regard themselves all the more as members of the greater community, the whole enterprise, for being given broad local autonomy.

## Size requirements

Federal decentralization was designed in response to a problem of size: the deterioration that begins in functional structures when they reach more than medium size. But federal decentralization also has size requirements. When the federal unit becomes so big that the functional subunits are too large to function well, the whole autonomous busines becomes unwieldy, sluggish and too big to perform. The 'brain', that is, the top management of the autonomous unit, may still perform. But the 'members', the functional components, turn rigid and bureaucratic and will increasingly serve themselves rather than the common purpose.

Du Pont has counteracted this in part by splitting autonomous businesses in two as they grow bigger and in part by setting up small autonomous decentralized businesses within large autonomous decentralized businesses. Another approach is that of Johnson & Johnson, the very large, multinational producer of health-care products ranging from absorbent cotton to birth-control pills. J & J for many years tried to limit the size of each business to 250 employees. Each business was run as a separate company with its own complete management and its own board of directors, and each reported directly to a small, central parent-company top-management team. While J & J, with worldwide sales of over a billion dollars and 40,000 employees, has been forced to accept individual businesses a good deal larger than 250 employees, it still limits the size of each business and will split it rather than permit it to grow large. As a result, functional units are still quite small in every J & J business.

But breaking up or subdividing autonomous businesses as they grow to large size is not always possible; or at least it is not always done. And the result is then the emergence of 'functional empires'.

The Chevrolet division of General Motors, for instance, has grown so large that it would by itself be the world's third or fourth largest manufacturing company if it were independent. It is a decentralized autonomous product business. But internally it is organized by function and is highly centralized. GM tries to counteract the resulting insulation of the huge functional units by frequently moving functional managers from Chevrolet into the other, smaller automotive divisions and moving functional managers from other divisions into Chevrolet. A good many GM executives, especially the younger ones, apparently believe that Chevrolet should long ago have been split up into a number of separate divisions, one, for instance, in charge of the large truck business; another one, perhaps, in charge of the smaller cars such as 'compacts' and 'subcompacts', with the original Chevrolet division confined to 'standard-sized' passenger automobiles.

## How small is too small?

But the decentralized autonomous unit also needs to be big enough to support the management it needs.

How small is too small depends on the business. A Sears store, or a Marks & Spencer store, can be quite small and yet support adequate management. All a small store needs is one manager and a few department heads who actually manage on the selling floor.

In other industries, the mass-production metalworking industry, for example, there is a minimum size. A metal-working business is rarely capable of supporting adequate management and its own engineering, manufacturing, and marketing work unless it sells twenty to thirty million dollars' worth of merchandise a year. Businesses with a significantly lower sales volume are likely to be understaffed, or staffed with inadequate people.

The decisive criterion is not size but the scope and challenge of the management job. A federal unit should always have enough scope so that a good manager can show his or her ability. It should have enough challenge so that the management group in the unit truly has to manage: that is, to think through objectives and plans, to build human resources into an effective team, to integrate the work, and to measure its performance. It should have enough challenge so that management will have to work on all major phases of a business, but also enough challenge that it can really develop a market, a product or service – and, above all, can truly develop people. The true criterion of size for an autonomous business unit is not economics. It is managerial scope and challenge, and managerial performance.

A decentralized organization needs effective 'conscience' work. It needs, especially if large and diversified, organized thinking and planning for top management. It needs strong central information and unified controls and measurements. It will have some common operating work, such as the supply and management of money, research, legal counsel, relations with the public, organized labour, and government, and perhaps purchasing. It may have to organize company-wide work on innovation in key activities whether marketing or managing people.

But the autonomous businesses of a decentralized organization should not have to depend on central service staffs, that is, on advisory and teaching activities operating out of headquarters. The decentralized operating units should be strong enough to stand on their own feet. Dependence on central staff services can only impose on a decentralized organization the weaknesses and vulnerabilities, without giving it the benefits and strengths, of functional design.

## What is a 'business'?

Federal decentralization is applicable only where a company can truly be organized into a number of genuine 'businesses'. This is its basic limitation.

But what is a 'business'? Ideally, of course, a federal unit should be a complete business in its own right.

This idea underlay Alfred P. Sloan, Jr's, organization of General Motors in the early 1920s. Each of the automotive divisions did its own design, its own engineering, its own manufacturing, its own marketing and its own sales. The divisions were limited as to the price range in which they could offer automobiles but were autonomous otherwise. GM's accessory divisions sold a large share of their output to the automotive divisions of their own company. But they were selling an even larger share directly to the outside market and indeed, very often, to General Motor's own competitors. They too were 'businesses' in every sense of the word. So are the autonomous companies into which Johnson & Johnson is organized. Each has its own product lines, its own research and development, its own markets and marketing.

But how much of the reality of a genuine business does there have to be for federal decentralization to work effectively? As a minimum the unit must contribute a profit to the company. Its profit or loss should directly become company profit or loss. In fact, the company's total profit should be the sum total of the profits of the individual businesses.

Perhaps even more important – and the real mark of autonomy – is that the federal unit must have a market of its own. The market may be only a geographic entity – as in the Sears or the Marks & Spencer stores, or in the case of the 'regional companies' into which several large American life insurance companies have divided themselves. But still there has to be a distinct market within which the unit is, so to speak, *the* company.

As long as a business can have full market responsibility and objective comparability of results, it can be an autonomous business even though it obtains its products from another autonomous unit or from a centralized company-run manufacturing source.

Neither the Sears stores nor the Marks & Spencer stores are true 'businesses'. They do not do their own buying, do not even decide what merchandise to carry and prices to charge. Yet in its geographic area each store stands on its own. And because all Sears or Marks & Spencer stores get the same merchandise at the same cost from the same central buying office, they can be compared to one another. Within the system, the Sears store manager is autonomous and can be measured by performance and results.

Where, however, no market test exists, we should not speak of an autonomous business. Federal decentralization then does not work.

So far we have been discussing federal decentralization of operating work, that is, of existing and known businesses. A decentralized unit for innovative work is structured and measured differently (see Chapter 37). But federal decentralization is also the most effective design principle for such work – as long as its performance and results can be objectively measured. A decentralized innovative unit also has to be a business – or must be capable of becoming one.

## Simulated decentralization

Whenever a unit can be set up as a business, no design principle can match federal decentralization. We have learned, however, that a great many large companies cannot be divided into genuine businesses. Yet they have clearly outgrown the limits of size and complexity of the functional or of the team structure.

These are the companies that are increasingly turning to 'simulated decentralization' as the answer to their organization problem.

Simulated decentralization forms units which are not businesses but which are still set up as if they were businesses, with as much autonomy as possible, with their own management, and with at least a 'simulation' of profit and loss responsibility. They buy from and sell to each other using 'transfer prices' determined internally rather than by an outside market. Or their 'profits' are arrived at by internal allocation of costs to which then, often, a 'standard fee' such as 20 per cent of costs, is added. Simulated decentralization is the one available design principle that copes with the structural problems of the big materials business, such as the chemical, steel, glass, and oil industries, in which all products come from a common source and out of a common process, but in which there are many different markets for each product.

Many chemical manufacturers have organized their business in three sets of units, each based on simulated decentralization. A research and development corporation is set up and organized by major fields of study and inquiry. Some companies, such as Monsanto, have set up separate marketing components and separate manufacturing components, both with profit and loss responsibility.

Simulated decentralization is equally applicable in single-product companies of similar size and complexity. IBM may be the leading example.

IBM, by and large, has one main product: computers. Only one of the markets can be split off as autonomous, the government and defence market. The bulk of IBM's business, 80 per cent or so, supplies one product to one market: computers to business. Yet the computer business, with its billions of dollars of sales and its great complexity is much too big to be organized by functions. Accordingly, IBM has split its computer business into two key units, each considered autonomous, on the basis of simulated decentralization. Marketing and services is one such business, and development and manufacturing is the other. Each unit is considered a profit and loss centre.

The most interesting attempts to apply simulated decentralization to very large businesses which cannot apply federal decentralization were the reorganizations of major New York commercial banks in the 1960s.

Both the First National City Bank (Citibank) and the Chase Manhattan Bank, respectively New York's first and second banks in deposits, have reorganized themselves into simulated decentralized structures. Citibank split itself into six autonomous units, each headed by a 'president': retail (dealing with the individual depositor and borrower), commercial (small and medium-sized businesses), corporate (large businesses), international, multinational, and fiduciary services such as investment management. Each unit has its own objectives, its own plans and its own profit and loss statements. The Chase organization, though developed independently, is roughly similar.

These bank examples show clearly some of the major problems of simulated decentralization. In both banks it is the large branch, such as the Rockefeller Center branch of each bank, or the branch in London, that is the geographic focus of the bank's business. Sometimes the branch acts merely as the landlord and facilties manager for the representatives of each of the six 'autonomous banks' that occupy space in the branch. Sometimes the branch is the 'banker'. At different times it is both. Clearly, the large branch is also itself a 'business' and a profit and loss centre. And who coordinates the different 'banks' and focuses them on the individual customer who often is a 'retail', a 'commercial', a 'fiduciary', and even a 'corporate' customer all at once? The head of a small fashion design business, for instance, will use the bank that finances her firm for her personal banking business and for her savings account. She will expect it to act as executor of her will, to be the manager for her investments and the trustee for her firm's pension fund. She does not want to deal with four different banks. Whose customer is she, and who gets the credit for her business?

Simulated decentralization is obviously difficult and full of problems. Yet it will be used even more in the future, because simulated decentralization is potentially most useful in the growth areas of economy and society, process industries and private and governmental service institutions. In these sectors neither functional organization nor federal decentralization can do the organizing job. Managers therefore need to understand the requirements and limitations of simulated decentralization. What problems can be expected in an organization built on it?

## The problems of simulated decentralization

Simulated decentralization is a poor 'fit' with respect to *all* design specifications. It is not clear. It does not make for an easy focus on performance. It rarely satisfies the specification that everyone should be able to know his or her own task. Nor do managers and professionals necessarily understand the job of the whole.

Least satisfactory in simulated decentralization are *economy*, *communications,* and *decision authority.* These weaknesses are unavoidable features of the design. Because the unit of simulated decentralization is not truly a business, its results are not truly determined by market performance. They are largely the results of internal management decisions. They are decisions on 'transfer prices' and 'cost allocations'.

*Communications* therefore are likely to suffer as a result. A tremendous amount of managerial time and energy will be spent working out the lines between different units that supposedly are autonomous; making sure that they cooperate; mediating between them. The smallest adjustment becomes a top-management decision, a trial of strength, and a matter of honour and sacred principle.

Simulated decentralization makes high human demands: on self-discipline, on mutual toleration, on subordinating one's own interest, including the interest in one's own compensation, to arbitration by higher authority; demands to be a 'good sport' and a 'cheerful loser'. These demands are far more difficult and, above all, far more divisive than the big demands that federal decentralization makes on people.

I once heard a candidate for a very senior position in a big bank turned down because his unit was doing too well at the bank's expense. 'He puts the performance of his own unit before everything else.' The next man was turned down because 'he is too willing to subordinate the performance of his unit to the needs and requirements of other units and, therefore, does not show a good enough performance'. Everyone admitted to confusion when I asked, 'Are they any guidelines for behaviour? Is there any way in which you can tell a man ahead of time what you consider "excessive cooperation"?' All admitted that this was the greatest worry of their own subordinates. 'You have to play it by ear,' the ranking officer finally concluded. But then he stopped himself and added, 'But by whose ear?'

In *scope,* simulated decentralization is limited to operating work. It clearly has no applicability to top-management work. And if innovative work cannot be set up as a federal decentralized unit, it requires either functional or team structure.

## Rules for using simulated decentralization

Simulated decentralization is a *last resort* only. As long as a functional structure – with or without teams added – works, that is, as long as a business is small or fair-sized, simulated decentralization is to be shunned. And beyond such size, federal decentralization is vastly preferable.

Even in the materials company, federal decentralization might be tried first – though it may not work forever. One example of an adaptation of genuine federal decentralization to a materials business is Owens-Illinois in Toledo, Ohio, a very large manufacturer of glass bottles. After World War II, when plastic bottles came into wide use, Owens-Illinois went into plastics to retain its leadership position in the bottle market. The company decided, after long soul-searching, to set up both the glass-bottle business and the plastic-bottle business as separate autonomous 'product' businesses, competing with each other for the same customers and in the same markets.

The Owens-Illinois strategy was a brilliant success. The company's growth was very rapid. And yet, fifteen years later, in the early 1970s, Owens-Illinois changed over to simulated decentralization. It retained the two divisions but confined them to manufacturing. Marketing of all bottles, glass and plastic, was put into a new marketing division. The reason given was that the customers demanded one source of supply for all their bottles. 'Glass' and 'plastics' are not meaningful to them; they want bottles and not materials.

With all its limitations, weaknesses and risks, simulated decentralization may therefore be the best available principle where constituent parts of the same large business have to work together and yet have to have individual responsibility. This applies especially where the organizing principle of the market is incompatible with that of technology and production.

A railroad or an airline has by definition no purely 'local' business. Hence, these businesses cannot be federally decentralized but have to organize themselves according to functions with, at best, a regional coordinator who intervenes between the functions, mediates and insures liaison. The decisions that affect performance of a transportation system must be made centrally. They are, above all, decisions on capital use, on the assignment of airplanes, locomotives, and freight cars, for instance. Yet transportation businesses, while incapable of being decentralized except for relatively unimportant tasks, are also clearly far too large to work well under functional organization.

This means, in effect, that there are businesses and service institutions for which we do not possess an adequate principle of organization.

In simulated decentralization, at least we know what to expect. It is therefore a major task of organization theory and organization practice to develop for these large, overcentralized functional structures, such as a railroad system or most government agencies, an organization design that works no worse for them than simulated decentralization works, for instance, for the large materials companies and the large commercial banks. This will probably have to be some application of the principle of simulated decentralization.

## The systems structure

Of the design principles of organization, only one, Fayol's functions, can be said to have started in a theoretical analysis. The others – the team, federal decentralization, and simulated decentralization – developed as responses to specific challenges and needs of the moment. This is true also of the systems structure visible as a principle of organization design, it has existed for a unique management problem: that of the American space effort in the 1960s.

Systems organization is an extension of the team design principle. But instead of a team consisting of individuals, the systems organization builds the team out of a wide variety of different organizations. They may be government agencies, private businesses, universities and individual researchers, and organizations inside and outside the parent organization. Systems design uses *all* the other design principles as the task demands: functional organizations and teams, federal and simulated decentralization.

Some of the members of the systems structure may have a specific task that does not change throughout the entire life of the venture. Others may change tasks according to the stage of the programme. Some will be permanent members. Others may be brought in only for one specific assignment.

Although the National Aeronautics and Space Administration (NASA), in its organization of the US space programme in the 1960s, first made the systems structure visible as a principle of organization design, it has existed for at least a century. It actually was first developed as a structure for businesses; and its major future application is probably in business. The large Japanese company and its suppliers and distributors have for decades worked in a relationship very similar to that in which NASA worked with its suppliers, subcontractors, and partners. The Japanese large company sometimes owns its suppliers. More often it has little or no ownership stake in them. Yet the suppliers are integrated into the 'system'. Similarly, the Japanese company usually depends upon a trading company that is both independent and integrated. The relationships among the large companies that constitute one industrial group are also comparable to the relationships which NASA developed for its own needs.

The systems structure may prove to be especially important in large multinational corporations. One example is the structure the Chase Manhattan Bank has developed for its worldwide banking system. Unlike the traditional approach, Chase decided not to rely on wholly-owned branches abroad. Instead, it has been expanding worldwide through acquiring minority interests in well-established, medium-sized, local banks. These banks are not owned or controlled by the Chase. Nor is the top management usually furnished by the Chase. But they are part of the 'Chase system'. They are integrated into the worldwide banking facilities and services of the bank while, at the same time, they keep strong local roots in their own community. They are both independent and integrated.

What organizations that use the systems structure have in

common is a need to integrate diversity of culture, values, and skills into unity of action. Each component of the system has to work in its own way, be effective according to its own logic and according to its own standards. Or else it will not be effective at all. Yet all components have to work towards a common goal. Each has to accept, understand, and carry out its own role. This can be achieved only by direct, flexible and tailor-made relationships among people or groups of people in which personal bond and mutual trust bridge wide differences in point of view, and in what is considered 'proper' and 'appropriate'.

NASA, for instance, faced the problem of the divergent values and cultures. NASA is a large government agency, but it was built of some major units staffed with men used to the ways of US military services, while others were built and run by German-born and German-trained space scientists like Wernher von Braun, raised in the tradition of the German *Herr Professor*. Businesses, some large (Pan American Airways for example), some small, were 'partners' on the 'team' rather than 'subcontractors'. They did not make and deliver a part to preset specifications but planned, designed, and operated the 'nervous systems' of the entire space effort. Other 'team members' were individual university scientists working independently in their own laboratories. Yet NASA had to integrate all these different traditions, values, and behaviour patterns into common performance.

### The difficulties and problems of the systems structures

Like simulated decentralization, systems design is a poor 'fit' with respect to all design specifications. It lacks *clarity*. It lacks *stability*. People neither find it easy to know what *their job* is, nor to understand the *job of the whole* and their relationship to it. *Communications* are a continuing problem. It is never clear where a certain decision should be made, nor indeed what the basic decisions are. *Flexibility* is great, and receptivity to *new ideas* is almost too great. Yet the structure does not, as a rule *develop people* and test them for top-management positions. Above all, the systems structure violates the principle of internal *economy*.

When NASA first started, the scientists who then dominated it believed that controls, especially computer-based information, would run the system. Their thinking soon changed as they learned the crucial importance of face-to-face personal relationships, of constant meetings and of bringing people into the decision-making process, even on matters remote from their own assignments. Key executives at NASA spent about two-thirds of their time in meetings, and mostly in meetings on matters not directly related to their own tasks.

Personal relationships are the only thing that prevents breakdown in the systems structure. There is constant need for arbitration of conflicts between various members of the system, on jurisdiction, on direction, on budgets, on people, and on priorities. The most important people, regardless of their job descriptions or assigned tasks, spend most of their time keeping the machinery running. In no other organizational structure is the ratio between output and effort needed for internal cohesion as poor as in the systems structure.

At the same time, the requirements for the systems structure to work at all are exceedingly stringent. It demands absolute clarity of objectives. The objectives themselves may well change, but at any one time they must be clear. The objective for the work of each of the members of the system must be derived from the objective of the whole and must be directly related to it. In other words, the systems structure can function only if the job of thinking through 'what is our business and what should it be' is taken seriously and performed with excellence. And then it requires that *operational* objectives and strategy be developed with great care from the basic mission and purpose. 'Get a man on the moon by 1970' is exactly the kind of clear objective that enables a systems structure to work.

Another requirement is a demand for universal communications responsibility. Every member of the systems structure, but especially every member of every one of the managing groups, has to make sure that mission, objective and strategies are fully understood by everyone, and that the doubts, questions and ideas of every member are heard, listened to, respected, thought through, understood and resolved. In projects like the NASA space effort the communications problem is enormous, involving the need to spread word of any problem, breakthrough or discovery immediately to hundreds of people.

A third requirement is that each member of the team, that is, each managerial unit, take responsibility far beyond its own assignment. Each member must, in effect, take top-management responsibility. To get any results requires, from each member, independent responsibility and initiative. At the same time, each member must try to know what goes on throughout the entire system and to keep the common goal in mind. Executives especially must always see their own assignments clearly in the perspective of the whole project.

No wonder that the systems structure has not, on the whole, been an unqualified success. For every NASA with a successful moon shot (but also with an almost unlimited budget to support it) dozens of systems structures have failed miserably to perform or have done so only through budgetary irresponsibility such as no private business could survive, as in the development of the Anglo-French supersonic plane, the Concorde, for example, and of various weapons systems in Europe as well as in the US. The attempt to use systems management to tackle major social problems – the much-touted promise of the sixties – is almost certain to be a total failure. Social and political complexities that are encountered whenever we move from outer space (where, after all, there are no voters) into the inner city and its problems, into economic development, or even into something seemingly so purely technical as mass transit, are almost certain to overwhelm the fragile cohesion of a systems structure.

But NASA's success and the success of systems-organized enterprises in Japan shows that the system structure can be made to work and can be highly effective. It needs, however, clear goals, high self-discipline throughout the structure and a top management that takes personal responsibility for relationships and communications.

For most managers, the systems structure is not of direct personal concern – though any manager in a multinational business who wants to function effectively will have to learn to understand it. The systems structure will never be a preferred form of organization; it is fiendishly difficult. But it is an important structure, and one that the organization designer needs to know and needs to understand – if only to know that it should not be used where other, simpler and easier structures will do the job.

## Summary

Both kinds of decentralization – federal decentralization and simulated decentralization – are organized around results. The systems structure is organized around relationships. Of all known design principles, federal decentralization comes closest to satisfying organization specifications. But it is severely limited in its applicability and has stringent requirements that must be met if it is to function. Otherwise we have to apply simulated decentralization – complex, unwieldy, difficult and far from satisfactory, but the only design principle we know for the organization of materials businesses, service businesses such as the very big banks, or government agencies. The systems structure is even more complex and difficult, but necessary to organize such multicultural enterprises as the American space programme under NASA or the multinational company.

# 37 The Innovative Organization

The need to innovate is mentioned – indeed emphasized – in every book on management. But beyond this the books, as a rule, have little to say about what management and organization need to be and need to do to stimulate, to direct, and to make effective innovation. Most discussions stress the administrative function of management, that is, the task of keeping going and of improving what is already known and what is already largely being done. Little thought is usually devoted to effectively and purposefully creating the new and different.

In neglecting the management of innovation, the books mirror business reality. Every management stresses the need to innovate. But few organize innovation as a distinct and major task. To be sure, since World War II, 'research' has become fashionable. Large sums of money are spent on it. But in many companies the outcome has been improvement rather than innovation.

This is even truer of the public-service institutions.

There were good reasons in the past for the focus on the administrative function to the neglect of innovation. When management first became a concern, in the early years of this century, the great need was to learn how to organize, structure, and direct the large-scale human organization that was suddenly coming into being. Innovation, insofar as it received attention, was seen as a separate job, a job done by an individual working alone, by the 'inventor' of the nineteenth century. Or it was seen as a predominantly technical job, that of research.

Moreover, there was little scope for genuine innovation in the years from 1920 to 1950 when most of the basic work on management was being done. For contrary to common belief, these were not years of rapid change, either in technology or in society. They were years in which, by and large, technology built on foundations that had been laid before World War I. While they were years of tremendous political turbulence, social and economic institutions were stagnant.

Now, however, we may be entering a period of rapid change more comparable in its basic features to the closing decades of the nineteenth century than to the immediate past with which we are familiar. In the late nineteenth century, as we need to remind ourselves, a major new invention, leading almost immediately to the emergence of a major new industry, surfaced every few months on average. This period began in 1856, the year that saw the invention of both the electric motor and synthetic dye. It ended with the development of the modern electronic tube in 1911. In between came typewriter and automobile, electric light bulb, man-made fibres, tractors, streetcars, synthetic drugs, telephone, radio, and airplane – to mention only a few. In between, in other words, came the modern world.

By contrast, no truly new major industry was started after 1914 until the late 1950s, when computers first became operational.

Between 1870 and 1914 the industrial geography of the world was in rapid change. A new major industrial area emerged on average every decade or so: the US and Germany between 1860 and 1870, western Russia and Japan during the next twenty years, Central Europe by 1900. Between World War I and World War II, however, no major new industrial areas joined the 'industrial club'.

Now, however, there are signs of rapid change, with Brazil and China, for instance, approaching 'the takeoff point'.

But the need for innovation will be equally great in the social field. And the public-service institutions too will have to learn how to manage innovation.

The need for social and political innovation is now also becoming urgent. Modern cities need new governmental forms. The relationship between human beings and their environment has to be thought through and restructured. No modern government governs effectively any more. The crisis of the world is, above all, an institutional crisis demanding institutional innovation.

The business enterprise, its structure and organization, the way in which it integrates knowledge into work and work into performance – and the way in which it integrates enterprise with society and government – are also areas of major innovative need and opportunity.

From now on, therefore, innovation will have to be built into existing organizations. Large businesses and large public-service institutions will have to become increasingly capable of organizing themselves for innovation as well as for administration.

These organizations have access to manpower and capital undreamed of a hundred years ago. But the ratio between the cost of invention or research and the cost of converting invention into new products has also changed significantly. It is now accepted as a rule of thumb that for every dollar spent on generating an idea, ten dollars have to be spent on 'research' to convert the idea into a new discovery or a new invention. For every ten dollars spent on 'research', at least a hundred dollars need to be spent on development, and for every hundred dollars spent on development, something between a thousand and ten thousand dollars are needed to introduce and establish a new product or a new business on the market. And only when a new product or a new business has been established in the market has there been an 'innovation'.

This means that the bulk of innovative efforts will have to come from the places that control the manpower and the money needed for development and marketing, that is, from existing businesses and existing public-service institutions.

But it does not mean that the small business or even the lone entrepreneur will not continue to play an important role. The innovative growth companies of the last twenty-five years all started as small businesses. And by and large the small businesses have done better than the giants.

In every industry, except those where monopoly is protected by government, small upstarts, unknown a few short years ago, have acquired major market positions and have proven themselves more than capable of competition with the giants. This is particularly true where the giants, through natural growth or deliberate policy, grew into conglomerates. In the chemical industry, in the electrical apparatus industry, and in many others, the traditional giant, a GE or an Imperial Chemical, has lost market position and market share in many markets – and largely to small or medium-sized newcomers with an innovative bent.

An established company that, in an age demanding innovation, is not capable of innovation is doomed to decline and extinction. And a management that in such a period does not know how to manage innovation is incompetent and unequal to its task. Managing innovation will increasingly become a challenge to management, and a test of its competence.

## Innovative examples

While in a minority, especially among big businesses, innovative companies do exist. One might mention Renault and Fiat, Marks & Spencer, Sony, 3M (Minnesota Mining and Manufacturing in St Paul, Minnesota), the Bell Laboratories of the Telephone Company, and Citibank in New York or the Bank of America. These firms apparently have no difficulty innovating and no difficulty getting change accepted in their organizations. Their managements, one would expect, rarely have to ask, 'How can we keep our organization flexible and willing to accept the new ?' These managements are much too busy finding the manpower and the money to run with the innovations their own people force on them.

Innovative organizations are not confined to business. Both the Manhattan Project in the United States which developed the atomic bomb during World War II, and CERN (The European Council for Nuclear Research) in Geneva, furnish examples of innovative organizations.

These examples indicate that an organization's ability to innovate depends more on management than on industry, size or age of the organization, let alone on that common excuse of poor managers, a country's 'culture and traditions'.

Nor is research the crucial factor. Bell Laboratories – perhaps the most productive industrial research laboratory – has indeed stressed fundamental inquiries into the laws of nature for many years. But Renault and Fiat are not particularly distinguished for their research; what makes them innovative organizations is ability to get new designs and new models into production and on the market quickly. The Bank of America, finally, innovated mainly in its customers' businesses, and in terms of financial structure and credit, inventory and marketing policies.

These examples suggest that the innovative organization somehow builds in an innovative spirit and creates a habit of innovation. At the beginning of these organizations there might well have been an individual, a great innovator. He might have succeeded in building around him an organization to convert into successful business reality his new ideas and inventions – as Edwin H. Land of Polaroid has been doing since World War II. But no such founding genius presided over Bell Laboratories, over 3M, or over Renault. The innovative organization manages to innovate as an organization, that is, as a human group organized for continual and productive innovation. It is organized to make change into the norm.

These various innovative organizations are very different in their structures, their businesses, their characteristics, and even their organization and management philosophies. But they all have certain characteristics in common.

1 Innovating organizations know what 'innovation' means.
2 Innovative organizations understand the dynamics of innovation.
3 They have an innovative strategy.
4 They know that innovation requires objectives, goals and measurements that are different from the objectives, goals, and measurements of a managerial organization, and appropriate to the dynamics of innovation.
5 Management, especially top management, plays a different role and has a different attitude in an innovative organization.
6 The innovative organization is structured differently and set up differently from the managerial organization.

**The meaning of innovation**

Innovative organizations first know what 'innovation' means. They know that innovation is not science or technology, but value. They know that innovation is not something that takes place inside an organization but is a change outside. The measure of innovation is impact on the environment. Innovation in a business enterprise must therefore always be market-focused.

Innovation that is product-focused instead is likely to produce 'miracles of technology' but disappointing rewards.

The outstanding innovators among the world's pharmaceutical companies define their goal as new drugs that will make a significant difference to medical practice and to patient health. They do not define innovation in terms of research, but in terms of the practice of medicine. Similarly, Bell Laboratories always starts out with the question 'What will make a difference to telephone *service* ?'

Nor surprisingly, however, it is precisely the most market-focused innovator who has come up with some of the most important technical or scientific advances. Bell Labs, for instance, created the transistor, produced the basic mathematics of information theory, and is responsible for some of the fundamental discoveries underlying the computer.

To start out with the consumer's needs for a significant change is often the most direct way of defining new knowledge and new technology, and of organizing purposeful and systematic work on fundamental discovery.

## The dynamics of innovation

Innovating businesses understand the dynamics of innovation. They know that innovation happens neither by chance nor according to some predetermined timetable.

They know that innovation follows the laws of probability. They know that it is possible to recognize an innovation, that if successfully brought about is likely to become a major product or process, a major new business, a major market. They know how to spot the areas where innovative activity is likely to enjoy success and to be rewarding.

One such mark of opportunity for innovation is basic economic weakness of a process, a technology, or an industry. Whereever an industry enjoys growing market demand without being able to turn the demand into profitability, a major innovation that changes process, product, distributive channel, or customer expectations is likely to produce high rewards.

Examples abound. One is the paper industry. Worldwide, it has enjoyed rapidly expanding consumer demands – on the order of 5 to 10 per cent a year, year in and year out – without apparently being able to earn a decent return on its capital. The steel industry is in a very similar position. But there is also life insurance, which is one of the few 'products' a customer is ready to buy – one of the few products, by the way, in which the interests of producer and consumer are completely identical – and which yet has to be sold through 'hard-sell' methods and against apparently very high buyer resistance.

Innovative opportunity also exists where there is glaring disparity between various levels of an economy or of a market.

The major growth industry in Latin America in the 1960s, for instance, was not manufacturing. It was retail distribution. Huge numbers of people flocked into the cities, from a subsistence economy into a money economy. Individually they were, of course, mostly very poor. But collectively they represented huge new purchasing power. Yet the distribution system in most Latin American countries remained in the pre-urban mould – small shops, undercapitalized, undermanaged, poorly stocked and with very slow turnover. Where an entrepreneur moved in to offer modern distribution – Sears, Roebuck was the first to recognize the opportunity – success was instantaneous.

Another area of innovative opportunity is exploiting the consequences of events that have already happened but have not yet had their economic impacts. Changes in population are among the most important. They are also the most nearly certain. Changes in knowledge are less certain, but they too offer opportunities. And then, most important but least certain, are changes in awareness, changes in vision, changes in people's expectations.

The pharmaceutical industry, for instance, earned its success largely because it anticipated the impact of fundamental changes in awareness. After World War II health care every place became a 'good buy'. And drugs are the only way to health care easily accessible to poor and poorly educated rural countries. Where physicians and hospitals are scarce, drugs can still be dispensed and will be effective for a great many health problems. The pharmaceutical company that understood this and went into the developing countries found that, with respect to drug purchases, these countries are 'fully developed'.

Finally, of course, there are the innovations that are not part of the pattern, the innovations that are unexpected and that change the world rather than exploit it, the truly important innovations. They are the innovations of a Henry Ford, who envisioned something that did not exist at the time, namely a mass market, and then set about to make it happen.

These innovations lie outside the normal range of predictability. They are also clearly the most risky ones. For every such innovation that succeeds, they are 99 that fail, 99 of which nothing is ever heard.

It is important for the innovating business to realize that these special innovations exist and that they are of supreme importance. It is important to watch for them. But, by their very nature, they cannot be the object of systematic, purposeful organized activity within the business enterprise. They cannot be managed.

And they are rare enough to be treated as exceptions, despite their overreaching importance. The business that understands the dynamics of innovation and organizes its innovation strategy to take advantage of it will innovate. And in the process it will become sensitive to the exceptional, the great, the truly historic innovation. It will be equipped to recognize it early and to take advantage of it.

To manage innovation, a manager need not be a technologist. Indeed, first-rate technologists are rarely good at managing innovation. They are so deeply engrossed in their specialty that they rarely see development outside of it. It is not metallurgists who are likely to recognize the importance of basic new knowledge in plastics even though it may, within a reasonably short time, obsolete a good many of their proudest products. Similarly, the innovative manager need not be an economist. Economists concern themselves with the impact of innovations only after they have become massive. The innovating manager needs to anticipate vulnerabilities and opportunities. The innovative manager needs to study innovation and to learn its dynamics, its pattern, its predictability. To manage innovation, a manager has to be at least literate with respect to the dynamics of innovation.

## Innovative strategy

Like all business strategies, an innovative strategy begins with the question 'What is our business, and what should it be ?' But its assumptions regarding the future are different from those of the ongoing business. There the assumption is that present product lines and services, present markets and present distribution channels, present technologies and processes will continue. The first objective of a strategy for the ongoing business is to take best advantage of what already exists or is being established.

The ruling assumption of an innovative strategy is that whatever exists is aging. The assumption is that existing product lines and services, existing markets and distribution channels, existing technologies and processes will sooner or later – and usually sooner – go down rather than up.

The governing device of a strategy for the ongoing business might therefore be said to be: 'Better and More'. For the innovative strategy the device has to be: 'New and Different'.

The foundation of innovative strategy is planned and systematic culling of the old, the dying, the obsolete. Innovating organizations spend neither time nor resources on defending yesterday. Only systematic abandonment of yesterday can free the resources, and especially the scarcest resource of them all, capable people, for work on the new.

Unwillingness to do this may be the greatest obstacle to innovation in the existing large business. The new and especially the as-yet unborn, that is, the future innovation, always looks insignificant compared to the large volume, the large revenue and the many problems of the ongoing business. It is all the more important, therefore, for an existing business to commit itself to the systematic abandonment of yesterday if it wants to be able to create tomorrow.

Second in a strategy of innovation is the clear recognition that innovation efforts must aim high. It is just as difficult, as a rule,

to make a minor modification to an existing product as it is to innovate a new one. In improvement work – adding a new product,
upgrading a product line, broadening the market, and so on –
one can assume a success rate of 50 per cent. No more than half
the projects should be total failures.

This is not the way innovation works. Here the assumption
must be that most innovative efforts will not succeed. Nine out
of every ten 'brilliant ideas' turn out to be nonsense. And nine
out of every ten ideas which, after thorough analysis, seem to be
worthwhile and feasible turn out to be failures or, at best, puny
weaklings. The mortality rate of innovations is – and should be –
high.

'Success' in innovating efforts is a batting average of one out
of ten. This is, of course, the reason for aiming high in innovative efforts. The one winner has to make up for the nine
losers in addition to producing its own results.

An innovation does not proceed in a nice linear progression.
For a good long time, sometimes for years, there is only effort
and no results. The first results are then usually meagre. Indeed,
the first products are rarely what the customer will eventually
buy. The first markets are rarely the major markets. The first applications are rarely the ones that, in the end, will turn out to be
really important.

The impacts of new technology are very difficult, and sometimes impossible, to predict. But this difficulty extends to everything connnected with the truly new – as demonstrated by the
example (given in Chapter 19) of the gross miscalculation of the
size of the computer market in the thorough market-research
study conducted around 1950. But even more difficult to predict
is the speed with which an innovation will establish itself. 'Timing is of the essence' – above all in innovation. Yet timing is totally unpredictable. The computer, antibiotics, the Xerox machine,
all swept the market. But for every successful innovation that has
results faster than anyone anticipates, there are five or six
others – in the end perhaps, equally successful ones – that for
long years seem to make only frustratingly slow headway. The
outstanding example may be the steam-driven ship. By 1835 its

superiority was clearly established, but it did not replace the sailing ship until fifty years later.

But then, after a long, frustrating period, the successful innovation rises meteorically. Within a few short years it becomes a new major industry or a new major product line and market. But until it has reached that point no one can predict when it will take off, nor indeed whether it ever will.

## Measurement and budgets

Innovation strategy requires different measurements and a different use of budgets and budgetary controls from those appropriate to an ongoing business.

To impose on innovating efforts the same measurements, especially the accounting conventions, that fit ongoing businesses is misdirection. It cripples the innovative effort the way putting on a one-hundred-pound pack would cripple a six-year-old going on a hike. It also fails to give true control. Finally, it may become a threat when the innovation becomes successful. For then it needs controls that are appropriate to rapid growth, that is, controls which show what efforts and investments are needed to exploit success and prevent overextension.

The successfully innovating businesses learned this long ago.

The oldest, best-known, and most successful managerial control system is probably that of the Du Pont Company, which, as early as the 1920s, developed for all its businesses a model focused on return on investment. Innovations were not subject to that famous standard. As long as a business, a product line, or a process was in the innovating stage, its capital allocation was not included in the investment on which the individual Du Pont division in charge of the project had to earn a return. Nor were the expenses included in its expense budget. Both were kept separate. Only after the new product line had been introduced in the market and had been sold in commercial quantities for two years or more were its measurements and controls merged into the budget of the division responsible for the development.

This made sure that division general managers did not resist innovation as a threat to their earnings record and performance. It also made sure that expenditures on, and investments in, innovative efforts could be tightly controlled. It made it possible to ask at every step, 'What do we expect at the end, and what is the risk factor, that is, the likelihood of nonsuccess?' 'Can we justify continuing this particular innovative effort or not?'

Budgets for ongoing businesses and budgets for innovative efforts should not only be kept separate, they should be treated differently. In the ongoing business, the question is always 'Is this effort necessary? Or can we do without it?' And if the answer is 'We need it', one asks, 'What is the minimum level of support that is needed?'

In the innovative effort the first and most serious question is 'Is it the right opportunity?' And if the answer is yes, one asks, 'What is the maximum of good people and key resources which can productively be put to work *at this stage*?'

A separate standard for innovative effort makes it possible to appraise the three factors that determine innovative strategy: the ultimate opportunity, the risk of failure, and the effort and expenditure needed. Otherwise, efforts may be continued and even stepped up where the opportunity is quite limited while the risk of nonsuccess is great.

Many broad-spectrum antibiotics were produced in the late 1960s with great scientific ingenuity by pharmaceutical companies. But by then the probability of synthesizing a new broad-spectrum antibiotic with properties significantly better than those already on the market had become fairly small. The risk of non-success was high, in other words. At the same time the opportunity had become much more limited than ten years earlier. Even an antibiotic with significantly better performance than the existing ones would have to compete against perfectly good products with which the physicians were familiar and which they had learned to use. Even a real breakthrough would in all likelihood have produced a 'me-too' product. At the same time, the expense and effort needed to find anything really new in a field that had been worked over so thoroughly were rising fast. Traditional market thinking, that is, thinking that looks at the size of the market and deduces from it great success for a new product that is 'better', would have been totally misleading. And indeed it did mislead several companies.

Nothing is more inconsistent with successful innovation than a goal of '5 per cent growth in profits' every year. Innovations for the first three or five years – some for longer – show no profit at all. And then their growth rate for five to ten years should be closer to 40 per cent a year than to 5 per cent a year. It is only after they have reached relative maturity that they can be expected to grow year by year by a small percentage. But then they are no longer innovations.

Innovative strategy, therefore, requires great discipline on the part of innovators. They have to operate without the crutch of the conventional budget and accounting measures that feed back fairly fast and reliable information from current results to efforts and investments. The temptation is to keep on pouring people and money into innovative efforts without any results. It is thus important in managing innovation to think through what one expects, and when. Inevitably, these expectations are changed by events. But unless there are intermediate results, specific progress, 'fallouts' to actual operation along the way, the innovation is not being managed.

When Du Pont engaged, in the late 1920s, in the polymer research that eventually led to nylon more than ten years later, no one could predict whether polymer technology would lead to synthetic rubber, to textile fibres, to synthetic leathers or to new lubricants. In the end it led to all of them. It was not until fairly close to the end of the work that it became clear that synthetic fibres would be the first major commercial product. But from the beginning Du Pont, together with Wallace Carrothers, the research scientist in charge, systematically laid out a road map of what kind of findings and results could be expected and when. This map was revised every two or three years as results came in. But it was always redrawn again for the next stages along the road. And only when the research came up with polymer fibres, which then made large-scale development work possible, did Du Pont commit itself to massive investment. Until then, the total cost was essentially the cost of supporting Carrothers and a few assistants.

## The risk of failure

A strategy for innovation has to be based on clear acceptance of the risk of failure – and of the perhaps more dangerous risk of 'near-success'.

It is as important to decide when to abandon an innovative effort as it is to know which one to start. In fact, it may be more important. Successful laboratory directors know when to abandon a line of research that does not yield the expected results. The less successful ones keep hoping against hope, are dazzled by the 'scientific challange' of a project, or are fooled by the scientist's repeated promise of a 'breakthrough next year'. And the unsuccessful ones cannot abandon a project and cannot admit that what seemed like a good idea has turned into a waste of researchers, time and money.

But many innovative efforts end up in near-success rather than in success or failure. And near-success can be more dangerous than failure. There is, again and again, the product or the process that was innovated with the expectation that it would 'revolutionize' the industry only to become a minor addition to the product line, neither enough of a failure to be abandoned nor enough of a success to make a difference. There is the innovation which looks so 'exciting' when work on it is begun, only to be overtaken, during its developmental period, by a competitor's more innovative process, product or service. There is the innovation which was meant to become a 'household word' that ends up as another 'specialty' which a few customers are willing to buy but not willing to pay for.

It is therefore particularly important in managing innovation to think through and to write out one's expectations. And then, once the innovation has become a product, a process or a business, one compares one's expectations to reality. If reality falls significantly short of expectations, one does not pour in more resources. One rather asks, 'Shouldn't we get out of this, and how ?'

## The innovative attitude

Resistance to change, by executives and workers alike, has for many years been considered a central problem of management. Countless books and articles have been written on the subject. Countless seminars, discussions and courses have been devoted to it. Yet little progress has been made in resolving the problem.

Indeed, it is incapable of being resolved as long as we talk of 'resistance to change'. Not that there is no such resistance, or that it is not a major obstacle. But to focus on resistance to change is to misdefine the problem in a way that makes it less, rather than more, tractable. The right way to define the problem is as a challenge to create, build and maintain the innovative organization, the organization for which change is the rule rather than exception, an opportunity rather than a threat. Innovation is, therefore, attitude and practices. It is, above all, top-management attitude and practices. The innovative organization casts top management in a different role and embodies a different concept of top management's relationship to the organization.

In the traditional managerial organization such as management texts discuss, top management is final judge. Management's most important power is the veto power, and its most important role is to say no to proposals and ideas that are not completely thought through and worked out. In the innovative organization, the first and most important job of management is the opposite. It is to convert impractical, half-baked and wild ideas into concrete innovative reality. In the innovative organization, top management sees it as its job to listen to ideas and to take them seriously. Top management knows that new ideas are always 'impractical'. It also knows that it takes a great many silly ideas to spawn one workable one, and that in the early stages there is no way of telling the silly idea from the stroke of genius. Both looks equally impossible or equally brilliant.

Top management in the innovative organization, therefore, not only 'encourages' ideas, as all managements are told to do. It asks continuously, 'What would this idea have to be like to be practical, realistic, effective ?' It organizes itself to study even the wildest idea for something new to the point where its feasibility can be appraised.

Top management in the innovative organization is the major 'drive' for innovation. It uses the ideas of the organization to stimulate its own vision. And then it works to make ideas a concern of the entire organization. Top management in the innovative organization fashions thought and work on the new into both organizational energy and innovative discipline.

This, however, requires a change in relations between top management and the human group within the enterprise. The traditional organization, of course, remains. Indeed, on the organization chart there may be little to distinguish the innovative organization from the most rigidly bureaucratic one. And an innovative organization need not be 'permissive' or 'democratic' at all. But the innovative organization builds a kind of nervous system next to the bony skeleton of the formal organization. Where traditional organization is focused on the logic of the work, there is an additional relationship focused on the dynamics of ideas.

In innovative companies senior executives typically make it their business to meet with the younger people throughout the organization in scheduled (though not necessarily regular) sessions in which there is no 'agenda' for top management. Rather, the seniors sit down with the younger ones and ask, 'What opportunities do *you* see ?'

In the period of its greatest growth and development, the 3M Company was anything but a permissive company. It was tightly run by two or three men at the top who made all the decisions. But even the most junior engineer was encouraged to come to top management with any idea, no matter how wild. And again and again he would be told, 'The idea makes no sense to me, but are you willing to work on it ?' If the engineer said yes, he would then be asked to write up his idea, together with a budget request – and more often than not he would be freed from his other responsibilities, given a modest sum of money for a year or two, and told to go ahead. As a result, the company grew from a small and obscure producer of abrasives into one of America's largest businesses.

The innovative organization requires a learning atmosphere

throughout the entire business. It creates and maintains continuous learning. No one is allowed to consider himself 'finished' at any time. Learning is a continuous process for all members of the organization.

Resistance to change is grounded in ignorance and in fear of the unknown. If change is seen as opportunity, then there will be no fear. It is seen as opportunity by the Japanese because they are guaranteed their jobs and are not afraid of putting themselves or their colleagues out of work by proposing something new. Fear and ignorance are also overcome in Japan by making continuing change the opportunity for personal achievement, for recognition, for satisfaction. The man who in a Japanese training session comes up with a new idea receives no monetary reward, even if his idea is a big and profitable one. But even if it is a very small improvement, he derives stature, recognition, intense pleasure.

We need not go to Japan to learn this. Every one of the 'suggestion systems' that are so widely used in American business teaches the same lesson. The suggestion system in which the reward is recognition, achievement, participation, is the successful system. And in those departments in a plant where the suggestion system is run this way, there is very little resistance to change, despite fears for job security and union restrictions. Where this does not prevail – as in the great majority – the suggestion system is not a success, no matter how well it pays for successful suggestions. It also has none of the effect on worker behaviour and attitude that the proponents of the suggestion system promise.

## Structure for innovation

The search for innovation needs to be organized separately and outside of the ongoing managerial business. Innovative organizations realize that one cannot simultaneously create the new and take care of what one already has. They realize that maintenance of the present business is far too big a task for the people in it to have much time for creating the new, the different business of tomorrow. They also realize that taking care of tomorrow is far too big and difficult a task to be diluted with concern for today. Both tasks have to be done. But they are different.

Innovative organizations, therefore, put the new into separate organizational components concerned with the creation of the new.

The oldest example is probably the development department at Du Pont founded in the early 1920s. This unit is concerned exclusively with the making of tomorrow. It is not a research department – Du Pont has a separate, big research lab. The job of the development department is to develop new businesses; production, finance and marketing are as much its concern as technology, products and processes. 3M, too, has set up a separate business development lab in parallel with, but separate from, its research labs.

This was not understood in 1952 when the General Electric Company embarked on the massive reorganization which became the prototype for major organization changes in large businesses around the world. Under the GE plan the general manager of every 'product business' had responsibility both for the ongoing business in his charge and for the innovative efforts for tomorrow's new and different business. This seemed reasonable. Indeed it seemed to follow from the idea that the general manager of a product business should, as much as possible, behave like the chief executive of an independent business. But it did not work – the general managers did not innovate.

One reason was the press of ongoing business. General managers had neither the time nor the motivation to work on obsoleting what they were managing. Another, equally important reason was that the true innovation is rarely an extension of the already existing business. It rarely fits into the scope, objectives, goals, technologies or processes of today. After ten years or so GE began to draw the proper conclusions from its frustrations and began to organize major innovation separately, outside existing product departments and product divisions. It adopted a structure very similar to the way innovative efforts had been organized at Du Pont for many years, that is, in a separate organizational 'business development' unit.

Experience in public-service institutions indicates that there too innovative efforts are best organized separately and outside existing managerial organization. Both the Manhattan Project, which developed the atomic bomb, and CERN, the European nuclear-research facility, were set up outside the existing academic and governmental structures precisely because their purpose was innovation.

## Innovation as a 'business'

At the same time, innovative organizations realize that innovation needs from the beginning to be organized as a 'business' rather than as a 'function'. This means setting aside the traditional time sequence in which 'research' comes first, followed by 'development', followed by 'manufacturing', with 'marketing' at the very end. The innovative organizations consider all these functional skills as part of the same process, the process of developing a new business. When and how each tool is put into play is decided by the needs of the situation rather than by any preconceived time sequence.

A project manager or business manager is therefore put in charge of anything new as soon as it is decided to pay attention to it. The project manager may come from any function – or from no function at all. And he or she can draw on all the functions right from the beginning; use marketing, for instance, before there is any research; or work out the financial requirements of a future business before there are even any products.

The traditional functions organize work from where we are today to where we are going. The innovative function organizes work from where we want to be, back to what we now have to do in order to get there.

The design principle of innovation is the team, set up outside existing structures as an 'autonomous unit'. It is not a 'decentralized business' in the traditional sense of the word, but it has to be independent and separate from operating organizations.

One way to organize innovative units within a large business might well be to group them together in an innovative group.

This group would report to one member of top management who has no other function but to guide, help, advise, review, and direct the innovating team at work. This is, in effect, what the Du Pont development department is. Innovation has its own logic, which is different from the logic of an ongoing business. No matter how much the innovative units may themselves differ in their technologies, their markets, their products, or their services, they all have in common that they are innovative.

Even such autonomous team organization may be too restricted for the kind of innovation that will increasingly be needed, innovation in fields that are quite different from anything that business has done so far. We may need to set up the innovating unit as a genuine entrepreneur.

Several large companies – GE, Westinghouse, or Exxon, for example – have set up innovative efforts in the form of partnerships with the 'entrepreneurs' in charge. The innovative effort is organized as a separate company, in which the parent company has majority control and usually a right to buy out the minority shareholders at some prearranged price. But the entrepreneurs, that is, the people who are responsible directly for developing the innovation, are substantial shareholders in their own right.

One advantage of such a relationship is that it eases the compensation problem. Innovative people can command high salaries in the managerial organization, as senior research scientists or as senior marketing people. Yet it is undesirable to saddle an innovative venture with high salary costs – it cannot afford them. At the same time, it is highly desirable to compensate the entrepreneurs for results. A method of compensation that induces these entrepreneurs to work for modest salaries until results are achieved, while promising substantial rewards in case of success, is therefore appropriate. A 'partnership' makes this possible.

Whether these 'confederations' in which the entrepreneurs become partners and shareholders will become general will depend as much on tax laws as on economics or organization structure. The principle, however, is important: compensation of the innovators should be appropriate to the economic reality of the innovating process. This is a process in which the risks are high, the lead time long, and the rewards, in case of success, very great.

Whether the innovating team is a separate company or simply a separate unit, an innovating company is likely to apply some of the design principles of systems management. There will be managerial units engaged in managing what is already known and what is already being done. And there will be innovative units, separate from them, working with them but also working on their own and charged with their own responsibility. Both will have to report independently of each other to the top-management group. To innovate within existing organizations will require acceptance of a rather complex organization design. It is neither centralized nor decentralized. Within such a company, functional organization, federal decentralization, simulated decentralization, and teams may all be found next to each other and working together.

## Summary

The innovative organization is a major challenge to management, private and public. We know that such organizations are possible; there are many of them around. But how to make such organizations general, how to make them productive for society, economy, and individual alike, is still largely an unsolved task. There is every indication that the period ahead will be an innovative one, one of rapid change in technology, society, economy, and institutions. There is every indication, therefore, that the innovative organization will have to be developed into a central institution for the last quarter of the twentieth century.

# 38 Top Management and Board

No business can do better than its top management will permit; the 'bottleneck' is, after all, always 'at the head of the bottle'. Of all the jobs in the enterprise the top-management job is the most difficult to organize. But it is also the most important one to organize.

## Top-management tasks

Every managerial unit other than top management is designed for one specific major task – whether the organization is structured on functional lines, in teams, on the basis of decentralization, or on the systems approach. Every building block of organization is defined by a specific contribution.

The one exception is top management. Its job is multidimensional. There is no one top-management task; there are only top-management *tasks*. And this is just as true for public-service institutions as it is for business.

1 There is, first, the task of thinking through the mission of the business, that is, of asking the question 'What is our business, and what should it be?' This leads to setting objectives, developing strategies and plans, and to making today's decisions for tomorrow's results. This clearly can be done only by an organ of the business that can see the entire business; that can make decisions that affect the entire business; that can balance the objectives and the needs of today against the needs of tomorrow; and that can allocate resources of people and money to key results.

2 There is need for standard setting, for example setting, that is, for what we have called the conscience functions. There is need for an organ of the enterprise that concerns itself with the gap – always a big one – between what the organization stands for and what it actually does. There is need for an organ concerned with

vision and values in the key areas. Again this can only be an organ of the enterprise that sees and comprehends the entire business.

3 There is the responsibility to build and maintain the human organization. There is need for work on developing the human resources for tomorrow, and especially for work on providing tomorrow's top management. The spirit of an organization is created by the people at the top. Their standards of conduct and their values set the example for the entire organization and determine its self-respect.

4 Equally important are major relations that only the people at the top of a business can establish and maintain. These may be relations to customers or major suppliers. They may be industry relations or relations with bankers or other outside institutions, such as government agencies or the Congress. These relations crucially affect the capacity of the business to perform. They are relations that can be made, again, only by someone who represents the entire business, speaks for it, stands for it, commits it.

5 There are countless 'ceremonial' functions – dinners, civic events – that must be performed by top management. They are actually more time-consuming and more difficult to avoid for the top people in a small or medium-sized business that is prominent in its local community than they are for the heads of the very big companies.

As the head of a fair-sized company said, 'As long as the president of General Electric sends a cheque, he can be represented by one of his vice-presidents – and he has sixty-five of them. I have to go myself; we are the largest employers in the place.'

6 There is need for a 'stand-by' organ for major crises, for somebody who is available to take over when things go seriously wrong. Then it is the most experienced, the wisest, the most prominent people in an organization who have to roll up their sleeves and go to work. They are legally responsible. But there is also a responsibility to knowledge that cannot be abdicated.

Every institution needs a top-management function. But every one has specific top-management tasks. The elements of the job are the same. But the specific top-management tasks depend upon the individual business. They have to be developed out of an analysis of the mission and purpose of the institution, its objectives, its strategies, and the key activities. The question to ask is not 'What is top management?' The question is 'What are the specific things to be done in *this* business that are of crucial importance to the success and survival of the business and that can be done only by top management?' 'What are the specific things that can be done only by people who see this business whole; who can balance the present needs of the business against the needs of the future; and who can make final and effective decisions?'

It therefore makes little sense to talk of an 'ideal' top-management structure. The ideal top management is the one that does the things that are right for its enterprise here and now. We do need a theory of top management. But each specific application must be developed individually on the basis of the needs of a particular organization. It must be tailored to the individual enterprise. It must be developed from an analysis of the specific enterprise. It must, above all, follow the strategies of the enterprise and be in harmony with them.

## To 'operate' or not to 'operate'

Only analysis of the individual business (or public-service institution) will bring out what key activities are properly top-management responsibilities.

The management texts agree that top management should not 'operate'. And most informed observers of top management agree that the most common reason why the top-management job doesn't get done is that top executives 'operate' and, in consequence, do not tackle the top-management tasks.

The first top management design was worked out in the 1870s. It was the design that a German, Georg Siemens, developed for the first of Europe's major banks – the Deutsche Bank. It is still the top management design for large companies in Europe, and increasingly in the US as well.

Yet Siemens in his top-management design included a good

deal of 'operating work'. He did not confine top management to directing others, to planning, to reviewing, to setting the direction of the bank. On the contrary, the first job of the members of his top-management team was specific work on the major industrial and financial investments the bank had decided to develop. It was not 'directing' the work of others but 'doing'. Far from isolating themselves from the 'nuts and bolts,' Siemens's top men were supposed to take direct personal responsibility for finding the right investment opportunities and for developing them into successful, well-managed businesses. Clearly this was one of the secrets of the success of the Deutsche Bank.

Effective top managements tend to follow the Siemens practice rather than the theorist's and consultant's preachings.

Here are some examples. A medium-sized French producer of nationally advertised consumer goods has gained, within the last decade or two, a strong position in the European markets. One of the reasons is that the head of the company is also the company's advertising and promotion manager. He himself writes most of the company's advertisements and designs the company's promotions. He also has assigned to himself direct responsibility for relations with the dealers throughout Europe, especially in France. He personally visits about thirty of the larger dealers in the course of a year, listens to them, studies their businesses and altogether manages the company's relationship with them. 'Our business is a promotion business. Our business, above all, depends on the willingness of the dealers to work hard at selling our merchandise. Our business, therefore, depends on knowing the dealers and on their knowing us, and on our willingness and ability to design products they want to sell and can sell, to deliver them the way they need them delivered, and to price them in line with the price preferences of their customers.' Yet the same man flatly refuses to have anything to do with manufacturing – even though his own background is manufacturing engineering.

Sears, Roebuck is a company that, from its early days, has insisted on keeping top management out of operations, and confined to top-management tasks. No one believed in this more firmly than General Robert E. Wood who presided over Sears expansion from an exclusively mail-order operation to a chain of successful retail stores. Yet when Wood systematized the top-management job and organized a three-man top-management team, he assigned to top management as a 'doing' responsibility the selection of sites for new major retail stores. This decision, he argued, had long-range and irreversible impact on the company's ability to sell and to make money. Once the site has been selected and a store has been built, there is a twenty-year commitment. A decision like this, though clearly an operating decision, has to be made by top management. To be able to make the decision intelligently, a member of top management has to work on the project from the beginning.

These are clearly dangerous precedents. If operating work can be legitimately included in the top-management job, then chief executives who open all the incoming letters or who themselves do the final inspection of the company's products – and I have seen both done, and in fairly large businesses – can claim that they are doing top-management work (as indeed both did).

The rules are simple:

1 Operating work is not top-management work if someone else can do it. Of course, most operating work will be eliminated as top-management work by the analysis of key activities; for top management should never be involved in any other activities. But key activities should then be subjected to the question 'Could anyone else in the organization do them just as well – or nearly as well? At least, should there be someone capable of doing them?' If the answer is yes, it is not top-management work.

2 People who move into top-management work should give up the functional or operating work they did earlier. That should always be turned over to someone else. Otherwise they are likely to remain functional or operating people.

## The characteristics of top-management tasks

The top-management function is especially difficult to organize. Every one of the tasks is a recurrent task. It needs to be done over and over again. But few of them, if any, are *continuous* tasks. Few of them have to be done every day from nine to five. When they arise, they are crucially important to the enterprise. They are the true 'life and death' decisions. But it would be foolish to 'plan' five days a week 52 weeks a year. Key personnel decisions also arise fairly infrequently. But they then require a great deal of time; few things are less likely to succeed than hasty personnel decisions. And the same applies to most of the other top-management tasks.

Another special characteristic of top-management tasks is that they require a diversity of capabilities, and, above all, of temperaments. They require the ability to analyse, to think, to weigh alternatives and to harmonize dissent. But they also require the capacity for quick and decisive action, for boldness and for intuitive courage. They require being at home with abstract ideas, concepts, calculations and figures. They also require perception of people, a human awareness, and altogether a lively interest in people and respect for them. Some tasks demand that a person work alone. Others are tasks of representation and ceremonial, outside tasks, that require the politician's enjoyment of crowds and protocol; the ability to represent and to make a good speech that says nothing.

The top-management tasks require at least four different kinds of human being: the person of thought, the person of action, the 'people person,' and the 'front man.' Yet those four temperaments are almost never found in one person.

Because the tasks are not continuous, the top-management job itself is often seen, even by people running sizable businesses, as something to be done if and when the need arises. But in the meantime, that is, day by day, the people at the top feel the need to do a continuing job. That, of course, means that they do functional work. For there is day-to-day work in manufacturing and marketing, in accounting and engineering, in advertising and in quality control. If they succumb the top-management tasks will not get done at all. There are simply too many of them to be done that way. While each individual task within the top-management function may require only a short time in the smaller and less complicated business, all the top-management functions taken together, even in the small business, are far too large to be handled on the side and in addition to functional work. Day-by-day operating work always has urgency – and many top-management jobs are for the long pull and look as if they can wait until the 'tomorrow' that somehow never comes.

The first requirement of effective top management, as Georg Siemens saw a century ago, is to identify objectively all the key activities and key tasks of top management in the business. The old saw that 'every chief executive has his or her own style and decides what top management is' is nonsense. Every chief executive – indeed, every person – has his or her own style and is entitled to it. But what decides what top management is or should be is an objective decision. It depends no more on individual style than the law of gravity depends on what the physicist had for breakfast.

The fact that the top-management tasks, or at least a good many of them, while continuous tasks are not continuous work and the fact that the top-management tasks demand a diversity of qualifications, skills and temperaments make it essential that every top-management task is clearly assigned to someone. Otherwise, important tasks will be overlooked. In fact, there should be a *top-management work plan* – especially in the small business – that spells out in considerable detail who is responsible for what; what the objectives and goals are with respect to each task; and what the deadlines are. Precisely because the top-management function differs in basic character from practically every other kind of work within the enterprise, it has to be made specific and has to be clearly assigned.

## Top-management structure

Top-management work is work for a team rather than for one person. It is quite unlikely that any one person will have all the divergent temperaments that the job requires. Moreover, it will be found, when the top-management tasks are analysed, that there is more work to be done than any one person can do. The tasks require, except in the smallest business, at least one full-time executive who does nothing else, and then one or two, at least for a major part of their time, who take on part of the task in which they are then the 'leaders' and have primary responsibility.

There are other reasons why the one-person top management tends to malfunction. Every top-management succession in a one-person top management is a 'crisis' and a desperate gamble. No one in the business except the former chief has really done the top-management work and been proven by it.

Henry Ford, as has been said, did not believe in managers at all. This, in large part, explains the decline and near-collapse of his company in his latter years. But as recent studies have brought out, the Ford Motor Company at the time of its greatest growth and success, that is, from 1907 to 1917, was in effect run by a true top-management team with James Couzens co-equal to Ford and the final authority in a great many clearly assigned top-management areas. After Couzens left – he later entered politics and became a greatly beloved liberal senator from Michigan in the New Deal Days – Henry Ford became a one-man top management. From that day on the Ford Motor Company began to go downhill.

On paper the top management of a company may look like a one-man job. But if the company is healthy, a closer look is likely to disclose that other people carry clearly assigned top-management responsibilities as well. The controller often takes on a part of the top-management function – usually the analytical, the planning, the objective-setting aspects. Or it may be the manufacturing head who takes on responsibility for the human organization in addition to the functional duties in the plant.

This works reasonably well as long as the business is simple and small. The larger and more complex business needs a clearly structured top-management team.

This team may be organized, as has become the fashion, as a 'president's office', in which a number of people serve as equals. All have their own assigned areas of primary responsibility within which they have final say. This is the structure Siemens designed; and for the large and complex business it is probably the best one – though it is not an easy one.

But it is also possible to have one person only, a president or a chairman, who carries the title of chief executive officer. This officer has then affiliated with him or her a small number of colleagues, perhaps with some such title as executive vice-president, each of whom has clearly assigned authority and responsibility for a part of the top-management task, and no other duties.

In another fairly common structure, there may be a three or four-person top, with each member carrying clearly assigned top-management responsibilities even though one of them is definitely number one. This is the structure which General Motors has had for fifty years – a chairman, a vice-chairman, a chairman of the executive committee, a president. What assignments each of these four officers carries is then worked out to fit their personalities. But the four positions are permanent.

But just because the organization chart shows a top-management team does not necessarily mean that there is one. There is need for safeguards against the danger of dictatorships disguised as a top-management team.

The only effective safeguard is to have every top-management task clearly lodged in a person with direct and primary responsibility for it. And in the larger company no one who carries any top-management responsibility should carry any responsibility that is not part of the top-management job.

The same lesson is taught by a more recent and perhaps less serious top-management malfunction, the operating 'group executive' who is supposed to work part-time on the top-management job.

The group executive in charge of a number of divisions who has become popular in large companies is supposed to be the operating head of his group but give some of his time – a common figure is 30 per cent – to the company's top-management tasks. This sounds plausible – but it has not worked out. The group executive is far too busy to have clearly assigned responsibility for a top-management task. As a result, he makes no top-management contribution.

One company that has recognized this is IBM. At IBM there are group executives for major areas (research, engineering, and manufacturing; domestic marketing and service; international;

and noncomputer businesses). But IBM also has a four-member management committee composed of the chairman, the president, and two senior officers, none of whom operates. Each of the four has clearly assigned top-management responsibilities and no other function.

And yet the group executive is a member of a top-management team. Only it is not the top-management team of the parent company. It is the top-management team of the divisions in the group, each a major and important autonomous business in its own right, and each therefore requiring its own top management.

We can now summarize the basic specifications for a functioning top-management structure:

The starting point is an analysis of the top-management tasks.
Each top-management task must be clearly assigned to someone who has direct and full responsibility for it.
This requires a top-management team, with responsibilities assigned to fit the personalities, qualifications, and temperaments of the members.
Whoever has assigned responsibility for a top-management activity is 'top management', whatever his or her title.
Except in the small and simple business no one who has top-management responsibilities does any but top-management work.
The complex business requires more than one top-management team, each structured according to these rules.

## Teamwork in top management

A top-management team has to satisfy stringent requirements to be effective. The team is not a simple structure. It will not work just because its members like each other. Indeed whether the members like or dislike each other is beside the point. A top-management team must function no matter what the personal relationships between its members are.

1 First, whoever has primary responsibility in a given area has, in effect, the final say. If top management is to function, no sub-

ordinate should be able to appeal a decision by one member of the team to another. Every member speaks with the full authority of top management.

2 No member will make a decision with regard to a matter for which he does not have primary responsibility. If such a matter is brought to him, he will refer it to the colleague whose primary responsibility it is. Indeed it is a wise precaution for members of the top-management team not even to have an opinion on matters that are not within their own areas of primary responsibility.

Alfred P. Sloan, Jr, was the undoubted head of General Motors with moral authority within GM's general management such as has rarely been equalled. Yet Sloan said again and again, 'I think you'd better take this matter up with Mr Brown or with Mr Bradley or with Mr Wilson' – his colleagues in the top-management group. 'I would be interested to hear what they decide; perhaps you'll let me know.' After the caller had left – and the callers were usually high GM executives – Sloan would sometimes take the telephone and quietly call up Mr Brown and ask him to come to the office to discuss the matter. Sloan usually had very definite opinions and fought for them. But he disciplined himself never to express an opinion outside the top group, unless he himself had direct responsibility in the matter under discussion.

3 Members of the top-management team need not like each other. They need not even respect each other. But they must not agitate against each other. In public, that is, outside top management's conference room, they have no opinions on each other, do not criticize each other, do not belittle each other. Preferably they do not even praise each other.

Enforcing this rule is the team captain's job – and he had better be strict about it. Even the most undisciplined man must not be allowed as a member of top management, to express in public criticism, dislike or contempt for any other member.

4 A top-management team is not a committee. It is a team. A team needs a captain. The team captain is not the 'boss'; the captain is a leader.

In times of extreme crisis the captain has to be willing and able – and has to have the legal power – to take over. In times of common peril there has to be unity of command.

5 Within his or her assigned sphere, a member of top management is expected to make decisions. But certain decisions should be 'reserved'. There only the team as a whole can make the decision. At least the decision has to be discussed with the team before it can be made.

Defining 'what is our business and what should it be' clearly is one such decision. Abandoning major product lines or adding new ones belongs here too, as do major capital appropriations and key personnel decisions.

Key personnel decisions are made neither by acclamation nor by taking a vote. They require careful thought, careful discussion and the pooling of the experience of different people within the organization. They are, properly, matters that top management considers as a group, even though it will then often leave the actual decision to one of its members.

6 The top-management task requires systematic and intensive work on communications among the members of the top-management team. It requires this precisely because there are so many different top-management tasks, each with decisive impact on the welfare of the entire organization. It requires it, above all, because members of top management should be able to operate with the greatest possible autonomy with their own spheres – and that can be allowed only if each makes every effort to keep his colleagues fully informed.

Respect for the task, and clear understanding of what it is and who has responsibility, are, in other words, the foundations for an effective top management.

## How to nourish the brain

Siemens's most distinct innovation in organizing the top management was the 'executive secretariat'. It may have been his most important contribution.

In most businesses all the world over there is a flood of data. There are constant reports, there are studies, there are researches of all kinds, there are presentations and meetings. Most of them are intended for operating management. The staff services within the typical business are set up to support the operating people. Indeed, it is the theory of staffs that their job is to support, service and educate operating managers. Who then serves top management?

What top managements get, by and large, are the same data, the same information, the same stimuli that operating managers get. Yet there are specific top-management tasks and specific top-management needs. Top management's needs are different in kind from those of the operating people. Top management is largely concerned with the future rather than solely with the present, and with the whole business rather than with any of its parts.

The questions 'What is our business?' and 'What should it be?' imply a very different view of the present enterprise from the one on which present objectives, present structure, present assignments are based. Genuine innovations never fit existing organization structures. They fall outside and beyond any existing organization scope. And tomorrow's key people should always be picked for reasons different from those for which one yesterday picked the key people of today.

A simple but telling example is that of a major manufacturer of electrical apparatus. Traditionally the company had been a leader in the steam-turbine business. During World War II, it went into jet engines. At first jet engines were seen only as power for aircraft, even though a jet engine, that is, a gas turbine, is just as much a producer of electrical energy as a steam turbine. Then the company entered the atomic energy field. Because each of these three means of producing electricity had a different technological origin, and at first also a different market, each was organized as a separate business. However, for the customer, the power company, the three are simply alternate ways of producing electricity. Any two of them together will give an electric utility a complete power supply. But none of the existing service staffs of the manufacturing company saw this, or could have seen it. Their job, after all, was to service the operating managements of each of the three divisions. The people who ran these divisions saw their own product as the prime generator and expected to get for it the lion's share of the growth in electric-power generation. A task force organized specifically to supply top management with new thinking about tomorrow's markets finally pointed out that these three divisions were in the same business. By that time the company's standing in one of its major markets had already been seriously eroded by the failure to supply information and thinking for the top-management job.

Georg Siemens's solution, the German 'executive secretariat', will not suit every company. Yet every company, beyond the very small and simple one, needs a specific organ to supply top management with thinking, with stimulation, with questions, with knowledge and, above all, with information. Top management work is a specific kind of work. Any kind of work requires the right tools; and the tools for the top-management job are information, stimulation, analysis, and questions.

Membership in Siemens's 'secretariat' was thought of as a distinct career. Great pains were taken to find the ablest, most brilliant, most intelligent young men in the bank's employ or to recruit such men from the universities or from government service. Then they stayed, as a rule, in the secretariat. Few of them ever moved out into operating work in the bank. A few made it into top management – but their number was small too. As a result, the secretariat tended to become insulated.

This is still a weakness of the secretariat as used in Germany. But it is an unnecessary weakness and one that can be remedied. The rule should be that no one gets into such a group designed to support top management with information, stimulation, and questions, unless he or she first has shown real performance in actual work. A secretariat assignment should be considered as a major training position for those who, at a fairly early age, have shown high capacity to perform. No one should stay in the secretariat for more than a few years before being moved back into performing work. And the secretariat as a whole should concentrate on key issues and not attempt to deal with everything.

## Needed: an effective board

Different countries have different names for the group that supervises top management, counsels it, reviews its decisions, and appoints top managers. In the US it is the board of directors, elsewhere, a supervisory board or *conseil d'administration*.

The law of different countries provides for different memberships. But there is one thing all boards have in common, regardless of their legal position. *They do not function.* The decline of the board is a universal phenomenon of this century. Perhaps nothing shows it as clearly as that the board, which, in law, is the governing organ of a corporation, has always been the last group to hear of trouble in the great business catastrophes of this century.

This happened in the collapse of the Austrian Credit Anstalt, the leading Austrian bank, which in 1931 triggered the first worldwide monetary crisis and, within a few weeks, brought down the English pound. It happend in the collapse of the big German banks which had a good deal to do with Hitler's ascent to power. It was true in the collapse of the Penn-Central Railroad in the United States forty years later. Only at the very last minute, if even then, did the boards of these companies find out that things were not going well.

Whenever one of the 'scandals' breaks, the board's failure is blamed on stupidity, negligence of board members, or on failure of management to keep its board informed. But when such malfunctions occur with unfailing regularity, one must conclude that it is the institution that fails to perform rather than individuals.

The board, whatever its name and whatever its legal structure, has become a fiction. The law may still treat it as the sovereign organ of the corporation but in reality boards are either simply management committees, or they are ineffectual.

Why have boards, regardless of their legal structure, lost their capacity to perform? One reason is the development of the large publicly held corporation. The original board, whether American, English, French or German, was seen as representing the owners. In the nineteenth century, when share ownership was concentrated among a few people or a few groups, each holding a substantial share of the total, the board really did represent them. Each board member had a sizable stake in the enterprise. Each could devote a good deal of time and attention to the company. Each sat on only a few boards.

But large companies in advanced countries are no longer owned by a small group. They are instead owned by many thousands of 'investors'. The boards no longer represent the owner, or indeed anyone in particular. As a result, board membership has lost its rationale. People are invited to sit on boards because of their names. Or worse, board members are recruited from people who do business with a company, such as the company's bankers or the company's lawyers. Above all, board members are now recruited from among successful corporate executives – and in return for the president of Company A accepting board membership of Company B, the president of Company B accepts board membership of Company A. These busy people do not have a large enough stake in the company to justify spending much time on it. If they are doing business with the company, they are understandably reluctant to probe into its affairs, to ask inconvenient questions or to appear critical. And they are likely to sit on so many boards that they cannot really do their homework.

A final factor in the steady decline of the board has surely been that top management, by and large, does not want a really effective board. An effective board demands top-management performance and removes top executives who perform inadequately – this is its duty. An effective board asks inconvenient questions. An effective board insists on being informed *before* the event – this is its legal responsibility. An effective board will not unquestioningly accept the recommendations of top management but will want to know why. It will not rubber-stamp the personnel decisions of top management but will want to know, indeed to get personally acquainted with, alternative candidates for senior appointments. An effective board, in other words, insists on being effective. And this, to most top managements, appears to be a restraint, a limitation, an interference with 'management prerogatives', and altogether a threat.

## Why top management needs an effective board

Allowing the board to fade into a fiction is exceedingly short-sighted. It is increasingly clear that top management will not be permitted to operate without an effective and strong board. If top management does not develop an effective board for its own needs and those of the enterprise, society is likely to impose the wrong kind of board, especially on the large corporation. Such an imposed board will attempt to control top management and to dictate direction and decision. It will indeed become the 'boss'. Because it is an *imposed* board, it must consider itself an adversary of top management. It will not, indeed, cannot, act in the interest of the enterprise. The first signs of this are clearly around us – indeed, it may already be too late to reverse the trend.

In the United States in the last few years, there has been mounting pressure to make boards 'relevant', that is, to appoint as board members representatives of all kinds of groups: blacks, women, the poor, and so on. These appointees, no matter how distinguished the individual, cannot function as board members. Their role is to represent this or that outside group, and to push special projects, special needs and special policies. They cannot be concerned with, or responsible for, the enterprise. Nor should they be expected to hold in confidence what they hear at board meetings. In fact their trust is not to the enterprise but to their constituents outside.

The development of these relevant boards shows that society will not allow top management, and especially top management of large and visible businesses, to exercise its power without an appropriate and effective board. But equally important is the push of the Securities Exchange Commission (SEC) for boards that are responsible, legally liable and capable of proving that they exercise control and have a clear programme of work. The board, as it was conceived originally, has indeed outlived its usefulness. This makes it an urgent top-management job to think through what kind of a board the enterprise and its top management need. The decay of the traditional board has created a vacuum that will not remain unfilled. Responsible top management will want to have a say in what replaces it.

## The three functions of the board

There are actually three different tasks for which a company, and especially a large one, needs a functioning board.

1 The enterprise, first, does need a review body. It needs a group of experienced people, people of integrity and stature, people of proven performance capacity and willingness to work, who counsel, advise, and deliberate with top management. It needs people who are not part of top management but who are available to it, and who can act with knowledge and decision in a crisis.

The big company is too important to society not to have a 'control' in its own structure. Somebody has to make sure that top management thinks through what the company's business is and what it should be. Somebody has to make sure that objectives are being set and strategies are being developed. Somebody has to look critically at the planning of the company, its capital-investment policy and its managed-expenditures budget. Somebody has to monitor people decisions and organization problems. Somebody has to watch the organization's spirit, has to make sure that it succeeds in using the strengths of people and in neutralizing their weaknesses, that it develops tomorrow's managers and that its rewards to managers, its management tools and management methods strengthen the organization and direct it towards objectives.

The board also meets an important top management need. It is an informed, intelligent outsider to talk to and confer with. Having someone to talk to is especially important in a small company where top management otherwise tends to be isolated. Small company managements, without easy, continuous access to outside advisers such as experienced lawyers and consultants, need to have available a few people who are experienced, who understand business, and who are still not part of the company. Small-company top managements need, therefore, a true board of directors – yet small companies as a rule, have an even less effective board than the large ones.

2 An effective and functioning board is needed to remove a top management that fails to perform.

A board capable of removing incompetent or nonperforming

top managements has real power. But only a weak top management is afraid of it. No society can tolerate top-management incompetence in its large businesses. If top managements do not build boards that will remove weak and incompetent chief executives, government will take over the job.

There is another alternative: 'takeover' by the 'financial raider'. Top managements – most of them seemingly all-powerful, seemingly deeply entrenched, seemingly in complete control – have been toppled by shareholder revolts organized by the financial raiders and their 'takeover bids'. The raiders do not aim at companies in trouble. They aim at companies that are not living up to their potential, companies the top managements of which do not perform adequately.

3 Finally, the enterprise needs a 'public and community relations' organ. It needs easy and direct access to its various 'publics' and 'constituents'. It needs to hear from them and to be able to talk to them. The need is readily apparent for the big company, but it may be even greater for the fair-sized company which is a major employer in a small or medium-sized community.

The modern enterprise has many constituencies. The shareholders are one, but they are no longer *the* one. Instead of being 'owners' they have become 'investors'. The employees are clearly also such a constituency, but they are not *the* constituency. There are also the communities where a major company has its plants. There are consumers, suppliers, and distributors. All of them need to know what goes on in a major business, what its problems, its policies and its plans are. The business needs to be understood by them. Top management needs to be known by them, respected by them, accepted by them. Top management needs even more, perhaps, to understand what these constituencies want, understand, misunderstand, see, question. A board involving these different constituencies could serve this two-way public relations need.

The governing board of directors must represent no one but the basic long-term interests of the enterprise. It must be capable of discharging its function as the review organ and as the supervisor of top-management performance.

But the enterprise also needs a board that is, in effect, an organ of information, advice, consultation and communication – that is, the public and community relations board. If the enterprise and its top management do not create this board, it will be imposed on them in the wrong form, that is, as an organ of antagonnism, control and restraint. This is what worker representation on the German board, government representation on the Swedish board, and minority-group representation on the American board are. This will not only further undermine the board, but it will also undermine the authority of company and top management and reduce their capacity to perform.

## What is needed

Clearly, two different organs are needed. One is the executive board that gives top management somebody to talk to, a review organ, a conscience, a counselor, and advisor. This board is an informed and prepared 'stand-by' in case there is failure of a company's top management or need to find successors to today's top management.

The other organ is the public and community relations board which gives a company, and especially a large one, access to its various publics.

There is no reason why these two could not legally be one body. But they have to operate differently. With its public and community relations board, top management needs to discuss what the various publics want, need to know and need to understand. With its executive board top management needs to discuss what top management itself needs to discuss, what top management itself needs to think through, needs to decide, needs to understand. One way to satisfy the need for two boards is to have the executive board operate as a special committee – an executive committee – of a big board that includes also the community relations group.

There are effective boards in existence. None so far adequately fulfil all three of the board's functions, but they do demonstrate the importance of an effective board and the contribution it can make.

What is needed for an effective board is first careful thinking through of the top-management function and of the function and work of the board. It requires objectives and a work plan for the board. Unless the board is set up to discharge specific functions with clear objectives, it will not perform.

## Who belongs on a board?

This requires thinking through who belongs on the board. Some of the people who today are being put on boards – the company's bankers, for example, belong on the public and community relations board. The financial community is a constituent. Management needs to have access to it, to be understood by it and to understand it. But very few other people who today sit on boards should be considered eligible for membership on either the public and community relations board or the review and appeals board.

Neither, for instance, should contain retired company officers. It will be argued that to exclude former senior managers from board membership is to deprive the company of a great deal of knowledge and wisdom. But the right way to keep available to a management the knowledge and wisdom of one of its retired elder statesmen is the Japanese practice of retaining such a person as a 'counselor'. Similarly, no one who sells anything to the company, whether goods or services, such as suppliers, lawyers or consultants, should be a member of the board.

Who, then, should be a board member ? So far we can answer this question only for membership on the review and appeals board.

The first requirement is competence. Board members should have proven ability as senior executives. Ideally, the board member of the future will be in his or her mid-fifties and willing to step out of operating to become an adviser, a guide, a conscience.

Second, board members should have time for the job. No one who sits on more than a small number of boards can really do the job well.

Finally, board members should be independent of management. This probably implies election for a limited term after which a person would not be eligible for re-election. If board members know that they will not be re-elected after five years, no matter how well they get along with the management they serve as a board member, they are less likely to find it necessary to be subservient. At the same time, board members should be elected for definite periods and should have reasonable security of tenure during that period.

How to build the communications and community relations board we do not yet know. But it is just as urgent. Politically, it may be more urgent. Surely the traditional attitude of management, that is, to resist any development that would introduce the public and community relations function into the board, can no longer be maintained. However justified it may have been, it will not work any longer.

The choice is no longer between having a nonboard, which is what we have today, by and large, and an effective board. It is between a board imposed on enterprise and both hostile and inappropriate to it, and a board that is an effective organ of the enterprise and appropriate to its needs.

## Summary

Of all the jobs in the enterprise the top-management job is both the most difficult to organize and the most important. The top-management job is multidimensional, but the tasks are different for each business, and each management needs to be tailored to its enterprise and to its needs.

Is operating work one of top-management's tasks? Top management tasks are recurrent but rarely continuing. And they require a diversity of temperaments. Every top-management task has to be assigned to someone since each is work. Top management therefore also requires a work plan. Top-management work is always work for a team, although there are different ways to organize it. But the specifications for a top-management team are the same, and they are stringent and rigorous. Top-management also has specific needs, especially for information. Just as a business needs a top-management, so top-management needs a supervisory organ, a board of directors. Yet boards have typically not performed their supervisory function. They need to be made functional – in the interest of top-management, of the enterprise, and of society.

# 39 Organizational Conclusions

Organization theorists have argued for years whether organization design should start with an 'ideal organization' or whether it should be 'pragmatic'. Should principles come first? Or should the first consideration be 'fit' to the special needs, the exceptional situations, the habits and traditions of an organization?

Our discussion of organizational building blocks, of design specifications and of design principles shows that the argument is pointless. Both approaches are needed. They have to be used in parallel. Organization design has to be grounded in an 'ideal organization', that is, in a conceptual framework. There must be careful work on defining the structural principles. This work, in turn, must be grounded in the purpose of the business, its objectives, its strategies, its priorities, its key activities. But there is no universal design principle. There is not even a best design principle. Each principle makes certain demands and has severe limitations. Each has only limited scope; none embraces operating work, top-management work and innovation work in a single design.

The reality of an enterprise, in all its complexity, has to be probed in designing organization. It has to be understood. The assumptions that are made, and especially the assumptions that underlie the 'ideal organization design' have to be tested. These assumptions always seem eminently reasonable to the people within a company, but rarely stand up under close scrutiny.

As long as one could assume that organization design meant one basic principle or a simple combination of two, developing an ideal organization could be considered the logical first step. Everybody knew of course that no ideal organization could ever really be achieved; reality always demands bending the rules. But one could hope to come close to the ideal – with exceptions infrequent and confined to purely local situations.

One can no longer assume this. Testing basic assumptions about organizational reality has to proceed parallel to the conceptual thinking about organization. Otherwise one ends up with an ideal organization that, while 'conceptually pure', is inappropriate and inhibits performance.

Two examples, both from the same major organizing task, illustrate this:

In the GE organization of the early 1950s, it was 'obvious' to everyone that any unit charged with 'product responsibility' was actually a 'manufacturing business'. Yet there were quite a few units that manufactured nothing but that were set up to develop a new process or a new product line. These units had a 'customer'; they had 'revenue' – usually a governmental research and development contract; they had 'performance responsibility.' But they were not manufacturing businesses; they were innovative organizations. Setting them up on the functional design of the typical manufacturing business stifled them. This would have been clear to everyone had the ideal design been tested. But it was far too obvious for that.

The other GE assumption was that the general manager of a product business would be an operating manager, like the heads of the automotive divisions of General Motors on which GE modelled its design. But all GM automotive divisions are alike. GM, while a multimarket business, is really a single-product business. GE, on the other hand, is one of the most diversified companies in the world, in its technologies, its processes, its products and its markets. Most of GE's product businesses are the leaders in separate, distinct, large industries. The GE general manager, therefore, is top management rather than operating management. Again, testing the assumptions would have shown this at once. But without such a test GE set up general managers who did not have the team they needed to do their top-management work and autonomous businesses far too small in volume and scope to support the top management they needed. That GE has been constantly reorganizing its supposedly 'definitive' organization structure – in sharp contrast to the stability of Alfred Sloan's design for GM – is largely the result of failure to test plausible assumptions. (Since these remarks may be read as criticism of the work at GE, it needs to be said that the author was closely connected as a consultant with the reorganization at GE, and that what seems so obvious now had yet to be learned in the early 1950s.)

The approach to organization design through the ideal model or organization structure is not 'theory'. It is eminently practical. But the pragmatic approach through explicit definition of assumptions and their testing in the reality of the organization is not 'muddling through' or 'patchwork'. It is theoretically sound in a situation where there are alternative possible models. Organization design requires both concept and experimental validation – or it is faulty design.

## The need for simplicity

The simplest organization structure that will do the job is the best one. What makes an organization structure 'good' are the problems it does not create. The simpler the structure, the less can go wrong.

But there is neither a perfect nor a universal design principle. All of them have limitations. Even the simplest business – a small to medium-sized company with one major product line for one major market – will use at least two design principles: functional design and teams, the teams for top-management and innovative work and as a complement to functionally organized work.

Using, for the sake of simplicity or symmetry, a design principle beyond its inherent limits is asking for trouble.

Using functional structure in tasks for which team structure is needed, in knowledge work or for genuine innovation, for instance, makes for a 'clean' structure. But it also makes for non-performance. Conversely, using teams as the structural units for unchanging, large-scale functional work causes only confusion. *Tasks*, in such work, can then be – and often should be – done in teams; but the work itself always has to be specific and specialized. And setting up a federally decentralized unit that is not a genuine business will only confuse; for all its limitations simulated decentralization will have to be used.

Some design principles are more difficult than others, but none are without problems. None are primarily people-focused or primarily task-focused; none are more 'creative', 'free', or 'more democratic'. Design principles are tools, and tools are neither good nor bad in themselves. They can be used properly or improperly; and that is all. To obtain both the greatest possible simplicity and the greatest 'fit', organization design has to start out with a clear focus on *key activities* needed to produce *key results*. These activities have to be structured and positioned in the simplest possible design. Above all, architects of organization need to keep in mind the purpose of the structures they are designing.

## Summary

Organization is a means to an end rather than an end itself. Sound structure is a prerequisite to organizational health; but it is not health itself. The test of a healthy business is not the beauty, clarity or perfection of its organization structure. *It is the performance of people.*

# Conclusion:
# The Manager of Tomorrow

Today's student in the college course in management will still be active and working forty-five or fifty years hence – well into the second quarter of the twenty-first century.

A century ago no one could have predicted the world of 1925 or 1930. And no one in 1930, when today's managers began their college studies or went to work, could have predicted the world of the 1970s. The one thing one can predict about the politics, society and economy that lie half a century ahead is that there will be great changes.

Yet one can also predict, with high probability, some important things in respect to the manager of tomorrow – that is, the management student of today. There will surely be new skills and, with them, a need for the manager of tomorrow to organize his or her own self-development and to acquire the habit of continuous learning. Yet the basic tasks of the manager will remain the same. Managers of tomorrow will have, as their first responsibility, the performance of the institution for which they work. They will be responsible for making work productive and the worker achieving. And the task of managing social impact and social responsibilities will hardly become less important or less demanding. The managers of tomorrow will, in other words, concern themselves with the same tasks as the managers of today, will worry about the same things, will face very similar problems and very similar demands – though they will be expected, I believe, to tackle these tasks with more knowledge, more thought, more planning and greater competence.

One can, however, also anticipate some real changes in managerial tasks. One of them will surely be a major thrust towards systematic management in the public service institution – whether government agency, hospital, school or university. Indeed the frontier of management in the next half century is likely to be in the public service institution, just as the frontier of management in the last fifty years was in business enterprise. But there are also major problems in respect to each of the major task areas that will, in all likelihood, demand systematic work on the part of the managers of tomorrow. In the first task area – that of the specific performance of business and of public service institution – the biggest immediate problem is to organize for systematic abandonment of the obsolete, the unproductive, the no longer appropriate. We have learned a great deal about innovation as an organized activity. At least we have learned that the making of a different tomorrow is a major responsibility of managers. Now we will have to learn that sloughing off yesterday is also a central managerial task. And this is something that managers in public service institutions in particular have yet to learn. So far, public service institutions have rarely abandoned, and almost never done so systematically.

In the area of work and working, the big job ahead is to make industrial relations within our organizations conform to social reality. Within the last fifty years, the 'working class' has changed dramatically in all developed countries. Today's 'worker' is likely to be 'middle class' in income and social position. He or she is likely to be a 'knowledge worker' rather than a 'manual worker'. Indeed the 'blue collar worker' in manufacturing industry – still the prototype of the 'worker' in most texts and in most discussions – is already a distinct minority in all developed countries, and likely to be a fairly small segment of the working population by the year 2000. But even the manual worker of today, the blue collar worker in manufacturing industry, is very different in income and above all in education, from the manual worker of yesterday. The traditional line between 'worker' and 'capitalist' is fast disappearing; it is already an anachronism, no matter how strong its emotional hold on our rhetoric. For, through the pension fund, employees (especially in the United States) are fast becoming the true 'owners' of industry. In the US today, employee pension funds own about one-third of industry, and a good deal more of the truly big companies. By 1985, pension fund ownership of the share capital of American business will have risen to fifty per cent or so – again considerably more in respect to big business. Other developed countries are reaching the same end through different routes and with different mechanisms.

This will not usher in Utopia in labour relations. All the old tensions, problems and conflicts of work and working discussed in this book will remain. But the emergence of the worker as a true 'owner' through pension funds – even though the worker does not directly control business – will make both possible and necessary systematic and purposeful work towards what this book has called 'the responsible worker': the worker who, regardless of job, takes a high degree of managerial responsibility for his or her own task, his or her own work group, and for the governance of the plant community and its concerns. Not much innovation is required. A good many businesses, for well over a hundred years, have been doing the job. But what has been isolated exception will have to become general rule. The needed changes will again be greatest in public service institutions. For in managing work and working, public service institutions, by and large, are well behind any reasonably well-managed business.

Finally, in respect to managing social impact and social responsibility, managers will have to learn how to think through systematically and carefully the difficult and risky 'trade-offs' between conflicting needs and conflicting rights. At the same time, managers will have to learn to think ahead in respect to the social impacts of the institutions – whether business enterprise, schools and colleges, hospital or government agencies; whether the impacts are technological or social; and whether they are impacts on individuals with the organization or on society, community and the environment outside. This is a leadership responsibility. And in a society of organizations, managers as a group are the leadership – however modest the personal role and individual power of a specific manager might be.

These are new challenges for management and new demands on it. But one can also predict a major change for the individual manager. The manager of tomorrow will increasingly have more than one career. Increasingly, men and women will change their work, their environment, their own role, some time between the ages of 40 and 50. And the more successful a person is as a manager or professional, the more likely that he or she will make such a career change. It may only be a move from one company to another or a shift from accounting work to sales management. But it may also be a move from one kind of institution to another. The successful controller of a fair-sized company may move, as administrator, into a hospital, for instance. 'Second careers' are by no means uncommon today. However, tomorrow they may well have become the accepted rule, where we still look upon them as an exception. One reason, though by no means the only one, is the employee pension plan – especially the pension plan of businesses. They now give the middle-aged manager and professional a substantial degree of economic security, where hitherto economic uncertainty alone tended to keep people in jobs and employment they had outgrown, had become bored with, had ceased to feel as challenging and enjoyable. And this, it is safe to predict, will put a high premium on continued learning by managers, on their taking responsibility for self-development as a person and as a manager, and on a thorough knowledge of a manager's work, managerial skills and managerial tools.

But the most important thing one can predict, in respect to the manager of tomorrow, is that there will be a manager of tomorrow. In all likelihood, there will be more managers tomorrow than there are today, and they will matter more. Unless mankind destroys itself in some such self-inflicted catastrophe as nuclear war, society will continue to be a society of organizations. And to the degree to which developing nations advance socially and economically they will increasingly become societies of organizations too. Organizations are far from perfect. As every manager knows, they are very difficult, full of frustration, tension and friction, clumsy and unwieldy. But they are the only tools we have to accomplish such social purposes as economic production and distribution, health care, governance or education. And there is not the slightest reason to expect society to be willing to do without these services which only modern organization can provide. Indeed there is every reason to expect society to demand more performance from all its institutions, and to become more dependent upon their performance.

And it is managers who make institutions perform.

*Peter F. Drucker*

# Bibliography

Management literature has become so voluminous that no one can hope to keep up with it. Even to pick out the 'best' books is a fruitless attempt. What I have tried to do is to prepare a list – admittedly overlong – of the books which a fairly large number of friends, experienced managers in a number of countries around the world, have found to be stimulating, readable, and worthwhile. Even so, the list suffers from being heavily biased towards American authors.

To make the list more useful, I have divided the books into major categories and have not hesitated to list a title more than once if it seemed to me to deserve mention in several categories. References are to the British edition wherever one exists.

Most management books take Western, and especially American, management for granted. For this reason, I have included a small list of six titles on Japanese management. They will not only help the Western reader to understand the one non-western managerial system in a highly developed country, but will also give him a better insight into the cultural and historical roots of his own system.

## 1 Origins, Foundations and Tasks of Management

Chandler, Alfred D., Jr. *Strategy and Structure*. London: MIT Press, 1962.

Chandler, Alfred D., Jr, and Salisbury, Stephen. *Pierre S. DuPont and the Making of the Modern Corporation*. New York: Harper & Row, 1971.

Drucker, Peter F. *The Future of Industrial Man*. London: New American Library, 1965.

Drucker, Peter F. *Concept of the Corporation*. New York: John Day, 1946. New Revised Edition, 1972. (Title of British Edition: *Big Business*. London: Heinemann, 1947.)

Drucker, Peter F. *The New Society*. London: Heinemann, 1951.

Eels, R. S. F. and Walton, C. C. *Conceptual Foundations of Business*. Homewood, Ill.: Irwin, 1961.

Emmet, Boris, and Jeuk, John C. *Catalogues and Counters*. London: University of Chicago Press, 1965.

Galbraith, John Kenneth. *The New Industrial State*. London: Hamish Hamilton, 1967; Penguin Books.

Landes, David S. *The Unbound Prometheus; Technological Change and Industrial Development in Western Europe from 1750 to the present*. Cambridge University Press, 1969.

Nevins, Allan, and Hill, Frank E. *Ford: Decline and Rebirth 1933–1962*. New York: Scribner, 1962/3.

Reader, W. J. *Imperial Chemical Industries: A History*, vol. 1, *1870–1926*. Oxford University Press, 1970.

Schumpeter, Joseph. *The Theory of Economic Development*. Harvard University Press, 1949. Original German Edition, 1911.

Schumpeter, Joseph. *Capitalism, Socialism and Democracy*. London: Allen & Unwin, 1950.

Siemens, Georg. *Der Weg der Elektrotechnik; Geschichte des Hauses Siemens*. Freiburg: Alber, 1961.

Sloan, Alfred P., Jr. *My Years with General Motors*. London: Pan Books, 1969.

Woodruff, Philip. *The Men Who Ruled India*. 2 vols. London: Macmillan, 1954.

## 2 Management as a Process and a Discipline

Drucker, Peter F. *The Practice of Management*. London: Heinemann, 1955; Pan Books, 1968.

Gantt, Henry. *Gantt on Management*. Edited by Alex W. Rathe. New York: American Management Association, 1961.

Merrill, Harwood, ed. *Classics in Management*. New York: American Management Association, 1960.

Koontz, Harold, and O'Donnell, Cyril. *Principles of Management*. New York: McGraw-Hill, 1972.

Urwick, Lyndall F., and Brech, E. F. L. *The Making of Scientific Management*. London: Pitman, 1966.

Urwick, Lyndall F., ed. *The Golden Book of Management*. London: Newman Neame, 1956.

## 3 Management in Japan

Abbeglen, James. *The Japanese Factory*. Glencoe, Ill.: Free Press, 1958.

Hirschmeier, Johannes. *The Origins of Entrepreneurship in Meiji Japan*. Cambridge, Mass.: Harvard, 1964.

Kobayashi, Shigeru. *Creative Management*. New York: American Management Association, 1971.

Nakane, Chie. *Japanese Society*. London: Weidenfeld & Nicholson, 1970.

Tobata, Seiichi, ed. *The Modernization of Japan*. Tokyo: Institute of Asian Economic Affairs, 1966.

Yoshino, M. *Japan's Managerial System: Tradition and Innovation*. London: MIT Press, 1969.

## 4 Managing for Performance

Crozier, Michael. *The Bureaucratic Phenomenon*. Chicago: University of Chicago Press, 1964.

Dean, Joel. *Managerial Economics*. Englewood Cliffs, N. J.: Prentice-Hall, 1951.

Drucker, Peter F. *Managing for Results*. London: Heinemann, 1964; Pan Books, 1967.

Penrose, Edith R. *The Theory of the Growth of the Firm*. Oxford: Blackwell, 1960.

Schumpeter, Joseph. *The Theory of Economic Development*. Harvard University Press, 1949.

Shackle, G. L. S. *Decision, Order and Time in Human Affairs*. Cambridge University Press, 1970.

## 5 Work and Worker

Herzberg, Frederick; Mausner, B.; and Snyderman, B. R. *The Motivation to Work*. New York: Wiley, 1959.

Herzberg, Frederick. *Work and the Nature of Man*. London: Staples Press, 1968.

Homans, G. C. *The Human Group*. London: Routledge & Kegan Paul, 1951.

Likert, Rensis. *The Human Organization*. New York: McGraw-Hill, 1967.

Maslow, A. H. *Motivation and Personality*. London: Harper & Row, 1970.

Mayo, Elton. *The Social Problems of an Industrial Civilization*. London: Routledge & Kegan Paul, 1949.

Mayo, Elton. *The Human Problems of an Industrial Civilization*. Boston: Harvard Business School, 1946.

McGregor, Douglas. *The Human Side of Enterprise*. New York: McGraw-Hill, 1960.

Taylor, F. W. *Scientific Management*. New York: Harpers, 1912, and many editions since.

Wiener, Norbert. *The Human Use of Human Beings*. London: Sphere Books, 1969.

Woodward, Joan. *Industrial Organization; Theory and Practice*. Oxford University Press, 1966.

## 6 Social Impacts and Social Responsibilities

Bowen, H. R. *The Social Responsibility of the Businessman*. New York: Harper & Row, 1953.

McGuire, J. W. *Business and Society*. New York: McGraw-Hill, 1963.

Steiner, George A. *Business and Society*. New York: Random House, 1971.

## 7 The Manager's Work and Job

Barnard, Chester I. *The Functions of the Executive*. London: Harvard University Press, 1938.

Drucker, Peter F. *The Effective Executive*. London: Heinemann, 1967; Pan Books, 1970.

Follett, Mary Parker. *Dynamic Administration; The Collected Papers of Mary Parker Follett*. Edited by Henry C. Metcalf and L. Urwick. London: Pitman, 1965.

McGregor, Douglas. *The Professional Manager*. New York: McGraw-Hill, 1967.

Mali, Paul. *Management by Objectives*. New York: John Wiley, 1972.

Simon, Herbert A. *Administrative Behaviour*. London: Collier-Macmillan, 1957.


## 8 Managerial Skills and Managerial Tools

Anthony, R. N. *Planning and Control Systems*. Harvard Business School, 1965.

Beer, Stafford. *Decision and Control*. New York: Wiley, 1966.

Churchman, C. W.; Ackoff, R. L.; and Arnoff, E. L. *Introduction to Operations Research*. New York: Wiley, 1957.

Ewing, D. W., ed. *Long-Range Planning for Management*. London: Harper & Row, 1965.

Forrester, Jay W. *Industrial Dynamics*. London: MIT Press, 1961.

Solomon, Ezra, ed. *The Management of Corporate Capital*. Glencoe, Ill.: Free Press, 1959.

Solomon, Ezra. *The Theory of Financial Management*. New York: Columbia University Press, 1963.

Steiner, George A. *Top Management Planning*. New York: Macmillan, 1969.


## 9 Organization Design and Structure

Dale, Ernest. *The Great Organizers*. New York: McGraw-Hill, 1960.

Drucker, Peter F. *Concept of the Corporation*. (Title of British Edition: *Big Business*. London: Heinemann, 1947.)

Fayol, Henri. *General and Industrial Management*. London: Pitman, 1967.

March, James G., and Simon, Herbert A. *Organizations*. New York: Wiley, 1958.

Sayles, Leonard R., and Chandler, Margaret K. *Managing Large Systems: Organizations for the Future*. London: Harper & Row, 1971.

Sloan, Alfred P., Jr. *My Years with General Motors*. London: Pan Books, 1969.

Webb, James E. *Space Age Management*. New York: McGraw-Hill, 1969.

Urwick, Lyndall F. *Notes on the Theory of Organization*. New York: American Management Association, 1953.

## 10 The Top-Management Job

Bower, Marvin. *The Will to Manage*. New York: McGraw-Hill, 1966.
Chandler, Alfred D., Jr, and Salisbury, Stephen. *Pierre S. DuPont and the Making of the Modern Corporation*. New York: Harper & Row, 1971.
Holden, Paul E. and others. *Top-Management Organization and Control*. New York: McGraw-Hill, 1951.
Sloan, Alfred P., Jr. *My Years with General Motors*. London: Pan Books, 1969.
Woodruff, Philip. *The Men Who Ruled India*. 2 vols. London: Macmillan, 1954.

## 11 Strategies and Structures

Chandler, Alfred D., Jr, and Salisbury, Stephen. *Pierre S. DuPont and the Making of the Modern Corporation*. New York: Harper & Row, 1971.
Dale, Ernest. *The Great Organizers*. New York: McGraw-Hill, 1960.
Guth, William. *Organizational Strategy: Analysis, Commitment Implementation*. Homewood, Ill.: Irwin, 1974.
Sayles, Leonard R., and Chandler, Margaret K. *Managing Large Systems: Organizations for the Future*. London: Harper & Row, 1971.

## 12 The Multinational Corporation

Brooke, M. Z. *The Strategy of Multinational Enterprise*. London: Longman, 1970.
Dunning, John H. *The Multinational Enterprise*. London: Allen & Unwin, 1971.
Rolfe, Sidney E., and Damon, Walter, eds. *The Multinational Corporation in the World Economy*. New York: Praeger, 1970.
Vernon, Raymond. *Sovereignty at Bay: The Multinational Spread of Private Enterprise*. London: Longman, 1971.
Eells, Richard. *Global Corporations*. New York: Interbook, 1973.

## 13 The Innovative Organization

Argyris, Chris. *Organization and Innovation*. New Haven, Conn.: Yale University Press, 1963.
Bennis, W. G. *Changing Organizations*. New York: McGraw-Hill, 1966.
Gardner, John W. *Self-Renewal: The Individual and the Innovative Society*. London: Harper & Row, 1964.

## 14 The Manager of Tomorrow

Boulding, Kenneth E. *The Organizational Revolution.* New York: Harper & Row, 1953.
Boulding, Kenneth E. *The Image.* New York: Harper & Row, 1956.
Drucker, Peter F. *The Age of Discontinuity.* London: Heinemann, 1969.
Drucker, Peter F., ed. *Preparing Tomorrow's Business Leaders Today.* Englewood Cliffs, N. J.: Prentice-Hall, 1969.

*Note:* British editions of books published by Prentice-Hall, McGraw-Hill, and Wiley are available from the UK companies at Hemel Hempstead, Maidenhead, and Chichester, respectively.

# Glossary

**Accountability** Responsibility for results.

**Accounting** The system of keeping records of financial transactions and of summarizing these data in appropriate reports for management, financial institutions, or government agencies.

**Affiliate** A company that works closely with another company in serving a particular market. A subsidiary of a multinational corporation that serves a country other than the larger company's home country is an affiliate.

**Allocate** To divide resources among competing interests. Allocating financial resources through a budgetary process is a prime example of such division.

**Antitrust legislation** Laws that prohibit the formation and operation of business monopolies. The Sherman Antitrust Law is the base of American antitrust law.

**Appraise** To assess the value of a property, a person's job performance, or other valuable.

**Assessment centre** A method of evaluating candidates for a managerial position that involves bringing the candidates to a central location for a series of tests and interviews.

**Assets** The items of value owned by a company or person. Also the items fitting this description that appear on the left-hand side of a balance sheet opposite the liabilities.

**Authority** The right to use assigned resources within one's discretion to accomplish an assigned task, including the right to direct people and other resources. Authority is always limited by the organization's policies and procedures and the rules of the larger society.

**Automation** The system of production that uses self-controlled machines to accomplish the task at hand. When further self-controlled devices are incorporated, one says that there is greater automation in the process.

**Autonomy** The ability to operate independently of other units. A manager may have great autonomy in his job, or one can speak of a subsidiary of a conglomerate having limited autonomy.

**Bankrupt** A legal or economic term that means insolvency or inability to pay one's debts.

**Basic strategy objective** A company or organization's central aim in trying to achieve its overall financial or other objectives. For example, Sears, Roebuck's basic strategy objective during its early decades was to merchandise true values to farmers and their families through mail-order merchandising.

**Behavioural psychology** The school of psychology that relies exclusively on the analysis of empirically observed behaviour in accounting for why people act as they do.

**Billing** The business function of giving customers or clients formal notice that payment is due on a certain date for goods or services provided.

**Brand name product** A product sold with a company's name or other specific name attached to it rather than being sold with only a generic name.

**Break-even point** The level of sales or production that is necessary to break even – that is, to lose no money and to make no money. Analysis whose objective is to determine this level is called break-even analysis.

**Budget** An approved scheme that specifies how much is to be spent on each category of expenditure during a given time period. The scheme is usually compiled in a document referred to as the budget.

**Budget allocation** The amount to be spent in a particular category as specified in a budget.

**Budget-based institution** An organization that receives relatively assured income rather than being subject to an immediately responsive market. Government agencies and nonprofit organizations are examples of such institutions.

**'Buying-in'** The process of getting approval to provide a product or service by underestimating the total cost.

**By-product** A substance, product or condition produced by a production process in addition to the primary item produced.

**Capital** Wealth that an organization possesses to employ in achieving its aims.

**Capital equipment** A company or organization's equipment or buildings whose purchase required the expenditure of substantial capital.

**Capital formation** The process by which capital is created in an economy.

**Capital investment decisions** Decisions regarding the employment of a firm's capital. Since capital is usually invested in plant or equipment for long periods, it is of utmost importance that decisions be made with as much knowledge as possible about the expected rate of return on the capital.

**Carrying costs** The costs incurred by holding inventory.

**Centralization** A method of organizing that concentrates decision making at the top of an organization's hierarchy.

**Common Market** The group of Western European countries banded together to provide a larger market open to all members, or any market formed in this manner.

**Communication** The transfer of meaning from one (the sender) to another (the receiver). The sender and receiver may be persons, corporate entities or other groups of people.

**Compensation** That which is given in exchange for work performed. Compensation is usually money but may include other items such as privileges.

**Computer program** An integrated set of instructions for a computer to use in performing a particular task.

**Conglomerate** A company made up of many other companies in a wide variety of industries. Many such companies were formed in the late 1960s.

**'Conscience' activities** The activities directed to giving vision and to setting standards and auditing performance against them.

**Constituencies** The various interest groups who vie for the attention of an organization.

**Consumerism** The social movement that insists that products and services be of unassailable quality and without any possible hazardous side effects.

**Control** The management function that aims to keep activities directed in such a way that desired results are achieved. Monitoring of performance is the starting point of all control. In case performance deviates from what is expected, corrective action must be taken.

**Coordinate** To integrate one's own efforts with those of others to achieve a desired result.

**Corporation** A legal entity formed by persons to enter a business while limiting their liability to the monies they have contributed to the enterprise.

**Cost accountant** An accountant whose primary responsibility is to determine the cost of goods or services. The cost figures are to be used in determining profit levels and in meeting other demands for judgements on what the costs are.

**Cost centre** In a business, costs are either assigned exclusively to the business as a whole, or the business is broken into parts each of which is responsible for certain costs. In the latter event, the parts are the cost centres. In a multidivision company, the divisions may be the cost centres.

**Cost effectiveness analysis** The method of analysis that compares the cost of alternative solutions for a problem with the relative benefits provided by each.

**Cost of capital** The rate of return that should be used as the minimum acceptable for considering a given capital expenditure; the 'rental' cost of money. Thus, projects must pay more than it would cost to 'rent' the money required, or no financial benefit has been produced.

**Credit** Ability to borrow funds, or the funds so borrowed.

**Critical path analysis** A method of analysing the scheduling of a project with multiple subactivities. The method uses network diagrams that represent the component activities. Time required to complete each activity is analysed, and the earliest and latest beginning date for each activity is specified. Finally the longest path through the sequence of activities (the critical path) is identified, and that path receives special attention so that the project will be completed on time.

**Data processing** The function of handling the masses of data involved in the multiple transactions related to a firm's business. Since most large firms use computers in this function, the department in charge of the computing is frequently called the data processing department. Similarly, the function is often referred to as electronic data processing (EDP).

**Decentralization** A method of organizing that disburses decision making to multiple locations and levels rather than concentrating it at the top of the organization's hierarchy.

**Decision theory** A body of analytical tools including logic, mathematical models (especially models that use probability theory) and diagrams to be used in decision making.

**Deficit** The amount by which expenses exceed the funds available to cover them.

**Delegation** The process a manager uses to assign a task or part of a task to a subordinate.

**Demographics** The study of populations as regards their numbers, births, deaths, etc., and the statistics so produced.

**Departmentalization** The process of grouping organizational activities into basic subunits, usually done using a common characteristic such as function, product or geography.

**Depreciate** The process by which the work or equipment or buildings are assigned decreased values due to deterioration, obsolescence or other considerations.

**Depression** A period of extremely low business activity, marked by high unemployment and extreme declines in demand.

**Direct labour cost** The cost that is attributable to the production process itself and that is so ascribed in accounting for the results of the business. Direct labour costs are frequently contrasted with indirect labour costs, which are costs counted in determining results but are not part of the production payroll.

**Discounted cash flow analysis** A method of allowing a stream of fund flows that are to occur over a period of years to be summarized into a single number so that alternative streams can be compared.

**Distribution** The function of dispensing the goods manufactured or warehoused to the locations where they will be consumed or received by customers.

**Distributor** A company or business agent who is the middleman between the manufacturer and the end user.

**Dividend** The amount of profit for a given period returned to the owner of one share of a company's stock.

**Division of labour** The method of dividing a task into specialized subtasks with different people doing different subtasks so that they may become very efficient at performing their subtask and thereby contribute to accomplishing the overall job at least cost.

**EDP (electronic data processing)** Data processing using computers.

**Effective demand** The demand that will be realized if the product or service is made available.

**Effectiveness** The extent to which the desired result is realized. Frequently compared with efficiency.

**Efficiency** Output divided by input, or the extent to which the result produced was produced at least cost.

**Entrepreneur** A person who starts and develops a business.

**Extrapolation** A method of forecasting that assumes that the future will continue to reflect already established trends.

**Factors of production** The elements necessary in order to produce goods and services in an economy, for example capital and labour.

**Federal decentralization** A mode of organizing a large multidivision company by decentralizing authority and centralizing control.

**Feedback mechanism** A mechanism to allow recognition of unexpected deviations in a process and prompt corrective action so that the process will stay at the level needed to obtain the desired results.

**First-line supervisor** A manager who supervises other employees at the lowest managerial level in the organizational hierarchy. These people are also referred to as first-line management.

**Fixed capital** Money invested permanently in buildings, machinery and equipment.

**Fixed costs** Costs that are incurred regardless of the level of production. Frequently contrasted with variable costs, which depend on the amount produced.

**Forecasting** Estimating the value of a certain variable in the future, such as sales for the coming year.

**Foreman** A manager who is in charge of one of the basic units of a production facility.

**Formal organization** The structure that indicates to whom each person in the hierarchy reports, frequently diagrammed in an 'organization chart'.

**Free enterprise system** The economic system that has private ownership of proerty and business units operated with a minimum of governmental interference.

**Functional authority** Authority based on a business function whose exercise may require compliance by persons who are not subordinates of the person exercising the authority.

**Function organization** A mode of organizing a business that makes the manufacturing, selling, engineering, accounting, and other departments defined by business functions the basic subunits of the organization.

**Gantt Chart** A chart to be used in planning and coordinating an activity that involves several parallel subactivities. A time line is depicted horizontally at the top of the chart. Below the time line are horizontal bars for each activity, with the length of each bar representing its duration and the left-end border representing the beginning time of the activity.

**Hierarchy of needs** A construct in Maslow's theory of motivation. The theory postulates that human needs consist of the hierarchy: physiological, security, affiliation, esteem and self-actualization needs. The theory suggests that the lower-level needs must be satisfied before higher-order needs come into play and that once lower-level needs are satisfied, they lose their motivational importance.

**Hygiene and housekeeping activities** Activities that do not contribute to the basic results of the business but that if done poorly could damage the business, for example keeping the premises clean, the employees fed, reporting to the government, etc.

**Impact** The consequences an action has in addition to those that constitute its raison d'etre, for example an action taken in one department may have consequences far beyond that department, or a production process may have polluting wastes as an impact.

**Incentives** The items provided as 'carrots' using a carrot-stick theory of motivation.

**Industrial engineering** The discipline that includes the scientific principles and research the industrial engineer applies in the work place.

**Industrial physiology** The subdivision of physiology that is concerned with the impact of specific industrial practices on the human body and its functioning.

**Industrial psychology** The branch of psychology that studies human behaviour in organizational settings, with special attention being given to behaviour in business firms.

**Industrial relations** An approach to management promoted by some behavioural scientists. The central theme is the relief or prevention of dissatisfaction among employees.

**Industrial sociology** The study of human institutions and groups and their operating characteristics in an industrial setting.

**Inflation** The process by which money loses some of its value.

**Individual professional contributors** Managerial personnel who may supervise no one (except possibly a secretary and an assistant) but who make major contributions to the results of the firm by applying their professional competence, for example an advertising specialist.

**Innovation** Activity or developments in a firm that result in the adoption of a new product, business, or way of doing things.

**Installment credit** Credit extended in exchange for the promise to repay the money with interest in equal payments at specified intervals until the money is repaid.

**Institutional investors** Investors who represent large organizations and as a consequence buy and sell very large blocks of stocks and bonds, for example, mutual funds, pension funds, university endowment funds. Since the late 1960s such investors have come to dominate the market, whereas individual investors were once a large part of the market.

**Integrate** A process by which a manager meshes his work with that of others (in his unit, in other units, above him, below him and laterally) in order to insure performance.

**Invention** A technological advance, either a product or a means of doing something.

**Inventory** The supply of goods or resources on hand at one time.

**Inventory models** Models that may be used to determine when inventories should be resupplied.

**Investment** An application of a firm's resources (especially money) in a means that is expected to pay off in future results.

**Investment banking** The function performed by financial institutions that underwrite and sell new issues of shares and bonds of a company and advise the company on such matters.

**Investment instruments** Vehicles that may be used to invest funds, for example shares, bonds, mutual funds, certificates of deposit.

**Irreversible decision** A decision whose impact cannot be removed or reversed, for example introducing a completely new technology (the secret of the technology cannot be reinstated).

**Job description** An exposition of the duties and responsibilities that are inherent in a particular job.

**Job enlargement** Including more tasks or more kinds of tasks in a given job in order to make the job more satisfying.

**Job enrichment** Changing some aspects of a job in order to have it satisfy more of a person's higher-order needs.

**Knowledge worker** An employee whose major contribution depends on his employing his knowledge rather than his muscle power and coordination, frequently contrasted with production workers who employ muscle power and coordination to operate machines.

**Labour economics** The branch or discipline of economics that concentrates its studies on the supply and demand of labour in an economy.

**Labour-intensive industry** An industry that, in comparison to other industries, requires large expenditures of labour per dollar of sales or production. Frequently contrasted with capital-intensive industry.

**Lateral mobility** Ability to move from one area of a business to another, as from production to sales. Frequently compared to vertical mobility.

**Lead time** The time that must pass between a decision and its coming to fruition, for example the number of years between the decision to build a new steel mill and the time when it can be placed in operation.

**Limited liability insurance** Insurance that covers only certain kinds of losses or only losses of a particular size.

**Linear programming** An operations research technique that can be used to determine the proper mix of products or ingredients to maximize profits or some other dimension of interest to management.

**Line management job** A managerial job that includes supervision and one of the central business functions such as selling or production. Frequently contrasted with staff jobs.

**Liquidate** To terminate an operation by disposing of all assets and inventory, returning the proceeds to the owners of the operation.

**Long-range planning** Planning with a multi-year time horizon. Contrasted with yearly plans and other short-range plans.

**Logistics** The function of moving, storing and distributing resources and goods.

**Management by objective (MBO)** The approach to management that emphasizes the central role of objectives for each unit of an organization and for each individual contributor. The approach emphasizes self-control as a consequence of having clear objectives for each individual.

**Management science** The approach to management that emphasizes the application of scientific methods for the improved understanding and practice of management.

**Managerial accounting** The accounting done in a firm to produce reports that will contribute to management decisions. Contrasted with tax accounting or financial accounting.

**Managerial economics** The subdivision of economics that emphasizes notions of direct relevance to managers; decisions such as investment and pricing decisions receive special attention.

**Manual worker** A worker whose primary contribution is a result of his or her muscle power and coordination.

**Marginal cost** The cost of producing and selling an additional unit.

**Marginal efficiencies** Efficiencies that if adopted would make very small changes in overall results.

**Marginal revenue** The revenue that would be produced by producing and selling an additional unit.

**Market** An area in which buyers and sellers may come together or an area of demand.

**Market standing** The relative ranks of various firms in a single market.

**Market research** The research produced by market analysts.

**Mass-distribution system** A system for distributing goods or services to large numbers of customers who are dispersed within an area.

**Matrix organization** A mode of organizing, especially of large technological projects, that includes persons having both task and function assignments and as a consequence being attached to two units of the organization at one time (with the possibility of having two bosses). The 'matrix' is suggested by a diagram that has functional units across the top and task units down the side with entries indicating persons from various functions assigned to a given task.

**Minimum profitability** The least level of profitability a particular industry should accept in order to take the risk inherent in that industry.

**Mission** An organization's paramount objective for its intermediate future.

**Model** A simplified replication of a problem situation that can be manipulated to explore the range and quality of solutions to the problem.

**Multinational corporation** A corporation that has significant production, markets, and operations in many countries.

**Multiproduct, multimarket, or multitechnology company** A company that produces multiple products, operates in many markets, or employs a wide variety of technologies.

**Mutual fund** An investment vehicle that allows the investor to have an interest in many companies without being the direct owner of their stocks.

**Network analysis** Analysis used in planning and scheduling, for example critical path analysis.

**Nonmanufacturing business** A business whose primary function is selling or some business function.

**Non-profit organization** An organization such as a university whose mission is other than to create a profit from its operations.

**Objectives** The levels of results to be sought within a specific time period.

**Obsolete** No longer in use; outmoded.

**Operations** The activities associated with the production of current results. Frequently contrasted with the preparations for future business opportunities.

**Operations research** The discipline that studies the application of mathematical tools and logic to the solution of industrial problems.

**Optimal solution** A solution to a problem that is the best one possible.

**Optimization** The process of finding the optimal solution to a management problem, usually using an operations research model.

**Organization chart** The pictorial representation of the formal organization.

**Organization design** The design principles incorporated in the formal organization of a company or the discipline that studies alternative ways to design organizations.

**Participative management** An approach to improving management practice that emphasizes participation of all impacted parties in decisions.

**Partnership** A mode of legally structuring a business that includes specifications of each partner's role and responsibility.

**Payback period** The period required for the proceeds from an investment to equal the amount invested.

**Performance** Actual results obtained. Sometimes used to denote the achievement of positive results.

**Personnel administration** The management role concerned with the hiring and training of employees and with keeping employee records.

**Personnel appraisal** The evaluation of employees' performance and interaction between a boss and subordinate to discuss the subordinate's performance and future objectives, a process frequently discussed in conjunction with MBO.

**PERT Chart (Program Evaluation Review Technique)** A planning technique that uses charts, created by the Navy to aid in planning a project and in evaluating progress after it is under way.

**Pilot plant** A plant built to test a new process, usually on a scale much less than that proposed for subsequent implementation. Frequently a pilot-plant test of a process, if successful, will suggest ways to improve the larger facility to be built later.

**Planned obsolescence** An approach to design that utilizes the expectation that the product design will become out of vogue before the product itself is physically unuseable; the approach includes subsequent designs that are intended to make previous designs unfashionable. Also, the design of products to become obsolete earlier than necessary in order to be able to introduce new designs.

**Plant** The facilities that a firm can use for production.

**Priorities** The relative order in which an organization intends to address a list of issues or areas.

**Probability mathematics** A subdivision of mathematics that is concerned with modelling situations with outcomes that have relative likelihoods of occurrence.

**Process industry** An industry that neither manufactures nor provides an intangible service; rather it subjects certain resources to a process, for example the oil refining industry.

**Product lines** The various basic categories of products produced or provided.

**Product manager** A managerial role that has responsibility for coordinating all of the activities that affect the results produced from the assigned product. Such a manager might coordinate all of production, advertising, selling and distributing.

**Product mix** The variety of products offered by one company.

**Productivity** The relative output for given levels of input, especially the production per production employee. The continuing challenge is to improve productivity.

**Profit** The difference between income and costs.

**Profit centres** In large multidivision companies, profits may be calculated in various subdivisions of the company to add up to the overall profit, compare with cost centres. A manager in charge of a profit centre (one of the subdivisions) has profit and loss responsibility.

**Proprietor** The sole owner and manager of a small business.

**Prototype** A model of a potential new product, used to evaluate the product's prospects.

**Public-service institutions** Institutions such as government and nonprofit institutions which exist to provide a service in a nonprofit manner.

**Purchasing power** The ability a person or a group of people has to purchase goods and services because of their income.

**Qualitative factors** Factors to be incorporated in decisions that cannot be quantified, such as values and beliefs.

**Quality control** The production function that sets quality standards and monitors the production process to insure that the process yields goods meeting the established standards.

**Quality of life** The qualitative assessment of the relative quality of living conditions, including attention to pollutants, noise, aesthetics, complexity, etc.

**Receivables** An accounting term denoting the amounts owed the company.

**Reserves** Monies held out of use by a company to meet certain demands or serve designated purposes, for example reserves for the replacement of worn out equipment.

**Result-producing activities** Activities that produce measurable results that can be related, directly or indirectly, to the results and performance of the entire enterprise. Among result-producing activities are revenue-producing activities such as selling, nonrevenue activities such as manufacturing (result contributing activities) and information activities.

**Return on investment (ROI)** The ratio of the amount earned per year to the amount invested in a particular project or business (stated as a percentage).

**Risk** The likelihood of success versus the likelihood of failure for any undertaking. Assessing a risk is the process of trying to quantify or judge which likelihood is the larger and by how much.

**Scientific management** The approach to management fathered by Frederick W. Taylor. Its core is the organized study of work, the analysis of work into its simplest elements, and the systematic improvement of the worker's performance of each of these elements, resulting in higher levels of output per worker.

**Service institutions** Organizations constituted to perform a public task not involving the production of a product. The service is provided in a nonprofit mode. Examples include the postal service, educational institutions and utility districts.

**Share [Stock]** Unit of ownership of a corporation.

**Shareholders [stockholders]** The owners of the shares of a particular company. The shareholders are generally a very large group, but theoretically they exercise control over the company through a smaller board of directors.

**Simulation** An abstract replication of certain of the dynamics of a problem situation. The replication usually involves the manipulation of a model using a computer.

**Simulated decentralization** A mode of organizing large companies that are too big to remain functionally organized and too integrated to be genuinely decentralized. One function or segment is treated as if it were an autonomous business relating to other units as if in an actual marketplace.

**Social impacts** The societal consequences of actions that go beyond the consequences that are the action's *raison d'être*.

**Social responsibility** An institution's obligations to the society in which it resides. Recent discussion has highlighted differing points of view about what these obligations are.

**Span of control** A number of persons who report directly to a given manager. In decades past, the question of whether this number had an upper limit or an ideal received much attention.

**Speculation** Investments that have high likelihoods of failure but promise high returns if successful.

**Strategic planning** The planning for a company's long-term future that includes the setting of major overall objectives, the determination of the basic approaches to be used in pursuing these objectives, and the means to be used in obtaining the necessary resources to be employed.

**Strategy** A company's basic approach to achieving its overall objectives. For example, Sears' early strategy was to become a major supplier of products to the rural population by means of mail-order sales utilizing attractive catalogues and efficient 'mail-order factories'.

**Structure** The arrangement of processes and functions within the company as regards their relationships to each other. The methods used vary including the functional approach, decentralization, simulated decentralization and matrix forms.

**Suboptimization** Producing ideal performance in one area of a business and thereby being unable to pro duce ideal or optimum performance for the business as a whole.

**Subordinate** A person who reports to a particular manager is said to be one of that manager's subordinates.

**Support activities** Support activities include 'conscience' activities (staff), and such functions as legal counsel, labour-relations activities. They are compared to result-producing activities, hygiene and housekeeping activities, and top-management activities.

**Supporting capital** Working capital, that is, capital used to bring goods and services to market or to finance the time between their production and the time the buyer pays. Frequently contrasted with 'producing' capital.

**Surplus** Profits and other savings that successful performance can produce.

**System** A set of interrelated parts. For example, one can speak about a distribution system, which might consist of a network of warehouses to be served in a particular manner by a number of plants and which, in turn, would ship to customers according to prescribed procedures.

**System thinking** Analysis that uses systems and their dynamics to examine problems and possible solutions.

**Tactics** Basic approaches to be used in carrying out a predetermined strategy.

**Task force** A group assigned to accomplish a task. Committees may limit their attentions to making recommendations, while task forces are expected to perform a job.

**Tax accounting** The subdivision of accounting that attends to keeping and summarizing records for tax purposes.

**Technology** A way or means to accomplish a task. The technology may or may not include the use of machines.

**Technology assessment** The function of trying to determine the impacts of utilizing a particular technology in advance of its introduction. Proponents argue that technology assessment is possible, and Congress has established an office to do technology assessment. Opponents argue that it is impossible to assess technology in advance of its introduction.

**Technology monitoring** Following the impacts of a technology as it is introduced in order to identify and combat the harmful impacts, if any. This process is recommended by some who think that technology assessment is difficult if not impossible.

**Theory X and Theory Y** Theories about human behaviour formulated by Douglas McGregor. Theory X assumes that people are lazy, dislike and shun work, have to be driven, and need both carrot and stick. It assumes that most people are incapable of taking responsibility for themselves and have to be looked after. Theory Y assumes that people have a psychological need to work and that they desire achievement and responsibility and will find them under the right conditions.

**Time and motion studies** Methods first promoted by the scientific management school. They include the study of physical work using stopwatches in order to break a task into segments that are redesigned in order to be performed more readily so that the productivity of the job is improved.

**Trade associations** Organizations that bring the companies of an industry together for the purpose of exchanging information and jointly promoting the interests of the industry.

**Union relations** The business function of conducting interactions with the unions to which a company's employees belong.

**Unity of command** A management notion emphasized by early thinkers. The concept states that each employee should have one and only one boss.

**Utility** The usefulness or inherent value of something as perceived by an individual or an organization. A branch of economics tries to empirically measure and compare utilities.

**Variable costs** Costs of a production process that vary with the level of production.

**Wage and salary administration** The business function that determines wage and salary rates and adjusts them in response to market conditions and changed assignments.

**Wholly-owned subsidiaries** Subsidiaries all of whose shares are owned by the parent company, as contrasted with a subsidiary that is controlled because of the parent's being the largest, but not the only, holder of shares in the subsidiary company.

**Zero-based budgeting** Budgeting that assumes that each project or activity must justify again any expenditures (above zero) for each new year even if the project or activity was justified previously.

# Index

# Management

*Books by Peter Drucker*

**Management**
The Changing World of the Executive
Concept of the Corporation
The Effective Executive
Frontiers of Management
Independent Director
Innovation and Entrepreneurship
Management: Tasks, Responsibilities, Practices
Managing for Results
Managing for the Future
Managing in Turbulent Times
Managing in a Time of Great Change
Managing the Non-Profit Organization
People and Performance
Practice of Management
Technology, Management and Society

**Economics, politics, society**
Age of Discontinuity
America's Next Twenty Years
The Ecological Vision
The End of Economic Man
The Future of Industrial Man
The Landmarks of Tomorrow
Men, Ideas and Politics
The New Realities
The New Society
Post-Capitalist Society
Technology, Management, Society
The Unseen Revolution
Towards the Next Economics

**Fiction**
The Last of All Possible Worlds
The Temptation to Do Good

**Autobiography**
Adventures of a Bystander